South Slav Nationalisms—Textbooks and
Yugoslav Union before 1914

South Slav Nationalisms— Textbooks and Yugoslav Union before 1914

Charles Jelavich

Ohio State University Press
Columbus

Library of Congress Cataloging-in-Publication Data

Jelavich, Charles.
South Slav nationalisms—textbooks and Yugoslav Union
before 1914 / Charles Jelavich.
p.   cm.
Includes bibliographical references.
ISBN 0-8142-0500-3 (alk. paper)
1. Nationalism—Yugoslavia—History—19th century.
2. Nationalism—Yugoslavia—History—20th century.   3. Textbooks—
Yugoslavia—History.   4. Education—Yugoslavia—History.
5. Yugoslavia—Politics and government.   I. Title.
DR1274.J45   1990
320.5'4'09497—dc20   89-36824
CIP

Printed in the U.S.A.

9   8   7   6   5   4   3   2   1

For Mark and Peter

Contents

Illustrations

Maps

Preface

In 1948, Slobodan Jovanović, Serbia's most distinguished historian, reflecting on the turbulent interwar years in the South Slav kingdom and the ensuing bitter civil conflict in World War II, observed that Serbia was not Prussia and could not impose its will on the other South Slavs as that state had done at the time of German unification in 1871. A viable, united Yugoslav state could be realized only if the South Slav nations enjoyed a century of peace in which education, mutual understanding, and respect for one another received the highest priority. Thus, he added, in order to understand why the interwar kingdom was less than successful, one had to examine what the educated youth, who had assumed positions of leadership in the interwar decades, had been taught before 1914. The purpose of this book is precisely that—to determine what the Serbian, Croatian, and Slovenian students respectively learned about their own nations and the other South Slavs from their grammar, geography, history, and literature textbooks in the half-century before World War I and to assess the degree to which the knowledge that they had acquired fostered Yugoslavism and contributed to the creation of a single South Slav state and nation.

The role that Yugoslavism has played in South Slavic affairs during the past 150 years cannot be minimized. To a greater or lesser extent it has influenced all areas of South Slavic activity—political, religious, economic, cultural, linguistic, social, military—and even sporting events. The concept was a paradox in the era of nationalism, in which individual nationalities worked to create unitary nation-states (for example, Germany, Italy, Greece, Bulgaria, Albania, and Romania). The idea of the nation-state was also strong among the Serbs and Croats, but many individuals, mainly intellectuals, dreamed instead of creating a new Yugoslav state, which would embrace Serbs, Croats, and Slovenes; some even included the Bulgars in it. The expectation was that in time its citizens would call themselves Yugoslavs, relegating their past national identity to history. One might say a new person—a Yugoslav—whose loyalty, traditions, customs, and standards would be exclusively attached to the new state—would emerge. The attraction of this utopian concept, commonly called unitarism, to individuals who saw their own history as one of centuries of subjection to foreign domination was understandable and appealing. They believed that strength through numbers could enable them to determine their own future. In reality, however, Yugoslavism was a nebulous concept, and lent itself to a number of dissimilar political programs. They can be divided into two broad categories—first, those that could be realized at the expense of the Ottoman and Habsburg empires, and, second, those which envisaged Yugoslav unity within the Austro-Hungarian monarchy.

Within the first category there were four basic programs— Illyrianism, Greater Serbianism, Greater Croatianism, and the state created in 1918. Ljudevit Gaj's Croatian Illyrianism, the genesis of Yugoslav unitarism, was based on a belief in the oneness of the Croats, Serbs, and Slovenes (it also included the Bulgars); it initially sought to create a common language for all the South Slavs, expecting that it would lead to their cultural and, subsequently, political unity. Inherent in both Greater Serbianism and Greater Croatianism was the basic premise that the Serbs, Croats, and perhaps even the Slovenes were one people who should be united in one state. Neither program held that name, language, and religion were valid obstacles to its goal, citing the fact that the existence of provincial names such as Bavarian, Prussian, and Saxon had not prevented German unification. Nor had Islam, Orthodoxy, and Catholicism been deterrents to Albanian unity. The state that was created in 1918 was based upon the concept of Yugoslavism, which stemmed from Illyrianism.

In the second category, the emphasis was on the unity of the Croats, Serbs, and Slovenes of the Dual Monarchy under the leadership of the Croats. This program excluded Serbia and Montenegro. It represented a form of Trialism, that is, the idea that once united, the South Slavs of the empire could become the equals of the Austrians and Hungarians. Others thought that, at the least, they would be able to extract more concessions from Vienna and Budapest. Powerful Croatian and Slovenian clericalist groups foresaw the possibility of reuniting all the South Slavs through Catholicism by having the Orthodox Serbs, whom they regarded as wayward Catholics, rejoin the fold. Others welcomed the annexation of Bosnia-Hercegovina, anticipating that it would strengthen Croatia's hand against Serbia. Some even speculated that in time the Serbs and Montenegrins would become a part of the monarchy. It is evident that South Slavic unity would not come easily. The issues raised did not disappear in 1918. The war, in fact, exacerbated most of them.

In 1918 the South Slavs were united in a state called not Yugo-slavia, as virtually every book in the West tends to identify it, but the Kingdom of the Serbs, Croats, and Slovenes, a name that accurately reflected its organization. However, within a year it was evident that South Slavic unity rested on a fragile foundation. The constitution adopted in 1921 met the wishes of the Serbs, but not of the majority of the Croats and Slovenes, nor, in fact, of many members of other groups within the kingdom. Given the political, economic, and social dislocation created by the war, one could hardly expect the state not to experience growing pains—one need only look at the history of the other states in Eastern Europe, or even at the postwar problems experienced by Britain, France, Italy, and Germany. However, in the South Slav kingdom the conflict between individual national interests—Serbian, Croatian, and Slovenian—came to the fore. Soon each nationality was accusing the others of responsibility for its countless problems, just as in the past the blame for internal difficulties had been placed on the Austrians, Hungarians, Ottomans, or Italians.

From 1921 to 1941, events seemed to go from bad to worse. In 1928 the leader of the Croats, Stjepan Radić, was shot in parliament by a Montenegrin Serb. The next year King Alexander proclaimed a dictatorship, designating his state the Kingdom of Yugoslavia, with the expectation that sometime in the future his subjects would become Yugoslavs and shed their Serbianism, Croatianism, or Slovenianism. In 1931 he promulgated his royal constitution. In 1934 he was assassinated by Croatian and Macedonian nationalists, abetted by foreign powers. Then, in 1941, Hitler attacked, plunging the nation into a tragic civil war. The Yugoslavia envisaged by the nineteenth-century idealists had failed to materialize. Instead, Tito's partisans emerged from the war triumphant, proclaiming that South Slavic unity, understanding, and brotherhood would be realized through socialism. Notwithstanding the other achievements of the new regime, events since 1945 reveal that the issue of nationalism in Yugoslavia is still far from being resolved.

This study is based on a reading of about three hundred fifty Serbian, Croatian, and Slovenian grammar, geography, history, and literature textbooks (many of which were revisions or new editions) authorized for use in elementary and secondary schools, teachers' colleges, theological institutions, and trade schools in the five decades before World War I. University textbooks have not been included in the study, however, since their content did not differ appreciably from that of the elementary and secondary school textbooks, and it was the latter that primarily molded public opinion. For example, in the only two South Slavic universities, at Belgrade and Zagreb, total enrollment in 1910 was about 2,100, whereas elementary and secondary school enrollment in Serbia and Croatia was over 400,000. If one adds the Slovenian, Dalmatian, Bosnian, and Montenegrin schools as well as those in the Vojvodina, the number of students was well over 450,000. Students who went beyond the secondary schools to the university, or to the teachers' colleges, and theological seminaries, collectively numbered about 3,700, less than one percent of the annual student enrollment.

I also examined about one hundred textbooks from Dalmatia, Bosnia, Hercegovina, Montenegro, and Vojvodina. They have not been directly integrated into this study, but it should be stressed that their content did not vary fundamentally from that of the Serbian and Croatian textbooks. Many Croatian books were used in Dalmatia, and the content of others was almost identical to that of those found in Croatia. In Bosnia-Hercegovina, Croatian readers were prescribed, but a few Serbian readers were also used. The Montenegrin books did not differ from the Serbian, except to include more information on Montenegrin affairs. On balance, thus, these books did not alter the basic facts, interpretations, and perceptions of the Croatian and Serbian textbooks.

In addition, I also reviewed about twenty-five almanacs (*kalendari*). Among the Serbian almanacs were *Kalendar Matice Srpske*, *Kalendar Narodni Novina*, *Vardar*, *Sveti Sava*, and *Orao*; the Croatian included *Danica*, *Bog i Hrvati*, *Zvonimir*, *Svačić*, and the Serbian *Srbobran*, which was published in Zagreb. Almanacs were very popular and found in most homes. They not only provided the usual facts about weather, seasons, horticulture, animal husbandry, and so on; in addition, almost all provided information of a primarily historical nature about the major events and personalities in the nation's history, announcements of historical anniversaries with their significance, excerpts from prominent authors, and some even commented on the major events of the preceding year. Their content was highly patriotic and nationalistic and, frequently, religiously inspired. In a sense the almanacs served as the link between what the family read at home and what the students learned from their textbooks about their nation. The content of the almanacs has not been extensively integrated in this study, because to do so would have expanded the scope of the study considerably, but examples are cited where the information in them reinforced the overall impressions and conclusions about South Slavic unity found in the textbooks.

I also examined course or curriculum catalogues (*izveštaji*) for the secondary schools of Serbia, Croatia, and Slovenia. They listed the courses taught, the names of the instructors, the textbooks prescribed, and, in many instances, even the names of the students, their place of origin, and their parents' occupations. In addition, the information found in the standard education journals, such as *Nastavnik, Napredak, Učitelj, Prosvetni glasnik, Nastavni vjesnik, Hrvatski učitelj*, and *Krščanska škola*, was invaluable. Not only did the articles discuss official directives to the schools, but, more important, they commented on the content of courses in history, geography, and literature. Often these journals also contained articles by teachers calling for more emphasis on religion, patriotism, and loyalty, all with the aim of indoctrinating the students.

Although this study focuses on textbooks, it also includes a brief introductory general survey of periods, events, and issues in South Slavic, mainly Serbian and Croatian, history that are discussed in the textbooks or influenced their writing. This survey is intended not as an interpretation of the Yugoslav idea or Yugoslavism, but to provide the reader with a frame of reference for the analysis of the textbooks.

The Library of Congress system for Serbo-Croatian has been followed, that is, Serbian is transliterated into Croatian. Names and places are given in their original spelling, except for those that have acquired a standard English spelling such as, for example, Belgrade rather than Beograd and King Peter rather than King Petar.

I have relied on the maps for the medieval period prepared by postwar Yugoslav scholars for their *Historija naroda Jugoslavije*, knowing well that many other scholars are not satisfied with them. They at least give an approximation of the medieval lands, because exact boundaries for that era cannot be verified.

Citations for Croatian elementary school readers (*čitanke*) present a problem, because their titles frequently change. For example, the third-year reader carried the title *Čitanka za treći razred pučkih škola i dodatak iz gramatike* for the editions published between 1880 and 1889, but in 1891 the title was modified to *Čitanka za treći razred obćih pučkih škola*. In 1892 a new edition of it was published, entitled *Čitanka za treći razred nižih pučkih škola*, with essentially the same subject matter. In 1903 the title again changed, to *Čitanka za treći razred općih pučkih škola u Hrvatskoj i Slavoniji*. There were similar alterations in the titles of readers of other grade levels. The critical factor in all these editions is date of publication. Hence, instead of providing a complete citation for each title revision in every note, I have used an abbreviated title, for example, *Čitanka za treći razred* (1903), with the date being the controlling factor.

A somewhat similar problem concerns secondary school readers. Franjo Marković and Franjo Petračić both compiled readers that were subsequently re-edited or revised by another author with the original author's name remaining on the title page. In citing these works in the notes, I have hyphenated the names of author and co-author or editor. For example, Franjo Petračić, *Hrvatska čitanka za više gimnazije i nalike jim škole-historija literature u primerah* II (1880), is cited as Petračić-Miler, *Hrvatska čitanka*, II (1895), to indicate that the work was revised by Ferdo Miler. Here the controlling factors are co-author and date of publication.

Different printings or editions of Serbian and Slovenian books are also identified by date of publication.

Acknowledgments

I am most grateful for the generous fellowship support of a number of institutions, which made it possible for me to conduct my research in the United States and Yugoslavia. They are the American Council of Learned Societies; the International Exchanges and Research Board (IREX); the National Endowment for the Humanities; the U.S. Office of Education, Fulbright-Hayes; the Russian Research Center, Harvard University. At Indiana University, the Russian and East European Institute, Research and Graduate Development, and the President's Council on the Humanities awarded grants for my research and the publication of this book. In Yugoslavia the cooperation and assistance I received from the different libraries were exemplary. The three principal repositories for material for my research were the Pedagoški muzej in Belgrade, Školski muzej in Zagreb, and Slovenski šolski muzej in Ljubljana. In addition, in Belgrade the Svetozar Marković (University) Library extended to me all possible courtesies, as did the Narodna i sveučilišna biblioteka in Zagreb; the university libraries in Sarajevo, Split, and Zadar; and the library of the Matica Srpska in Novi Sad. Among the many individuals in these libraries who assisted me, I would like in particular to acknowledge the support of Deziderija Bosnar, Svetomir Gačić, Stanija Gligorjević, Branko Hanž, Milena Marković, Slavica Pavlič, Branko Pleše, and Lydia Subotin. Two colleagues, Ivan Čizmić and Dragan Živojinović, were similarly generous with their advice and assistance.

I wish to thank the press's two anonymous readers, who made valuable suggestions. My greatest debt, however, is to my wife, Barbara, who came to know this subject as well as I, who made invaluable suggestions throughout the course of my research, and whose criticisms of the manuscript and suggestions for its revision were indispensable.

I am grateful to Debbie Chase, who typed the final versions of the manuscript, and to John Hollingsworth, Indiana University cartographer, who drew the excellent maps. I wish to thank Alex Holzman, Acquisitions Editor at the Ohio State University Press, for his encouragement and understanding. I also profited from Sally Serafim's careful editorial reading.

1

The Historical Background

Before we proceed to an analysis of the contents of the textbooks, a brief survey of the historical background of the Serbs, Croats, and Slovenes is necessary. The emphasis here will be on those aspects of the individual national movements that brought the three peoples together and those that drove them apart. As will be shown, centuries of living in close proximity resulted in feelings both of mutual attraction and of competition and enmity.[1]

THE SOUTH SLAVS IN 1914: THEIR EARLY HISTORICAL DEVELOPMENT

At the time of the outbreak of World War I, the largest portion of the South Slavic population was Serbian. According to 1910 statistics there was a total of approximately 6,568,000 Serbs living under various political jurisdictions. Of this number 2,911,000 were citizens of independent Serbia. In 1913, after the Balkan Wars, they were joined by the 1,500,000 Serbs inhabiting Macedonia and Old Serbia. Of the 1,957,000 Serbs in the Habsburg lands, there were 105,000 in Dalmatia, 644,000 in Croatia-Slavonia, 383,000 in Vojvodina, and 825,000 in Bosnia-Hercegovina. In addition, the 200,000 inhabitants of the independent kingdom of Montenegro were considered as Serbs in the nineteenth century.

Although the Croatians lived in the Habsburg empire, they were in fact under different administrative authorities after the Ausgleich or Compromise of 1867, which divided the state into separate Austrian and Hungarian divisions. In 1910 the total Croatian population numbered about 2,789,000. Of these the 1,638,000 inhabitants of Croatia-Slavonia and the 93,000 of the Vojvodina were in the Hun-

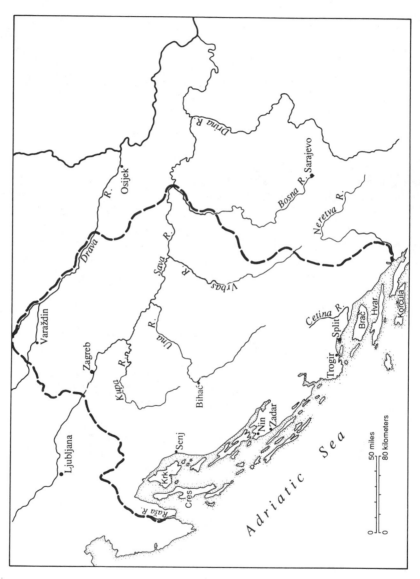

Croatian Lands in the Tenth Century

garian part of the empire. The 505,000 Croats in Dalmatia and the 168,000 in Istria were considered part of Austria. In Bosnia-Hercegovina, which was under the joint control of Austria and Hungary, Croats were a minority of 385,000.

The Slovenes inhabited principally four provinces under the jurisdiction of Vienna. Of the total of 1,252,000 Slovenes, there were 491,000 in Carniola, 410,000 in Styria, 82,000 in Carinthia, and 266,000 in the Littoral, which included Gorica, Istria, and Trieste. In addition, 5,000 Slovenes lived in Prekomurje, which was part of the Hungarian kingdom.

It is important to emphasize in regard to these population figures that in some regions the individual South Slav nationalities formed only a minority of the general population. There they shared the same political jurisdiction not only with other South Slavs, but also with outside, contending nationalities, such as Bulgarians, Greeks, and Albanians in Macedonia; the Italians in Dalmatia; and the Hungarians and Germans in many Habsburg regions. Because of the intermixture of populations, it was impossible to draw neat national borders. As will be seen, this situation not only caused friction among the various nationalities; it also formed a basis for nineteenth-century arguments calling for Yugoslav unity.

The Yugoslav movement was a relatively recent development in the long history of the three peoples. In the medieval era each had led a separate political existence. Whereas the Slovenes had had a brief period of self-rule in the eighth century, both the Serbs and the Croats had formed important medieval kingdoms. The Croatian state, which at times had included all or part of present-day Croatia, Slavonia, Dalmatia, Bosnia, and Hercegovina, maintained an independent existence from 910 to 1102. Having accepted the Catholic faith, the Croatian leaders felt henceforth close to Western developments. Croatia's three greatest kings, Tomislav, Krešimir, and Zvonimir, provided heroic figures for later national development. Of particular significance was the organization of the Croatian *sabor*, or assembly, which was the single political institution to remain in existence during the years of foreign domination; it became the symbol of national continuity into the modern era.

The Serbian kingdom under the Nemanja dynasty was in existence from 1169 to 1389. In different periods the state controlled present-day Serbia, Macedonia, Old Serbia, Bosnia, Hercegovina, Montenegro, and parts of Dalmatia. During the reign of Dušan (1331–55) all of Albania, much of northern Greece, and most of western Bulgaria were included in the kingdom. The Serbian adherence to the Orthodox faith, like the Croatian conversion to

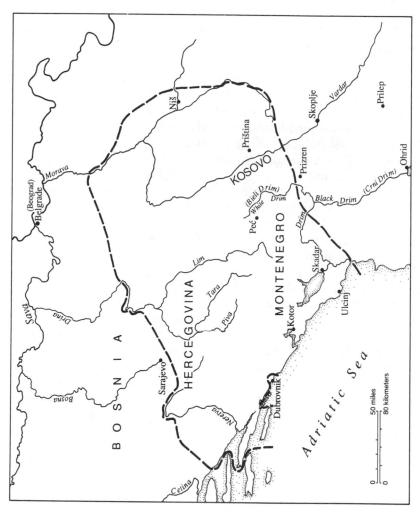

Serbian (Nemanja) Lands in the Twelfth Century

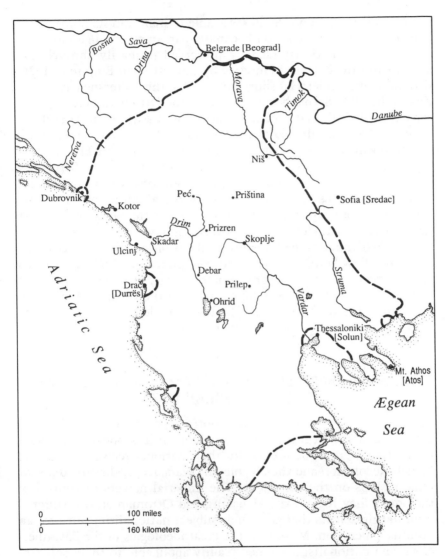

Tsar Dušan's Empire in the Fourteenth Century

Catholicism, was to have a determining influence on its future civilization and political development. The Serbian church, initially founded in the thirteenth century under Saint Sava, was to be the institution that served to preserve the national identity when the state fell under outside domination. It also acted as a bond uniting all Serbs no matter where they lived.

Neither Croatia nor Serbia was able to maintain its political independence. In 1102 Croatia became a part of the Hungarian kingdom, with its national identity preserved primarily through the sabor. After the defeat of Hungary by the Ottoman Empire in 1526, Croatia came under Habsburg rule. After the watershed battle of Kosovo in 1389, Serbia became a part of the Ottoman domains. The separate political roads taken by the Serbs and Croats further deepened the divisions already created by their adherence to different religious organizations. Croatia, as a part of the Habsburg Empire, was not only Catholic but shared in Western developments. Serbia, by contrast, with its Orthodox Byzantine traditions, was to remain for over five centuries under the control of the Muslim empire. These events made a deep impression on the view the Serbs and Croats held of each other. Henceforth Croats often saw themselves as representatives of the advanced Western civilization, and they looked down on their fellow South Slavs as Orthodox heretics who had acquired an Ottoman veneer. The Serbs, for their part, often considered the Croats as tools of the Catholic church and the German-dominated Habsburg Empire, both of which they regarded as enemies of the Serbian Orthodox religion and the nation.

THE NINETEENTH-CENTURY NATIONAL REVIVAL: THE YUGOSLAV IDEA

For the South Slavs under foreign control, the end of the eighteenth century and the beginning of the nineteenth witnessed developments that were to be crucial for their national reawakening. The French Revolution and the Napoleonic wars deeply disturbed power relationships on the continent. The imperial powers in control of the South Slav region, the Habsburg and Ottoman states, suffered humiliating defeats that gave their subject nationalities hope for an eventual liberation. Moreover, the great ideologies of the day, liberalism and nationalism, seemed readily applicable to their political situation. Although a conservative system was reestablished in most of Europe after 1815, both the Serbs and Croats won notable advances in their national programs in the next half-century. Serbia achieved autonomous status by 1830; in Croatia, the Illyrian movement defined Croatian national goals. What is most important to the understanding of the contents of the textbooks is to review these national programs, rather than the specifics of South Slav political events.

Serbia, 1804–1848

Although the initial Serbian revolt under Karadjordje Petrović in 1804 was unsuccessful, his successor Miloš Obrenović, with Russian backing, was able to secure Ottoman recognition of certain autonomous rights, and in 1830 the state received full autonomy. In the reigns of Miloš (1815–38) and Alexander Karadjordjević (1842–58) state institutions were developed and a national program defined. In this period the work of two men, Vuk Stefanović Karadžić and Ilija Garašanin, was of decisive importance to the development of specifically Serbian national ideals and goals.

Karadžić, the preeminent Serbian scholar, was a self-educated man who excelled in many fields. He compiled the first modern Serbian grammar and dictionary, and collected folk poetry. However, his most important contribution was the standardization of the Serbian language. Believing that the literary language should be based on the phonetic principle "write as you speak," he established the štokavian vernacular dialect as the standard. Since a majority of Croats also spoke this dialect, a common linguistic bond was forged between the two people. Karadžić's views on linguistics were widely praised by Croatian scholars, especially those with Yugoslav convictions, who recognized the importance of a common literary language.

Although certain aspects of Karadžić's work helped bring Serbs and Croats together, others had the opposite effect. Accepting an idea that was commonly held in Europe at the time, that a nation was identified by its language, Karadžić wrote an article in 1836 entitled "Serbs All and Everywhere"; it was published only in 1849, after the Croatian Illyrian movement was well established. In it he argued that all South Slavs who spoke štokavian were Serbs, a generalization that, of course, embraced the majority of Croats. This conviction led logically to the next conclusion, that those lands where štokavian was spoken—namely Croatia, Slavonia, Dalmatia, Istria, Bosnia, Hercegovina, and Vojvodina—belonged to Serbia. He considered religion a minor factor in identifying a nation, arguing that since Catholics and Protestants alike considered themselves Germans, and since Catholics, Lutherans, Calvinists, and Unitarians alike called themselves Hungarians, then all Catholic, Muslim, and Orthodox speakers of štokavian could be designated as Serbs. Although his views in later years were not accepted even by all Serbian linguists, his immense prestige gave weight to his arguments. His views on this question were thus incorporated into all Serbian grammar, geography, history, and literature textbooks.[2]

Whereas Karadžić's writings provided the Serbs with a sense of cultural and literary unity, his contemporary Garašanin was concerned primarily with designating which lands were to be finally included in the Serbian state. In 1844, in a secret document called the *Načertanije*, he made clear that his goal was the unification of all Serbs, not all South Slavs. His views of the future Serbian state centered on the lands that had been included in Dušan's medieval empire, but he also favored the acquisition of territory in which there were large Catholic or Muslim populations—for instance, Bosnia, Hercegovina, Dalmatia, and Vojvodina. Avoiding the word Croatian, he referred, for instance, to the Catholics of Bosnia as Bosnian Catholics, Roman Catholics, or simply Catholics. Garašanin's importance in Serbian politics—he served several terms as foreign minister— made his views of particular importance. His conclusions, like those of Karadžić, were reflected in the textbooks.[3]

Croatia, 1790–1848

In contrast to Serbia, which won its autonomy through revolution and diplomacy, the Croatian leaders in the same period had to fight to preserve their autonomous rights against Hungarian pressure. The Croatian nobility, which in general had served the nation well in the past through the sabor, jeopardized its position by agreeing to make Hungarian compulsory in Croatian schools. Because of their elders' lack of resolve here and in regard to other questions, a new generation of young men took over the leadership of the national cause. They sought first to define its goals and later to implement them.

The group's leader was Ljudevit Gaj, whose name has become synonymous with the Illyrian movement. Though his paternal ancestors were French Huguenots and his mother was German, he became a staunch Croatian patriot. By 1830, at the age of twenty-one, he had already assumed a position of leadership among those who opposed the increasing Hungarian pressure and championed Croatian autonomous rights. His studies, particularly of the works of Czech scholars, led him to believe that all of the Balkan Slavs—Bulgarians, Croats, Serbs, and Slovenes alike—were descendants of a single illustrious race, the Illyrians. The basis thus existed for a future political unity. Even more important were his views on language.

Sharing the widespread contemporary belief that a nation was definable by its language, he was concerned by the fact that among the Croats there were not only speakers of the štokavian dialect, but also kajkavian and čakavian speakers.[4] Believing that linguistic conformity was essential to attaining his principal goal, the political unity of Croatia, Slavonia, and Dalmatia (the lands of the Croatian Triune Kingdom), he persuaded influential Croatian intellectuals to adopt štokavian as the standard language. He expressed his opinions in a weekly, *Danica*, which appeared in 1835.[5]

Gaj's arguments had obvious political implications. Not only did they provide an intellectual basis for resistance to Hungarian cultural pressure, but also and even more important, they provided a bridge to closer cooperation with the Serbs. Like Karadžić, Gaj used the common štokavian dialect as a direct link between peoples, but with entirely different implications. Since the vast majority of Croats and the Serbs spoke a common language, Gaj envisioned a linguistic union, which could in time lead to a political union. To further this goal, he believed that every educated Croat should learn the Cyrillic alphabet in order to read the works of Serbian writers. His concepts laid the basis for the unitarist idea of a single Yugoslav people or nation. Gaj's Illyrianism also raised the issue, which was to be so important later, of whether the Serbs, Croats, and Slovenes were three separate Slavic peoples, or one nation with three names.

Gaj's activities had little effect on the Serbs or Slovenes. Certainly, Serbian leaders could find little to attract them in the nebulous Illyrian idea. The movement was, however, important in developing Croatian national consciousness and underlining the importance of language. In 1847 the sabor took an important step, declaring Croatian the official language of the nation. Thereafter the Illyrian idea continued to play a major role in the development of a national culture. In the textbooks, the idea of a common language of the Serbs and Croats received attention; the students were urged to respect each other's religions, traditions, and cultures.

The Revolution of 1848–1849

The first instance of practical political cooperation between Serbs and Croats for a common goal occurred during this revolutionary period. When the Hungarian revolution threatened the integrity of the Habsburg lands, the Croats, under the leadership of Ban Josip Jelačić, came to the aid of the imperial government. At this time both the Serbs and Croats of the Habsburg Empire supported the concept of Austroslavism, that is, that the monarchy should be restructured in a manner that would allow the Slavs a greater role in government. In the fighting, the Croats and Serbs coordinated some of their military operations. In a symbolic display of unity, Josip Rajačić, the Serbian patriarch of Sremski Karlovci, went to Zagreb and gave his blessing to Jelačić. A Belgrade newspaper commented that such a scene had "not been seen since Christianity has been in the world; such a scene is only possible in the nineteenth century."[6]

The Serbian government, by contrast to the Habsburg Serbs, found itself in a dilemma. Obviously, the Habsburg government opposed Serbian national territorial goals, but the Serbs of the Vojvodina were calling for assistance against the Hungarians. Eventually the Serbian government allowed 10,000 so-called volunteers under the command of a Serbian officer to cross the frontier. The objective was to aid the Serbs, not the South Slavic cause. After a brief period the volunteers were recalled.

The only significant development involving South Slav understanding in the post-revolutionary decade was the adoption of the Literary Agreement, or Vienna Accord, of 1850. A number of prominent scholars, including Karadžić and Djuro Daničić for the Serbs and Ivan Kukuljević-Sakcinski, Ivan Mažuranić, and Dimitrije Demeter for the Croats, agreed that the ijekavian variant of the štokavian dialect should be adopted as the literary language of both Serbia and Croatia. Their decision was based on the consideration that, first, most Serbs and Croats used it and that, second, it was the language of the great period of Dubrovnik literature and of most folk poetry. It was also the form commonly used by contemporary authors.[7] The Literary Agreement adopted by the scholars received official sanction from the Serbian government in 1868 and from the Croatian authorities in 1892. By that time, however, both the Serbian government and scholars had come to prefer the local eastern Serbian variant, ekavian. Nevertheless, štokavian, in one or the other of its forms, was to be the official literary language of both the Serbs and Croats.

POLITICAL REALITIES, 1849–1878

The next quarter-century, 1849–78, witnessed marked changes both in Serbia and in the Croatian political leadership. The national movement in Serbia made great advances, culminating in the achievement of full independence in 1878. Whereas in Belgrade there was general agreement on policy among the leaders, in Croatia three opposing parties, with different programs, emerged. Finally, in 1878 the dispute over Bosnia and Hercegovina forced both Serbs and Croats to define more closely their mutual relations and to face the thorny question of exactly which state was entitled to possess lands occupied by both people.

Serbia

The Serbian government had to face directly its relationship with the Croatian national leadership for the first time during the reign of Prince Michael Obrenović (1860–68). During this period Garašanin was again foreign minister. With an ambitious foreign policy, the monarch and his minister attempted to organize the Balkan peoples—Serbs, Bulgarians, Greeks, and Romanians—in a common front whose first goal would be to end Ottoman control of the peninsula. In 1866–67 Serbia signed bilateral agreements with their governments or representatives.

Garašanin also began negotiations with Croatian leaders. Obviously, discussions could not be carried on openly with the authorities in Zagreb, who were subject to Habsburg authority. In 1866–67 secret talks were, however, held between Josip Strossmayer, the Croatian bishop of Djakovo, a man who enjoyed wide confidence and respect, and Antonije Orešković, Garašanin's intermediary. Although Orešković was able to report that Strossmayer had accepted the Serbian foreign minister's proposal "concerning the common efforts between the Triune Kingdom and Serbia for the formation of a Yugoslav state independent of Austria and Turkey," it was soon apparent that the two sides had different conceptions of their relationship.[8] Orešković, a former Habsburg citizen who entered Serbian service, drew up a program for cooperation on a joint, Yugoslav basis. Garašanin, however, refused to accept several of its central provisions. In reply to the suggestion that Belgrade direct all activities involving the inhabitants of the Ottoman Empire and that Zagreb be given similar responsibilities for the Habsburg Empire, Garašanin insisted that Serbia should assume the leadership of the Serbs of the monarchy. When Orešković proposed that all decisions should be made jointly, the Serbian minister would agree only that the Croatian leaders could "assist" in the process. He also refused to commit himself on the political and administrative structure of a future joint state. Similarly, the disposition of Bosnia and Hercegovina could not be settled.[9] In 1867 Garašanin was dismissed and a year later Prince Michael was assassinated. These events brought at least a temporary end to the ambitious plans for a radical reordering of conditions in the Balkan peninsula under Serbian leadership.

Strong Serbian national views remained, of course, predominant in the principality. The ideas of the majority of intellectuals were reflected in the program of the *Omladina*, or Youth Movement. Although its domestic program called for the introduction of liberal reforms, including a truly representative government and civil liberties, in foreign policy the ideal was the re-creation of Dušan's empire. The goals thus included acquisition of Bosnia, Hercegovina, Old Serbia, and Macedonia, and a union with Montenegro. Should a South Slav state be created, it should be under Serbian leadership. Even Svetozar Marković, the founder of Serbian socialism, who had little sympathy for the idea of the re-creation of the medieval empire or the leading role of the Orthodox church, believed that Bosnia "was a land in which the Serbian nation was divided into three parts by religion."[10]

Croatia

Croatian internal affairs were radically altered by the reorganization of the monarchy, which occurred in 1867. In the Ausgleich creating the Dual Monarchy, Croatia and Slavonia were placed under the jurisdiction of Budapest, whereas Dalmatia and Slovenia were administered from Vienna. Faced with this situation the sabor was forced to negotiate its own compromise with Hungary. In the *Nagodba* or Compromise of 1868 Croatia was granted administrative autonomy, an independent judiciary, and, what is essential for this study, control over its educational system. This agreement, of course, did not meet even the minimum demands of Croatian nationalists. In the sixties, three major political parties had been formed, all representing conflicting viewpoints: first, the Magyarone or Unionist Party, which was pro-Hungarian; second, the National Party of Bishop Josip Strossmayer and Canon Franjo Rački, which supported the principles of the Illyrian movement; and, third, the Party of [Croat State] Right (Stranka prava) founded by Ante Starčević and Eugen Kvaternik, which stood for an independent Croatia.

The Unionist Party believed that Croatia's interests would be best served by retaining its historic ties with Hungary, which dated from 1102. Their program was anti-Serbian, anti-Orthodox, and opposed to measures supported by those with a Yugoslav orientation, such as the teaching of the Cyrillic alphabet in the schools. In control of the sabor after the rigged elections of 1868, the Unionists were responsible for the adoption of the *Nagodba*. They remained the predominant party until 1873.

The National Party, in contrast, championed the restoration of the political and administrative unity of the lands of the Triune Kingdom. Although proponents of the Illyrian idea that the South Slavs were one people, the party's leadership believed that for the present each nationality should retain its individual identity but should, at the same time, work to remove the barriers between them. The common literary language, agreed upon by the Serbs and Croats, was a major step. The party now strongly supported the teaching of both alphabets in the schools so that Serbs and Croats could share a common literature.

The National Party leadership also stood behind the creation of institutions to foster South Slav or Yugoslav understanding. Its major undertaking was the organization of the Yugoslav Academy in Zagreb, whose goal was to foster scholarly cooperation through publication and dissemination of works by not only Serbs and Croats, but also Slovenes and Bulgars. Nationalist convictions also were responsible for the appointment of Djuro Daničić, a Serb and Karadžić's closest collaborator, as the editor of the *Dictionary of the Croatian or Serbian Language*, a multivolume undertaking that took over a century to complete. It should be noted that the National Party, while strongly supporting Serb and Croat unity, believed that Croatia should be the nucleus of any future South Slav union.

Strong Croatian national convictions were represented by the anti-Serbian Party of Right. Its leader, Ante Starčević, born in Lika, was the son of a Croatian father and a Serbian mother. In his youth he was a strong supporter of the Illyrian movement and of Jelačić's actions in 1848–49. Later he remarked that in those years "no one had been for Croatia." Thereafter, believing that Croatia had been treated unfairly by the monarchy, he claimed that the state had the right to sever its ties with empire and reestablish the independent status that had existed in the Middle Ages. However, before independence could be achieved, the Croatian national identity had to be reaffirmed and the spirit of the nation revived.

Whereas Starčević considered the Habsburg Empire to be the major outside political enemy, those in the Croatian community who held Illyrian or Yugoslav ideas were his main domestic opponents. Reversing the claims of those in Belgrade who considered all South Slav lands as Serbian, Starčević declared them to be Croatian instead. In his opinion, "the entire population between Macedonia and Germany [the Austrian German-speaking areas], between the Danube and Adriatic Sea, has only one nationality, one homeland, one Croatian being." In other words, he considered not only Croatia, Slavonia, and Dalmatia but also Serbia, Montenegro, Bosnia, Hercegovina, Vojvodina, and Slovenia to be Croatian domains. He declared further that: "In the principality of Serbia, the nationality is the same as among us . . . which some in recent times called Serbian." As far as the Slovenes were concerned, he wrote: "the ordinary population was called Slovenes. Since when I do not know . . . The population speaks Croatian, or, as others say, a dialect [of Croatian, that is, kaj-kavian]." In all these lands, however, there was only one "political nation" and one language—Croatian. The Serbs and Slovenes were Croats who used regional, geographic names to identify themselves. Starčević thus could speak of the medieval "Croatian" Nemanja dynasty, the "Croatian" ruler Dušan, and the "Croatian" Orthodox Saint Sava. Just as the Serbian Orthodox were Croats, so too were the Bosnian Muslims.[11]

The two strongly nationalist views, the Croatian as represented by Starčević and the Serbian as expressed in the works of Karadžić and others, were soon placed in sharp relief by two events: the passage of a new education law in Croatia in 1874 and the Habsburg occupation of Bosnia and Hercegovina in 1878.

The education law had two primary goals. First, it sought to remove the control previously exercised by the church over the schools and place them under the jurisdiction of the sabor. The state was to determine all aspects of education, except those which dealt directly with religion. This secularization of education, which brought Croatia in step with most of Europe, was bitterly resisted by the Catholic church. Similarly, the Serbian Orthodox church, which had controlled the education of its followers, opposed the new system. Its request that an exception be made for its schools was naturally rejected by the sabor.

The second objective of the law was strictly political. Since Serbian and Croatian students would now use the same textbooks and learn more about each other, it was hoped that Serbian children would grow up to be loyal citizens of Croatia and not be attracted by the neighboring Serbian kingdom. This aspect of the reform was particularly unsettling to nationalist Serbs in the monarchy. Their attacks on the law and demands for its suspension for Serbian students aroused suspicions among Croat leaders, who sought either an independent Croatia or a Yugoslav solution under Croatian direction.

The Bosnian Controversy, 1878

For obvious reasons the fate of Bosnia, which had been under Ottoman control before 1878, was a matter of extreme importance to Serbs and Croats of all political persuasions. The crisis in the Balkans between 1875 and 1878—involving an uprising in Bosnia and Hercegovina, the war of Serbia and Montenegro against the Ottoman Empire, and finally the Russo-Turkish War of 1877–78—made the disposition of the lands of international importance. At the Congress of Berlin in the summer of 1878, the great powers recognized the independence of Serbia, Romania, and Montenegro and created an autonomous Bulgarian state. The two provinces of Bosnia and Hercegovina were placed under Habsburg occupation and administration. The *sanjak* or district of Novi Pazar, a strip of land separating Serbia and Montenegro, was also to be occupied by the monarchy. Although Serbia gained some territory to the south, this settlement caused extreme bitterness in the country. Serbs in the principality and the monarchy alike looked on these lands as rightfully theirs, despite the fact that in Bosnia and Hercegovina the Orthodox constituted only 44 percent of the population, with the remaining 33 percent Slavic Muslim and 22 percent Catholic Croatian.

The occupation of Bosnia and Hercegovina received a mixed reaction in Croatia. Starčević condemned it as yet another example of the Habsburg seizure of Croatian lands. Strossmayer too disapproved, but his influence had waned. A majority of the sabor, welcoming the occupation as a liberation of South Slav lands from Ottoman control, passed a resolution supporting the action. Croatian nationalists were also enthusiastic about the occupation, since they could hope that sometime in the future the provinces might be joined with the rest of the lands of the Triune Kingdom to form a strong Croatian state. Moreover, should the territory be joined to Croatia, then it would have the upper hand in any contest for the leadership of the South Slav movement.

The contrasting reactions of Serbs and Croats to the occupation naturally embittered relations between them. Nothing better illustrated this situation than the controversies that arose in Dalmatia, where previously the two peoples had had good relations. Until this time the Serbs in the Dalmatian sabor, who represented 16 percent of the population, had regularly supported the Croatian demands for the reunification of Dalmatia with Croatia-Slavonia to reconstitute the Triune Kingdom. Because of the controversy that arose over the two provinces, as well as other matters, however, the Serbian representatives in 1879 abandoned their backing of the Triune concept and instead called for the unification of Dalmatia with Bosnia and Hercegovina to form an autonomous unit. As a result of these conflicts, relations between the Serbs and Croats in Dalmatia remained strained until the first decade of the twentieth century.

THE ERA OF SOUTH SLAV CONFLICT, 1878–1903

With this background it can be understood why mutual relations between Serbs and Croats became worse over the next quarter-century.

Moreover, having achieved independence in 1878, it was natural that
the Serbian government should concentrate on other national goals.
After the Habsburg occupation of Bosnia and Hercegovina, and faced
with the monarchy's strong opposition to any movement to the west
or north, the Serbian government placed its hopes in expansion
southward. National enthusiasm continued to be fostered through
the press, the church, and the schools.

Whereas the Serbian government could point to concrete
achievements in its national program, the Croatian leadership had
obviously not made major gains. The Austro-Hungarian Compromise of 1867 appeared to be firmly entrenched. Its provisions placed
an apparently permanent block to attempts to reunite the lands of
the Triune Kingdom. Although Croatian opinion continued to be
divided, political failures made more nationalistic programs appear
increasingly attractive, and they encouraged the maintenance of
conflict and tension between Serbs and Croats.

Serbian Nationalism

Although most Serbian nationalists still regarded Bosnia and Hercegovina as their primary territorial goals, they also expected to
acquire at some time Macedonia and Old Serbia, the heart of Dušan's
empire. Here they ran directly into conflict with another South Slav
people, the Bulgarians. In 1878 in the Treaty of San Stefano between
Russia and the Ottoman Empire, Macedonia had been included in a
Greater Bulgarian state. Although it was subsequently partitioned at
the Congress of Berlin, the regaining of this province became the
goal of the Bulgarian nationalists. The conflict over Macedonia and
the bad relations between the neighboring Slavic states resulted in a
war in 1885 in which the Serbian army was defeated. Despite this
failure the emotions generated by the achievement of independence,
joined with the general awareness that the Serbian national program
was far from completed, created an atmosphere of extreme national
enthusiasm in the state.

These patriotic sentiments were fostered by the Serbian leadership through the educational system and the press. As in other European states, the government through its officials and institutions
worked to strengthen national self-consciousness and to prepare the
population to make sacrifices for the sake of territorial expansion.
In this endeavor, official sources often portrayed the neighboring
Greeks, Bulgarians, Turks, Albanians, Germans, and Hungarians as
historical enemies in possession of Serbian lands. This interpretation caused no immediate problems; except for the Bulgarian con-

flict this expressed enmity did not involve other South Slav peoples. The major difficulties arose when it became apparent that Croatian national aspirations were in direct conflict with those of the Serbs.

The immediate result of this situation was a sharpening of Serbian judgments of the Croats. Typical of the Serbian critical reaction was an article by Nikola Stojanović, entitled "Serbs and Croats," which was published in 1902 in *Srpski književni glasnik*, the leading literary periodical in Belgrade. Here the author, while glorifying Serbian past achievements, restated earlier Serbian denunciations of the Croats as tools of the Serbs' enemies: the Catholic church, the Hungarians, and the Habsburg government. The Croats did "not have their own language, nor common customs, nor a strong common identity, nor, what is important, consciousness of belonging to one another, as a result of which they cannot be a separate nationality." He concluded with the inflammatory statement that the struggle between the Serbs and Croats would go on "until either we or you are eliminated. One side must surrender. That it will be the Croats is assured by their [numerical] inferiority, geographic position, circumstances . . ."[12]

This article, which was in part a response to similar Croatian declarations, inflamed opinion in Croatia when it was printed in *Srbobran*, the principal Serbian periodical in Zagreb. It gave credence to the opinions of Croatian nationalists such as Starčević's followers, and it further embittered Serb and Croat relations both within and without the monarchy.

Croatian Nationalism

Croatian nationalism was fueled not only by conflicts with the Serbs but also by the activities of Károly Khuen-Héderváry, who was *ban* (governor) of Croatia from 1883 to 1903. Representing Hungarian interests, he sought to thwart Croatian national goals such as the efforts to unite Dalmatia with Croatia-Slavonia. Most important, invoking the principle of divide and rule, his administration catered to the Serbian minority in religious, educational, and economic matters in return for its support in the sabor. Although he enjoyed considerable political success, his actions strengthened Croatian national feelings and the Party of Right.

In this period Starčević's party, which had been relatively weak previously, emerged as the dominant political influence. His demands for Croatian unity and autonomy and his strident anti-Serbianism appealed to many sections of the Croatian population. Whereas earlier the educated youth had been drawn to the Illyrian

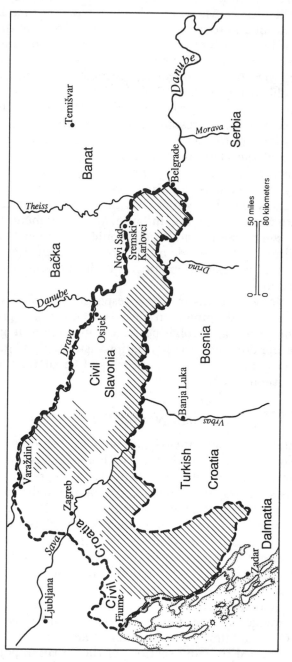

The Habsburg-Croatian Military Frontier

movement and the Yugoslav idea, the new generation, similar to the members of the Serbian Youth Movement, were more attracted by strong national appeals. In addition, Croatian suspicions had been aroused by the conflict over Bosnia-Hercegovina and by persistent demands of the Serbian Orthodox church that the schools be returned to church jurisdiction. Fears about Serbian influence were increased not only by the tactics of Khuen-Héderváry but also by the rise in the Serbian population in Croatia-Slavonia. In 1881 the Military Frontier, which had been under Habsburg administration since the seventeenth century, was returned to Croatian control. This measure added 190,000 Serbs to the state, thereby increasing the Serbian share to one-quarter of the entire population. Although the negative effect of Starčević's ideas on South Slav relations was obvious, his activities did serve to increase the sense of national identity and consciousness among the Croats. When his influence began to wane in the early nineties, his cause was taken up by one of his followers, Josip Frank, a Jewish lawyer who converted to Catholicism.

Whereas Starčević had seen the Austro-Hungarian Empire as the principal impediment to Croatian national interests, Frank, at the head of the newly organized Pure Party of [Croatian State] Right, directed his major attacks against the Hungarians and the Serbs. He called for cooperation with Vienna against both Budapest and Belgrade. His supporters and those of Starčević took part in violent anti-Hungarian flag-burning demonstrations in 1895 on the occasion of Franz Joseph's visit to Zagreb. In the next years Croatian nationalists participated in other confrontations with the Habsburg Serbs. The climax was reached in 1902, after the publication of Stojanović's article "Serbs and Croats." Throughout the area Croats took to the streets, beating up Serbs, breaking their store windows, and generally harassing them. The policy of divide and rule, together with the increase in Croatian nationalism as shown in the popularity of both Starčević and Frank, created an atmosphere of hostility between the Serbs and Croats unparalleled in the century.

THE YUGOSLAV IDEA REEMERGES, 1903–1914

With this background of increasing antagonism between Serbs and Croats, it would appear that concepts of Yugoslav unity would have been permanently weakened. Yet in the next decade these ideas won renewed support among various groups in Serbia and among the South Slavs of the Habsburg Empire. A number of reasons account for this development. First, in 1903 an army coup resulted in the assassination of Alexander Obrenović and the accession to the throne of Peter Karadjordjević. A grandson of the leader of the first Serbian revolution, King Peter was believed to be sympathetic to ideas of South Slav cooperation. Second, in Croatia the replacement of Khuen-Héderváry as *ban* ended two decades of officially orchestrated hostility between the Croats and Serbs. Third, in contrast to the previous period, the new youth movements became South Slav oriented. For example, many young students, primarily from Croatia, but also from Slovenia and Serbia, were deeply influenced by their studies with the Czech professor Thomas Masaryk, who urged them to unite behind a Yugoslav program. These developments did not mean that the great majority of Serbs, Croats, and Slovenes turned away from their national convictions. Those who favored a unified Yugoslav state remained a small minority, consisting primarily of intellectuals. Nevertheless, discussions concerning the possibility and advisability of Yugoslav unity became increasingly frequent. Some parties and organizations even included this goal in their programs.

Serbia, 1903–1914

After the accession of the new dynasty in 1903 the major attention of the political leaders was directed toward the achievement of the national program. The platforms of all of the major political parties identified this goal as the liberation and unification of the Serbian nation; none called for South Slav unity. These views were shared by all elements of the population. Expressing these sentiments, the minister of education in his appeal for more funds from the parliament in 1908 stressed that his request was "based on the needs of Serbdom . . . on the preparation of students who are the future of Serbdom." Serbia's successes would also have an impact on "the distant enlightened Serbian regions, in Vojvodina and the Triune Kingdom, [as well as] in Bosnia, Hercegovina, Macedonia, and Old Serbia."[13]

With these convictions it is understandable why Serbian nationalists regarded the Habsburg annexation of Bosnia-Hercegovina in 1908 as such a disaster. As long as the provinces remained under Ottoman suzerainty, there was hope that they might sometime join Serbia. Full Habsburg control made such an event a remote possibility indeed. It must be remembered that almost all the Serbs believed that the population of the region was solidly Serbian. Thus the independent newspaper *Odjek* stated that not only were these provinces ethnically purely Serbian, but so was Dalmatia, which was "populated in the majority by Serbian inhabitants of the Orthodox and

Catholic faiths."[14] *Delo*, the organ of the ruling Radical Party, earlier had declared that "Bosnia is our Alsace-Lorraine."[15] The loss of the two provinces, of course, greatly intensified the national animosity toward the Dual Monarchy and ultimately affected Serbian attitudes toward the South Slav question.

The disappointment over the loss of Bosnia was at least partially assuaged by the large territorial gains in the Balkan Wars of 1912–13. Serbia was almost doubled in size, and its population was increased by 50 percent. The state now included Macedonia, the heart of Dušan's empire, Old Serbia, with the historic battlefield of Kosovo, and Peć, the site of the former patriarchate. Despite the Serbian claims on these regions on the basis of historic rights, the population, although largely Orthodox, was not in the majority Serbian. At this time the emphasis was entirely on the Serbian national program. Although the Macedonian population was largely "South Slavic," this aspect of the annexation was entirely ignored.

The strength of Serbian national sentiment can be measured in a number of ways. For example, the most popular Serbian almanac, *Vardar*, the organ of the Circle of Serbian Sisters, in 1908 published a large multicolored map that identified all the South Slav lands—Croatia, Slavonia, Dalmatia, Vojvodina, Istria, Bosnia, Hercegovina, Montenegro, Old Serbia, and Macedonia—as being Serbian. Only Slovenia and Bulgaria were excluded. In a 1911 editorial, *Vardar* repeated the claim that Croatia, Slavonia, Dalmatia, and Istria were Serbian lands. A similar viewpoint was taken by the patriotic organization Narodna Odbrana (National Defense), formed in 1908 to combat the annexation. In 1911 it adopted as its motto "All for Serbdom and the Fatherland."[16]

Whereas these organizations operated openly, another organization, Union or Death, commonly known as the Black Hand, was a clandestine, conspiratorial group. Founded in 1911 by Serbian officers, many of whom were closely associated with the 1903 coup, the Black Hand stood for a militant national program. The first article in its secret by-laws stated that its goal was "the unification of Serbdom." Article VII identified the Serbian lands still to be acquired as "(1) Bosnia and Hercegovina, (2) Montenegro, (3) Old Serbia and Macedonia, (4) Croatia, Slavonia, and Srem, (5) Vojvodina, and (6) the Littoral [Dalmatia]."[17] South Slav unity was obviously not even considered. What should also be noted is that the lands identified by *Vardar* and the Black Hand as being rightfully Serbian were precisely those listed in the Serbian textbooks.

Although, as can be seen, in the majority official and public opinion strongly backed Pan-Serbian goals, there were voices raised in another direction. In both the Habsburg Empire and Serbia, student groups were organized that supported South Slav unification on an egalitarian basis. In Serbia the most important was that associated with the Belgrade periodical *Slovenski Jug*. In 1903 it called for "an immediate alliance of Serbia, Bulgaria, and Montenegro and later all the South Slavs" based on the "identity of language, culture, education, economy, laws, and customs, as well as common interests."[18] The student group deplored Greater Serbianism, Greater Croatianism, and Greater Bulgarianism, concepts which it regarded as reflecting sterile past policies. The future would instead bring South Slav unity.

Those associated with *Slovenski Jug* were well aware that their policy of South Slav cooperation did not enjoy popular support in Serbia. In an editorial published in 1911, entitled "Serbian Frankovites," the author attacked those Serbs who held ideas which paralleled those of the followers of Frank in Croatia:

> Serbian Frankovites are Serbs who commit on the Serbian side those acts against the Croats which are committed on the Croatian side against the Serbs by the followers of the late Josip Frank. . . . There are Serbian Frankovites. Those are the people for whom there are "no Croats" in Bosnia-Hercegovina, nor, perhaps there aren't any in Croatia, but "there are" Serbs on all sides. For our Frankovites even Istria is Serbian, Trieste is Serbian (!), and for them, in general there are no Croats. If they do exist, they do so with the permission of these people, but only as a branch of the great and powerful Serbian race![19]

Aside from those who supported either a Greater Serbian or a Yugoslav program, there were some who doubted the practicality of a South Slav orientation. In a 1912 editorial *Pravda*, the newspaper of the Progressive Party, raised some of the questions that disturbed Serbian nationalists concerning the Yugoslav idea. Questioning the idealism of the students who spoke of South Slav unity, *Pravda* asked if it was "Dušan's Greater Serbia or Yugoslavia" that they sought. If it was the latter, there were several options for its achievement. One was the union of the South Slavs of the Dual Monarchy, a step that could lead to the eventual conquest and absorption of Serbia. This result was in fact favored by some Croats and Slovenes. Serbs thus had reason to be suspicious of plans for a South Slav union.[20]

The difficulty in achieving a Yugoslav goal was also commented upon in 1909 by Ljubomir Stojanović, the minister of education: "The realization of the Yugoslav ideal is in the distant future, because before then many obstacles and misunderstandings must be overcome, the intrigues that the enemies had sown among the South Slavs must be cast aside and the need for unity must be developed and strengthened."[21] It must be remembered also that until 1914 the Latin alphabet was not taught in Serbian elementary schools and that the Gregorian calendar was not adopted until after the war. There were many simple, practical measures that still needed to be taken on both sides in order to further better understanding.

The principal spokesman of Serbian national policy was Nikola Pašić, the leading Serbian political figure of his day. A strong patriot and nationalist as well as the leader of the Radical Party, he wrote in his unpublished memoirs that his goal was to have Serbia become an independent, constitutional, parliamentary state that would lead in "the unification of the Serbian nation." Serbia was to be "the center of Serbdom" and the "Piedmont of all Serbdom."[22] Yet early in his career he recognized the importance of the Croatian issue. In an unpublished manuscript, probably written in the 1890s, entitled "The Unity of the Serbo-Croats," he wrote that the principal conflict centered around the question of who would lead in the task of unifying the Yugoslav lands and whose influence and traditions would subsequently prevail. Understandably, he believed that Serbia, as an independent nation, was best suited for this role. Moreover, "the Serbian nation has preserved many more characteristics of the Slavic peoples than has Croatia, which is under foreign cultural influences." Among these, the Catholic influence was of major importance, since Austria-Hungary and, by implication, Croatia were in "constant collusion with the Vatican."[23]

From 1904 to 1918 Pašić held the office of prime minister almost continually. In those years his policies both toward his domestic opponents and in foreign relations were characterized by pragmatism and realism. He followed the events in Croatia, in particular the formation of the Croatian-Serbian coalition (to be discussed in the next section), but he did not want its activities to compromise Serbian relations with the Dual Monarchy. He recognized that "the question of our liberation and unification will not be decided by the politicians of the Serbo-Croatian Coalition; rather, it will be decided by Serbia and Russia. Neither one nor the other is yet prepared for war."[24] He thus clearly recognized that a South Slav movement led by Serbia implied war with the Habsburg Empire.

Although the emphasis in Serbia was thus on the achievement of specific national aims, some efforts were made to strengthen Serbo-Croatian understanding. In January 1912, Ljubomir Jovanović, the minister of education, issued a directive (whose details will be discussed in the next chapter) whose aim was to acquaint Serbian students with Croatian cultural achievements. The war, of course, interrupted the implementation of this program. Since no efforts had been made in this direction before this date, it can be seen why the top Serbian military and civilian leaders were in the vast majority educated in the spirit of and thoroughly convinced of the justice of the Serbian national program. In 1914 the goal remained the unification of lands that they considered Serbian.

Croatia

In contrast to Serbia, where the South Slav idea had limited appeal, in Croatia there was a resurgence of interest in reviving Serbo-Croat cooperation, in part due to the easing of tensions after the departure of Khuen-Héderváry. Moreover, the remembrance of the discord that had characterized his administration caused some political leaders to recall a better previous era. For example, Mihailo Polit-Desančić, who had been a Serbian representative in the sabor for many years, recalled in his eulogy to Franjo Rački, who died in 1895, what it had been like in the 1860s, when Serbs and Croats had together fought against the restrictions of the *Nagodba*: "God grant that the young generation of Croats and Serbs will again follow the path that once was taken by sensible Croats and Serbs, when they jointly defended the rights of their nation in the scholarly and political arena."[25] Another Serbian leader, Svetozar Pribićević, a prewar advocate of South Slav union, noted that if indeed the Serbs and Croats were two different people, with different cultures and national interests, their disputes could be resolved within this framework. However, "the Serbo-Croatian quarrel cannot be taken as a national question, because the Serbs and Croats are not two different nations, but are part of one and the same."[26] In the same spirit Lovre Monti, a prominent leader in the Dalmatian and Viennese parliaments, argued that if Bavarian Catholics and Württemberg Protestants were members of one and the same German nation, then why could not Catholic Croats and Serbian Orthodox similarly belong to the same nationality. Concepts such as "unity, brotherhood, freedom, and nationality" were meaningless until Croats and Serbs, divided by ideas of "Croatianism" and "Serbianism," finally understood that they could not survive without one another.[27]

Such convictions were the basis of the so-called new course introduced in 1904–05. Although this political direction stressed the right of each nation to determine its own future, it called for some form of united action between them. However, those who supported the concept did not have a common understanding of its precise implications. For example, Stjepan Radić's Peasant Party, which became the dominant party in Croatia in the postwar era, accepted the premise that the Serbs and Croats were one people, but it stressed that each had developed a separate historical identity. Their unity could only be realized after the Croatian state was united and Croatian national consciousness fully developed. Nor could there be any compromise at the expense of the name "Croatia" or the "Croatian language." Unity could be achieved only between political and cultural equals.

Despite the reservations of some of the political leaders, in 1905 five Croatian and Serbian parties and some prominent but unaffiliated politicians joined to form the Croatian-Serbian Coalition. Its fundamental principle was *narodno jedinstvo*, national unity. Implicitly or explicitly those who associated themselves with the movement accepted the idea that Serbs and Croats were one nation with two names—or three if the Slovenes were included. The three peoples together thus constituted a single nationality, the Yugoslav. The spokesmen for the Coalition thought primarily in terms of the cooperation of the South Slavs of the monarchy. The union was thus a political association that did not seek to jeopardize the territorial integrity of the Habsburg Empire. Subsequently others, in particular youth groups and some intellectuals, sought to expand the unity concept to include the Serbs of Serbia and Montenegro, with the recognition that the center would be Belgrade. In other words, their goal was a South Slav state organized at the expense of the Habsburg Empire.

The strength of the Coalition was demonstrated in the sabor elections of May 1906 when it gained a plurality of thirty-seven seats, controlling 42 percent of the votes. Thereafter, in every free election (1908, 1910, 1911, and 1913), it secured either an absolute majority or a plurality. The Coalition gained particular cohesion and strength when it was faced with political or economic pressure from Vienna or Budapest.

Although Serbs and Croats could easily cooperate in opposing Austrian or Hungarian policies, they did not share similar common interests when the fate of Bosnia-Hercegovina came into question. The annexation in 1908 raised some of the same issues that had surfaced in 1878. Baron Pavao Rauch, the new *ban* of Croatia, was able to some degree to exploit the disagreements, but he did not succeed in measurably weakening the Coalition. Nevertheless, the issue did cause tension. Many Croats after the annexation envisioned a future Croatian political unit encompassing the Triune Kingdom and Bosnia-Hercegovina. This state could well become the center of the Croatian-dominated Yugoslavia so feared by Serbian nationalists. Moreover, Croats of all persuasions were disturbed by the claims coming from Belgrade that the entire population of the two provinces was exclusively Serbian; they were even more alarmed by similar claims in regard to Dalmatia. Of course, in the opposite camp, many Habsburg Serbs, conscious of Serbian state interests, wished the provinces to remain under Ottoman rule, since autonomy would make a future annexation by Belgrade easier.

The emphasis on Serbo-Croatian cooperation, represented by the Coalition, was also reflected in the ideas of the influential South Slavic youth organizations in the Habsburg Empire. Many university students in Croatia, who strongly admired Serbia and its achievements, became ardent Serbophiles. Their sentiments were well expressed by Augustin Ujević, a prominent Croatian author, who in various letters to Pašić hailed the victories of the Serbian army. He saw its triumphs in the two Balkan wars as the result of "the national conscience and the general common Serbocroatian culture."[28] To those that charged that a political union would only result in the Serbianization of the Croats, Ujević replied that the common goal was a Yugoslavia based on the equality of the Serbs, Croats, and Slovenes. These general sentiments were shared by Ivan Meštrović, a prominent Croatian sculptor, and Ivo Vojnović, a major Croatian dramatist. Of course, even among the intellectual youth, there was no unanimity of opinion. Some saw the goal of a Yugoslavia as something that could be achieved only in the distant future; others, more radical, favored the absorption of the Croats and Slovenes into the Serbian nation. Although extremely active and vocal, the Habsburg youth did not have political strength and, of course, were not represented in the sabor.

The opposition to the Yugoslav program of the Coalition was led primarily by the Frankovites. Opposed to Hungarian control as well as to cooperation with the Serbs, they denounced anyone who accepted the *Nagodba*, worked for South Slav understanding, or conceded that Serbs lived in Croatia-Slavonia. In one of their best-known brochures, "The So-Called 'Serbian' Question," the Frankovites stated categorically that in Croatia there was only one political nation, the Croatian, and that only the Croatian crown, flag, coat-of-arms, and public inscriptions should be displayed. The Serbs were accused of flaunting the Serbian flag and of using its coat-of-arms; even their use of Cyrillic was attacked. These "so-called Serbs," the pamphlet continued, were devoted "body and soul" to the king of Serbia. Within the Habsburg Empire they were creating a state within a state that could eventually be fatal to the Croatian kingdom. They even denied them their right to call themselves Serbs: "*Nations are not divided nor differentiated by religion*; thus, even if they are of different faiths, nevertheless they can and must be Croats, because all those who live off the Croatian land and speak Croatian are obligated to acknowledge that they are loyal sons of this homeland, that is, that they are Croats."[29] Although the Frankovites never won a majority or even a plurality in the sabor, they did at different times have about a dozen representatives, or about 15 percent of the entire body.

Similar views were held by another party, the Milinovci, named after Mile Starčević, the nephew of the former leader of the Party of Right. Its members too believed that the Croats were the only political nation, but they were willing to recognize Serbian "ethnic" and "religious" differences. At times cooperating with the Frankovites in the sabor, they had considerable political influence. In the 1913 elections the Milinovci and the Frankovites together elected twenty representatives. Thus about a fourth of the membership of the sabor at this time held pronounced Croatian nationalist views and opposed a common front with the Serbs of the monarchy.

As we can thus see, despite the opposition of these two parties, there was considerable sentiment in Croatia for a closer understanding among the South Slavs of the monarchy. The success of the Coalition assured that result. However, even though the Croatian leaders professed respect for their Serbian counterparts and called for the equality of the two people, at no time did they envisage this cooperation as being other than within the framework of a Croatian state. Ideas of unity were limited to the Slavs of the Habsburg Empire, among whom the Croats formed the plurality. The quarrels over Bosnia and Hercegovina well illustrated the tenuous nature of the Croatian-Serbian relationship. As Pašić had earlier observed, the question of who would lead in the quest for Yugoslav unity was the essential issue, and one unsettled at the outbreak of World War I.

THE SLOVENES

The Yugoslav movement from its inception had operated under the assumption that not only would the Serbs and Croats unite, but they would be joined by the Slovenes. Despite this conviction both the Serbian and Croatian intellectuals, with their strong emphasis on the connection between language and national identity, did not apply this standard to their fellow South Slavs. For example, Rački in the sixties urged the Slovenes to abandon their kajkavian dialect and learn štokavian, the common language of the Croats and Serbs. Before the war Frano Supilo, a strong advocate of the Coalition and of South Slav cooperation, shared the same opinion. In Serbia Jovan Skerlić, the leading literary critic, and many of his colleagues made the same suggestion. The basis for their arguments was their opinion that the Slovenes could retain their Slavic identity only by joining with the Serbs and Croats in a linguistic union; the alternative would be total assimilation by the Germans.

By the end of the nineteenth century, however, the preservation of their kajkavian dialect had become a central element in the awakening Slovenian national consciousness. Unlike the Serbs and Croats, who could look back to medieval kingdoms and had preserved certain national institutions, the Slovenes had except for a brief period in the eighth century been continually under foreign rule. Even more important, the Slovenes lived in four separate provinces—Carniola, Styria, Carinthia, and the Adriatic Littoral. Here German was the primary language of administration, commerce and education. Faced with these conditions, it can be understood why the Slovene leadership in the nineteenth century concentrated on achieving two goals: the preservation of their language through control of their schools and the unification of their people in a single administrative unit. South Slav unity was not a major issue for a people who needed to take the first steps toward asserting their national identity.

By the nineteenth century, the Slovenian kajkavian dialect had become a standardized literary language. In the sixteenth century, Primož Trubar had translated the Bible; in the eighteenth and nineteenth centuries, Marko Pohlin and Jernej Kopitar provided grammars, and Anton Linhart wrote a history of the Slovenian people. Convinced of the importance of the Slovenian dialect and rejecting Gaj's appeal for a common South Slavic language, France Prešeren, Slovenia's greatest poet, wrote in kajkavian.

For the Slovene nationalists, however, the critical issue was the language of instruction in the schools. Education in the Slovenian lands was regulated by Austrian education laws. Although these authorized the use of any language if forty or more students living within four kilometers in circumference of the school demanded it, the implementation and enforcement of the provision was at the discretion of the provincial and regional authorities. Language was not a problem in Carniola, where the population was overwhelmingly Slovenian. However, in Styria and Carinthia, where forty percent of the Slovenes lived, they were in the minority. The local German authorities attempted to block any measure that called for specifically

Slovenian advantages. This conflict persisted until 1918 and was a central issue for all the Slovenian political parties.

In the programs of the three parties—the Slovene People's Party (or Clerical Party), the Liberals, and the Social Democrats—the greatest attention was directed toward local issues. However, their leaders too had to consider the issue of Yugoslav cooperation. Although in 1870 about a hundred Slovenes, Croats, and Serbs met in Ljubljana and drafted a Yugoslav program, initially there was little interest in the South Slav question among the population. The first serious consideration of these issues came in the eighties and nineties. As might be expected, the Liberal Party, representing 25 percent of the electorate, was sympathetic toward the aims of the Croatian-Serbian Coalition and its efforts to further South Slav understanding. After the annexation of Bosnia-Hercegovina, some of its members expressed sympathy for the Serbian attitude, but most favored the Habsburg action. With few links to Belgrade, the party leaders considered Yugoslav unity only as it applied to the Habsburg South Slavs.

The other two parties were even less inclined to seek radical solutions. The Clericalists, who regularly won about 65 percent of votes in local elections, felt at home in the Catholic Habsburg Empire. In regard to the Serbs, their chief interest was in winning over the Orthodox to Catholicism. The Social Democrats, who received 10 percent of the votes, similarly supported the monarchy, although they believed in cultural autonomy and favored the reorganization of the state on a federal basis. They rejected any links with Serbia, which they regarded as politically and economically backward. In 1913 one Social Democrat, expressing a general Slovenian viewpoint on South Slav unification, commented: "We never put forward the idea of Yugoslavism so that we could someday set aside our own language, our own national manners and customs in order to become something new overnight, that is, that we become a so-called nation, which does not as yet even exist."[30]

The one exception to this trend was to be found in the Slovenian youth movement, Preporod, which was active in the two years before the outbreak of war. Within its ranks there were indeed individuals who were pro-Yugoslav, pro-Serbian, and anti-Habsburg. However, as was also the case with similar associations in Serbia and Croatia, the Slovenian students expressed their views loudly and strongly but exercised little political influence.

It can thus be seen that by 1914, although the Slovenian leaders had come out strongly in the defense of their language and their national identity, they were loyal to the monarchy. As one Slovenian authority has stated: "On the eve of the First World War the anti-Austrian movement was only in its incipient stage in the Slovenian areas of the monarchy, although it was already beginning to spread rapidly."[31] The limited support for the Yugoslav cause in Slovenia was well known in Belgrade and Zagreb.

THE DEGREE OF SOUTH SLAV UNITY IN 1914

From this brief survey, whose purpose has been to provide the political background within which to analyze the role of education and the textbooks in the development of nationalism and Yugoslavism, it can be seen that broad support for South Slav unity was limited at best. Neither the Serbs nor the Croats nor the Slovenes embraced the concept unreservedly. Instead they looked to their own nation's past achievements to provide the inspiration for future progress. Indeed, many writers who used Yugoslav terminology were in fact advancing their own nation's interests. Thus, for example, Gaj's Illyrianism had as its main aim to provide a linguistic basis for the unification of the Croatian lands. Similarly, Garašanin's *Načertanije* was actually a blueprint for Serbian unification. Although Karadžić's claim that all štokavian speakers were Serbs was based on his understanding of linguistic principles, his views in later years were given a political interpretation. Starčević's Greater Croatian convictions were based on the premise that the Serbs and Slovenes were all Croats. Without their numerical inclusion, Croatia's geopolitical weaknesses were obvious. Strossmayer and Rački believed in the necessity of South Slavic unity, but their program too was conceived with Croatia's interests first in mind. The differences that surfaced between Serbs and Croats over the occupation of Bosnia and Hercegovina revealed the fragility of South Slav unity. Leaders in each nation recognized the importance of the two provinces to their respective national programs and the advantage they would gain in dealing with the other nation if these lands were under their own control. Other general issues that came into sharp focus at this time similarly intensified Serbian and Croatian nationalism.

Although support for the Yugoslav idea grew in the decade before the war, its most enthusiastic adherents were a relatively limited number of intellectuals and students. Ignoring the realities of historical forces and politics, these individuals believed that through goodwill and understanding Serbs, Croats, and Slovenes would make political, religious, social, cultural, and economic sacrifices in behalf of the common good. Few others shared their optimism. Even the program of the Croatian-Serbian Coalition, which of all the political parties, including those in Serbia, came closest to accepting the concept of Yugoslav unity, concentrated its efforts on achieving Croatian and Serbian understanding within the monarchy, ignoring, for all practical purposes, the Slovenes. Moreover, the Coalition did not explicitly or implicitly advocate closer ties with the Serbs in the neighboring kingdom.

Among the Slovenes whatever support there was for Yugoslav unity was confined to a belief that the South Slavs of the empire should work together. The dominant Clerical Party believed that such cooperation would be a means to convert the Serbs to Catholicism. None of the parties advocated any arrangement that included Serbia, save a handful of students.

As far as Serbia was concerned, as we have seen, its leaders throughout the nineteenth century concentrated on gaining those lands which they claimed as theirs on historical or ethnic bases. The political and military victories, particularly in the Balkan Wars, heightened Serbian national enthusiasm and served to attract the support of the Serbs of the Habsburg Monarchy. Although there were some signs of support for a Yugoslav program, particularly among youth groups, the official Serbian goals were to enlarge and enhance the state, not to create a Yugoslavia.

2

The Serbian, Croatian, and Slovenian Educational Systems

In this section a brief analysis of the educational systems in Serbia, Croatia, and Slovenia will be given. In addition, the principal issues affecting the writing of textbooks and education in general will be discussed. The emphasis will be on those questions which affected the contents of educational material available to students in the South Slav lands.

EDUCATION IN SERBIA

On March 1, 1880, the Serbian *skupština* (assembly) passed a law creating the Chief Educational Council. The regulation stated that the minister of education and religious affairs would "administer higher and elementary education in accordance with the state idea and contemporary scholarship." As the minister's principal advisory body, the Council's main function was to provide him with "its views on all important questions of higher and lower education, educational developments at home and abroad, school curricula, and scholarly literature."[1] Among the many issues that the Council was empowered to consider were educational planning, teacher certification, student examinations, the review and recommendation of textbooks, and library acquisitions. Its broad responsibilities were expanded in later years so that finally there were few aspects of education that it did not consider. The government and the minister set the goals; the Council devised programs and plans to achieve them.

The Council consisted of eight to twelve members, who served two-year terms with the possibility of reappointment. According to law, its membership was to include four professors, two from the Philosophical Faculty and one each from the Law and Science faculties of the university (called the Velika Škola or Great School until 1905, when it was officially designated the University of Belgrade); the director of the National Library; one school superintendent; one professor each from the school of theology, the teachers' college, and the Belgrade *realka* (high school); two professors from the Belgrade gymnasium; and a doctor.[2] Since it was considered an honor to serve on this board, some of the most distinguished scholars as well as cultural and public figures in Serbia participated in its deliberations between 1880 and 1914. Among this group were, for example, Jovan Cvijić, Jovan Djordjević, Achimandrite Ničifor Dučić, Bogdan Gavrilović, Sima Lozanić, Josip Pančić, Bogdan Popović, Pavle Popović, Jovan Skerlić, and Nikola Vulić.[3]

In addition, the Council had ten to twenty associate members or consultants, who served one-year terms. Some were drawn from the same institutions as the regular members, but there were also four elementary school teachers and six gymnasium professors from outside Belgrade. The members of this group provided advice in their fields of specialization. Within this group were several well-known authors of textbooks, for example, Uroš Blagojević, Mihailo Jović, Mihailo Stanojević, and Milenko Vukičević.[4]

The initial Council was appointed by Stojan Novaković, the first minister of education and religious affairs. A historian and philologist, he had a distinguished career, serving as an ambassador, minister of foreign affairs, prime minister, and president of the Serbian Academy. The author of over four hundred scholarly works, he also wrote the first *Serbian Reader for the Lower Gymnasiums and Realkas*, which was used until 1909. After Karadžić, Novaković was perhaps the leading authority on the Serbian people and their history. At the initial meeting of the Council he demonstrated his devotion to Serbian national goals. Declaring that the body had assumed a major responsibility, he defined its task as aiding "the national progress . . . in every sphere of national life. . . . The source of everything was without doubt education." What Serbia had achieved historically could be attributed to its intellectual, creative endeavors. Furthermore, the "unity . . . and the future of the entire nation . . . depended on the education of the people." Progress in politics, military affairs, industry, agriculture, and trade could not be achieved "without education, without literacy, schools, [and] books." If Serbia were to have "a better and more brilliant future," he added, great attention would have to be paid to education.[5]

In a subsequent speech Novaković explained the need to draw

up a precise program and coordinate all educational endeavors behind a single goal: "the entire future of the nation depends upon schools, and schools will become a strong and powerful organism in the life of the nation only when there is one soul and one goal in every part of the fatherland."[6]

It has been estimated that the Council held about 1,100 meetings before 1914. In the initial period through 1894, 604, or an average of about forty a year, were held. At this time the educational system was thoroughly evaluated.[7] As directed by law, the council considered educational programs, curriculum revisions, the content of textbooks, handbooks, and teachers' guides, the qualifications of teachers, examinations for teachers, discipline in schools, the political views of teachers, as well as questions involving school buildings, their furnishings and hygienic facilities, the size of school yards, the standards for classrooms, the types of student benches, and residences for teachers.

The Council's major undertaking, however, was to develop a new program for elementary and secondary schools and teachers' colleges. There were also vocational schools, a theological school, and the University of Belgrade. Reforms were made in all the basic institutions, but for our study those enacted in the elementary and secondary schools and the teachers' colleges are the most important.[8]

The first fundamental reform occurred in elementary education, where no basic change had taken place since 1862. In 1882, a new law, commonly called the Novaković Law, which decreed that there were to be four years of compulsory elementary education, was passed. In 1880 there were about 200,000 children between the ages of six and twelve; about 36,000 of them started the school year, but only about 80 percent completed it. The goal was to have 100,000 students enrolled by 1890; to do so would depend, in part, upon such things as the construction of new schools and the availability of qualified teachers.[9]

The major reform in secondary education was to make the realka, whose curriculum consisted of general subjects, the principal secondary school institution. A large number of those who completed this program eventually became teachers. To the disappointment of many, the Council decreed that classical and humanistic studies should be confined to the gymnasium, which would serve as the preparatory school for the university.

It was not the schools, however, but their curriculum that was basic for the development of Serbian nationalism. The Council decided that the core of instruction in elementary schools was to be "the Serbian language"; hence the most hours were allocated for its study. Whereas in the early years grammar was emphasized, by the end of the century composition was being stressed. History and geography, including "the study of Serbian lands outside the kingdom," were also stressed.[10]

There were four basic revisions of the elementary school curriculum—in 1883, 1891, 1899, and 1904—and two in the secondary schools, in 1881 and 1899. In the prewar years, there were minor changes, but none involved the entire program of study. Here the curriculums will be examined from the point of view of the number of hours devoted to the study of the Serbian language, history, and geography.

In the 1883 elementary school curriculum, each student who completed the four-year program spent ninety-three hours in class. Of this, twenty-six were devoted to study of the Serbian language, eight to a combined course of "geography with history," and four to Serbian history, for a total of thirty-eight hours. Those three subjects represented 40 percent of the student's total hours in school. If one adds the eight hours for religion, a compulsory subject in all schools, in which the Orthodox faith and the study of the Serbian church were stressed, 50 percent of class hours were devoted to subjects dealing with Serbia.[11]

In the 1891 curriculum, five class hours were added, for a total of ninety-eight. Now the student studied thirty hours of Serbian, up from twenty-six. Geography, a separate course, was taught for nine hours, and Serbian history was taught for three hours, instead of the previous four. These three subjects represented 43 percent of the curriculum. In 1899 the total number of hours remained the same—ninety-eight. The course on the Serbian language was twenty-eight hours, but it now included reading in Church Slavonic, which in 1883 and 1891 was taught as a separate subject for two hours. A combined course of geography and Serbian history was studied for seven hours. These three subjects represented only 36 percent of the curriculum, a drop of 7 percent. More emphasis was placed on practical subjects such as mathematics, agriculture, and manual training for boys, and home economics for girls. The only significant modification in 1904 was that history and geography were again taught as separate subjects.[12]

In 1881 there were two kinds of secondary schools, the realka, which emphasized sciences and modern languages in preparation for the professions, and the gymnasium, which stressed the classics required for entrance into the university. Each had seven grades. In 1886 another year was added to the gymnasium, but this did not occur in the realka until 1898. In 1881 the curriculum was identical in the first four years of both. It included 122 hours, of which the Serbian language and Serbian grammar represented seventeen hours, Serbian history six, and geography, which included cosmology, twelve. In the last three years the curriculums of the two schools diverged, each emphasizing the subjects that corresponded to its stated goal. In 1886, when another year was added to the gymnasium, the changes in the curriculum were mainly increases or decreases in hours for some subjects. However, what had formerly been a course on the history of general literature was now called "the history of Serbian literature."[13]

In 1893 a strong effort was made to restore classical and humanistic studies in the realka, but it was defeated. However, the controversy continued until a compromise was reached in 1898. Now there were three types of secondary schools—the gymnasium, the realna gymnasium, and the technical gymnasium. The gymnasium retained its former program; the realna gymnasium stressed general subjects but also included Latin and Greek; the technical gymnasium emphasized training for the sciences and professions. In all three, study of the Serbian language occupied more hours than any other course, with the exception of Latin in the gymnasium and realna gymnasium. Geography and history were prominent in all three curriculums.[14]

Similar comparisons can be made for the teachers' colleges, whose curriculum was reformed in 1881, 1887, and 1896. In 1881 the schools had a four-year program; it was reduced to three years in 1887 but increased again to four in 1896. Here also, Serbian language, geography, and history were emphasized. In 1881 "the Serbian language with Church Slavonic and literature" was given eleven hours, geography four, and Serbian history three. In the three-year program of 1887, "Serbian language and literature" were taught for nine hours, "physical geography and the political geography of the Serbian lands and the Balkan peninsula" three hours, and Serbian history three hours. In 1896 Serbian language and literature were studied for twelve hours, geography for four hours, and Serbian history three; a new two-hour course entitled "Understanding Civil Rights and Responsibilities" was introduced. Of course, students in the teachers' colleges were required to take a variety of courses such as psychology, pedagogy, and methodology, in preparation for their profession. Nevertheless, the teachers were expected to be well versed in the language, history, and geography of both the Serbs of the kingdom and those who lived outside the kingdom.[15]

Another fact in connection with the curriculums which should be mentioned concerns alphabet. The Latin equivalent of the Cyrillic alphabet (Latinica) was not taught in the Serbian elementary schools before 1914. In previous years prominent Serbs had repeatedly brought up the question. However, the measure was never adopted. Students learned the Latin alphabet in the advanced schools—secondary, teachers', vocational, etc.—when they were required to study Latin, German, or French. Thus students in the elementary schools, who in 1910 represented 95 percent of the enrollment, could not read Croatian books, journals, newspapers, calendars, etc., unless they had learned the Latin alphabet on their own.

Although the Council devoted considerable effort to curriculums, most of its attention was devoted to textbooks. In the opinion of the authors of the recently published *One Hundred Years of the Educational Council of Serbia, 1880–1980,* "Of all the matters with which the Chief Educational Council was concerned, it appears . . . most dealt with those which directly related to textbooks and other books intended for schools, and also those [books] which could in some sense be of value to the students or teachers of the most diverse specialized interests."[16] As noted earlier, Novaković had stated that Serbia needed to produce textbooks that were appropriate for its educational program. Hence the government provided general guidelines of the topics it wished to include in textbooks for each subject. It did not specify the exact content; the author decided that.

An example of how the Council operated can be seen in the instructions involving readers. Since language was the most important subject, the Council's guidelines to authors were clear. The content of the reading textbook should "focus on the study of the Serbian language"; its purpose was gradually to introduce students to "the national literature."[17] The language in the readers should provide examples that could be models for speaking and writing. Readers for the lower elementary-school grades were expected to contain subject matter dealing with family, school, and church, as well as stories, songs, fables, folktales, and selections from Serbia's "newer literature." Readers for the upper grades were to include subjects dealing with the nation and state, taking into account the geography and history being studied at the time. The readers were also expected to have illustrations depicting historical events whenever appropriate. The authors were further instructed to include information of importance to girls. In other words, the subject matter of language, history, and geography courses was to be coordinated. Based upon this information, each author was free to select his own material.[18]

After receiving manuscripts submitted by competing authors, the Council appointed two to four experts to review them and to submit written evaluations. These reports, published in *Prosvetni Glasnik*, disclose that the specialists took their assignments seriously. Using these recommendations and their own assessment of the manuscripts, the Council submitted its report to the minister of education and religious affairs. In almost all instances he followed its advice. The textbook adopted was published by the state and became its property for five years, with royalties paid the author. Six months before the expiration date, the author was informed if his textbook was to be republished. If the competition was reopened, he could revise his book and resubmit it. This procedure was followed for all textbooks. The government also approved supplementary readings.[19]

The minutes of the Council, published in *Prosvetni Glasnik*, indicate that its members were generally in agreement with the experts' recommendations. When opinions differed, a vote was taken, sometimes by secret ballot. However, it must not be assumed that the Council was immune to factors other than merit when it and the minister made their decisions. For example, in 1905, Stanoje Stanojević, a major historian of the period, published a critical review of the officially approved secondary-school textbook *History of the Serbian Nation*, by Milenko Vukičević. Stanojević questioned Vukičević's competence as a scholar, his use of sources, and the book's presentation. Nevertheless, Vukičević's textbooks continued to be approved. In fact, when Stanojević and L. Zrnić submitted their own textbook in the competition, Vukičević was asked to evaluate it. He replied in kind. Vukičević was a teacher in a Belgrade gymnasium who had become a member of King Peter's inner circle and often accompanied the monarch on his trips. He also had been shown favor by the government when he was given permission to publish Garašanin's *Načertanije* in 1906.[20]

In another example, Novaković's *Serbian Reader*, first published in 1870 and revised later by Svetislav Vulović, was regularly approved by the Council and was in use into the twentieth century. In 1909, the three experts appointed by the Council—Jovan Skerlić, Pavle Popović, and Milutin Dragutinović—recommended against further authorization of Novaković's book. It had been a valuable reader and had served its purpose well in the past, they noted, but it was written more from a philological point of view, whereas the students of today should be exposed to new currents in contemporary Serbian literature. Similar criticisms had been made earlier of Novaković's reader, but they were discounted, most probably because, as noted above, he was a prominent public figure.[21]

The Council acted with remarkable unanimity in the selection of textbooks. Novaković's admonition in 1881 that it should coordinate its choices to conform to Serbian national aims was indeed implemented in the grammars, readers, geographies, and history books. Their purpose was to educate loyal, patriotic citizens who would enthusiastically support the national goals of the Serbian state. An example of how the Council furthered current government objectives came in 1913. In 1912 Ljubomir Jovanović, the minister of education, issued a directive that steps should be taken to achieve "the ideas of cultural unity with the Serbs outside Serbia and at the same time with the Croats, the first priority being to become better acquainted with their literary heritage. . . . Hence publications of the Matica Srpska (the Serbian Literary Foundation), Matica Hrvatska (the Croatian Literary Foundation) and the Society of Croatian Writers . . . should be purchased for the public, school, and teachers' libraries and reading rooms."[22] This shift in direction from a purely Serbian emphasis toward some form of South Slav awareness was incorporated in some textbooks. In 1913 a committee of experts headed by Jovan Skerlić, an exponent of South Slav cooperation, was asked to review a number of elementary school readers for the Council. This board subsequently recommended that "more space should be given to Croatian literature, at least as much space as there was in Croatian school readers for Serbian literature."[23] In other words, the textbooks should reflect the decision of the government that the students should know more about the Croats. However, only about half a dozen textbooks were printed that carried this new theme before war broke out.

Notwithstanding the intentions of the government and the outstanding work of the Education Council, the achievements fell short of the goals. Two of the basic provisions of the education law were never fully implemented. The first mandated that compulsory education be provided for all children, initially for a period of four years, which was later extended to six. The statistics, however, indicate that about 95 percent of children never went beyond the fourth grade. The exceptions were children who lived in urban areas, where fifth and sixth grade classes were available. A second provision made each community largely responsible for the financial implementation of the law. However, since the bulk of the population lived in rural areas where communities lacked the funds necessary to construct and maintain schools, these communities had to appeal constantly to Belgrade for assistance. Rural teachers, many of whom were underpaid and poorly trained, often had to supplement their incomes with menial jobs. Thus, although all sections of the population recognized the importance of education, the schools never received adequate financial support.

In 1880 the budget for education was approximately 1,193,000 dinars, with 607,000 dinars, or 51 percent, coming from the central administration. By 1900 the budget was 3,487,000 dinars, with the state's share 2,134,000, or 61 percent. In 1910 the budget increased to 5,519,000, with Belgrade contributing 3,612,000 dinars or 65 percent. In other words, as the economy improved, the state increased its assistance.[24]

In 1880, when the population of Serbia numbered 1,724,000, there were 680 elementary schools, with a total enrollment of 36,314. By 1900 the population had risen to 2,492,000 and 321 new schools had been constructed, for a total of 1,102; enrollment had almost tripled, to 103,000. A decade later, when the population was 2,911,000, there were 1,328 schools, with 145,000 students in attendance. The statistics are not clear concerning the number of children of school age who attended school, but it appears that the figure was below 50 percent.

In 1880 there were twenty-five secondary institutions (including realkas, gymnasiums, teachers' colleges, theological schools, and trade schools); the number had increased to thirty-two by 1910. Total enrollment in the realkas and gymnasiums was 2,498 in 1880, 3,851 in 1900, and 8,858 in 1910. When the students from the theological schools, teachers' colleges and higher girls' schools are included, the total for 1910 was over 10,000 students. The university, however, was not large. In 1880 it had 130 students, in 1900 415, and in 1910 941, numbers that represent only 0.6 of one percent of the students who were attending elementary school in the same year.

One major aim of education, of course, was to eradicate illiteracy. Here again the statistics are somewhat misleading. A literate was defined as anyone above the age of six who could read and write. Thus in 1900, for example, only 17 percent of the population, or 423,433, were classified as literate. Of this group, 53 percent were in the age group 11–30. By 1914 it is estimated that literacy nationwide had increased to approximately 40 percent. The figures also show that literacy rates were more than four times higher in the cities and towns than in the rural areas.

On the eve of the war, Serbia thus had a four-year elementary school system functioning throughout the land and secondary schools that met the basic needs of the nation. The teacher cadre was generally well trained, and elementary and secondary-school textbooks for all subjects were available.

EDUCATION IN CROATIA

In some respects, educational development in Croatia was similar to that in Serbia. As an independent state, Serbia formulated its own educational policy and created a system to implement it. Croatia, as a result of the Nagodba of 1868, had also gained control of its school system, but with limitations. As noted in chapter 1, Vienna and Budapest could influence Croatia's internal affairs. Moreover, without the counter-signature of the Habsburg monarch, no fundamental changes in any law could be implemented. Other differences between Serbia and Croatia also affected education. Even though education had been secularized in Serbia, there the Orthodox church was a state institution. It provided the unifying link between the Serbs of the kingdom and those who lived under Ottoman and Habsburg rule. Church and state coordinated their efforts, which included education, on behalf of the nation.

In contrast to the close ties between church and state in Serbia, in Croatia the law that secularized elementary education pitted the Catholic church authorities against civil authorities. The reasons advanced on behalf of secularization varied. First, although the church hierarchy and clergy perceived themselves as the sole custodians of the nation and its heritage, they were always subordinate to the papacy. Whenever national issues engulfed the Habsburg Empire, Rome tended to side with Vienna against the nationalities. Second, in part because of the church's influence on education in the empire, the demand for secularization became a cardinal principle of nineteenth-century German liberalism. As a result, education was secularized in Hungary in 1868, in Austria in 1869, and even in the Military Frontier in 1871. A similar development in Croatian education would put Croatia in step with the other areas of the empire. Third, the Croatian teachers' association was a major force behind this goal. It cited all the traditional arguments on behalf of secularization—the poor quality of religious education, the paucity of schools, the lack of qualified teachers, the outdated curriculums and textbooks, and the inadequate salaries. Finally, others contended that non-confessional state schools would in fact break down the religious and other barriers that had divided Croat from Serb: "the inhabitants of one land will be offered the opportunity mutually to come together and to get to know one another, to learn to love one another as sons of one mother should."[25] Ivan Filipović, the founder of the teachers' association and a passionate champion of secular education and South Slavic unity, stated: "Croats and Serbs, in our unity is our hope, and the school must, it alone can, clear the way to creating that national unity."[26] His sentiments echoed those expressed by Rački in his inaugural presidential address to the Yugoslav Academy, in which he stressed the importance of education.

The Catholic church and the Orthodox church opposed secularization because each would lose control over its respective schools. Equally important, Strossmayer and Rački, both of whom worked unswervingly for South Slav understanding and some form of unity, objected to the reforms. Strossmayer wanted the church to continue to exercise control over the curriculum and the contents of textbooks. Rački charged that the reformers were being influenced by "kike-German (*čifutski-njemačko*) liberalism."[27]

Notwithstanding the opposition, in 1874 the educational law was approved. It had been drafted the preceding year by a committee that represented the different points of view. The clerical position was defended by Father Franjo Klaić, the head of the clerical teachers' association, a principal and teacher of bookkeeping and penmanship, whereas Ivan Filipović, the leader of the lay teachers, advocated the secularization of schools. Filipović was the author of primers, readers, dictionaries, and scores of nationalistic works. The other committee members were Pavao Muhić, the minister of religion and education; Janko Jurković, an education specialist; Živko Vukasović and Andrija Knezević, school inspectors in the Military Frontier; Canon Adolfo Veber-Tkalčević, a member of the Yugoslav Academy, author of readers and a Croatian grammar, and inspector of the Zagreb archdiocesan schools; Franjo Petračić, another author of readers and the principal of the Zagreb gymnasium; and Ivan Stožir, a professor of mathematics and science in a realka. The ban, Ivan Mažuranić, presided over the committee.[28]

In an address to the sabor, Ban Mažuranić, presenting the draft of the law on education, stated the principles on which the government's policy was based.[29] His arguments were aimed at the church and were designed to justify the secularization of education.

> The new relations into which the state had entered vis-à-vis the church as regards public schooling, which have already been strengthened in practice by the educational legislation of almost all European states and particularly of the Austro-Hungarian Monarchy, cannot be disregarded in the reorganization of public schools in this land, for the very same reason that they arose elsewhere. . . . Above all, the Croatian-Slavonian state government cannot renounce the rights to ultimate administration and supervision [of the schools].

The church, Mažuranić continued, was not "excluded from that influence in the public schools which belongs to it by fairness and rights and, in the interest of the state, it must be more vigorously desired." Yet in "defending the rights of the state over public education," the government reserves for the church "as much influence as is deemed necessary, so that through a common effort the goal of the public schools is reached, as defined in Article 1 of the law." Article 1 stated that "the task of the public school is to educate children religiously and morally; to develop their mental and physical powers; and to instruct them in the general knowledge and skill necessary for civil life."

To reassure the church, Mažuranić added that not only would it have control over religion and morals, but one of its representatives would also serve at each level of the school administration—the local school board, the county school system, and the State Education Commission. He hoped that the law would not split church and state, but rather "guarantee the harmonious work of both these factors in the state system which are naturally divided into spheres of responsibility." Furthermore, "the public school, on which this law is based, takes into consideration the modern demand of the community and public to the extent that in its principles it does not exclude the community of children of different faiths." On the critical issue of language, he affirmed that the "language of instruction is Croatian, but the right to use as the language of instruction the mother tongue of another group in the state is guaranteed, so long as the local commune builds and supports a public school at its expense." For those who did not know Croatian, it must "be taught as a compulsory language in the school." He concluded his address by repeating that just as the church was responsible for the religious and moral upbringing of the students, so the state had reserved for itself the right to provide a general education for its citizens.

The principal provisions of the law were the following: there were to be four years of free, compulsory education; each locality was required to support a public school, even if there were already religious or private schools in the community; Croatian was to be the language of instruction in all schools, except in localities where the mother tongue of the children was another language, in which case Croatian was to be taught as a compulsory language. Readers were to have identical selections in Latin and Cyrillic. The state was to set the curriculum, and only state-authorized textbooks would be permitted. The sole exception was for the course on religion, for which the church could prescribe the textbooks. All teachers would be selected by the local school boards, based upon an advertised public competition and approved by the state. Teachers were to be employees of the state, except for instructors of religion, whom the church would appoint. Each community would have its own local school board, composed of the principal, one teacher, two to five citizens, and a member of the church, usually the priest. The supervisor of the county schools, who was appointed by the state, would administer them with the help of a committee composed of one member of the church, two teachers, and six citizens. Final authority was to be invested in the State Education Commission, headed by a state official, one representative of each religion, and six teachers selected from the public schools. Among its responsibilities, the Commission was to set the curriculum, authorize textbooks, and supervise the schools.

In addition to the basic four years of elementary school, for which there was to be a set curriculum, there were to be three additional grades of upper or middle school, which would prepare students for advanced work in crafts, trade, and farming. The law also prescribed a three-year program for teacher training and set its curriculum.[30]

The government had prepared its case carefully and lobbied effectively. Knowing that the opposition did not have the votes to block the law, the parliamentary leaders let the opposition, which came mainly from supporters of the church, state its case. Thus Stjepan Vučetić, argued that the church

> had the indisputable right to direct all education in the schools, and protect and defend its daughter the school. . . . The church has to look after not only the study of religion, but also all school books, because if religion does not penetrate all knowledge, then, as with yeast in dough, teaching will not be successful. The present failures in public schools are the responsibility of not the clergy but the state. . . . It is sad that the school is being taken away from the church in our homeland, when the church civilized the Croats and created the schools . . . and with this law [the state] expresses a lack of confidence in the church and priesthood.[31]

Other arguments were also made, but to no avail. The revisions that were accepted in the proposed law did not in any manner affect its aim. The opposition's frustration was perhaps best expressed by one member who, referring to the fact that the government had stressed that the church would have one member on each level of the school administration, remarked that it reminded him of the man who told a mother whose daughter had been abducted: "Mother, you can go to the child, but you are only allowed to say three words, one in the morning, the other at noon, and the third in the evening."[32]

Having disposed of the Catholic church's opposition, the sabor was confronted by strong objections from Serbian Orthodox church spokesmen. They argued that the integrity and identity of the Serbs in Croatia would be compromised if they did not have complete control over their schools—with their own curriculum, textbooks, and supervisors—as they had had in the past.[33] Obviously, this demand could not be met without compromising the basic aim of the law—the secularization of education. More important, the same provisions would have to be extended to the Catholic schools. The only concession granted the Serbs was an article stating that "wherever in this law the Croatian language is mentioned as the language of instruction, it is understood that this language in the Serbian school communes is identical to the Serbian language."[34] Furthermore, Cyrillic was to be taught in the public schools. In fact, Cyrillic had been taught in the Croatian schools since 1861, beginning with the second grade of elementary school. As for the interchangeability of Croatian and Serbian, this notion too was welcomed by those who supported a close understanding between Croats and Serbs. In their view the national public schools would bring together the children of the nation, notwithstanding religious differences, thus contributing to the defense and development of political unity, which was the purpose of the law.[35] The law, they believed, would strengthen the Croatian nation and contribute to South Slav understanding. In part, at least, however, it would have the opposite effect.

Whereas in the past, education had not been a major issue between the Croats and Serbs, since each church had controlled its own schools, set its own curriculum, and prescribed its own textbooks, now the law set the churches in opposition to one another. From 1874 to 1914 the Serbian patriarchate in Sremski Karlovci and the Serbian Church Congress never gave up their efforts to regain absolute control over their schools. While not objecting to the Orthodox attacks on the law itself, the Catholic prelates increasingly came to regard the Serbian demands as more than just a religious issue. They perceived the Serbian goal to be the creation of a Serbian "political-religious" entity within the Croatian state—in other words, they saw a threat to the integrity of the nation. This view was held especially by the Starčevićites and Frankovites, but also by many individuals of other political persuasions. As a result, in both Serbia and Croatia the clergy came to play a vital role in identifying national interests and questioning the wisdom of South Slav unity.

Following the lead of the other lands in the empire, secondary education in Croatia had been secularized two decades earlier; it enrolled less than 5 percent of the students. The major issues considered in 1874 involved the teaching of language, history, and geography and the question of teachers' salaries and pensions. As in Serbia, Croatia had two types of secondary schools, an eight-year classical, human-

istic gymnasium and a seven-year realka, which stressed the sciences and prepared students for the professions. In addition, there
were teachers' colleges and trade schools. In 1875 the University of
Zagreb was constituted. It had three faculties—theology, law, and
philosophy.[36]

In 1888, during the administration of Ban Khuen-Héderváry, the
elementary school law was revised. The principal reason for doing so
was that the teachers sought to extend the 1874 law to the Military
Frontier lands, which had been restored to Croatia-Slavonia in 1881.
Their aim was to make six years of education compulsory and to
have an eight-year program for the upper or middle schools. This
step, however, revived the divisive issue of church-state relations,
with the focus now on the Serbian Orthodox church and its supporters in the sabor.[37]

In 1887 the emperor had signed a law stating that the Cyrillic
alphabet was equal to the Latin and could be used in all governmen-
tal communications. Moreover, in those localities where a majority
of the population used Cyrillic, correspondence and proclamations
were to be in Serbian. Although this measure was welcomed by the
Serbian leaders, their goal was to regain control over their schools.
Since Khuen-Héderváry had been able to implement most of his
policies only with the support of Serbian members of the sabor, the
latter now pushed for a revision of the school law. Thus, in November 1887, the representatives of the Serbian Club in the sabor stated
their demands in a memorandum.[38]

Without controlling their schools, the Serbs contended, they
would be unable to defend their "nationality, religion, and alphabet." Subjects that were essential to educating "Serbian children
in the Serbian Orthodox spirit" were being neglected, namely, the
Cyrillic alphabet, Church Slavonic script, national history, religion,
and religious singing. They wanted Serbian instructors to teach these
subjects in the public schools. Communities with their own religious schools should not be required to support a public school. And
in the teachers' colleges they wanted the curriculum expanded to include church singing and the reading and interpretation of religious
works, which should be taught by Serbs to Orthodox students. The
implementation of these measures would "best guarantee the indi-
viduality and distinctiveness of the Serbian people" in those regions
in which Serbians had lived for "hundreds of years in union with the
brotherly Croatian people," but from whom the Serbs through their
"distinctive customs, distinctive alphabet and religion" were separated "from the Croatian nation of the same race. . . ."[39]

In April 1888 the Serbian Orthodox National Church School

Council, at a session presided over by Patriarch German Angelić, submitted its views on the same subject to the sabor. It reaffirmed the basic arguments made by the Serbian Club but concluded with the admonition that "unless the Serbian national schools are permitted to revive, to be strengthened and allowed to flourish—by this means and this means only will there be real unity and true love between the two brotherly tribes, between Croats and Serbs."[40]

In 1888, after acrimonious debates in which the Starčevićites condemned what they called the Serbianization of the Croatian schools, the Mažuranić law of 1874 was replaced. The new law divided elementary schools into a lower and higher public school, the latter being for four years. The teachers' college would also have a four-year program. The language of instruction was to be "Croatian or Serbian." Communities with their own religious and autonomous Serbian schools were no longer required to support public schools, a concession that partially satisfied the demands of the Serbian representatives. The sabor rejected a provision stating that "every book in the religious schools, before it could be introduced, must be approved by the state government." The concern was that, in order to appease the religious authorities, all textbooks would again come under the control of the church. Instead, the sabor decreed that, excluding the religious textbooks, only those books prescribed by the government would be permitted, and "any others are prohibited." Subsequent to this law no major reforms in elementary education were enacted until 1914, although revisions were made in the curriculum.[41]

The effect of the 1888 law was to revive the Serbian schools. No longer would Serbs be required to support both religious and public schools. Also, whereas in 1874 the curriculum had simply listed "religion" as a subject, the new requirement was for "religion and, for students of the Greek-Eastern faith, the reading of Church Slavonic texts." The Serbs also gained the political advantage of having the language of instruction called "Croatian or Serbian."

As for the secondary schools, in 1894 they were divided into three units—the gymnasium, the realna gymnasium, and the realka. As had happened in Serbia, disputes arose between the advocates of the classical gymnasium and the proponents of the realka. The same solution was reached as in Serbia. The eight-year classical gymnasium was retained, but the eight-year realka was divided. The lower realka remained at four years. Thereafter, the students either attended, for an additional four years, the realna gymnasium, which emphasized a broad, general program plus classical languages as preparation for the university, or continued in the realka, where they studied scientific and practical subjects in preparation for a profession.[42]

In all of the reforms, the study of language, history, and geography was given a prominent role in the various curriculums. In Croatia, as in Serbia, the goal of the educational system was not only to prepare students for the technical and scientific changes taking place in the modern world but also to instill in each student a love for his homeland. Of the subjects taught, language was the most important. Repeatedly it was stated that language represented the soul of the nation. In the Croatian curriculum, as in the Serbian, language was always listed immediately after religion. More hours were devoted to the study of language than to any other subject. The 1874 law for the public elementary schools stated that students were required to study "the mother tongue—reading, writing, grammar, and practice in speaking and expressing one's thoughts in writing." History and geography were included in the readers, together with physics and natural science. In the upper elementary school the language was called Croatian, and there was a separate course for "geography and history, with special emphasis on the homeland and its constitution."[43] The new education law of 1888 mandated the study of "the mother tongue—reading, writing, grammar, and exercise in speaking and expressing one's thoughts in writing, and, where Croatian or Serbian is not the language of instruction, they are to be studied as compulsory subjects." "The most important topics from geography, history, physics, and natural science" were included in the readers. In the upper elementary school the curriculum called for "Croatian or Serbian and its components" and "geography and history, with special attention to the homeland and its constitution."[44]

In 1895 geography and history were dropped from the curriculum, but they were reintroduced in 1900 in a new course entitled "general education based upon readers," which included, in addition to history and geography, natural science and general subjects. In 1905 history and geography again became separate subjects.[45]

In the secondary schools, where the programs of study were directed toward specific goals, Croatian did not have the highest priority. In the eight-year gymnasium, where the program stressed classical and humanistic training, more hours were devoted to Latin (47) and Greek (28), than to Croatian (27). However, twenty-eight hours were devoted to history and geography, which were taught in the first four grades as separate subjects and in the other four in a combined course. In the realkas, because of the emphasis on science and technology, the concentration was on German (20 hours) and French (14), with the hours varying due to frequent changes in the distribution of courses in the curriculum. Neither language exceeded Croatian in emphasis. Geography and history, which at times were taught separately and at times jointly, equaled or exceeded the hours devoted to Croatian.[46]

Understandably in the teachers' colleges language, geography, and history were prominent. Only the course on pedagogy exceeded Croatian in the number of hours devoted to it. The 1874 law stipulated that future teachers be taught "the Croatian language and the history of its literature" and "geography and history, with special emphasis on the homeland and its constitution." The 1888 law mandated identical requirements, with the language now called "Croatian or Serbian."[47]

For every course in the curriculum, the Education Commission provided a specific outline of topics to be presented in each semester and authorized textbooks. This information served as a guide for the authors of textbooks, who were not instructed what specific information should be included, only the subjects to be presented. For example, among the many topics in history mentioned in the curriculum for the first semester of the fourth grade of the public schools in 1900 were "The Life and Homeland of the Ancient Croats and Serbs," "The Christianization of Croats and Serbs," "Tomislav," and "Saint Sava." Second-semester topics included "The Fall of Serbia and Bosnia," "The Military Frontier," "Dubrovnik," "The Arrival of the Serbs under Crnojević," "Literary Revival," and "Franz Joseph I." Using these directives, the author wrote his book.[48]

In contrast to Serbia, where there was open competition among authors, in Croatia many textbooks were commissioned. Some were written by individual authors, whereas others were collaborative works, especially readers for the elementary schools, where information from different subjects was included. The Education Commission reviewed the books and, if they were accepted, authorized their adoption.

In December 1874 the minister of religious affairs and education requested the Croatian Pedagogical Literary Association to prepare new readers for the lower schools. Since Ivan Filipović, a prime mover behind the education reform in 1874, had founded the association, it was evident that the new textbooks would reflect the intent of the law. Skender Fabković, Filipović's closest collaborator and now president of the association, who was also an author of textbooks, sent a circular letter to all the teachers requesting their cooperation and assistance. He opened his appeal by noting that "the more eyes, the more one sees" hence "the more wisdom there is, the better the foundation and the better the results." He asked teachers to send individual reports to the association detailing the information they had found most useful in their classrooms. For example, they were asked to indicate the most effective stories, fables, riddles, proverbs, songs, and the like, that should be included in the readers. The teachers were also asked to write their reports "in the orthography used by our academy," that is, in štokavian.[49]

These reports were made available to the authors selected to prepare the new textbooks. All of them supported Vuk Karadžić's linguistic reforms and closer South Slav cooperation. The new primer (1878) was written by Ljudevit Modec; the reader for the second grade (1878) by Fabković; the third and fourth grade readers (1879) were a collaborative effort of members of the association. Fabković also wrote the grammar section for each reader. A committee of the association reviewed the books and incorporated the revisions suggested for the primer. The evidence indicates that the Education Commission regularly sought advice and was not hesitant to reject books or ask for revisions. Its greatest problem, however, dealt with criticism of the books based on political and religious, rather than scholarly and pedagogical, criteria.[50]

The criticisms directed against the first textbooks were representative of views expressed in subsequent years as well. The supporters of the church found that Modec's primer lacked religious significance. J. Glaser's textbook on psychology for the teachers' college was condemned by Bishop Stadler as "a masterpiece of materialism and of anti-Christian spirit." S. Basariček's volume on the theory of pedagogy was "a true masterpiece of naturalism." These comments were directed as much against the substantive content of the textbooks as against what the church supporters called "German liberalism," which they believed had permeated the Croatian school system and which they considered responsible for the secularization of education. Some authors were even accused of not acting in the best interest of Croatia, and their patriotism was challenged.[51]

At the same time, legitimate questions were raised. For example, Modec, in his primer, wrote about "our" cities, naming Zagreb, Zadar, Novi Sad, and Belgrade. What did "our" mean? Clearly Novi Sad and Belgrade were Serbian cities. As one observer noted, there were circumstances in which Zagreb and Belgrade could be discussed together, or Nikola Zrinski and Miloš Obilić, but these were subjects for historians and specialists in literature. They should not be included in the primers, where a child who was learning by rote and was not yet able to make comparisons might draw the wrong conclusions. It was apparent that a main objective of the critics was to undermine the 1874 reforms by criticizing the textbooks. In fact, the minister of education appointed a special committee to investigate these charges and issues.[52]

The content of textbooks became a prime issue also in politics. In the 1880s and 1890s, when tensions between the Croats and Serbs were at their peak, Croatian nationalists sought to have the sabor do away with the teaching of Cyrillic, but without success. Charges were also made in the sabor that the contents of the textbooks should not be such as to lead one to believe "that we are in the Serbian kingdom." Students must be "inculcated with love for the fatherland, so that they know that this is the Kingdom of Croatia and Slavonia."[53] To the charge that in the elementary and especially the secondary schools, Croatian history was taught poorly, Tomislav Maretić, the leading Croatian Slavicist of the period, a professor in the university and eventually president of the Yugoslav Academy, and at this time a member of the sabor, replied that history should be taught the way it happened and not the way Starčević's Party of Right wanted it presented: "The student must understand the history of his nation and of his people, because without knowing it, he cannot love it; he must understand it in its historical as well as its geographical context." Historians must not, continued Maretić, present Nikola Zrinski and Krsto Frankopan as though they were members of the Party of Right. The Party also wished to have Andrija Kačić-Miošić, the eighteenth-century author, represented "as the bard of the Party of Right. It is necessary not to master his works, but only to glance through them, to see that he expressed equal love toward the Serbs, Croats, and Bulgars, and he even favorably mentions Hungarian heroes, because he was interested only in glorifying the Christian struggle against the half-crescent."[54]

Another sabor representative quoted from the teachers' manual for the primer, which explained why the word Croatia was not mentioned even once in the book. The reason offered was that "it is not necessary that children read and write an infinite series of meaningless names, which they have not yet heard; therefore, the name of our homeland is not mentioned in the primer, because it is not possible to explain to children in the first grade the concept of the homeland; much less the concept of the Kingdom of Croatia, Slavonia, and Dalmatia." If the children could not understand these concepts, then why, asked the representative, include proverbs with philosophical connotations, such as "shame is the reverse of goodness"; "one is blind who cannot read"; "every bird is strong in its own nest"; and "it is foolish to want something, but not know how to get it"?[55]

Most of the criticisms were made by those who objected to the textbooks' extensive presentation of material on the Serbs and the support given to South Slavic understanding. However, even Pavao

Jovanović, the editor of the Zagreb *Srbobran*, a Serbian newspaper, who was the most outspoken defender of Serbian rights in the sabor, criticized a section in a third-year reader entitled "Croats Arrive in the South and Create Their Own State." He objected in particular to one sentence: "The people in present-day Croatia, Slavonia, and Dalmatia are by origin one and the same Croatian people." Were there no Serbs? he asked. He also quoted from the Apprentice School textbook, which stated that "the first Croatian printing press was in Cetinje in 1493." "Gentlemen," he added, "this shows you that the Montenegrins are Croats. Are they? Ask some Montenegrin if he is a Croat and you will hear what he will tell you."[56]

The secularization of Croatian education in 1874, in accordance with prevailing nineteenth-century liberal principles, had two basic purposes—first, to modernize the educational system in accordance with European practices and, second, to create amicable relations with the Serbs, who represented one-fourth of the population in Croatia-Slavonia. It is difficult to fault the provisions of the law because it did not exhibit preference for any group. In fact, if it was prejudicial, it discriminated against the Croats, because its initial goal was to break the power of the Catholic church in education. The Serbs, however, sought preferential treatment for their schools, and when it was not granted many assumed that the sole intent of the law was an attempt to subvert their rights and identity as Serbs. As a result, many in Croatia questioned the Serbs' motives and even had reservations about their loyalty in Croatia-Slavonia. This assumption was especially prevalent during the era of Khuen-Héderváry, when the Serbian leaders regularly sided with Hungarian authorities in implementing measures that in the eyes of many Croatian spokesmen went contrary to the interests of the Croatian state.

The revised education law of 1888, which appeared to favor the Serbian minority, exacerbated relations between Croats and Serbs. Consequently, as time passed both the Catholic and Orthodox church leaders were more concerned with defending the interests of their respective nations and faiths than they were with reconciling national differences. The Starčevićites and Frankovites in particular perceived the law as a threat to the integrity of the Croatian nation-state. Even during the years when the Croatian-Serbian Coalition scored impressive political victories, it was not successful in resolving the educational issues dividing the two peoples. In fact, in 1909 a serious attempt was made in the sabor to suspend the teaching of the Cyrillic alphabet, which, as we have noted, had been taught regularly since 1861. The argument advanced was that since 95 percent of all Croatian children completed only elementary school, few would ever have occasion to read Cyrillic as adults. The measure failed, but it exposed the intensity of feeling that persisted among many Croats. It also revealed that the support for South Slav unity was considerably less than its spokesmen sought to convey.

The educational goals that the Croatian authorities set for their nation were never realized, in part because their resources were limited. According to the terms of the Nagodba of 1868, 55 percent of all taxes collected in Croatia-Slavonia were allocated to the Kingdom of Hungary for expenses common to the realm. From the remaining 45 percent, the Croatian state met all its obligations, including the salaries of state officials, members of the judiciary, the police, and the teachers, as well as the maintenance of roads and the construction of public buildings and other public works. Although the localities were obligated to cover the basic cost of education, most, especially those in rural areas, where most of the children lived, were unable to meet their needs. Therefore, like their Serbian counterparts, they looked to the central administration for assistance. Because teachers were underpaid, they often had to hold two jobs and live with a village family. The low level of teachers' salaries was a constant source of grievance. Nevertheless, despite these and other problems, there was a gradual improvement in all aspects of Croatian education.

In 1885 there were 1,263 elementary schools and 223,063 children of school age, of whom only 143,450 (64 percent) attended classes. In 1900 there were 1,407 schools, with 318,584 eligible students, of whom only 199,292 were enrolled (63 percent). In 1910 there were 1,596 schools, with 396,119 students of school age, of whom only 265,972 attended school (67 percent). In other words, in these years approximately one-third of all children did not attend school. For these same years the budget for elementary schools increased from 2,445,264 crowns in 1885 to 3,540,635 crowns in 1900 and 6,160,210 in 1910; thus, there was an increase of about 250 percent in a quarter-century.[57]

In the secondary schools there were 5,947 students enrolled in 1886, 6,693 in 1900, and 7,212 in 1910. The expenditures for these years were 941,402 crowns in 1886, 1,057,642 in 1900, and 1,607,513 in 1910, for an increase of 170 percent. When the enrollment figures from the other schools—teachers', girls', agriculture, trade, commerce, theology, maritime, music, and art—are added to the secondary school numbers, the total enrollment in 1910 was well over 10,000.

The University of Zagreb had 307 students in 1880, 677 in 1900, and 1,179 in 1910. As an illustration, and as was the case in Serbia, in 1910 only 0.4 of one percent of the number of students enrolled in the elementary school attended the university.

The figures for literacy are somewhat misleading. Anyone above the age of five who could read and write was defined as literate in the 1880s and 1890s, and anyone over six in the twentieth century. Accepting this criterion, in 1880, from a population of 1,564,150 above the age of five, 390,253, or 25 percent, were designated as literate. In 1890, of 1,806,439 individuals, 582,927, or 32 percent, were in the literate category. In 1900 of 2,011,790 individuals older than six, literates represented 887,878, or 54 percent. In 1910, of 2,194,669 people, literates accounted for 1,153,784, or 52 percent. Even if one accepts this criterion for the definition of literacy, it is evident that only about half of the population met the necessary standards on the eve of the war.

A comparison of Serbian and Croatian statistics is revealing. Collectively, these two states in 1910 had about 400,000 children enrolled in elementary schools and 16,000 in gymnasiums and realkas. The two universities' combined enrollment was 2,120. There were, of course, Serbian and Croatian students studying in universities abroad, but their numbers do not appreciably alter the basic situation. Although both Serbs and Croats had made substantial progress in education, they still had much to accomplish.

EDUCATION IN SLOVENIA

In contrast to Serbia and Croatia, each of which had their own education laws, in Slovenia, which was associated with the Austrian half of the Dual Monarchy, elementary education was chiefly affected by the Imperial School Law of 1869 and secondary education by the Imperial Resolution of 1849. Beginning in the eighteenth century the Habsburg government supported education and had achieved considerable success in its development. With the emergence of the national question in the mid-nineteenth century, the Austrian government was confronted with an educational issue that it never was able to resolve. Each nationality was determined to have its own language used for instruction in the schools. Without their own schools, language, teachers, and textbooks, the minority nations would continue to be subordinate to the culturally dominant Germans. Hence in time the issue became more political than pedagogical.

Whereas Serbia was independent and Croatia-Slavonia had the Nagodba with Hungary in 1868, the Slovenes, as noted earlier, lived in four Austrian provinces—Carniola, Styria, Carinthia, the Adriatic Littoral—as well as in southwestern Hungary. With the exception of Carniola, they were a minority in each province. Numbering at most 1,200,000 in 1869 and about 1,252,000 in 1910, they never were able to exert the same degree of political pressure on the Habsburg government as did the Czechs, the Poles, or even the Croats and Serbs in Dalmatia. Control of the schools thus became a primary concern through which the national leaders sought to forge a cohesive consciousness.

By the imperial law of 1869, which provided for secularized education, the provincial authorities, in consultation with those of the city or commune, determined the language of instruction in the elementary schools. In the non-German regions, German was offered as an elective subject in the fifth through eighth grades. In secondary schools, the resolution of 1849 no longer mandated German as the sole language of instruction in gymnasiums and realkas; instead, the language was left to the determination of provincial and local authorities. However, in order to graduate from the gymnasium, each student was required to pass exams in both reading and writing German.[58]

Whereas these laws appeared to be straightforward, perhaps no regulations were subject to more litigation in the remaining years of the empire than those involving education, especially in the elementary schools. The issues were complex and real. They represented a struggle for political power. For the Germans, who had dominated the empire since its creation, political control was a matter of national survival. For non-Germans, such as the Slovenes, education represented the first step in the battle for national revival. For all the minority nations, and especially for the numerically weak Slovenes, German was the language of commerce, trade, industry, technology, and advanced education. In other words, for Slovenes to be competitive in the modern world, they had to know German. Yet they came to believe that in Styria and Carinthia, where about 491,000 or 40 percent of their population lived, their national identity was compromised by German provincial and local administrations that favored their own co-nationals in disputes involving education. Therefore, in many districts the language of instruction in elementary schools attended by Slovenian children was German, notwithstanding a provision in the law of 1869 stipulating that every national group could have its own school if forty children of school age lived within an area four kilometers in circumference.[59] The law was often not enforced, or protracted litigation delayed its implementation. Equally important, this provision did not apply to secondary schools; thus, for advanced Slovenian students the language of instruction was German. To appreciate the impact of these disputes in education, one need only recall that the fall of the imperial Windischgrätz government in 1895 was precipitated by the educational controversy in Celje (Cilli) between Slovenes and Germans.

According to the law of 1869 there were two levels of elementary schools—the four-year curriculum and the upper or public school (that is, fifth through eighth grades). The law mandated eight years of compulsory education, but for the Slovenes this was only feasible in the wealthier German provinces of Styria and Carinthia. In the other lands, four years of schooling was most common, with some children having six; however, the overwhelming majority of children completed only the basic first four grades. In the upper public schools, mainly found in cities and industrial centers, the curriculum was directed toward preparing the students to learn a trade.[60]

The secondary schools followed essentially the same pattern found in Serbia and Croatia. The eight-year gymnasium was oriented toward the classics, to prepare the student for the university. The realka, which was introduced in the Slovenian areas in 1870, had a seven-year curriculum (which in 1908 was expanded to eight) as the prerequisite for the professions.[61]

Whereas the education laws of 1849 and 1869 permitted either Slovene or German as the language of instruction, the curriculum for the elementary schools was set by the imperial law. From the point of view of this study, the subjects taught in Slovenia did not vary appreciably from those taught in Serbia and Croatia. As in those two states, the aim of the law was to provide for the moral and religious training of the children. Hence the first subject listed in the curriculum was religion; the second was language. In contrast to Serbia, where history and geography were taught as separate subjects in the elementary schools, in Slovenia, as in Croatia, history and geography were combined in one course, which also included natural sciences and "special consideration for the Fatherland and its constitution." Since the schools attended by Slovenian students were in different provinces, the number of hours devoted to each subject varied. However, the study of language, whether Slovenian or German, received the most attention, followed by geography and history. These courses, together with religion, were the core of the curriculum, and it was their purpose to instill citizenship and develop patriotism. The other subjects were arithmetic, penmanship, drawing, singing, and physical education.[62]

In the gymnasium and realka, religion, language, history, and geography were compulsory courses. Although the hours in the eight-year gymnasium differed at different periods, in relative terms they did not deviate from those of the Ljubljana gymnasium in 1880. The student studied religion for 26 hours, Latin for 86, Greek for 38, German for 41, Slovenian for 34, geography and history for 44, mathematics for 40, natural sciences for 36, and physics for 22. In the realka the emphasis was on German and French, rather than Latin and Greek, and extensive hours were devoted to the sciences and mathematics.[63]

Serbia and Croatia each had its own university, but the imperial authorities rejected numerous petitions to establish one in Ljubljana. Hence the vast majority of Slovene students who pursued a university education were compelled to attend either the University of Vienna or the University of Graz, with some also enrolling in Prague or Zagreb.[64]

Notwithstanding the obstacles that Slovenian education faced, by 1914 Slovene national consciousness had taken root throughout all the provinces. In large measure this was due to the success of their schools. Thus, for example, in 1910 illiteracy among Slovenes above the age of ten was only 15 percent nationally; the highest rate was in Istria, 47 percent. In Carniola, with the largest Slovene population, 491,000, illiteracy was only 12 percent.[65] The Slovenes had made impressive progress in the publication of newspapers, journals, and books, which the public supported. Hence on the eve of the war, the reading public was well aware of their Slovenian identity, but also of their attachment and loyalty to the Habsburg Empire. The issues raised by South Slav unity in Serbia and Croatia did not have a high priority in Slovenia.

CONCLUSION: TEACHERS AND TEXTBOOKS IN SOUTH SLAV NATIONAL DEVELOPMENT

Before we proceed to an examination of the content of the educational material, some comment is necessary about the influence of the teacher, whether lay or clerical, and the printed word in the development of the national movements. It is most important to emphasize that teachers and priests, aside from their professional functions, were usually leaders in their communities in this regard. The role of the teacher was particularly central. Although there were teachers who were social critics, and some even lost their positions because of their criticism, they almost unanimously favored national unification objectives. They did so not only because they were civil servants, expected to be loyal and patriotic, but also because they personally believed in the cause they supported. Their attitude was particularly important because of the prestige they enjoyed, especially in rural communities. Here the teaching profession was held in high repute; many peasant parents urged their children to follow their teachers' example and even acquire a higher education. An intellectual in the family was a source of pride and prestige. The teacher also fulfilled another important function. In the rural areas he served as a source of information about current events for the people; thus he served as a link between the state, the student, and the parents.

The priest served similar educational and informational functions. For Serbs, Croats, and Slovenes alike, religion was compulsory in all grades of the elementary and secondary schools, with these classes taught by members of the clergy. Despite the secular convictions of the political leaders, none suggested that religious instruction be excluded from the curriculum. As we have seen, representatives of the church were always included in the membership of the various education committees. Many times their views were ignored, but their very presence signified that religion would retain a central place in the school system.

Like the teachers, the clergy had certainly in the past played a major role in national movements. The importance of Orthodoxy for the Serbs and Catholicism for the Croats has already been described. As was the case with the teachers, the clergy could either support their own group's national development or seek to build bridges with the other South Slav people. We have thus seen on the one hand Strossmayer and Rački as leaders in the Yugoslav movement and on the other the People's Party in Slovenia with its national outlook. The supporters of Starčević and Frank in Croatia also came from among the Croatian Catholics. In fact, with a few obvious exceptions, the clergy and their followers gave their undivided loyalty to their nation. There were very few among them who were convinced adherents of the Yugoslav idea.

Together with the teacher and the priest, the textbooks and almanacs provided the population with much-needed information about the nation and its achievements. Newspapers and journals, which are not covered in this study, were, of course, also important. For the individual his first acquaintance with his nation's history and culture came in school. Here the textbooks presented the student with a picture of his past and his place in the community, painted in glowing colors. As we shall see, emphasis was placed on historic achievements and national heroes. Given such an ancestry and feeling a part of what was pictured as a noble society, the student naturally accepted the written word. Most students, during their school years and afterward, believed that the books told the truth and that within their covers the reader could find a true expression of the nation's wisdom.

The same generalizations can be made about the almanacs, the average person's "treasury of knowledge." Displayed prominently by every family who owned one, the almanacs provided practical information about the calendar, the phases of the moon, planting and harvesting, and similar subjects. They also included articles commemorating the anniversaries of historical, religious, cultural, and literary events. The volumes also contained poems, usually with romantic, nationalist themes, written by popular poets. Through a careful examination of each issue over a decade, a reader could obtain a good knowledge of his nation's history based on the latest scholarship.

Although the almanacs were designed to fulfill a variety of needs, the most popular were those with strong nationalist orientations. There are two excellent examples. In Serbia *Vardar*, named after a river running through Macedonia, sought to educate the public about Serbian national goals. Its contents spanned the Serbian horizon. It was, in fact, more a textbook than an almanac, numbering several hundred pages and containing scores of articles about the nation, its history, its religion, and its great historical figures. *Vardar's* counterpart in Croatia was *Danica*, published by the Society of Saint Jerome. Providing its readers with similar information, but from a Croatian viewpoint, it too exceeded in size the normal almanac. By 1914 these, the two most popular almanacs in their respective lands, both conveyed strongly nationalist messages.

For the development of nationalism, of course, the organization of an educational system was of the first importance. This chapter has described the steps by which this goal was achieved among the three South Slav groups. As we have seen, the first task, successfully accomplished, was to break the church's hold over the schools and establish a secular system. The second was to assure that the schools produced patriotic citizens. The emphasis on nationalism did not cause problems in relatively homogeneous areas, but it brought about conflicts in, for instance, Croatia-Slavonia with a population that was one-quarter Serbian. The contents of the textbooks presented similar difficulties. A clear national message could be presented in ethnically similar regions, but in mixed areas the students obviously needed to know something about one another.

The following chapters will through an analysis of the contents of the textbooks concentrate on determining how well the educational systems prepared the students to eventually become citizens

of a Yugoslav state. The main emphasis will thus be on not only
what the textbooks taught the pupils about their own national back-
grounds, but also what they taught them about the other South
Slavs. The subjects covered will be history, geography, and literature,
including the study of language. As in all European states, each of
these school subjects could be used to promote national sentiments.
History presented the nation's heroes and its place in world developments; geography described the richness and beauty of the lands;
through literature the students learned about the uniqueness of
their language, the past cultural achievements, and the rich heritage
of folk customs and traditions. We will demonstrate how these subjects, presented in different ways, provided both bridges toward unity
and grounds for dispute among the South Slav peoples.

3

Readers—Serbian and Croatian Literary Traditions

INTRODUCTION

The South Slav leaders, scholars, and teachers repeatedly emphasized the importance of language; consequently, the students learned about their own society and their national literature, above all, from their readers. As the first book to which a student was exposed, the reader provided the foundation for his education. Starting with the elementary primer, each succeeding book expanded on the information previously presented and introduced new material. The student read selections from the best-known native authors, in the process learning both style and subject matter. The readers dealt with a wide range of subjects—among them history, the fatherland, patriotism, loyalty, geography, regions, cities, nature, seasons, religion, morals, manners, customs, folklore, proverbs, fables, and riddles. The accounts were concise, most often written in a dramatic style, which made a greater impression on the student than the presentation of the same subjects in the history books. In other words, the student who completed elementary school had received information about the world, his nation's place in it, and his own role within the nation, presented from moralistic, romantic, and patriotic points of view. Those who went on to secondary school built on this base, but for most children, elementary school was the extent of their formal education. Therefore, of the textbooks studied, the readers were the most instructive and influential in shaping the minds of students.

Before discussing the role played by readers in the development of Serbian and Croatian national consciousness, let us compare two influential secondary school grammars. Stojan Novaković's *Serbian Grammar* and Tomislav Maretić's *Croatian or Serbian Grammar for*

61

the Secondary Schools, will be compared to demonstrate their respective approaches to the study of language. Novaković's work was published in 1894, Maretić's five years later, in 1899.[1] Both thus appeared in the era when Serbian and Croatian nationalism were at their peak and when relations between Serbia and Croatia were strained.

As stated in his preface, in 1869 Novaković began to write the grammar for his students in the Belgrade gymnasium. Because of interruptions, it was completed in 1894, to be reprinted in 1902.[2] One recent scholar has described it as being Novaković's "most significant work in language," although it should be noted that the author was primarily an historian, not a linguist.[3] In 1869 he published the first part, entitled *Serbian Syntax for the Lower Gymnasiums and Realkas in the Principality of Serbia,* and as other parts were completed in subsequent years, they too were published. In 1879, the fourth expanded edition, now entitled *Serbian Grammar for the Lower Gymnasiums and Realkas in the Principality of Serbia,* appeared, followed by its third edition in 1890.[4] Novaković noted in the 1894 completed work that "all these editions were published as individual books, for school use. . . . A whole series of generations both in the kingdom and in the other Serbian lands . . . learned from this grammar."[5] Then in 1892, the newly founded Serbian Literary Association (Srpska književna zadruga) appointed Novaković to a committee whose task was to standardize the orthography for the association's projected publications. Not only was the orthography modified in Serbia, but in the same year, Novaković noted, "In the western, Croatian, part of our literature, the same question was being settled more through official means, because there the need was much greater than among us, since there were many serious, difficult questions to be settled."[6] He was referring to the appearance of Ivan Broz's major work, *Croatian Orthography,* in which Broz stated the Croatian government decreed that there should be a single orthography for the schools, based upon phonetic principles.

The point to be noted here is that Novaković used the phrase "in the western, Croatian, part of our literature," where the pronoun "our" does not refer to Croatian and Serbian literature, but to Serbian literature. As noted earlier, Novaković's grammar was published in 1894, a year when he did not hold public office. In the previous year, 1893, he was the Serbian foreign minister, and in 1895 he was appointed prime minister. After serving as minister of education from 1880 to 1883, he was minister of internal affairs in 1884 and from 1885 to 1892, the ambassador to Constantinople. In other words, he held every major position in the Serbian government.

His views on Serbian nationalism and his perception of Croatia in relation to South Slav understanding and cooperation can best be seen by citing from the contents of his grammar. The first sentence in his book was "Language is the means by which individuals convey their ideas to one another."[7] Subsequently, he stated that "All the nations in the world have their own national language," but they belong to groups or families of languages.[8] "The Serbian language is, for example, a branch of the Slavic family of languages in which are included: *Old Slavic* (which is in our church books), *Bulgarian, Slovenian* (Kranjski), *Russian, Polish, Czech,* and *Lusatian-Sorbian.*"[9] Croatian was not listed.

Concerning the letters of the Cyrillic alphabet, Novaković wrote, "In addition to these letters, the Serbian language is written in Latin letters among the Serbs of the Western (Catholic) church and the Croats, who, because of their literary unity with the Serbs, have accepted, instead of their own regional dialect, our Serbian language, and which they now even call Croatian (pa ga sad i hrvatskim zovu). The letters with which we write are called Cyrillic in contrast to Latin."[10] Novaković further noted that when Djuro Daničić began to edit the *Dictionary of the Croatian or Serbian Language*, which the Yugoslav Academy published, he introduced the letters *dj, lj, nj,* and *dž* into the Latin script.[11]

Novaković's book is 512 pages, 405 of which consist of explanatory text. In it the word "Croats" is mentioned only once and "Croatian" nine times. The first instance is the reference to alphabets mentioned above. "Croatian" is next used when Novaković describes the formation of adjectives—Beogradski, Srpski, Hrvatski, Carski, etc.[12] On seven other occasions, Novaković mentions Croatian when he discusses the ending of cases and notes that Croatian writers use certain forms that are considered archaic.[13]

The significance of the above information for the study of South Slav understanding can be demonstrated in a number of ways—by citing Novaković's use of historical names, his use of geographic place names, and the construction of simple and complex sentences. About half of Novaković's grammar is filled with quotations from historical episodes, literature, or folklore, almost all of which deal with Serbia's struggle against the Ottomans. As a gifted historian, he skillfully presented historical names that would evoke pride among the Serbs—Sava, Kosovo, Dušan, Obilić, Mother of the Jugovićes, Jug Bogdan, Njegoš—or would recall misfortunes, such as Murad, Bayezid, Bechir-Pasha, Čengićes, Ljubovićes, and especially the word "Turks." The section on syntax is especially effective. Here one finds the following sentences: "Even without him they know that there are Turks in Bosnia"; "Skanderbeg had the heart of Obilić, but he died in sad exile"; "He who is a Serb and of Serbian birth, but did not come to the battle of Kosovo, does not have the heart of his family"; and "I am going, Tsar, directly to Kosovo; for our holy religion, I will shed blood."[14]

There are frequent references to Old Serbia, Bosnia, Hercegovina, Dalmatia, Boka Kotorska (The Bay of Kotor), and Montenegro, all of which the Serbs claimed as their own lands. Yet when Novaković gives examples of the use of hyphens in Serbian he cites "Dalmatian-Dubrovnik, Western-Christian, Hellenic-Serbian, Eastern-Slavic, Russian-Slavic, political-satirical, German-Serbian, etc.," but not Serbian-Croatian.[15] His book is called the *Serbian Grammar*, and he states in the preface, "I thought it was foolish to demand from educated Serbs that they write more clearly and correctly in their language, if a book were not prepared that would simplify the implementation of this responsibility, which, today, Thank the Lord, is dear to everyone."[16]

Novaković was also the author of a secondary school reader, *Serbian Reader for the Lower Gymnasiums and Realkas*, which was published in 1895, the year he was appointed prime minister.[17] In the preface to his second volume, he revealed his intent to bring Croatian writers into the readers. His reader was first published in 1870 and was expanded to three brief volumes in the 1870s by his colleague Svetislav Vulović. In the 1880s Novaković reduced it to two volumes so that it could be used in "all grades of the gymnasium or realka." Novaković wrote in the introduction that the reader, "in addition to cherishing the national language, must have the aim of informing the student about the life of the nation in the present and past. Under these influences the Serbian language was formed; and it must be continuously studied under these conditions."[18] Hence in the first volume of the reader, the emphasis was on prose, national poetry, and other selections from authors such as Karadžić, Branko Radičević, Jovan Jovanović Zmaj, Milan Dj. Miličević, and Josip Pančić.

In the second volume, selections were taken from the best Serbian writers, among whom were Karadžić, Matija Nenadović, and Milan Miličević, who in prose described aspects of Serbian life, events in Serbian national history, and the Serbian lands. To this group he added "two writers of the western lands, Andrija Kačić and Matija Reljković, who, back in the previous century, were among the first western writers to acknowledge the influence of national thought and songs, which were published and read among the eastern parts of our people."[19] He then listed the other Serbian authors,

some of whom were Djuro Daničić, Ljubomir Novaković, Jovan Subotić, Čedomil Mijatović, and Vladan Djordjević, whose works are
reproduced in the reader. He concluded his preface with this sentence. "Of the new western writers, Lj. Gaj, Ivan Mažuranić, Petar
Preradović, Ivan Trnski, and August Šenoa are recognized with thorough examples of their style of writing, so that the more mature
youth in the third and fourth grades could become acquainted with
the true representatives of Croatian writing in literature."[20]

In addition to the seven Croatian writers mentioned above, he
quoted from three other authors—Bogoslav Šulek, Milan Šenoa, and
Mijo Kispatić. Of the one hundred selections in the reader, twenty-
two were from Croatian authors, of which eleven were from Kačić-
Miošić and Reljković. Of these twenty-two, half were printed in
Cyrillic and half in Latin. Five selections were cited as coming from
Tomislav Maretić's Croatian reader and three from Mirko Divković's Croatian reader. Of the twenty-two selections only one, Gaj's
"From the Youth of Ljudevit Gaj," can be considered to deal strictly
with a Croatian subject.[21] All of the others—which, for example, included maxims, fables, folk poems, and articles on nature—could
readily be assimilated into Serbian literature. This was especially
true for the selections from Kačić-Miošić and Mažuranić's "Četa,"
which came from his epic work "The Death of Smail-Aga Čengić."
In other words, the selections not only gave the gymnasium and realka students an opportunity to gain an appreciation for Croatian
writers, but the selections also served to strengthen the impression
that the "western writers," who were of course Croatian, wrote in
"our language," meaning Serbian, and were a part of the Serbian literary tradition.

The differences in the respective approaches of the Serbian and
Croatian grammars and readers, and the influence which each approach could have on Croatian and Serbian understanding among
students, can be seen by examining Tomislav Maretić's grammar,
and to a lesser extent his reader. Unlike Novaković, Maretić never
held any prominent political position in Croatia, although in the
1890s he was a representative in the sabor, where he took an active
part in the debates on education and the role of textbooks. Maretić
studied Slavic and classical linguistics, taught in a gymnasium from
1879 to 1885, was appointed a docent at the University of Zagreb in
1885, and became a professor of Slavic philology in 1888. From 1915
to 1918 he was president of the Yugoslav Academy. For three decades, from 1907 until his death in 1938, he was the editor of the
Yugoslav Academy's monumental *Dictionary of the Croatian or
Serbian Language*, whose first editor had been Daničić. Maretić was

responsible for six volumes—from *maslo* to *pršutina*—which to-
taled about six thousand pages.[22]

Maretić's scholarly career was devoted to the study of the Croatian and Serbian languages, which he considered to be one, and their
national poetry. An avowed adherent of Karadžić's emphasis on phonetic orthography, Maretić worked unceasingly on behalf of establishing a single štokavian literary language for the Croats and Serbs.
In the recent words of an eminent scholar, Maretić's "great *Grammar and Stylistics of the Croatian or Serbian Literary Language*
(1899, 1931, 1962), which was written on the basis of Karadžić's and
Daničić's works, was to serve as the foundation of the next literary
language." Although criticized by some, "it remains to this day un-
surpassed."[23] He also wrote on orthography, poetry, accent, the
sources of names and surnames, the history of the language, stylistics, and he translated the Iliad, the Odyssey and the Aeneid, among
other works. It is understandable, then, that Maretić would be considered "the central figure in linguistic scholarship in Croatia."[24]

For this study he is important because of the grammar and reader
he wrote for the secondary schools. Both appeared in the same political era as Novaković's two works. In 1900 Maretić's grammar became the compulsory textbook for secondary schools in Croatia,
and, in the following year, in Dalmatia as well, and it was used
through the interwar period. In contrast to Novaković's *Serbian
Grammar*, Maretić's book was entitled *Croatian or Serbian Grammar for the Secondary Schools*. Immediately after the preface, in
which he acknowledged his debt to Karadžić and Daničić, he presented the Cyrillic alphabet in printed and written form. The first
two sentences of Maretić's textbook state: "One person says to another what he thinks in sentences composed of words. Therefore, a
sentence is an expression of one's thought."[25] Novaković had said essentially the same thing in his first sentence—"Language is the
means by which individuals convey their ideas to one another." Yet
what Maretić and Novaković conveyed in their respective grammars,
which could influence Croatian and Serbian students in understanding one another, was not identical.

Throughout his grammar Maretić used the term "Croatian or
Serbian language" (*Hrvatsko ili srpski jezik*). Thus he wrote that
"Croatian and Serbian have 30 sounds . . . and 27 letters" which he
presented in Latin, and then added that "Cyrillic has the same number of sounds and letters . . . as are in the Latin alphabet," which
was also printed. He explained that "Croats and Serbs" were identified by whether they spoke the ijekavian, ekavian, or ikavian variants of the štokavian dialect.[26]

Although Maretić also used quotations from literature to demonstrate grammatical points, in contrast to Novaković, Maretić presented many more examples that he wrote himself. One need only glance through his grammar to see how he used Serbian subjects to illustrate grammatical points. Some of the best examples can be found in the section on syntax: "Dušan is proclaimed the Serbian Tsar"; "Hunting in the mountains, Tsar Dušan saw where the lower branches of a tree were bending and those on the top were soaring upward; when he reached the place, a child, tending a few sheep, had swung his ax into a log and lay down to sleep"; "After the death of Tsar Dušan"; "Hardly had the prince instructed his army, when the Turks attacked at Kosovo"; "It is known that Marko Kraljević lived in the time of Prince Lazar"; "The plowing of Marko Kraljević"; "All the *vojvodas* (military commanders) accepted the new leadership and took an oath to Karadjordje"; "At the end of 1806 the Serbs entered into Belgrade"; and "When the Turks heard that Miloš was in Belgrade."[27] For each one of these examples, the subject could just as well have been an event from Croatian history, involving Croatian rulers.

Perhaps the best illustration of Maretić's reliance on Serbian themes is found in the following paragraph.

> For example, Stefan Dušan, the Serbian tsar, took from the Greeks Macedonia, Thessaly, Aetolia, Arcadia, Epirus, and Albania and proclaimed himself emperor. He divided his extensive and unconsolidated empire among his *vojvodas* and princes, whom his eighteen-year-old son and heir, Uroš, was unable to keep in check. Hence each one became autonomous, and Vukašin, the most powerful among them, disregarding Uroš, became king. Then the Turks attacked the Serbian empire, which was torn asunder by domestic disunity. When Vukašin lost his life defending his kingdom from the Turks, the Serbian prince Lazar ascended the throne. The Turks brought to an end the Serbian empire and kingdom on the field of Kosovo in 1389. After the death of Lazar, a Serbian despotate was established under Turkish suzerainty. Soon, however, the Turks drove the despotate from Serbia into Srijem, where subsequently it too ceased to exist. And thus the Turks little by little conquered all of Serbia and Bosnia and Hercegovina.[28]

It was precisely the inclusion of this type of information that caused some members of the sabor in the 1890s to protest that the textbooks made it seem as if Croatia were a part of the Serbian kingdom.

The illustrations cited above were in Maretić's grammar. His reader, *Croatian Reader for the Second Grade of the Secondary Schools,* did not reflect the same degree of emphasis on Serbian subjects for several reasons. First, the original author was Tade Smičiklas, who was commissioned to write it in 1875. In 1884 Maretić was requested to prepare a new, revised third edition. Subsequent editions by Maretić appeared in 1890, 1899, and 1906. Second, in Croatia there were separate readers for each grade, and, as noted before, the State Educational Commission chose the subjects to be studied in each grade. Hence, Maretić did not have the liberty he had had in writing his grammar. Third, the readers for the other grades had more information about the Slavic peoples, as will be seen below. Nevertheless, Maretić's second grade reader is instructive.[29]

Its selections were divided into three categories—prose, folk poetry, and proverbs. The prose section contained stories, tales, fables, articles on geography, history, natural science, and plant life, and miscellaneous items. In the geography section there were articles on Mount Ararat, the Nile River, the Sahara Desert, the Red Sea, ancient Greece, and Thessaloniki. The history articles dealt with Greek or Roman history. Contributions to the stories and fables included those by the Serbian authors Daničić, Ljubiša, Karadžić, and Obradović. The interesting point, however, is that some of the works by Serbian writers—Daničić, Karadžić, Ljubomir Nenadović, Obradović, and Jovan Jovanović-Zmaj—were printed in Cyrillic whereas others were in Latin, as was also the case in the selections by the Croatian writers J. R. Tomić, S. S. Kranjčević, and Petar Preradović. Thus of the one hundred selections in the reader, twenty-eight were in Cyrillic—some by Serbian writers, some by Croatian. The reader also contained selections from Tolstoy, Turgenev, and Hans Christian Andersen. Yet even though the emphasis in the second grade reader was not on the South Slavic world, from this volume the student learned about Serbian customs, folk poetry, and heroes, such as Marko Kraljević.[30]

The purpose in comparing the works of Novaković and Maretić has been to indicate the respective approaches to South Slav relations and the issue of Yugoslavism in the grammars and readers of these two influential prewar scholars. The differences in presentation and understanding in their books were also found in the Serbian and Croatian readers. They will be examined in greater detail.

SERBIAN READERS OR ČITANKE

The Authors

Although this study concentrates on the readers used in Serbia after independence, they nevertheless were influenced by those published before 1878. Primers and readers were produced from the beginning of the nineteenth century, but the major advances in education came in the second half of the century. Since some of the readers available before 1878 continued to be used into the 1890s, they serve as a measure by which to compare the shift in emphasis and interpretations. It is apparent that the few students who went to school between 1850 and 1885 actually read more about the other South Slavs, especially the Croats, than did their successors who were educated in the decades up to the Balkan Wars.

The authors of the textbooks were able men, most of whom were teachers, although some became administrators and others served in the national government. Among the authors of the elementary readers, several are especially prominent. Filip Hristić dominated the field from the 1850s through the 1880s. He wrote the readers for all four elementary grades in the 1850s. Although his second grade reader was displaced in 1873 by one by Djordje Natošević, Hristić's first grade reader was used until 1885, the third grade reader to 1893, and the fourth to 1890. As was the case with many successful individuals in nineteenth-century Serbia, Hristić had a broad and rich career. He began as an official in the ministry of education, in time became the secretary to the ministry, and for a period in the 1870s served as minister. He also was active in diplomacy, serving as the Serbian delegate to the Danube Commission, the minister of foreign affairs and the ambassador to Constantinople, Vienna, and London. He also served as a member of the State Council and the governor of the National Bank.[31]

Another prominent author was Ljubomir Protić, who, with Vladimir Stojanović, wrote textbooks for all four elementary grades. They were published in the first decade of the twentieth century. Protić, a conservative who had studied at the University of Jena, believed that religion was the most important subject in the school curriculum. He was a teacher; he served as superintendent of schools of the Kragujevac district; and from 1906 to 1925 he was the director of the girls' gymnasium in Belgrade. He also served as the secretary of and consultant to the ministry of education and religious affairs.[32] Stevo Čuturilo was another popular author, whose primer, first published in 1886, was used for over three decades. He was a teacher and school superintendent in Niš.[33]

At the other end of the political spectrum was Pera Djordjević, who belonged to the Radical Party. He began his career as a gymnasium teacher in Kragujevac and Belgrade. Eventually he became the secretary of the ministry of education and religious affairs and a government consultant. His scholarly work dealt with grammar,

syntax, and theories of literature. In 1893 he was elected to the Serbian Academy. Together with Uroš Blagojević he wrote a fourth
grade reader that was used for over fifteen years beginning in 1891.[34]

As noted above, Stojan Novaković produced the first successful
reader for the secondary schools. When he became preoccupied with
other duties, he asked Svetislav Vulović, who first taught Serbian
literature in the Belgrade gymnasium and then Yugoslav literature
in the university, to revise the reader.[35] The other important author
in the secondary field was Milan Šević, who was most influential in
the two decades before the war. Šević studied philosophy, Slavistics
and German in Budapest, Geneva, Zurich, Munich, and Leipzig. He
was a gymnasium professor in Požarevac, Kragujevac, Belgrade, and
Niš. He published extensively on different aspects of education
and was a student of the literary and cultural history of the Serbs and
Croats. Together with Sreten Pašić, the director of the Paraćin gymnasium, he published readers for the first four grades of the secondary schools.[36] In 1913 Vojislav Jovanović, a docent at the University
of Belgrade, and Miloš Ivković, a professor at the Belgrade gymnasium, published readers for the third and fourth grades, which replaced those of Pašić and Šević.[37]

Although not all the authors wrote prefaces in which they stated
their goals, some provided this information. Given the fact that the
ministry of education controlled all facets of the educational system
and approved the curriculum, including the textbooks, the views expressed by the authors of the secondary textbooks are also helpful in
understanding what was expected of the elementary textbooks.

The difference in approach to the treatment of the Croats in the
readers published before Serbia's independence in 1878 and after the
adoption of the educational reforms in the 1880s can be demonstrated by comparing what Novaković stated as his purpose in writing his books in 1870 and again in 1895. In the 1895 preface to his
reader, he stated that it differed from the first edition of 1870. In the
earlier edition, he wrote that because of the prolonged and divisive
controversy over the Serbian literary language and orthography,
which was finally won by Karadžić, the study of language had suffered in the Serbian schools. In the elementary grades, students had
learned to read and write, but not well enough. In 1870 the government sought to remedy this situation by stating that the aim in the
secondary schools was to have the students learn the grammatical
rules, learn to write correctly, learn to enunciate clearly, and to be
able to read intelligently. The reader was aimed at achieving this
goal. At the same time, its purpose was to introduce and stimulate
the student's interest in literature. Thus the government directed

that readers should be divided into four sections: (1) entertaining passages in verse and prose, (2) national history and ethnography, (3) natural sciences, and (4) quotations stressing morals, proverbs, and anecdotes.[38]

Novaković believed that "in the elementary schools one should retain the dialect of the region in which the school is located"; he acknowledged that to do so would necessitate the printing of books in the different dialects. "Then in the secondary schools the students can be shown the small differences in our language." Perhaps his most significant comment was: "Similarly we maintained that it was not necessary to conceal from the children the fact that our language is written in two scripts [Cyrillic and Latin]." The students must know this "because of our common relations with the Croats, who in their readers teach Cyrillic alongside Latin," and also because the children should "not judge their kinsmen by foreign symbols but by reality. For these reasons we have printed some brief articles in Latin as written by the Croats."[39] The content of the reader depicted the Croats as a separate but related nation. In the new 1895 edition, Novaković remarked that he was including selections from "the Western Writers . . . in order that more mature students in the third and fourth grades could recognize them as real representatives of the Croatian style of writing in literature."[40] Two points should be noted. First, the term "Western writers" had become the commonly used euphemism among Serbian authors to define Croatian authors who wrote in the štokavian dialect. Second, his remark implied that the other students, in particular students in the elementary schools, were not cognizant of the differences in Serbian and Croatian developments.

The new direction in Serbian readers was more pronounced in the four secondary school readers by Šević and Pašic, which soon displaced Novaković's textbook. In the 1894 preface to their first reader, Šević and Pašić stressed that "the greatest attention was being paid to the mother tongue." Everyone seemed to concur, they added, "that the [study of the] mother tongue was the core of education in the secondary schools." Then the two authors added that "political and cultural development could not remain without influence on the school and that the contemporary demands to which it [the school] must respond differ in many respects from those of the past. In particular, national feelings and needs emerged, and to these feelings there must be given a somewhat firmer content. This [goal] can be achieved . . . through the study of the national linguistic treasures, national characteristics, and the best works of national literature. . . . A good reader is the most trustworthy guarantor of success. It is the principal means by which the designated goal can be attained."[41]

In the introduction to the third grade reader, which Šević produced alone, he wrote that the volume's emphasis was on events after Kosovo. The goal was "to stress from these most tragic pages of Serbian history those events which will be able to fill the heart of the student with justifiable national pride."[42] In his fourth grade reader, Šević stated

> that this fourth book of the "Serbian readers" relies . . . on the earlier books. With this book the projected plan is carried out whereby the readers for the lower classes described the best-known events from the history of the Serbian nation, how they are seen in national tradition and in national literature . . . All four books . . . comprise one whole, and each in itself is a separate entity with its own subject matter. The core of this book, which can be seen at first glance, is national liberation and the desire for national unification, as they appeared back at the beginning of the past century and gave direction to further national aspirations.[43]

From these statements it is clear that Šević and Pašić took into the consideration the "political" and "contemporary" considerations and "national feelings" of the 1890s and first decade of the new century, when manifestations of Serbianism were the strongest. Thus they concentrated on Serbia and its history, traditions, literature, and national aspirations. The South Slavs as such did not fit into this scheme. When the writings of non-Serbian authors were incorporated into Šević's books, the goal was to further Serbianism, not South Slavic understanding, as will be noted below.

The Serbs: Their Lands and History

As would be the case with the geography and history books, the readers emphasized national and patriotic themes. Of importance were the selections dealing with the origin and relationship of the Serbs to the other Slavs, the Serbian lands, and the emphasis on loyalty to the fatherland (*otadžbina*). Under the first heading, the Serbs were described as members of the Slavic family. However, Hristić in the elementary textbook and Ivković and Šević in their secondary school texts declared that the Slavs originally were all called Serbs and only subsequently did the name Slav come to denote the different nations. Thus in 1872 Hristić stated that scholars had discovered in chronicles that several thousand years before the birth of Christ, the Slavs "were then called Serbs."[44] Ivković emphasized in 1911 that the Slavic peoples had had different names in their ancestral home,

but that "of the names the best known were two—the older name
Serb and the younger name Slav. All the above-mentioned peoples
are called by this latter name, and they are called this by other nations. The older name 'Serbs,' at one time the common name for all
the Slavic peoples, today is only the name for us and the Lusatian
Sorbs."[45] Šević repeated the same statement almost verbatim in his
other readers. The intent of these statements was, of course, to establish the primacy of the Serbs and their historic tradition among
the Slavs.[46]

Hristić, however, did not belabor this point. His views on the
Serbs and Slavs were presented in the form of a dialogue in which a
grandson requested his grandfather to tell him about his country and
people. When asked about the Slavic peoples, the grandfather replied
that they numbered 80 million, of whom "about 55 million were
Russians, up to 4 million Bulgars, about 4 million Serbs, nearly one
million Croats, approximately 1,200,000 Slovenes, over 7 million
Slovaks, Moravians and Czechs, who are very closely related, up to 9
million Poles, and approximately 150,000 Lusatians Sorbs."[47] Notwithstanding their numerical strength, the grandfather told his
grandson, the fate of the Slavs had not been a happy one.

> It is a great pity and misfortune for the Slavic peoples that they are
> not united either in literature, in religion, in a state, or in the place
> where they live. Instead they have different literatures, they are di-
> vided and separated from one another by vast expanses, in which
> other peoples live, and what is worse, they are fragmented into dif-
> ferent Christian faiths or churches.[48]

The religious division of the Slavs disturbed the grandfather:

> There was a time when almost all the Christian Slavs belonged to
> Eastern Orthodox Christianity and they used the old Slavic lan-
> guage in the liturgy. But the Slavic tribes, which were under west-
> ern religious authorities, were after a short time compelled to
> abandon the Slavic language and Eastern Orthodoxy and to accept
> the Latin language and Western Christianity.[49]

As a result, the grandfather continued, 20 million Slavs, "Poles,
Czechs, Moravians, Slovaks, Croats, Dalmatians, and Slovenes," became Roman Catholic. There were about 1,500,000 Protestants
among the Slovaks, Lusatians, Czechs, and Poles. There were also
about a million Slavs "of the Muslim or Turkish faith, mainly in
Bosnia and Bulgaria. They accepted this religion in order to escape
Turkish oppression."[50] The only fortunate Slavs were the Russians,
who, 55 million strong and being "of one blood, one language, and
one religion," lived in one state under one ruler. The other Slavs

lived under German, Austrian, or Ottoman domination. Of those who lived under the Turks, there were "7 million Slavs, who were of one faith, who lived as neighbors, and who were divided in speech by two related [languages]—Serbian and Bulgarian."[51]

Hristić's purpose was to impress upon the children the numerical strength of the Slavs, whose potential, however, could not be realized primarily because of their religious differences. Within the context of the grandfather's remarks, the Bulgars, whom Hristić identified by name as a separate Slavic nation, were depicted as more closely akin to the Serbs than were the Croats.

The readers also defined the Serbian lands. Thus in his 1855 book Hristić wrote that the Croats had their own kingdom, which comprised "present-day Dalmatia, the Croatian littoral, the Bosnian region up to the river Vrbas, present-day Croatia and Slavonia, excluding Srem." In his 1872 third grade reader, he gave the same description, but the reference to Srem was omitted. In a revision of his fourth grade reader in 1885, he asserted that the Croatian kingdom included "northern Dalmatia, the Bosnian region to the river Una, and present-day Croatia and Slavonia."[52]

The modifications were not inconsequential. First, by confining the Croatian lands to northern Dalmatia in the 1885 edition, he excluded Dubrovnik. Although the precise boundaries of northern Dalmatia were not defined, one may assume that he referred to the area north of the river Neretva or even further north to the Cetina River, which flowed into the Adriatic Sea at Omiš, south of Split. This boundary was used by the Serbian geographers and historians to define the limits of the lands originally inhabited by the Serbs. Second, by shifting the frontier westward from the river Vrbas to the Una, he made the boundary coincide with the prevailing Serbian interpretation that their people had inhabited all of Bosnia with its westernmost boundaries being the Una and Cetina rivers. The presentation in Hristić's 1855 reader was more in line with the Croatian interpretation of their medieval history, whereas, in the 1885 edition, Serbia's territorial claims were extended at the expense of lands that Croats regarded as historically and ethnically theirs.

Two decades later, in 1907, the two most influential prewar authors of elementary readers, Protić and Stojanović went much further than Hristić had in asserting claims to the Croatian lands. They wrote that "the Serbian people have had bad luck," because only two Serbian lands—Serbia and Montenegro—were free. On the other hand, "in the beautiful Serbian lands of Bosnia, Hercegovina, Srem, Banat, Bačka, Croatia, Slavonia, Dalmatia, Istria, Old Serbia, Macedonia, and the Vidin and Sredac [Sofia] provinces, foreigners rule

over the Serbian people. . . . It was difficult for our brothers in these
Serbian regions," they added, because in some areas their lands were
seized, they were persecuted and even killed. Worse yet, in some
places they were not allowed to say "that they were Serbian and that
their language was Serbian."[53] Four years later, in 1911, Šević in the
secondary textbook was not so direct. He wrote that by A.D. 650 the
Serbs had settled in the Balkans "in association with the Croats."
However, during the last Serbian migration, "the most warlike Serbian tribes arrived and with the force of the sword cleared the way
and seized the land." The Serbs then became "the masters of the
western half of the Balkan peninsula and settled it." The lands that
were occupied then were "*Serbia, Old Serbia, Macedonia, Bosnia,
Hercegovina, Dalmatia with Dubrovnik, Montenegro,* and northern
Albania." The Serbs had also preceded the Magyars in settling
"*Bačka, Banat* and *Slavonia.*"[54] Although Protić and Stojanović in
1907 included Croatia as a Serbian land, unlike Šević in 1911, the student in the elementary and secondary schools who accepted what he
read would naturally believe that Slavonia, Bosnia, and Dalmatia
were Serbian.

Having identified the Serbian lands, the students were next
taught their relationship to them. Consequently, the idea that permeated all the textbooks was loyalty, patriotism, and devotion to
one's fatherland. There could not be any wavering on these principles, which were repeatedly expressed in various forms—in essays,
through folk poetry, in accounts of the deeds of national heroes, by
simple declarations of individuals, and in proverbs. The student was
thus told that he should devote his life to his country and that the
supreme test of his individual worth was his readiness to sacrifice
his life for Serbia. His fatherland was described as "a beautiful and
dear land. God endowed her with the greatest worldly goods. . . .
Serbia, you are beautiful and dear to me. I love you as I do my father
and mother, as I do all of my good and dear people."[55]

In his second year elementary reader in 1872, Hristić emphasized the theme of personal responsibility:

> Children! A Serb gave birth to you, as a result of which you are
> called Serbs. You will carry this name with you until you die. You
> will boast about it before the world. Should anyone seek to impose
> another name on you in place of it, you would sooner die than ac-
> quiesce to this. . . . When you become grown-up you must love
> your fatherland, Serbia, and you will gladly do everything that
> is necessary in order that the Serbian nation be progressive and
> fortunate. . . .
> This idea henceforth must be constantly in your mind, if you

wish to be worthy sons of your ancestors, who loved their country and people so much that many of them died in order that they free it of the enemy.

  Listen very carefully to me, and I will tell you the main events in Serbian history. I will tell you what we were a thousand years ago, how at first we were eminent and well-known under our kings and emperors; how, later, because of treason, we suffered; how for a long time we labored and struggled until again with the Grace of God and the heroism of our own people we were liberated.[56]

Two years later, in 1874, Vulović in his reader for gymnasium students quoted from Milan Dj. Miličević's essay entitled "Lesson in Civic Rights and Responsibilities," to define further the concept of fatherland.

  If you ever see any person who scorns his fatherland, you know that such a person is no good, is a tyrant, or a servile slave. These individuals have not been given [the opportunity] to know the sweetness of that feeling which this word [fatherland] awakens in a noble and honorable soul. . . . And what is a fatherland? Is it some piece of land between designated boundaries? Or a city? Or a region? Or a state? Or the place where one was born?

  No. The fatherland is something more than all that. It is a part of mankind, a part of humanity tied by some special bonds; it is a society of men who live in one land, under the same laws, with more or less the same customs.

  The fatherland is an abbreviated expression of all our affection. Our parents, our children, friends, our paternal house, the memories of those whom we loved—all of these are included in the word fatherland.

  It gives us the cradle and it opens the grave where our bones are laid to rest in eternal peace, alongside the remains of our fathers, when our earthly life expires. It looks at our first games, our first happiness, and our first sorrows; it hears our forgiveness and our last breath. We are a single child of our fatherland, and in the love which we have for it, we embrace ourselves.[57]

Almost four decades later, the same themes were repeated. Thus in the first year gymnasium reader, Ivković in 1911 quoted a poem by Vojislav J. Ilić, "Conversation of a Small Serbian Girl with the Fatherland." Ilić has been eulogized as "the best poet born in Serbia," who perfected the "poetic form and enriched the poetic language."[58] In his poem he described how Serbian was spoken from Budapest to Thessaloniki, from the Timok River to the Una and on Mount Lovćen. Yet the Serbs were not free.

  My children shed tears
  Because an old enemy torments them

The enemy drinks their blood:
Turks, Germans, and Magyars.
Because he is not free everywhere
That is why the Serb sheds tears.[59]

In 1913 in their fourth grade gymnasium reader, Jovanović and Ivković quoted from Isidora Sekulić, the best-known woman author in Serbia. Inspired by the Balkan Wars, she wrote patriotic articles and prose poems. One, entitled "Question," centered on the fatherland. In part she wrote:

We went [to war] for the fatherland, we served the fatherland, we loved the fatherland. . . .

What is the fatherland? What is love for the fatherland? What brutal force drove innocent men into the storm and into an impasse? What monster sought you that you charge death and fire? What pretension drove you to seize with your bare hands thunder and lightning? What wickedness drove you to be discoverers, who with your own blood and brains covered your path and illuminated it with fire?

. . . . . .

What is in the heart of that fatherland which conjures up fiery visions before tiring eyes and bloody brow?

In the heart of the fatherland, there is neither truth nor justice. We love our fatherland.

Love for the fatherland is an obstacle to human love. We love our fatherland.

The heart of the fatherland is great, selfish, and warm, and in it is the loyalty of all our hearts. We love our fatherland.

The fatherland must be guarded, it must be defended, it must be loved until the grave and coat-of-arms are covered by ivy.

Her [Serbia's] victory is resounding. We all march. Nobody asks who will return. We love our homeland even when our blood freezes with fear and even when we must carry our guts in our hands.[60]

Also in that same year, 1913, Jovanović and Ivković in their third grade reader reproduced Djura Jakšić's poem "Fatherland," which described the nation's historic struggle against its enemies.[61]

Such eloquent tributes in behalf of the fatherland were always coupled with examples of heroism, whose purpose was to inspire pride in the students and to set examples to be emulated. Thus, Ivković quoted the well-known national folk-poem "Stevan Mušić," to which he had added the subtitle "It Is Glorious to Die for the Fatherland." This is a stirring, dramatic poem describing the battle of Kosovo and how Stevan Mušić killed three pashas before the fourth killed him. After most of the essays, articles, and poems in his textbook, Ivković included questions, some to test the students' factual knowledge, others to appeal to their emotions. In this particular instance, he asked: "Tell me the name of another hero who died for his country" and "what would you have done in his [Stevan Mušić's] place?"[62]

Among the writers whom Ivković most highly recommended to students was Stevan Sremac, whose work "The Forgotten Obilićes," was included in the readers. This story discussed the fate of eight young Serbs who were converted to Islam during the Ottoman invasion and then became servants in the sultan's court at Adrianople.

> However neither the brilliance of the court, nor the wealth, nor the gold-embroidered suite made them happy. They all yearned for their land of birth and their own dear families. They withered as a delicate flower that was moved from a rich and cultivated climate to another land, to a frozen terrain, under a dark climate.

One day, as they discussed their homesickness, one of them remarked that "if they were to kill this great sultan [Mehmed the Conqueror], we will free our relatives, our nation, and all of Christianity and the gray-haired *guslars* will sing songs about us as they do about Miloš Obilić. . . . And if our right hand should fail us, we will become martyrs for our faith and nation before God in heaven and before men on earth." All eight then took oaths, vowing to carry out the deed and not to betray one another. However, one of their number, Dimitrije Tomašić, dazzled by the wealth and brilliance of the court, "forgetting his faith and blood, betrayed his brothers" and told Sultan Mehmed of the conspiracy. A clever trap was set and the seven were caught. When questioned by the sultan on the reasons for their action, they replied that it was "only their great homesickness for their relatives and friends." The sultan then ordered his aides never again to allow any individual "of that criminal Serbian race" to be one of his servants. He added: "My grandfather, the late Murad-han, was killed by the criminal Obilić at Kosovo," and now he too was almost assassinated by Serbs. The seven Serbs were tortured for a year; then they were beheaded and their bodies dumped on a heap without burial. But another young Serb, a janissary, seeing what had happened, solicited the aid of some other Serbian janissaries and they buried the seven Serbs secretly near a church.[63]

For the Serbian teenager in 1911, after the annexation of Bosnia and on the eve of the Balkan Wars, this was a powerful, emotional story. By connecting the lives of these young men to that of Miloš Obilić, considered one of Serbia's greatest heroes, and the betrayal, in popular legend, at Kosovo by Vuk Branković, Sremac simultaneously evoked hatred for the enemy and loyalty for the fatherland and one's faith. This point was best expressed in two brief poems included in the Protić and Stojanović reader. The first, entitled "The First Wish of a Serb," read:

> Sun, let me warm my son's hands
> That I may drive the Turks from Kosovo.

The second, "The First Curse," read:

> He who does not see a rainbow
> And the sorrow of Kosovo
> May his Mother not see him
> Until judgment day.[64]

In the books, the author repeatedly returned to the theme that Serbia had been betrayed by one of its own. Hence, over and over again, the slogan "Only unity saves the Serb" (*Samo sloga Srba spasava*) was repeated. When the authors wrote about the fatherland, patriotism and loyalty, there was no ambiguity—the reference was exclusively to Serbia and the Serbian lands, with examples chosen from Serbian history.

The Serbian Language

The importance of language has been repeatedly emphasized in this account. As noted above, in 1894 Šević wrote in the preface to his textbook that the study of "the mother tongue was the core of education in the secondary schools," and that "the goal was the study of national linguistic treasures, national characteristics, and the best works of national literature." This statement was equally applicable for the elementary schools. As could be expected, the work of Vuk Karadžić received prime attention. In 1913 Jovanović and Ivković, in their fourth year reader, quoted from Jovan Skerlić, who explained in detail Vuk's place in Serbian literature.

> Vuk Karadžić is one of the most original and most powerful personalities in all of Serbian literature. . . . By collecting national folk literature and by describing national life in all Serbian areas, without regard to religious and political divisions, he gave the Serbs the idea that they are one large spiritual entity and in this manner strongly contributed to the formation of one general popular Serbian feeling. By praising the national past and magnifying old glories through epics, he had great influence on the strengthening of national consciousness in the Serbian nation. . . . Vuk Karadžić became the principal creator of Serbian nationalism in the nineteenth century.[65]

These comments by Skerlić reflect the respect that Karadžić enjoyed in Serbia. For a people steeped in tradition, who cherished their heroes, Vuk appeared as a national savior after centuries of Ottoman domination. His views on the importance of the national language, literature, history, and customs were accepted by the nation as articles of faith. Consequently, there was not a textbook that did not cite from his scholarly works or the collections he had compiled.

Karadžić's general views on the importance of language were echoed by Stojan Novaković. Thus, Protić and Stojanović in their elementary textbook and Pašić and Šević in their secondary reader used the same quotation from Novaković on the role of language in defining national identity.

> Nations are recognized by their language. However many thousands of families [there are] who speak one language and understand one another, they comprise one nation. For example, when you leave here you can easily know how extensive is the nation in which we live. Go north, west, east, and south, and wherever you travel, wherever you hear people who speak as we do or you can easily understand them, that represents one nation. But there is also something else by which a nation is identified. For example, if you were to go far from here, you would see many people who not only do not speak our language, but also are not proud of Miloš Obilić and do not sing about Kraljević Marko, they do not celebrate our glories, they do not go to church meetings as we do, and they do not lament our Kosovo. Frequently, they do not even know about these things. Consequently, people who speak one language, who share one national pride and everywhere remember one another, who have one and the same customs are called a *nation*.[66]

The readers also concentrated on the importance of the correct use of language. As the 1907 Protić and Stojanović reader explained: "A well-educated and respected person will never go into the street in slippers and the clothes" that he wears in his house,

> because it is indecent. It is the same with language. What clothes are to your body, language is to your thoughts. In the same manner that you have to pay attention to the clothes you wear, so you must pay attention to the [language] you use to express your thoughts.
>
> Therefore, when you speak or write be very careful how you express yourself and do not be indifferent. Listen carefully and keep in mind the words and speech of educated people when they speak in society. Be very careful that you do not imitate the vocabulary and speech of indifferent and uneducated men and children.

The children were also admonished to use only those words they understood. Certain individuals wished to show off by "mixing words from other languages into their beautiful Serbian language." Frequently, they did not know the real meaning of the words or how to use them. By doing this, they "introduced into our beautiful Serbian language erroneous words and thereby corrupted it [Serbian]." As a result of this development, many foreign words which were not understood by the great majority of people had entered into Serbian books, journals, and newspapers. Consequently, one should "always only use pure Serbian words." By so doing, "you also demonstrate that you are a patriot and that you love your national language."

These admonitions were not intended to discourage the study of foreign languages. On the contrary, the more foreign languages one knew, "the more worthy he was." But in the process one should not "underestimate his own language." Should one do this

> it is a sign that you do not love our Serbian people; that you do not wish Serbian to be heard everywhere where Serbs live. It means that you do not want a Greater Serbia (*da ne želiš Veliku Srbiju*) in which will be united all the Serbs, however many there are. That is what the foreigner and our enemy wish and desire, that is why they purposely do not call our language in Bosnia the Serbian language, but "Bosnian" and why they intentionally say that in Montenegro they speak Montenegrin and not Serbian. Therefore, beware that you do not give aid to the enemy's wishes and the foreigner's intentions.[67]

The importance of the role played by language in Serbian affairs is clear. The emphasis throughout the readers was on the Serbian language, its beauty, and what it meant to the Serbs and the Serbian nation. Within the broad context of the term literature, the students were exposed to all its forms and a broad spectrum of authors.

Croatia in the Readers

Croatia was presented in the readers through language, literature, and its writers. The readers published before the Balkan Wars will be analyzed first, and then a few that were published immediately before the world war will be examined, in order better to appreciate the extent to which the concept of South Slav understanding had developed by this time. Furthermore, the comparison in the treatment of Croatia and the other South Slavic provinces will be evident.

Once again Hristić's works are instructive. In the 1855 fourth grade reader, he wrote

> *The language of the ancient Croats* was wholly related to the Serbian language and the difference between these two Slavic dialects

was totally unknown. This is evident from the old Croatian inscriptions and also because the Croats today are everywhere intermingled with Serbs who, during the Turkish wars, settled there
[Croatia]. In the most recent times, the Croats have accepted into
their literature the Serbian dialect, which they write in Latin letters. Since they did this, literary activity among them has greatly
developed and their nationality has been happily revived, which
hitherto had almost been totally extinct.[68]

The same statement was repeated in 1872 in the third year reader.
In 1885, instead of stating that the Croats had "accepted the Serbian
dialect into their literature," Hristić wrote, "in literature the Croats
use the same language as the Serbs."[69] The interpretation presented
by Hristić reflected the point of view of Karadžić's supporters concerning the Serbian character of the štokavian dialect. It disregarded
any role played by the Illyrian movement in the standardization of
the Croatian literary language.

In the 1911 edition of his first year gymnasium reader, Ivković
quoted a paragraph from the Serbian geographer Jovan Cvijić, entitled "The Greatness of the Serbian Nation." It stated:

Among us it is frequently forgotten that we, with the Croats, are
proportionately a large nation, of whom there are over nine million
who have the same basic spiritual characteristics and one language.
From the German border to Constantinople there is not a larger nation than ours. We are larger than the Czechs, Magyars, Romanians, Bulgarians, and Greeks. Every year we increase significantly.
Excluding Bačka and Banat, the yearly increase of our population is
either almost the same as or larger than that of any of our adversaries. Our language is heard in the western part of the Balkan peninsula around Trieste, in Istria, in Rijeka and Skadar, and a language
that is related to ours is spoken around Thessaloniki and Seres. Excluding Greece, Epirus, Thessaly, and southern and central Albania, one can cross the Balkan peninsula and a significant part of
Austria-Hungary with the Serbian language.[70]

Although Cvijić wrote about the numerical strength of the Serbs
and Croats, who spoke one language, it was identified as "the Serbian language," not Serbo-Croatian. Coming from the pen of a distinguished scholar who was known as a supporter of South Slavic
cooperation, his views were accepted by both students and teachers
as those of an authority.

Perhaps the most revealing point concerns the extent to which
Croatian authors were presented to the elementary school students
in the readers. Of the forty readers examined, only two had works in
which the author was identified as a Croat. One was in the 1907 Pro-

tić and Stojanović volume, which represented the best example of the Serbian emphasis in the readers. The book, which numbered 329 pages, included a single selection by Davorin Trstenjak entitled "Croatia." It was a glowing tribute: "Croatia is a wonderful land. It is filled with natural beauties. It has everything a people need for a fortunate and decent life. It has high mountains, large forests, fertile and beautiful valleys, and rich plains." After identifying the geographic features, Trstenjak wrote that the

> greatest fortune and beauty for Croatia was the Adriatic Sea, which opens the way to all parts of the world. Fortunate is the nation that can be proud of the sea. . . . Croatia is beautiful; that is why the national anthem begins with these words—"Our beautiful homeland—oh, our heroic land, the glory of our ancestors."
>
> The heroic Croatian people fought for centuries a life-and-death struggle against many terrible enemies. Ever since Croatia was proclaimed a kingdom, through a thousand years, not for a moment has she ceased to be a kingdom. Once she had kings of her own blood, and she was then the most free and most fortunate and most renowned.
>
> The Croats and Serbs settled in these lands as one people, as they are in fact today. They are of the same blood; they have the same customs, the same national poetry and folk literature, and the same education.
>
> The Serbs and the Croats are twin brothers and if each did not have his own name they could not be distinguished from one another.
>
> The Croats and Serbs are doing much to become united spiritually, because in their unity, brotherhood, and love is their national fortune, freedom, and better future. Blood is not water![71]

Two points should be made. First, however laudatory of Croatia, the selection was included in the section of the reader entitled "Serbian Lands." Second, the significance of this evidence can be better understood when it is remembered that it represented only one of two excerpts found in the elementary school readers whose author was specifically identified as a Croat.

The situation was different, however, in the secondary schools, where students read selections from "Western" or "Catholic" Croatian literature. Although most of these consisted of essays or poems about nature, seasons, and the like, which did not have any explicit political or nationalistic implications, some of them did carry these connotations. The latter were so similar in content to works of Serbian authors that they could be integrated into the heritage of Serbian literature. Generally, these Croatian works could be divided into two groups—those that were descriptive of nature and those that were written in praise of events or heroes in Serbian history.

An example of the first was Stojan Novaković's second year gymnasium reader published in 1895, which contained twenty-two selections from eleven Croatian or "Western" authors. Examples of writings that did not have political connotations were Reljković's "Harvesting" and "Slavonia." The latter was a poem about the cities, towns, rivers, and beauty of Slavonia. Also included were Mija Stojanović's "The Badger," Bogoslav Šulek's "The Linden Tree," Milan Šenoa's "Ocean Waves" and "Ocean Water," Mija Kispatić's "Rosemary," and Preradović's "Greetings to the Homeland" and "Traveler." Although the Croats were emotionally attached to Preradović's poems, the Serbian student could also understand their underlying meaning.

In the second category, those selections with nationalistic implications, two dealt with the Ottomans—Kačić-Miošić's poem "Djuradj Kastriotić," about the Albanian leader Skenderbeg, and an excerpt from Mažuranić's "The Death of Smail Aga Čengić." From the medieval period there were two poems by Kačić-Miošić—one about the Serbian king Vladimir, who had been the prisoner of the Bulgarian ruler—and Ivan Trnski's essay "Kulin Ban," about the Bosnian ruler. The only selection which was related to Croatia specifically was an excerpt entitled "From the Youth of Ljudevit Gaj," based upon Gaj's account of how he became interested in his nation, through the tale of the three brothers Čeh, Leh, and Meh. It also described how his mother stressed the importance of the "mother tongue" rather than the Latin and German spoken by the nobility. In addition, she emphasized the value of books. "In my mind and my heart were my mother's words: 'Books, books for the people in the national language.'"[72]

Of the six basic secondary readers published between 1894 and 1911, all had works by Croatian authors with the exception of Ivković's first grade reader published in 1911. None, however, had the quantity of Croatian selections or the topical diversity offered by Novaković. The most popular Croatian author found in each of the other readers was Petar Preradović, with twenty-five selections, some being repetitions. Next came Stjepan Basariček with seven, Janko Jurković and Mija Kispatić with four each, Vjekoslav Klaić with three, and one each for Ivan Gundulić, Andrija Kačić-Miošić, Ivan Mažuranić, Ante Reljković, and August Šenoa.

Given Preradović's career, his popularity is paradoxical. He was an officer in the Habsburg army who rose to the rank of a major general, which he held at the time of his death in 1872. He first wrote romantic verses in German and only later turned to Croatian, which he had almost forgotten. He became a passionate supporter of the Illyrian movement and champion of South Slavic unity. He saw a bright future for all Slavdom. He was a lyric poet who was an idealist and optimist. Fully aware of the delicacy of his position as an officer in the Habsburg army, he was circumspect. Yet his poems caught the imagination of not only the Croats but the Serbs as well, in particular his drama *Kraljević Marko*.[73]

Some of the selections from his poems were "Good Night," "Storm," "Prayer," "Four Springs," "Two Birds," "Night Poems," "Fall," and "Traveler." Others carried more explicit political messages. In his "To the Nation about Language," he extolled the importance of the "mother tongue," remarking that one should love one's own language above all else, live for it, and if necessary die for it. It was a language that was heard from Constantinople to Kotor and from the Black Sea to the Adriatic. Throughout all these areas, he noted, poems about Marko Kraljević were to be heard. In another poem, entitled "To the Dear Departed," he paid tribute to five prominent men—three Serbs, one Montenegrin, and one Croat. The Serbs were Patriarch Josip Rajačić, Branko Radičević, the poet, and Stevan Knićanin, the general who led the Serbian forces against the Hungarians in 1848–49. The Montenegrin was the poet and ruler Njegoš; the Croat was Ban Josip Jelačić. All five men had been involved in the revolutions of 1848–49 in some capacity. Preradović lauded Knićanin for his work on behalf of "Serbian and Croatian unity." Rajačić's blessing of Ban Jelačić in 1848 was praised. Njegoš was honored for his poetry, and his major work, *Mountain Wreath*. Radičević was recognized for the excellence of his patriotic poetry. These were eloquent tributes to five men who had expressed appreciation for and understanding of the need for South Slavic unity.

Some of the selections by other authors included Stjepan Basariček's "Three Brothers Travel the World," "Fall," and "The Value of Salt"; Vjekoslav Klaić's "Adriatic Sea"; Mija Kispatić's "Donkey," "Horse," and "Salt"; Janko Jurković's "Harvest" and "Reconciliation"; August Šenoa's "My Shield"; Ivan Mažuranić's "Storm"; and Kačić-Miošić's "Saint Sava."

The selections from these Croatian authors were excellent examples of their writings, but they did not convey Croatian national sentiments. Hence in the broader context of this study they did little to further South Slavic understanding. This point becomes more evident when the content of the readers discussed above is compared with that of those published after the Balkan Wars, following the shift in Serbian policy and the instructions by the minister of education that more attention should be given to Croatian subjects. The best illustration of this point is found in the 1913 fourth year secondary school reader by Jovanović and Ivković, which was recommended for continued use to the Educational Council by its committee of consultants, whose chairman was Skerlić. As we noted in chapter 2, this was the committee that had suggested in 1913 that more space be given to Croatian literature.

The euphoria over the successes of the Balkan Wars was conveyed in the Jovanović and Ivković reader, particularly in a selection entitled "The Educational Progress of the Serbian Nation," in which Jovan Skerlić described in enthusiastic terms the great achievements of the past century. He did not confine his comments to the successes of the Serbian kingdom, but extended them to include a discussion of the Serbs in the Habsburg Empire, the issue of South Slav unity, and relations with the Croats. Thus he wrote:

> The spiritual ties between Serbia and the other areas where Serbs lived are stronger than they ever have been. Serbian books were read in larger numbers in all Serbian regions . . . not only among the Catholics . . . but also among the Muslims in Bosnia and Hercegovina since the end of the nineteenth century. Until the end of the nineteenth century national activity was experienced in Serbia and in Vojvodina; today it is spread out in all Serbian regions, especially in Croatia and in Bosnia and Hercegovina. . . . The movement to bring together the South Slavs, which took on greater dimensions after 1904, grows stronger. . . . That which was expected long ago and had to come about has finally arrived. The idea of the national unity of the Serbs and Croats has engulfed almost the entire real intelligentsia and virtually all educated men of both parts of our people. The idea of national unification is being implemented in the political arena and the literary field. The cooperative work between the Matica hrvatska and Srpska književna zadruga, between the Belgrade and Zagreb theaters, the constant contributions of Serbian writers to Croatian journals and Croatian to Serbian— all contribute to the assimilation of the literary language, the reading of Serbian authors by the Croatian public and Croatian by the Serbian—[and] these are all indications that we are moving toward the formation of one Serbian Croatian literature (*književnost srpsko hrvatske*), a literature of all our people.[74]

In addition to the material contained in this book, the third year reader also included four Croatian selections. The poem by Vladimir Nazor, "Zvonimir's Ship," was a selection from his larger work entitled "Croatian Kings," which related the most important events in medieval Croatian history. The most novel inclusion, however, was

an excerpt entitled "Matija Gubec, Peasant King," from August
Šenoa's major historical novel *Peasant Revolt*. Šenoa was a patriotic
writer whose subject matter and narrative skills appealed to the nationalistic feelings of the Croatian nation. Hence, by including Šenoa
in their reader, in particular a selection about Matija Gubec, Jovanović and Ivković were introducing the Serbian students to the best of
Croatian nationalistic writings.[75]

The passage included in the reader is most dramatic. Briefly, the
peasants under Matija Gubec rebelled for socioeconomic reasons
against the nobility in 1573. Eventually the revolt was crushed. The
selection describes the last stages of the battle when Gubec and his
followers were finally cornered in a church in Stubica. To save his
men, Gubec, without identifying himself, agreed to reveal the hid-
ing place of Gubec, if the rebels were spared. When Alapić, the head
of the nobility, gave his word of honor, Gubec replied: "I am Gubec."
The men were saved, but Gubec was taken to Zagreb, where he was
drawn and quartered.

The third selection was Preradović's popular "Traveler" (Put-
nik), concerning a man who is lost, seeks overnight shelter in a
home, but the woman who lives there, although sympathetic, points
out that all the available space is occupied by her own children. The
traveler longs for his own mother's house, vowing never to leave it.

The last selection was a poem entitled "Prophecy," by Ivan
Trnski. Trnski, whose life spanned most of the nineteenth century
(1819–1910), was a translator, novelist, poet, and product of the Illyrian movement. In this brief poem he described how the Serbs and
Croats were neighbors who shared a common fate. At times they
hated and even killed one another, but this was now at an end. "Let
us go forward in brotherly embrace." This poem was preceded by a
brief introduction by Jovanović and Ivković, who wrote:

> The Croats and Serbs are one and the same people, with two names,
> divided especially by religion and alphabet. Relations between us
> have not always been as good as they are now, because there was
> deep dissension and hatred, especially instigated by foreigners, our
> common enemies. At the time when there was movement toward
> reconciliation, this is how the patriotic Croatian poet Ivan Trnski
> expressed his feelings.[76]

Thus, on the eve of World War I the secondary school readers for
the first time contained information about the Croats that was both
sympathetic and coincided with the aspirations of the advocates of
Yugoslavism. The need for understanding, harmony, and unity
among the Serbs and Croats now found a place in the readers. As

noted, Skerlić even foresaw the development of a common Serbo-Croatian literature, which had been the dream of Ljudevit Gaj and the Illyrians. But, more significant, Skerlić also had observed that the idea of national unity was confined to the ranks of the "intelligentsia and educated men."

Although there was a perceptible shift in emphasis in the Jovanović and Ivković reader, which was in sharp contrast to the Serbianism found in the 1907 fourth year elementary reader by Protić and Stojanović, in its totality the Jovanović and Ivković book still retained strong Serbian sentiments, which buttressed the points found in the elementary textbooks. Thus in another selection from Skerlić, entitled "The Beginning of New Serbian Literature," the authors quoted Skerlić, who had written that modern literature began among the Serbs in Vojvodina in the eighteenth century. The medieval religious Serbian literature, which had died out by the end of the eighteenth century, "did not influence the creation of the new Serbian literature."

> It was the same situation with the other regional literatures of the Serbo-Croatian language. The Dalmatian, and in particular the Dubrovnik, literature of the fifteenth century to the beginning of the nineteenth century, the Bosnian literature of the seventeenth and eighteenth centuries, and the Slavonian literature of the eighteenth century, all these, our regional and Catholic literatures—nationally vague, mostly class-based and religious, almost all written in Latin script—did not have any influence on the Orthodox part of our nation. The religious chasm between the individual parts of our people was so deep that in effect there was no spiritual contact between the Orthodox and Catholics. The Orthodox Serbs, persecuted religiously in the eighteenth century, forced to accept Catholicism, were extremely suspicious of all books printed in the Latin alphabet. Only in rare exceptions were there translations from Catholic literature into Serbian, as there were also some cases of the reverse situation. These were different literatures of one and the same language, which had developed completely independently.[77]

Thus, Skerlić continued, modern Serbian literature developed independently of the medieval religious literature and "of the contemporary regional and Catholic literature." Although the new literature originally had a regional and religious bias, it soon was influenced by Western culture and education, and it then became "contemporary, cosmopolitan, 'secular,' national, and universal." By the mid-nineteenth century, the center of literary activity had shifted from Vojvodina to Serbia proper, where "the literature ceased to be regional and became universal, Serbian, for all the Orthodox, and for one part of the Catholics and Muslims in our nation. Contemporary Serbian literature was formed exclusively from this literature." [78]

The fact to note from this selection of Skerlić's writings are his repeated references to "Catholic" literature. Not once was this identified as Croatian literature. This point cannot be minimized, because throughout the readers, as well as in the geography and history textbooks, there was one constant theme: that although the Serbs suffered at the hands of the Turks, the persecution by the Catholics in some respects was even more onerous. The term Catholic was used to designate the Austrians, the Magyars, and the Italians in Dalmatia, but it also referred to the Croats. Skerlić was a known advocate of South Slav understanding; however, as was demonstrated, excerpts from his writings could be used to buttress the historic Serbian hostility to Catholicism and thereby to the Croats. The final point that must be stressed is that the immediate prewar shift in emphasis found in the secondary school Jovanović-Ivković reader, which sought to convey better understanding of Serbian and Croatian relations, applied only to their treatment of Croatia-Slavonia. As will be shown, the readers continued to present the other lands inhabited by Serbs and Croats as Serbian domains as they had in the past.

The Other South Slavic Lands

As for the other South Slavic lands under Austro-Hungarian rule, Bosnia, Hercegovina, Dalmatia, and Vojvodina, they were analyzed and discussed as part of the "Serbian lands" in all the readers. No concessions were made regarding Serbia's claims to these regions. The contrast between the way information was presented on these provinces and the way it was presented on Croatia is instructive and revealing.

Bosnia was represented as completely Serbian in the readers as well as in the geography and history textbooks. All of them claimed that the South Slavic inhabitants who were Muslims and Catholics and spoke the što dialect were Serbs. Moreover, the authors stated that the Serbs had occupied the lands up to the Una and Cetina rivers from the early medieval period on.

The feelings about Bosnia were best expressed by Stevan Vladislav Kačanski, a fervent nationalistic poet, in his poem "Wretched Bosnia," published in the fourth grade elementary reader. It read:

Proud Bosnia has bowed her head
And sheds tears into the murky Sava

She sheds tears and bitterly laments
From great misery and heavy pains
Oh, the poor one wails louder and louder
Listen, Serbia, Bosnia is crying!

The arrogant foreigner oppresses and shames her,
So that the wretched one dare not even complain
If she utters a sound, then misery befalls her
The chains are tightened and bones break
From bitter suffering and heavy pain
Listen, Serbia, Bosnia is wailing.

So that her bitter sorrow pass
She looks, ah, wistfully across the Drina
With her look she beckons, with her heart she sighs
She almost shouts, I can't any longer
Bear sorrows, carry shackles!
Serbia, Serbia, Bosnia beseeches you.[79]

Kačanski's theme is repeated in Mihailo Jović's "Drina, Beautiful Drina," about the river that forms the boundary between Serbia and Bosnia. In this prose poem, the Drina, when asked why its waters glistened, replies that "it was of Serbian tears, slave tears." When asked why the river meandered, it responds, "I seek Serbian unity from shore to shore, but, like last year's snow, it is nowhere to be found." When asked if it flowed swiftly to escape someone, it retorts: "I'm not chasing anyone, or anyone me. I flow in order not to see divided sisters: beautiful and proud Serbia and Bosnia, Hum [Hercegovina] and Montenegro—that is why I flee to the sea."[80]

In another story entitled "Among the Homes in Bosnia," a young Serb describes how he could hear his co-nationals on the Bosnian side from his village on the Serbian bank of the Drina. In the summer they swam together in the river while tending their flocks. "We sing the same songs, we and they. . . . But there was something different in Bosnia, something even better than we had." They had more and darker forests. They seemed to have more and healthier sheep, cattle, and horses. The houses in their village were together in a row; at night beside each house there was a huge bonfire tended by several individuals. Furthermore, at night the Serbs could hear the Bosnians beating on drums and wood and shouting: "Get away, get away, don't let it in, it is over there." The young Serb thought these were Bosnian children enjoying a wonderful custom, but his father explained that these were unfortunate individuals who were deprived of their firearms by the Austro-Hungarian authorities. Moreover, only those individuals could purchase rifles "to whom the government gave permission, and they do not approve this for any good Serb." Yet the Bosnian forests were filled with wolves. The bonfires and shouting were the only way to keep them away from the livestock. "Now everything is clear to me, our unfortunate brothers," lamented the young Serb.[81]

In another story, entitled "Abroad One Came to Know His Brothers: Recollections from a Trip," a young Serb tells of his experiences with the Bosnian Muslims. At one time the Orthodox and Muslims looked upon one another as enemies. "We spoke the same language, but we called them Turks. . . . We hated them [because of their religion]. We did not know we were brothers, and our elders did not tell us this. In school, however, the teacher taught us that 'he is my brother regardless of his religion.' In school we also learned where all our brothers lived and which were the Serbian lands."

Soon he began to like his Muslim brothers. He would speak to them as "brother to brother, but they only spoke to me as a neighbor. I was not of their faith and they were afraid of me." They regarded themselves as Turks. They did not go to school, nor did they learn from anyone "that they were Serbs." Yet he asked them "if they would like to have Bosnia united with Serbia. They said they would like to be united with Serbia and not to remain under Austria-Hungary. They know they are closer to us than to the Germans and Magyars. They feel it. . . ."

Some time passed before he again met some "Serbs of the Muslim faith." Then one year in July he was returning from a trip, and at the border railroad station he spotted two Muslims who he could tell were Bosnians. He even knew the area from which they came. The Bosnians heard the Serb talking to a friend and came over. The following dialogue took place.

> "Greetings brothers. You are Serbs," one of them said to us.
> "Greetings! And who are you?" I asked.
> "We too are Serbs from Bosnia."
> "Are you not Turks?"
> "No, by God. We are Serbs like you. During our trip we saw some people dressed as we are. They told us they were Turks. We wanted to talk to them. We spoke to them but they did not understand us, nor we them. We do not know Turkish. We are not Turks. We are Serbs even if we are of the Muslim faith. We recognize this now, traveling in foreign lands." [They had just been to the Ottoman Empire.]
>
> Thus it was that brothers came to know one another in a foreign place. But have they reconciled and united themselves at home?
>
> This is how my friend finished telling these cherished recollections about his trip from the past.[82]

The textbook also included a letter written in 1891 about Sarajevo, "our most important and most beautiful city in Bosnia," by a Serbian Muslim, Ahmet Mahmudagić, to his friend Omer. Ahmet began by describing his anticipation and feelings upon finally visiting Sarajevo. Situated in a narrow valley between mountains, the city glistened like a "mound of pearls" as one entered it. There was the beautiful Gazi-Husrev-Begova mosque, and a hundred others. In the distance one could see old and new Orthodox churches and the residency of the Orthodox Metropolitan. Of its 40,000 inhabitants, "More than half . . . were Serbs of the Turkish-Muslim faith, and over 5,000 Orthodox Serbs. There were 3,000 Catholics and 2,500 Jews. In Sarajevo the well-known Serbian Simo Milutinović Sarajlija was born."[83]

The province of Dalmatia did not receive the same attention in the readers that it would in the geography and history textbooks, yet the readers made clear that it, too, was considered a Serbian land. In 1907 Protić and Stojanović included Dalmatia among "the beautiful Serbian lands," which Šević in his 1911 reader claimed the Serbs had occupied when they entered the Balkan peninsula. Yet it was Serbia's insistence that Dubrovnik was their city which generated the bitterest controversy with the Croats.[84]

The readers provided extensive information on the formation of the medieval Dubrovnik republic, its administration, and its architectural achievements. They also stressed Dubrovnik's extensive commercial ties with Serbia in the pre-Ottoman era. Departing from factual information, Djordjević and Blagojević in their fourth grade elementary reader wrote about "the ancient glory of the Serbian maritime state, the Dubrovnik Republic," which was founded 1,300 years earlier. Whereas the majority of the Serbs preferred to live under a monarchical form of government, "the state of Dubrovnik, which from its foundation until the beginning of this century [nineteenth] was independent, was the only republic in the history of the Serbian people." The population of Dubrovnik was "all Serbs, but of these only one-fourth were of the Orthodox faith, and the remainder Catholic. However, even if the majority of the inhabitants of Dubrovnik are of the Catholic religion, nevertheless they think and feel themselves Serbs as do the Serbs of the Orthodox faith."[85]

The readers also stressed the Serbian character of Dubrovnik's literature. Djordjević and Blagojević wrote that "in the sixteenth and seventeenth centuries Dubrovnik reached the peak of its fame, because at that time scholarship blossomed there more than in any other Serbian city." It was the home of the poets Ivan Gundulić, Djono (Junije) Palmotić, and Stijepo Djordjić and the scientists Marin

Getaldić and Rudjer Bošković. "These are authors of whom all Serb-dom is proud, and whom other educated people admire." The crown-ing moment came in 1893, when a statue of Gundulić was erected in Dubrovnik. "When it was unveiled, there were Serbs present from all Serbian regions, who came to see the ceremony and to place wreaths at the statue. Of all the wreaths that were presented, the one that stood out for its beauty was that of the late king of Serbia, Alexander I [Obrenović]."[86] The significance of these statements can be appreciated when it is remembered that Gundulić, Palmotić, Djordjić, Getaldić, and Bošković were all Croats, and were ranked by the Croatians among the most prominent men in their history.

Perhaps the most important statement was by Pavle Popović. It was printed in the same 1913 fourth year gymnasium reader of Jova-nović and Ivković that contained the favorable information about Croatia and the selections from Skerlić. Popović was an eminent professor at the University of Belgrade who specialized in South Slavic, not just Serbian, literature. He eloquently described the physical setting of Dubrovnik with its massive walls and architec-ture and noted that Dubrovnik through many centuries in the medi-eval and modern periods had been "wealthy, cultured, and free." It ruled the coastal land from Kotor in the south to the Neretva River in the north. "From the end of the fifteenth century, literature devel-oped in the Serbian language in Dubrovnik and continued inten-sively to the end of the eighteenth century, when it began to fade and die, together with the reputation and freedom of the Dubrovnik re-public, which was abolished in 1808." Popović went one step further and declared that "it was destined that Dubrovnik take over Serbian literature at the moment when the old Cyrillic literature began to wane, and to sustain it [Serbian literature] until the new literature began to flourish."[87] The importance of this statement, coming as it did from a distinguished scholar, is clear. It placed the final stamp of authority on all the statements that described Dubrovnik as a Ser-bian city. Thus, on the eve of the war, precisely in the period of the strongest support for Yugoslavism by Serbian intellectuals, a state-ment from one of them, a specialist in Serbian and Croatian litera-ture at the University of Belgrade, was included in the reader that made no concession to the Croatian character of the city or to the Croatian origins of its distinguished authors and scientists.

The other South Slavic land under Habsburg rule that was given considerable attention was Vojvodina. Citing a work by Bogoboj Ata-nacković, a romantic story writer, entitled "Serbian Vojvodina," the Protić-Stojanović fourth grade reader eloquently described the Ser-bian character of the area. "It really is a beautiful land, that Serbian

Vojvodina! It is proper that it be a Serbian land! It truly is also a center of heroes! God indeed created a beautiful land for a beautiful
people!"[88]

The students learned of the major Serbian migrations into the
area in the seventeenth century and the emergence of Novi Sad as
the principal Serbian city. Even so, out of a population of 24,000,
Novi Sad contained only 8,000 Serbs; the others were mainly Magyars and Germans. The cosmopolitan character of the city was evident from the fact that, in addition to the five Orthodox churches,
there were two Catholic churches as well as individual Armenian,
Lutheran, and Calvinist churches and a synagogue.[89]

The term Vojvodina had come to include not only Banat and
Bačka, but also Srem, which technically was the eastern tip of Slavonia, and hence a part of the Triune Kingdom. Its Serbian character
was indicated in two ways. First, the textbooks stressed the migrations from the Ottoman lands in the seventeenth and eighteenth
centuries, which resulted in an overwhelming Serbian population in
the provinces. Consequently, the Djordjević-Blagojević reader emphasized that in Srem "live only Serbs, who speak the same language as is heard in all the northern and eastern regions of our
[Serbian] kingdom." But the students also read that in the province
"here and there live those of our brothers who long ago accepted the
Catholic faith."[90] Second, on Fruška Gora, in Srem, there were sixteen Serbian monasteries. They never rivaled the southern medieval
Serbian monasteries in splendor or significance, but they nevertheless had great importance for the Serbs. Thus, for example, the remains of Prince Lazar, Tsar Uroš, the son of Dušan, despot Stevan
Stiljanović, Princess Ljubica, the wife of Prince Miloš and the mother
of Prince Michael, and many others were buried in these monasteries. These facts clearly helped confirm the Serbian character of
Srem and Vojvodina and what the students would also read in the
geography and history textbooks.[91] However, the attachment that
the Serbs had to Srem was best expressed by Atanacković. In vivid
terms, he described the physical beauties of the province and its
principal city, Sremski Karlovci, the seat of the Serbian patriarchate.
"Karlovci—Karlovci with its surroundings—God's splendor. Has
a mother given birth to a Serb who does not know of Sremski
Karlovci?"[92]

As for the Slovenes, they were largely ignored in the readers. The
only reference to them was when they were listed, along with the
Russians, Poles, Czechs, and Bulgars, as Slavic nations, or when linguists classified their language as kajkavian. Even the gymnasium

readers, which contained writings from other countries, did not have any selections, even geographic descriptions or folk poetry, attributed to a Slovenian author. Yet they did include excerpts from Edmondo De Amicis, Thomas Carlyle, Alphonse Daudet, Nikolai Gogol, Nathaniel Hawthorne, Heinrich Heine, Victor Hugo, Charles Marie Leconte de Lisle, Prosper Mérimée, William Shakespeare, Friedrich Schiller, Alfred Tennyson, Leo Tolstoy, and Ludwig Uhland. It should also be recalled that in the quotation from Skerlić, which Jovanović and Ivković cited in their 1913 reader, the Slovenes were not included in his comment that "the idea of the national unity of the Serbs and Croats has engulfed almost the entire real intelligentsia and virtually all educated men of both parts of our people."[93]

Although the provinces of Macedonia and Old Serbia did not directly involve the Croats and Serbs and the question of South Slav unity, their acquisition was a major point in the Serbian national program. Hence the information in the readers about these two provinces was very important. The selections concentrated on the medieval period, especially the reign of Tsar Dušan, when these lands were the heart of the Serbian empire. The task was made easier by the richness of Serbian folk poetry, much of which centered on the exploits of Miloš Obilić and Marko Kraljević. As noted earlier, Serbia's attention was focused on these lands after the Congress of Berlin primarily to counteract the Bulgarian claims to Macedonia, which were being successfully fostered through religious, cultural, and educational means. Hitherto the information about Macedonia and Bulgaria had been largely factual, as evidenced in Hristić's readers.

In the 1855 and 1872 editions of his readers, Hristić repeated the same information about Macedonia. In the seventh century, the Bulgars gained their independence from Byzantium and soon established their rule over almost "all of Thrace, Macedonia, and Albania." In the ninth century, under Tsar Boris, the Bulgars were converted to Christianity by Methodius. Boris's successor, Simeon, encouraged the development of literature "in the Slavic language. . . . That is why at that time the most important books in Old Slavic literature were written in Bulgarian." Thereafter, the Bulgars succumbed to Byzantium. Although there was a subsequent revival, Bulgaria never regained her former greatness. Then at the end of the fourteenth century, Bulgaria was conquered by the Ottomans. In other words Hristić acknowledged that at one time the Bulgars ruled over Macedonia and that they had developed a literature, but he gave the impression that this was a transitory development. Subsequently, Serbian authors ignored this and saw Macedonia as only Serbian.[94]

As cited previously, in 1907 Protić and Stojanović in their fourth year elementary reader wrote that in the beautiful Serbian lands, which included "Old Serbia, Macedonia, and the Vidin and Sredac [Sofia] provinces, foreigners rule over the Serbian people." In 1911 Šević in his second year secondary school reader stated that when the Serbs entered the Balkans they occupied the western half of the Balkan peninsula, which included "*Serbia, Old Serbia, Macedonia, Bosnia, Hercegovina, Dalmatia* with *Dubrovnik, Montenegro*, and northern *Albania*."[95] The Serbian claims to Macedonia were reinforced in the selections found, for instance, in the prose poem "Macedonia," by Vladimir Jovanović, included in the Protić and Stojanović reader. Written in fifteen stanzas, it touched on all aspects of Macedonian history. It began: "And you were always famous!—no one land was your equal! Your renown spread throughout the world—and once you were proud!" Macedonia was praised as "a monument of Slavic glory," which Serbs had settled. The Nemanjas fought for and united Macedonia. Tsar Dušan was crowned in Macedonia; he made Skopje Serbia's capital. It was there that the Serbs received their law code. It was the land of Jug Bogdan, Momčilo, and Preljub. Veles, Thessaloniki, Seres, and Voden looked different under Serbian administration. It was a great Slavic era when "Serbdom" reigned there. At Kosovo Serbian pride ceased, and Macedonia together with Serbdom became Turkish slaves. "And now you are still in a difficult situation. There is still no one to avenge you, you are still being dismembered by enemies, in order to subject you to a NEW YOKE." But the dawn will arrive "as soon as Serbdom raises its banner." Then "all your long pains will end, your fame will again glisten; your reputation will rise, you will achieve all your aspirations. Prilep [Marko Kraljević's birthplace] will be what it once was, Macedonia!" Jovanović believed that the days of Ottoman rule were numbered, but he feared the "new yoke," which was Bulgaria.[96]

Other selections described Macedonian cities and regions, with Ohrid receiving particular attention. Djordjević and Blagojević noted that at one time Ohrid "was in the hands of the Romans, Greeks, and Bulgars, before it was liberated by Dušan." It did not remain long in Serbian control because the Turks conquered it. Nevertheless, the Serbs had lived in Ohrid ever since they arrived in the Balkans in the seventh century.[97] More dramatic were the comments found in the Protić-Stojanović reader about Ohrid by Jovan Jovanović Zmaj, one of Serbia's most distinguished authors and poets, who was known for his strong anti-Ottoman and anti-Habsburg views. "Do you know, children, the city which Dušan the Great conquered, in which he subsequently was crowned with the Serbian and Greek crown? It is Ohrid, a beautiful city, a monument to all the Serbs." On the mountains above Ohrid, he continued, an eagle soars.

> What—does only a bird remember the old Serbian glory?—In Ohrid there are twice as many Serbs as non-Serbs. In Ohrid and throughout these vast Macedonian lands there are many Serbs—Serbs who are not warmed by the Serbian sun. For long they have prayed to God that their real mother find them, and today they still pray— but the prayer is weakening. It is not a joke that centuries of ordeal have crushed spirits (*stisli grudi*); and it is a wonder that long ago consciousness did not lapse into unconsciousness. Soon the mother will remind the child—then, look out! White Ohrid will be Serbianized, where Dušan reigned![98]

In addition to Ohrid, the cities of Prilep in Macedonia and Prizren in Kosovo, with whom Marko Kraljević and Tsar Dušan respectively were associated, were extolled in the readers. "Will [Prizren] have to wait even longer for its freedom, for its old and dear rulers?" asked one reader.[99]

Whereas some authors stressed Serbia's historic claims, others based their justification on both historical and ethnic principles. Thus Jovan Cvijić, who had traveled extensively throughout the Balkans and knew the peninsula well, was cited in reference to Old Serbia, which included Kosovo and the historic patriarchate of Peć. His impressions following one of his trips were quoted by Ivković in 1911 in his first year secondary reader. Cvijić stated that

> No other part of the Serbian people is so lacking in basic rights and so oppressed as that in Metohija around Peć, Dečani, and Djakovica, which is subject to the savagery of the Albanians. . . . On the eve of a great holiday I saw this population gathered around the Holy Patriarchate outside Peć, afraid and some terrified. It is evident that among them prayers are not only a consolation but also a hope, when one does not have other comfort or other hope. They pray for their salvation, and that precisely is the substance of their prayers. They pray not only to God, but to the Nemanjas and Tsar Lazar, then to Serbia and Montenegro."[100]

The message was clear; Old Serbia was one of the most cherished centers of Serbdom.

Capitalizing on the rich Serbian literature, authors used selections from folklore, geography, history, language, and literature to create a positive, glowing image of the Serbian nation. With more than half of the lands where Serbs lived still under foreign domination and with reports of the mistreatment of Serbs in these lands, one can understand the power of the readers' emotional appeal. The liberation of the Serbian lands and national unity, not South Slavism, surely were the paramount issues confronting the nation.

CROATIAN READERS OR ČITANKE

As was the case with the Serbian readers, the Croatian books covered every conceivable subject—the universe, religion, flora and fauna, geography, history, language, literature, government, customs, manners, morals, folklore, fables, proverbs, and riddles. The Croatian elementary and secondary school students, like the Serbian, were imbued with a romantic, patriotic view of their nation in which good citizenship was rewarded by a merciful God and a benevolent king. Unquestionably, the readers played a major role in preparing the students for adulthood.

Before we analyze their contents, a number of general observations must be made. First, language was the central issue, because it was a means by which the Croats could oppose Magyarization, and it was the common denominator that would unite, culturally and politically, not only the Croats but all the South Slavs of the Habsburg empire. The major emphasis was placed on the development of the standard literary language. Consequently, the historical background of the Croatian and Serbian language and literature from the middle ages through the nineteenth century was discussed extensively. The purpose was to demonstrate their interrelationship.

In contrast to Serbia, which was independent and had its own native ruler, Croatia, it will be remembered, was an autonomous kingdom whose king was also the Habsburg emperor, Franz Joseph. Moreover, the link to the emperor went through Budapest, since Croatia was a part of the Hungarian kingdom. Thus when the Croats wrote in praise of their ruler, it was the Habsburg monarch who was exalted, not a native son as in the case of the Karadjordjevićes and Obrenovićes in Serbia. But when they spoke of patriotism and loyalty, it meant primarily their attachment to their *domovina* or homeland, the Triune Kingdom of Croatia, Slavonia, and Dalmatia. Because of the political situation, the readers did not directly comment on the major political issue that confronted the Croats in the nineteenth century, namely, their perennial struggle with Budapest to avoid Magyarization. The politicians discussed it and it was an issue in the electoral campaigns and parliamentary debates. In the textbooks, however, it was presented through the emphasis on the primacy of the Croatian language in the Triune Kingdom and the repeated criticism of the Hungarians for their failure to heed the advice of the Croats on how to meet the Ottoman threat. The Croatian writers had to be circumspect in this matter because of the political and economic influence that Budapest could exert on Croatia, notwithstanding the fact that the Nagodba of 1868 specifically guaranteed Croatia control over her own educational system.

The Authors

Many of the leading scholars of the period were authors of readers. They championed the idea of South Slavic cultural unity. Even those who were not as prominent shared these sentiments. In other words, commencing with the Illyrian movement, the concept of Croatian and Serbian linguistic unity was propagated through the readers. It was to be the base upon which to achieve cultural and political unity.

After the Nagodba was ratified, committees were appointed by the government to study the question of readers, including their purpose and content. When the reports were approved, either a single individual or a group of authors were commissioned to prepare the readers. The men who played the dominant role in the preparation of the readers were all influenced by the Illyrian movement. Within their ranks were Stjepan Basariček, Skender Fabković, Ivan Filipović, Vjenceslav Mařik, Matija Mesić, Ljudevit Modec, and Ivan Šah.

Unquestionably, the dominant member of this group was Ivan Filipović. He was a teacher in several Croatian cities, including Zagreb, and was a school superintendent from 1875 to 1886. However, his importance was based on two factors: his championing of Yugoslavism and his role in establishing the teachers' asssociation in Croatia. As a young man he became a passionate partisan of the Illyrian movement and South Slavic unity, and he supported religious tolerance. In the 1850s he was imprisoned for writing a Croatian patiotic poem. In the 1860s he organized the Teachers' Societies and in 1871 he was the principal founder of the Croatian Pedagogical Literary Association. These two societies were the major organizations behind the secularization of education. In addition, Filipović was the chairman of the committee commissioned to prepare new textbooks. He had, in fact, published a *Grammar and Reader for the First Grade* in 1851, which was used throughout Croatia until the new law was enacted. In 1875 he prepared the *First Grammar and Reader*. In the same year he also published his well-known *Short History of Croatian and Serbian Literature for the Public and Upper Girls' Schools*, which is one of the best contemporary surveys of

Croatian and Serbian literature written from the Illyrian and Yugoslav point of view. His advocacy of South Slavic unity was rewarded by his election as corresponding member of the Serbian Learned Society, the precursor of the Serbian Academy of Sciences.[101]

Filipović's close collaborator on the textbook committee was Skender Fabković. After studying education and philosophy at Prague, he taught in a number of Croatian cities before becoming a professor at the teachers' college or school in Zagreb. He too was instrumental in organizing the Teachers' Societies and fought hard for the 1874 law. His scholarly research centered on the study of language and pedagogical questions. He was responsible for the *Reader for the Second Grade* and worked closely with the committee that produced the third and fourth year readers.[102]

Another author was Ljudevit Modec, who also studied education in Prague, taught at a girls' school, and then at the teachers' college in Zagreb, where he eventually became the principal. He supported Filipović's policies, worked closely with the teachers' organization, and was involved with the textbooks. Thus he published the first and second readers and revised the primer. It should be noted that, notwithstanding their authors' advocacy of the secular control of education, the Catholic Croatian confessional schools in Bosnia used the readers by Filipović, Fabković and Modec.[103]

Ivan Šah was a Czech who studied in Prague but obtained a teaching position in Croatia, which he came "to love as his own country." He became very active in the various teachers' organizations. He served as principal of the girls' school in Zagreb and was a member of the Croatian Educational Commission. He wrote for Czech and Serbian newspapers and was a follower of Gaj's Illyrianism. He wrote the reader for the fourth grade.[104]

Stjepan Basariček, well known for his numerous contributions in the field of Croatian education, wrote some of the basic works on pedagogy. He was also the author of the *Reader for the Upper Public Schools* and the *Croatian Primer*, which enjoyed considerable success. In addition, he was a member of all the teachers' organizations.[105]

Although the readers were revised and new editions prepared (1895 and 1906), their basic emphasis did not change. The first year reader stressed love of family, patriotism, and loyalty; the second emphasized the fatherland and nationality; the third introduced the student to the political geography of the Croats, a cursory history of the Croats and Serbs, and their heroes; and the fourth elaborated on their heroes, introduced the students to all the South Slavic lands, the Austro-Hungarian empire, and Europe. This steady progression meant that when the students completed their elementary schooling, which was the extent of education for about 95 percent, they had a good basic knowledge of their language, literature, history, and geography, as well as an appreciation for the other South Slavs and the Habsburg empire.

The authors of the secondary school readers represented some of the best-known scholars of the era. Although supporting South Slavic cooperation and the use of the što dialect, they disagreed on orthography. The early writers, Antun Mažuranić, Matija Mesić, and Adolfo Veber-Tkalčević, who were Illyrians, supported an orthography that was somewhat flexible, because their purpose was to entice the Slovenes, and possibly the Bulgarians, to develop a common literary language with the Croats and Serbs. The others, who were active mainly after 1874, Hugo Badalić, Ivan Broz, Mirko Divković, Tomislav Maretić, Franjo Marković, Franjo Petračić, and Tade Smičiklas, were avid followers of the orthographic reforms for the što dialect stressed by Vuk Karadžić, which involved only the Croats and Serbs. The scholars who subscribed to Vuk's views gained the appellation of "Vukovites." Thus the difference between the early reformers and the Vukovites was not over the question of South Slavic understanding and unity, which they all favored, but over the best means to achieve it. Notwithstanding this difference in approach to Yugoslav unity, the readers used before the reform of the 1874 and those prepared by the Vukovites were in agreement on the importance of understanding both Croatian and Serbian literature. Some of the authors even considered it a single literature.

Of the three "Illyrians," Adolfo Veber-Tkalčević was perhaps the most controversial. After studying Slavistics and Latin in Vienna, he taught in the Zagreb gymnasium and was its principal from 1860 to 1867. He was also a founding member of the Yugoslav Academy. A firm believer in the Illyrian movement, he ardently defended the ijekavian variant of the štokavian dialect, but preferred to use variations of the older orthography, which he believed would rally all the South Slavs behind a common literary language, which he called "Illyrian or Yugoslav." In support of his views he wrote many studies, including the first syntax of the Croatian literary language and a number of textbooks, the best known of which was *Illyrian Reader for the Upper Gymnasium*, which he produced with Mažuranić and Mesić. Veber engaged in sharp polemics with Vatroslav Jagić, Tomislav Maretić, and Mirko Divković over orthography and stubbornly adhered to his views until his death in 1889, even though the battle had been lost by 1867, when the Yugoslav Academy sided with the Vukovites.[106]

Veber's colleague, Matija Mesić, was a well-known historian. He also wrote readers, which was not an uncommon practice, because so much of the material in the textbooks dealt with history. Mesić studied theology, history, and geography in Vienna and Prague, and then taught law and history in Zagreb. In 1874 he was elected the first rector of the University of Zagreb. He was the first scholar to discuss seriously the issue of the periodization of Croatian history. In addition to the *Illyrian Reader*, which he co-authored with Veber and Mažuranić, Mesić wrote the *Grammar and Reader* for the second, third, and fourth elementary grades. Like Veber, he did not endorse all of Vuk's reforms.[107]

The last of the Illyrian triumvirate, Antun Mažuranić, who was the brother of Ivan Mažuranić, also was a gymnasium teacher. He was a close collaborator of Ljudevit Gaj, a contributor to *Danica*, and in 1839 he published a grammar. He helped found the Matica Ilirska (Illyrian Literary Foundation) and he played a major role in the production of the *Illyrian Reader*. In addition, these three scholars prepared *The Reader for the Third and Fourth Grade*, which was used until new readers were published in the 1870s.[108]

The opposition to the Veber group was led by Tomislav Maretić, Tadija Smičiklas, Franjo Petračić, Ivan Broz, and Mirko Divković, all of whom accepted Vuk's reforms and wrote readers. The two most distinguished members were Maretić and Smičiklas. Maretić was the greatest Croatian linguist of the period, and his role in producing the *Croatian or Serbian Grammar*, the *Croatian Reader for the Second Grade*, and his major work, *Grammar and Stylistics of the Croatian or Serbian Literary Language* as well as his role as editor of the *Dictionary of the Croatian or Serbian Language* were discussed at the beginning of this chapter. Here it is only necessary to reassert that he was a confirmed supporter of Karadžić and believed strongly in Croatian and Serbian literary unity.[109]

Smičiklas, on the other hand, was not a linguist but a historian whose interests centered especially on Croatia's relations with the Austrians and the Magyars. During his career he was a professor at the University of Zagreb, its dean of theology and rector, the president of the Yugoslav Academy, and the president of the Matica Hrvatska. For seven years he also served in the Croatian sabor as a representative of the Independent National Party. He wrote an outstanding history of Croatia and numerous studies of prominent nineteenth-century Croatians—including Ivan Drašković, Mažuranić, Mesić, Rački, Kukuljević, Strossmayer, Gaj, and Vjekoslav Babukić—which reflected his interest in Illyrianism and Yugoslavism. Given his abilities, it is understandable that after the enactment of the 1874 education law, Smičiklas was asked to prepare the gymnasium readers for the first (1875), second (1875), and third (1880) grades. Although later other scholars revised or prepared new editions of his readers, Smičiklas's imprint remained through World War I.[110]

Franjo Petračić studied philology, Greek principally, at the University of Vienna, where he came to know Vuk and became one of his converts. After a number of years as a gymnasium teacher in various Croatian cities, he became a professor of Greek at the university. In the 1870s he was invited to prepare two volumes of readers for the advanced grades of the gymnasium, both entitled *Croatian Reader for the Upper Gymnasium*. The first volume dealt with poetry, style, and prose (1877), and the second with the history of literature (1880). They were remarkably successful, being used until World War II. Although later other scholars—Hugo Badalić, Ivan Broz, Ferdo Ž. Miler, Djuro Zagoda, Josip Pasarić, and D. Bogdanović—made additions or revisions to his books, the title page always carried his name: for instance, *Fr. Petračić's Croatian Reader for the Higher Grades of the Secondary Schools.*[111]

The most successful textbook writer was Mirko Divković. He studied in Vienna and taught in gymnasiums for over forty years, twenty-four of which were spent as the principal in Zagreb. His political views were those of Strossmayer, and he engaged in sharp polemics with Veber over Croatian grammar. His fame rests, however, on his textbooks. From 1879 to 1881 he published *Croatian Grammar for the Secondary and Similar Schools*, which went through twelve editions by 1917. In 1888 he reedited Smičiklas's *Croatian Reader for the First Grade*, which had twelve editions by 1923. In 1889 he revised Smičiklas's *Croatian Reader for the Third Grade*, which in 1918 was in its eighth edition. In 1891, he revised *Croatian Reader for the Fourth Grade*, initially written by Franjo Marković; by 1918 it was in its seventh edition. In other words, the students who attended the gymnasium in the quarter-century before the war were taught using readers that Divković had either written himself or edited. They contained some of the best examples of support for the common Serbo-Croatian language and Strossmayer's ideals.[112]

Other well-known authors were Ivan Broz, Hugo Badalić, and Franjo Marković. Broz was a brilliant linguist who studied with Vatroslav Jagić in Vienna and collaborated with Maretić. In 1892, a year before his death, Broz was elected a corresponding member of the Yugoslav Academy. His scholarly work was in phonetics, morphology, and syntax, and his major work was his study of phonetic orthography, published in 1892. His views on the unity of the Croatian and Serbian literary language are evident in his editions of Petračić's reader (1888) on poetics, style, and prose.[113]

Hugo Badalić also studied in Vienna and became a gymnasium teacher. He is best known for his libretto of Ivan Zajc's patriotic romantic opera titled *Nikola Šubić Zrinski*, but he also produced excellent editions (1888, 1895, 1899) of Petračić's readers. Franjo Marković studied Slavistics and philosophy in Vienna and subsequently taught philosophy at Zagreb. A prolific writer, many of whose epic poems were regarded by his contemporaries as the best in Croatian literature, Marković wrote the initial *Reader for the Fourth Grade* (1874), which Divković was to revise after 1891.[114]

There was no ambiguity among the authors of either the elementary or the secondary readers concerning the importance of language and literature. The Illyrian movement had charted the course and set the goal; their task was to follow it and bring about the cultural unity of the South Slavs. The key to their success, they believed, was language, because, as the fourth grade elementary reader emphasized, "the principal criterion" that differentiated nations in Europe was language.[115] An 1891 grammar and phrase book informed the students that "the language of the Croats is identical to the language of the Serbs" and that "Vuk Karadžić and Ljudevit Gaj reformed our orthography."[116]

Although the elementary school readers did not have prefaces, their intent can be seen in part from the contents of the second year reader. In 1861, the Cyrillic alphabet was introduced into the Croatian schools, and it was mandated in the 1874 law. Thereafter, schoolchildren read variations of two statements. The Croatian students read: "We have books that are not printed in these letters, which you learned in the 'primer' (*početnica*) and which were called Latin. Our books are also printed in Cyrillic letters." The Serbian children read in their readers in Cyrillic: "We have books that are not printed in these letters, which you learned in the 'primer' (*bukvar*) and which are called Cyrillic. Our books are also printed in Latin letters." In other words, the only difference in the two statements was in the word for "primer."[117] Each statement was followed by the two alphabets, together with words and phrases. In some books the Latin words and phrases were on one page and the identical Cyrillic on the opposite. It was clear to the students that the language was the same, but written in two alphabets. Thereafter, in all elementary and secondary school readers, both Latin and Cyrillic were used. No precise formula was employed, but anywhere from 15 to 30 percent of each textbook was in Cyrillic. In time Croatian students read accounts of their own country, rulers, heroes, and literature in Cyrillic, and Serbian students found themselves reading about their nation in Latin, measures aimed at furthering mutual understanding.

Whereas the authors of the elementary readers did not write explicit prefaces or introductions that indicated their purpose and points of view, the authors of the secondary readers provided such information. The general views of these authors were perhaps best expressed by Petračić, who in 1880, in the first edition of his reader, wrote that "the history of language cannot be divorced from the history of literature, because language is the vehicle of literature." Furthermore, he continued, "now virtually everywhere it is maintained that Croatian with Serbian are one and the same language. . . . Consequently, the development of Croatian and Serbian literature will be equally studied and presented here."[118] In the 1895 edition, Ferdo Ž. Miler, the new editor of Petračić's book, carried the theme further. He explained that when the Croats and Serbs arrived in the Balkans from their ancestral home, "they were divided by name, but in language they were as two natural-born brothers." After their conversion to different branches of Christianity, "each developed its own literature and thus even today these two brother tribes are not totally united in a single enlightened entity." The Ottoman conquest complicated the issue and further contributed to the emergence of two literatures so that "today one can speak of Croatian and of Serbian literatures as being two separate cultural manifestations, whereas by blood and language the Croats and Serbs are in fact one nation."[119] In 1910 Antun Pechan, another successful author, stated that his history of literature "was formulated from the point of view of the unity of the Croatian and Serbian people."[120]

To support the idea of the similarity of language, literature, blood, and nation, many Croatian readers carried a selection written by Daničić in 1874 for the well-known Belgrade newspaper *Vidov Dan*. Here he sought to provide a logical explanation of the issues involving the Croats and Serbs. Not everyone, he wrote, understood the differences between Serbs and Croats. At one time in Serbia it was most frequently believed that the Croats lived in the three western provinces where the kajkavian dialect was spoken. There was a tendency among some, for linguistic reasons, to regard the Croats as Slovenes, which they were not. In fact, wrote Daničić, they call themselves Croats because "they feel and know that they are Croats." On the other hand, others, who included Karadžić—and Daničić admitted that he himself at one time shared these views—assumed that the Croats were only those who spoke the čakavian dialect and who lived in the western part of the Croatian Military Frontier, parts of Dalmatia, and the neighboring islands. Now, Daničić added, he knew that the minor linguistic differences between the čakavians and the others who lived in Croatia and Dalmatia did not justify the contention that only the čakavian speakers were Croats. In fact, Daničić informed his readers, in addition to the kajkavian and čakavian Croats, "there are people, who speak exactly the way we [Serbs] do, who are not called Serbs, but Croats, and they love this name and are proud of it just as we love the Serbian name and are proud of it. Consequently, I believe it cannot be otherwise than that the Serbs and Croats are one people, who have two names, one part of whom are called Serbs and the other Croats."

Next Daničić entered into a discussion of when the Serbs and Croats came to have two names, speculating that this probably occurred in ancient times. Thereafter, the tribal elders retained these names, and they became part of the nations' subsequent political development. Thus, although the same people lived in two states, they came to be known by two different names. Moreover, even when their states were destroyed and the people intermingled, each retained its old name. Then Daničić came to the crux of his argument: "And since the Serbs and Croats are one people, who speak the same language, it is not strange then, but completely normal, if those who call themselves Serbs, call as Serbs those who call themselves Croats seeing that they [Croats] speak the same way as they [Serbs] do, or if those who call themselves Croats call as Croats those who call themselves Serbs also seeing that they [Serbs] speak the same way as they [Croats] do." He concluded his discussion with a call for understanding and cooperation.

> Truthfully, it might be difficult for some individual when someone calls him by a name other than the one by which he calls himself. However, this is not offensive only to one party but it is the same for the other also. This difficulty could be minimized, and could be further reduced, if it is taken into consideration that it was the history of our people that brought it about, and thus it belongs, along with so many other national misfortunes, to those which we must bear heroically until we overcome them. They cannot be mastered by learned treatises but only by great historic deeds. We must work at it, so that the people can achieve these goals. I believe that we will pursue these goals most confidently only when every individual applies himself with all his strength to advance the task to which we are committed.[121]

This eloquent appeal for South Slavic understanding became a mainstay in Croatian readers. However, it is significant to note that Daničić's statement was not in the Serbian readers examined, although he was frequently cited by Serbian authors as an authority on their language.

The Croatian Kingdom

The main objective of the readers was to instill in the students love for their homeland by presenting articles about the people, their religion, patriotism, loyalty, heroism, and language. But to define the territorial limits of the homeland or fatherland was a more complicated problem for Croatia than it was for independent Serbia. The Croats in effect had two national centers—first, the Triune Kingdom of Croatia, Slavonia, and Dalmatia and, second, the Habsburg Empire, of which they were an integral part. Their king resided in Vienna, not Zagreb, and ruled through Budapest. As his subjects they were obliged to fight for whatever goals were deemed vital to the empire, not just for Croatian interests. Moreover, Croatia's union with Hungary in 1102 and Austria in 1527 spanned more than eight centuries, and thus it placed, in some respects, a greater imprint on the character of the Croatian nation than did the previous five centuries. Thus, much of Croatian history was seen as part of the larger Habsburg-Hungarian complex. Consequently, concepts of fatherland, loyalty, patriotism, and heroism could become blurred at times.

As was the case with the Serbian readers, the Croatian books relied heavily on historical information. Thus, the first point impressed on the students by the third grade elementary reader was that they were members of one of "the most numerous peoples in the world," the Slavs.[122] In their original ancestral home, which was identified as being located in what is present-day Ukraine-Poland, the Croats lived together with the Serbs, Russians, Ukrainians, Poles, Czechs, Slovaks, Bulgars, Slovenes, Polabians, and Lusatian Sorbs. In the sixth and seventh centuries the Croats and the Serbs migrated southward into their present homelands. The transition was not easy because the Avars, "a terrible and wild people," who occupied these lands had to be subdued. The Croats responded to the appeal of the Byzantine ruler for help against the Avars, as did the Serbs, who had migrated southward about the same time as the Croats. The Serbs, "settled to the east of the Croats. In no respect did they [the Serbs] differ from them [the Croats]. In other words, they had the same language, same religion, same institutions and customs, virtues and vices." As soon as the Avars were defeated, the Croats settled in the land that they now occupied and proclaimed it "Croatia," which originally was composed of two states—Dalmatia and Posavska (the land between the Sava and Drava rivers). These

states were organized into fourteen districts by the middle of the
ninth century, each ruled by a *župan* (district administrator). Subsequently, the Croats created their own kingdom and had their own
king. "The Serbs organized their lands in the same way. They too
had their great *župans*, princes, and kings, and later tsars." In other
words, the unity of the Croats and Serbs could be traced back to
their known origins.[123]

After their settlement in Croatia, Slavonia, and Dalmatia, the
next great event in Croatian history was their conversion to Christianity. Since religion was a compulsory subject in school, it is understandable that great emphasis was placed on it. The third year reader
noted that some of the Croats who settled in Dalmatia were converted in the middle of the seventh century—an important point because it implied that they were among the first Slavs to become
Christians. Thereafter, young Croats were sent to Rome for training,
returning home as missionaries. The greatest emphasis, however,
was placed on the missionary role of Cyril and Methodius, two
ninth-century brothers from Thessaloniki who not only translated
the Bible for the Slavs but also devised the Cyrillic alphabet. Their
work among the Slavs, especially in Croatia, was lauded, in particular, because of their role in obtaining the Pope's approval for the
Croats to have their religious services in their own "Croatian language" or "Croatian Glagolitic," rather than in Latin.[124]

However, the fourth grade reader reminded the students that not
all Christians were Catholics. The Serbs were identified as belonging to the Orthodox Christian faith, as were the Russians, Romanians, Bulgarians, Greeks, and Montenegrins. Moreover, the students were admonished "that all men on earth, regardless of religion
and nationality, were our fellowmen whom, in the words of our Savior, we must love and respect—'Love your fellowman as you love
yourself.'"[125] Finally, to underline the significance and importance of
one's religion, the second grade reader included a story in which
Napoleon asked his guests when they thought he had been "most
happy and most successful." Some mentioned his military victories,
others the time when he became emperor. All were wrong. "'Believe
me, Gentlemen! In my whole life I never had a more joyous moment
than that instant when I had Holy Communion for the first time.'"[126]

Notwithstanding the fact that the church lost its control of education in 1874, Catholicism remained an integral part of Croatian
education. Not only were there the mandatory courses on religion in
all the schools, but the readers contained material with religious
themes, as for instance, a poem of nine stanzas called "Catholic."
The first verse read:

I am a Catholic Christian
And the Holy Church is my mother
And thank God for all of eternity
That I am allowed to call myself her son
Before the entire world I acknowledge her
And my faith I proclaim loudly
I shall be thankful to God for eternity
That I am a Catholic Christian.[127]

Each subsequent stanza concluded with the same two lines.

Following the romantic, nationalist tradition of all East European peoples, the Croats looked back to the period when they had had their own kingdom. The readers thus described how the Pope sanctioned the crowning of Tomislav (r. 910–28) as king in 925, and he became "the real founder of the Croatian state." Among Tomislav's achievements, prominence was given his aid to the Serbs. They too were in the process of developing their state, Divković noted in his third year gymnasium reader, when the Serbs were attacked by Tsar Simeon, the great ruler of the first Bulgarian empire. Anxious to expand his domains throughout the Balkans, Simeon invaded and conquered "Serbia" in 924, which caused its leader Zaharija "to flee to Tomislav's Croatia, which received him kindly and entertained him. With him came many people and Serbian notables, who put themselves under the protection of the Croatian king expecting [that Tomislav would] invade Serbia and liberate it from the Bulgarian yoke." The Croatian offensive was successful and Tomislav led the Serbs back into their homeland. Three years later, in 927, Simeon attacked the Croats, who "beat him to his knees and on the same day of the battle he died of grief," which was "one of the most glorious days in the history of Croatia's early history." Simeon's successor, Peter, accepted Croatia's peace terms, which guaranteed that "Serbia remained independent of Bulgaria."[128] This theme of Croatia's aid to the Serbs was to be repeated in connection with other episodes in their common history. The same point would be made in relation to the Hungarians and Habsburgs. The students were taught that the Croats were great fighters and honorable people who came to the aid of their friends and allies.

The tenth and eleventh centuries were trying times for the Croatian kingdom, the readers reported. Independence did not bring peace. Croatia was constantly under pressure from its neighbors, in particular the Venetians and Hungarians. The leadership of the nation soon found itself divided, and even the reigns of two prominent monarchs, Krešimir (1058–74) and Zvonimir (1075–89), could not overcome the split. In 1091 the last descendant of the Croatian dynasty died, and the Hungarian chapter of Croatian history began. Although the question of whether Croatia was conquered by the Hungarians or whether the association of 1102 was a personal union by two consenting political entities is an issue still debated in Croatian and Hungarian historiography, the readers were clear about the event. The second year reader emphasized that "Our fatherland . . . joined (sjedinila se)" with Hungary, "whereas hitherto it had its own princes and kings." In the third year reader the children were told that Koloman, the Hungarian ruler, had sought to conquer Croatia but realized he would fail. Subsequently, the Croatian notables elected Koloman, who was crowned king of Croatia in 1102. Before the assembled bishops, notables, and citizenry, he took an oath to uphold the laws and defend Croatia's independence. Thus the personal union between the Croats and Hungarians, which endured to 1918, was the result of a free choice by the Croatian nation.[129]

The Croats, the Hungarian Kingdom, and the Habsburg Empire

With the end of the Croatian kingdom, the focus in the textbooks shifted to the role which the Croatian nation played in the Hungarian kingdom and the Habsburg empire up to the nineteenth century. Without always being explicit, it was nevertheless clear from the textbooks that whatever decisions and actions the Croatian leadership took were made principally with Croatian interests in mind. Consequently, the Croats' political support and the military contributions that they made in behalf of the Hungarian kingdom and Habsburg Empire, while serving the interests of these two entities and demonstrating Croatian loyalty, were in fact aimed principally at defending the Croatian state and nation. In other words, loyalty was a virtue that served both the empire and Croatia.

The readers were quick to point out that the Croatians played a prominent role in defending the Kingdom of Hungary and subsequently the Habsburg Empire against its enemies. One of the principal tests of the union came in the thirteenth century, when the Mongols overran the Hungarian lands and advanced into Croatia. In a story in the third grade reader entitled "Croatian Loyalty," the students learned that Bela IV, the king of Hungary and Croatia, was forced to flee before the Mongols and withdrew first to Trogir, near Split in Dalmatia, and then to some adjacent Adriatic islands. Batu-Khan, the Mongol leader, called on the Croats not to perish defending their foreign ruler. The Croats rejected this appeal, fought bravely, and defeated the Mongols. As a result "for the rest of his life King

Bela remained grateful to the Croatian people, who had saved his life and royal crown."[130] The reader also claimed that the Croats had saved not only their own fatherland "but also the other West European states from the great misfortune, because the defeated Mongols were forced to retreat to their own homeland in Asia."[131] Divković, in the third year gymnasium reader, went into greater detail, described the role of the nobles, and added that "the rich royal [Bela's] gifts [to the Croats] proved that Croatian muscles saved the king and defeated the most feared enemy of Europe, which saved Italian and west European culture. . . ." "At least national tradition asserts that the Croats defeated the Mongols," Divković concluded.[132] Whatever the Croats' actual role in the defeat of the Mongols, the students learned that they had saved their king, the Hungarian ruler, as well as Europe from the Mongols.

The readers also pointed out the disaster that befell both Hungary and Croatia when the Hungarian leaders failed to heed Croatian advice at the battle of Mohács in 1526. In his fourth grade gymnasium reader, Divković cited an account by Matija Mesić, the well-known Croatian historian and the first rector of the University of Zagreb, to explain what happened. "There was not one Magyar who was experienced even in leading a company, much less an army, because the Magyars had lost their military spirit and skills." In preparation for the battle, King Louis appealed to Ban Bačan of Croatia and Krsto Frankopan, a leading noble. Frankopan was alarmed by the fact that there was no well-conceived plan for the engagement. He "was the only one who could achieve this, which is why everyone awaited his arrival anxiously." His advice was to prepare carefully and, if the Christian forces were not ready for battle, to retreat to another location. The king's advisers argued against this strategy, and the Magyars proceeded to their battle stations, even though the forces of Frankopan and others had not arrived. Brodarić, a Croatian noble who was privy to the deliberations, reported subsequently that the king's counselors had insisted that "the glory in their kingdom had always gone to the Magyars and not to anyone else." Both the king and Hungary would be disgraced if it were said that they could not defeat the Turks, but had "to wait for Frankopan and his Croats." If this were to happen, then "the fame of victory, which we counted on, would go to him." Their view prevailed. In a two-hour battle, over twenty thousand Hungarian troops perished. When his ranks broke, even the king tried to flee, but he was drowned when his horse fell on him as he tried to cross a swamp.[133]

The immediate effect of this disaster was that the Croatian sabor exercised its independent prerogative by electing the Habsburg ruler, King Ferdinand, as their monarch. The long-range consequence was that Hungary and most of Croatia-Slavonia fell under Ottoman control, which lasted until the end of the seventeenth century. On the other hand, the Ottoman conquest served "to unite" the Croats and Serbs against the Islamic power. Evidence of this was not only their common military actions against the Ottomans, but also the development of the popular folk songs in which the Turks were the enemy. It was this oral literature that played a major role in the emergence of Karadžić's and Gaj's plans for a common literary language for the Croats and Serbs. Finally, the disdain toward Magyars evident in Mesić's account of Mohács would resurface in the narration of other events involving the Croats and Hungarians.

The readers also discussed Croatia's relations with the Habsburgs. Two basic themes predominated—first, the role played by the Croatian nation in the defense of the empire, and, second, the devotion and kindness exhibited by the Habsburgs toward their subjects. The first theme, which is found in Divković's gymnasium reader, is reflected in an account from the Croatian historian Smičiklas, who wrote that in 1532 Suleiman sent his top military leader, Ibrahim, to capture the fortress of Kiseg (Köszeg), which was being defended by Nikola Jurišić. Jurišić had no possibility of defeating Ibrahim without reinforcements from Vienna, which never arrived. All that Jurišić could hope to accomplish was to delay the enemy units, and to do so would give his Christian monarch more time to prepare for the next attack on Vienna. For three days a fierce battle raged and to each appeal to surrender, Jurišić retorted: "As long as I'm alive I will not give up." With his gunpowder almost depleted, his troops almost annihilated, and he himself wounded, Jurišić, in desperate condition, faced another Ottoman assault. Then, suddenly, the Turkish troops broke ranks and retreated in panic, claiming that a horseman with a flaming sword had driven them off the ramparts. The citizenry of Kiseg attributed this miracle to Saint Martin. From this account the students gained the impression that their Catholic faith and Jurišić had saved Croatia and the empire, a theme that was to be repeated frequently in the textbooks.[134]

Although the battle of Kiseg was extolled as a major triumph for the Croats, it was Nikola Šubić Zrinski's defense of Siget (Szigetvar) in southern Hungary in 1566 that took on epic proportions in Croatian folklore, history, and literature; it was also used as the plot for the best-known Croatian opera. Having distinguished himself militarily in numerous campaigns against the Ottomans, Zrinski was directed by the emperor to halt the advance of Suleiman's army at the strategic city of Siget; the students were told that this was Suleiman's seventh attack on "our fatherland," that is, on the Habsburg Empire. Zrinski appealed to the emperor for reinforcements, but, at the urging of his advisers, Maximilian decided to make his stand farther north at Györ, leaving Zrinski to cope with the situation at Siget as best he could. "The Turks did not fear anyone as much as they did our Nikola Šubić," which is why they sought to avoid a battle with him. First they tried to bribe Zrinski to surrender Siget, in return for which they would assign him Croatia to rule. When that failed, they appealed to his paternal instincts, showing him the standard and coat-of-arms of his son, whom they had captured earlier and whom they offered to release, together with his followers. However, nothing could cause Zrinski to dishonor Croatia and betray his monarch. "As an honorable Croat he could not even think of such a thing." Hence, he is said to have replied that "the city had been entrusted to him by the king and that he would defend it even if it meant his own life."

Within the walled fortress of Siget, surrounded by moats, Zrinski had about 2,500 troops, mainly Croats, with a few Magyars, whereas Mehmed Sokolović, the grand vizier, led an Ottoman force of 100,000. The ailing, aging Suleiman was in the vicinity. The siege began on August 6 and ended September 7. All accounts, including the Turkish, agree that it was a classic confrontation. Zrinski's forces succeeded in capturing the military commander of the janissaries, but they could not win the battle of attrition. When the end approached, with only a handful of troops left, Zrinski dressed himself in his best uniform and led the final charge, even though the Turkish janissaries "shouted loudly in Croatian 'Don't lose your head— throw yourself on the mercy of the Sultan.'" Zrinski and his followers perished, and over 20,000 Turkish troops were lost. Two days earlier the aged Suleiman had died. Under the circumstances, the Turks called off their campaign against the empire.[135]

Although Zrinski was their adversary, the readers state that the Turks gave him a hero's funeral, because of the respect they "had for him." For the Croats, "thus died the greatest hero of our nation. Through his heroic death he saved not only our empire from misfortune but all of Christendom."[136] The clear image conveyed by the readers is that the brave and honorable Croats were loyal to their king and country and fought for Christendom.

In a sense Zrinski and Siget came to represent for the Croats what Miloš Obilić and Kosovo represented for the Serbs. Although a cycle of folk poetry equal to that of Kosovo did not develop around Siget, many Croatian writers looked to this episode with pride and for inspiration. In analyzing its significance, a leading Croatian historian in the recent postwar era has written that justifiably, Zrinski was called the "'Slavic Leonidas,' whose importance as a Croatian national symbol has remained to the present."[137]

Parenthetically it should be noted that the battle of Siget contributed to a classic paradox, examples of which can be found in most nineteenth-century nationalist literature. The villains of modern Croatian literature, as well as of Serbian, Bulgarian, and Greek, were the Turks. Not only were they infidels, but also "wild people." Yet this reprobation did not extend to the grand vizier, Mehmed Sokolović, who defeated Zrinski. From an account by Leopold Ranke, the students learned that Sokolović was a young Serb from Bosnia who was a product of the Ottoman *devshirme* system, by which young Christian boys between the ages of five and ten were forcibly recruited by the Ottoman government and converted to Islam, and then served the sultan as soldiers or administrators. As a converted Christian, Sokolović could not become a sultan, but he could rise to the exalted office of grand vizier, the second highest position in the Ottoman Empire. In other words, in the entire empire Mehmed was "the only ear to hear and the only head that would decide." Thus, even though he was faithful to Islam, was loyal to the sultans, and waged war against the Christian Serbs, he was not one of the "wild people." "Anybody, even the most humble person, could talk to him."[138] The fact that he was a converted South Slav, with a dominant position in Ottoman society, appeared to exonerate, or at least to mitigate, the reality that for many years he had command of troops who had killed South Slavs and devastated their lands.

Croatia's support of the empire was not confined to fighting the Turks. Croats responded with equal enthusiasm against other adversaries and distinguished themselves especially in the Thirty Years' War, according to both the fourth year elementary reader and Divković's gymnasium reader. Twenty to thirty thousand Croatian troops, mainly cavalry, were employed as the advance guard, and for patrolling, surprise attacks, and initial assaults. Divković cited an account from Smičiklas in which the latter stated that the Croats succeeded in terrorizing their opponents in part because they employed tactics they had learned from the Turks, which contributed, in the eyes of Europeans, to "a stain on our name." Nevertheless, the Europeans could not "suppress their admiration for the heroism of the Croats." Nor could they forget the Croats' distinctive uniforms: "Above the blue frock coat, decorated with silver buttons, one notices a wide red cloak and a high-plumed red hat, decorated with silver, on the head. Besides a carbine, there are two pistols at the belt, and then a sword and a fierce khanjar dagger, before which trembled the soldiers of every nation." It was these troops who were in Wallenstein's forces, who fought at the battles of Breitenfeld (1631) and Lützen (1632). "The Germans report," Divković added, that in the battle of Lützen, in which Gustavus Adolphus was killed, "he fell at the hands of the Croats."[139]

When the empire was threatened again, in Maria Theresa's reign, by Frederick the Great, whom the third year reader described as "the worst and most dangerous" enemy, she appealed to the Croatian nobles in the Pressburg (Bratislava, Poszony) parliament to rally to the defense of the empire. Unanimously they shouted: "We will die for our sovereign Maria Theresa." Thus thirty thousand "Croatian heroes" were recruited to fight in the War of Austrian Succession (1740–48) and the Seven Years' War (1756–63). The most colorful of these were Trenk's pandurs (frontier militiamen), named after their commander Baron Franjo Trenk. Composed of Serbs and Croats they came mainly from the Croatian Military Frontier area around Pakrac in Slavonia, where they maintained law and order and fought the Turks. They dressed in distinctive, gaudy uniforms, with shaved heads, and their reputation as fighters against the Turks, whom they rather resembled, preceded them in Central Europe. They asked no quarter and gave none. Popular legend states, according to the third year reader, that "everyone trembled when just the name of Trenk and his pandurs was mentioned." On their return through Vienna, after their successful campaigns, Maria Theresa invited the Croatian nobles to a reception where she decorated "our troops." At the end of the Seven Years' War, she sent eight captured Prussian flags to Croatia in honor of her troops.[140]

The only blemish in the Croats' record of loyalty to the empire occurred in 1664, when Petar Zrinski, the grandson of Nikola, and his brother-in-law, Krsto Frankopan, were accused of treason and of conspiring with Louis XIV of France and others against Leopold, their king. After a lengthy trial, they were beheaded. There are subtle implications in the readers that the emperor had helped precipitate the conspiracy by his actions against the nobility. Since Zrinski and Frankopan perished without male heirs, "with them died out two brave Croatian families, who, through the centuries, defended Austria, Hungary, and Croatia from the Turks and who were the jewel and pride of our Croatian homeland."[141]

The impression conveyed by the readers was that the Croats were reliable and courageous. Students were taught in the second grade reader that military service was honorable. A soldier had the opportunity to become acquainted with other lands, peoples, and customs. After completing his service, he could return home to a "good job" because the emperor was very concerned about the welfare of his soldiers. Thus, when "our emperor and master" issued an order "everyone must jump to his feet to defend the fatherland." Some might lose their lives "in fulfilling their duty," as Zrinski had done, yet it was "beautiful to protect and defend the emperor and homeland."[142]

The second theme, the goodwill of the Habsburg monarchs toward their Croatian subjects, was demonstrated repeatedly in the elementary school readers by citing events, stories, and anecdotes associated in particular with three rulers—Maria Theresa, Joseph II, and Franz Joseph—which all conveyed the deep concern the Habsburgs had for each individual. Many stories were told about Maria Theresa, whom the third year reader affectionately identified as "the mother of her people." An example of her concern is the story about a young soldier, Vukasović by name, who attended the military academy. When told about his abilities, the empress asked that he demonstrate his skill as a swordsman. She was so impressed with his performance that she gave him twelve ducats. Several days later, when she requested to see him again, he became frightened. "Why? Are you afraid to say what you did with your money," she inquired. With tears in his eyes, he informed the empress that he had sent it to his poor father, who had been a lieutenant but now lived in poverty. Maria Theresa dictated a letter to the soldier, addressed to his father, in which she praised his son. In addition, she issued an order granting the father a yearly pension of 200 forints. "Soon Vukasović became an officer in the army and so distinguished himself that he became a vice-marshal."[143] In other readers the students learned that the empress had regulated the obligations and duties of the serfs, created elementary schools, "an Academy of Sciences [in Zagreb] for the Higher Education of the Croatian Youth," returned the port city of Rijeka (Fiume), and reunited Slavonia with Croatia.[144]

Her son Joseph II was presented in a similar manner. Once, while going about in disguise, he came upon a young girl crying. When he inquired about her unhappiness, she replied that her father had died, and that she and her mother were destitute. "Why don't you ask the emperor" for help, he responded. Over the objection of his aides, Joseph II then gave her three ducats, and told her to call on the emperor the next day. Only then did she realize who her benefactor had been.[145]

On another occasion, Joseph II saw a peasant plowing. He asked if he might be permitted to do some plowing, and the peasant, not recognizing him, agreed. Only later did he learn the stranger's identity. After the harvest, the peasant took some wheat to the emperor,

who "received this gift with great pleasure and rewarded the peasant. . . . Thus even the emperor was not ashamed to plow and thereby
demonstrate that one must respect the peasant who produces our
daily bread."[146]

Given his long period of rule, there were even more frequent references to Franz Joseph. The story most often quoted concerned an
episode in his childhood. One day, according to the second and third
grade readers, while walking with his grandfather, Emperor Francis I,
he saw a soldier standing guard at the palace. Believing the man to be
poor, he asked his grandfather for a coin to give to him. The emperor
agreed. Twice the young prince offered money to the soldier, who
stood at rigid attention looking straight ahead. The grandfather told
Franz Joseph, who was bewildered by this behavior, that the soldier
was on duty and was not allowed to accept money. However, he suggested that Franz Joseph put the coin in the soldier's pocket. The emperor was so pleased by the soldier's behavior that he gave him his
discharge "and enough money that he was able to buy a parcel of land
in his hometown, where he lived happily thereafter until his death."[147]

Another time an epidemic struck the city, and the hospitals
were filled with patients, whom Franz Joseph decided to visit. His
aide sought to accompany the emperor, but Franz Joseph refused,
"because the aide had children and if their father died, what would
become of them." But, the aide replied, "the emperor ruled over mil-
lions." To which Franz Joseph responded, "he was the father of the
sick as well as the healthy and since the aide's children were well, he
should go home to them." The aide did as commanded, and the emperor alone called on the ailing in the hospitals.[148]

Another story reported on a flood in Vienna that left many
stranded. One family took refuge on the roof of their house, but no
one dared rescue them because the current was swift. Then, suddenly, a rowboat appeared, manned by four soldiers, under someone's command. All wondered who had the courage to undertake
this hazardous mission. "That noble man was our most gracious
emperor and King, Franz Joseph the First."[149]

The elementary readers made clear that the Croatian nation was
responsible and loyal, that it was ready and eager to serve its king,
and that it appreciated his keen devotion to the welfare of his subjects. Equally important, whereas the Croats were contemptuous of
the Ottoman Empire and what it had wrought in the Balkans, they
were proud to be a member state of the Habsburg Empire, whose civilization they regarded as in the mainstream of European culture.

Whereas the historical parts in the readers emphasized the loyalty of the Croats and their political and military contributions to

the empire, the information on the nineteenth century focused on the ideas of the Illyrian movement, in particular on language and literature. Thus, beginning with the first elementary school reader and through all the secondary school readers, the Illyrian concepts were presented.

Croatian Language and Literature

As noted previously, modern Croatian nationalism began with Gaj's Illyrian movement, whose goal was to preserve the nation and its language from Magyarization. He sought to give a historical basis to his program by linking the South Slavs to the ancient Illyrians. The authors of the readers ignored this part of his work and concentrated instead on proving that Croatia's language and literature had a long tradition emanating from Dalmatia, and, in particular, from the writings of the Dubrovnik authors. The readers, therefore, stressed the importance of Dalmatian literature, which was the historical link to Gaj's linguistic reforms. Furthermore, since the authors of all the readers believed in the existence of a common Croatian and Serbian language, they conceived it as the base from which South Slav linguistic-cultural unity would emerge.

The author who best expressed the importance of literature and language and set the pattern for others to follow was Franjo Petračić, in his 1880 gymnasium reader. He began his book with a brief discussion of Croatian literature, which he divided into three eras. The first was the medieval, in which both language and literature were strongly influenced by religion. The second covered roughly the years 1500 to 1800, when a Croatian nationalist literature emerged in Dalmatia, especially in Dubrovnik, and to a lesser extent in Croatia and Slavonia. The third period began at the end of the eighteenth century and led to the Illyrian movement and its Yugoslav legacy. The latter period "was characterized by the fact that gradually it embraced all the lands in which the Croats and Serbs lived, and thus among both, one and the other, it led to the creation of a single literary language that had shed its more regional characteristic."[150]

Petračić dismissed the medieval period in a few pages, because he saw it as primarily influenced by religion. He asserted that "no documents from this period were written in the pure national language, and thus there can be no discussion of such a literature here."[151] Instead, Croatian national literature emerged first in the early modern period. Petračić stressed the importance of external factors in this development in both Dalmatia and Croatia-Slavonia. After Dalmatia fell under Venetian control, the center of its literary activity shifted from Split, Hvar, and other islands, southward to Dubrovnik. The Dalmatian writers had been greatly influenced by the lyric poetry and drama of the Italian Renaissance. Much of their writing was in Italian; Latin was used by the multilingual educated class and nobility. Yet the beginning of a Croatian national literature was evident through popular folk poetry, which was inspired by themes from the period of Ottoman domination.[152]

In their treatment of Dalmatia, the readers were clear on two points: first, they all considered Dalmatia a Croatian land, and, second, the literature of Dalmatia was Croatian written in the ijekavian variant of the štokavian dialect. It never occurred to any author to counter the argument in the Serbian readers, which considered Dalmatia to be Serbian. It was not that the existence of a Serbian population in Dalmatia was either denied or overlooked. The readers made clear that Serbs lived in Dalmatia, that they had a bishopric and Orthodox seminary in Zadar, and that "Croatian or Serbian" was spoken in Dalmatia. They also acknowledged that Italians lived in Dalmatia, but said that the province was Croatian, not Italian or Serbian.[153]

Dubrovnik was treated in a similar manner. Not only was it Croatian, but it had played a unique role in the emergence of a national Croatian language and literature, which in turn partially inspired the cultural and political developments of the Illyrian movement. Thus, Petračić wrote that "Dubrovnik became the center around which gathered other Croatian authors from different parts of Dalmatia and the islands."[154] In his reader, Filipović observed that Dubrovnik shed the Old Slavic Church literature and "embraced and adopted the national language."[155]

In his various readers, Divković wrote: "All the citizens of Dubrovnik loved their dear Croatian language." To substantiate the significance of Dubrovnik for Croatia, Divković quoted extensively from two members of the Yugoslav Academy, Ivan Kukuljević-Sakcinski and Vjekoslav Klaić. Kukuljević, a writer, historian, and active supporter of Croatian and Serbian cooperation and Yugoslavism, wrote that "we call it our Athens. . . . The literature and art, commerce and crafts, and the national characteristics of all the South Slavs created its permanent center there for many centuries. . . . Dubrovnik remained loyal to its Slavic nationality. . . . The love of freedom that is inherent among all the Slavs was mostly rooted in Dubrovnik," whose motto was "Precious freedom is not sold for all the gold." Furthermore in previous times it was the women of Dubrovnik in particular who were "the sole defenders of honorable family life, the national language, national customs, stories, songs, proverbs, and so on."[156]

Klaić, also a historian and a strong Croatian nationalist and patriot, wrote, "It is well known to every Croat how important Dubrovnik was and is for Croatian cultural history, how in the sixteenth and seventeenth centuries it acquired the illustrious name 'Croatian Athens.'" When the rest of Croatia was fighting the Turks or lived under their domination, "Dubrovnik was the only oasis where a Croat could enjoy freedom and peace." It was the "only home where the Croatian spirit and language was entrenched." Croatia may have had its Zrinskis and Frankopans, but "Dubrovnik was producing the wise Croatian poets Gundulić, Palmotić, and others."[157] In his reader Pechan quoted the linguist Vatroslav Jagić that "in the seventeenth and eighteenth centuries many Dalmatian authors gladly used the name Croatian; but it is significant that the name Serbian was never customary in Dubrovnik."[158]

All these sentiments were crystallized in a poem entitled "Dubrovnik."

> Dubrovnik—illustrious city
> and for long glorious,
> God richly endowed it
> with every known grace,
>
> He adorned it with gentlefolk,
> laws and justice,
> He exalted it in all manner
> of goods and treasure.
>
> Everywhere full of glory,
> everywhere celebrated,
> It is called the crown
> of the Croatian cities.[159]

In support of the second point about Dalmatia, the emergence of a Croatian national literature, the readers pointed with pride to a number of their authors. They included Dinko Zlatarić, "our poet," whose poems are known for "the beauty of their Croatian language," and Djono Palmotić, who stressed the purity of the language.[160] The best known was Ivan Gundulić, who wrote in ijekavian, as did the other authors. In his works Gundulić championed "Slavdom," which, in the nineteenth century, meant South Slavic unity.[161] Similarly, Filipović stated in his reader that Andrija Kačić-Miošić, an eighteenth-century Dalmatian monk, was the first person who, through his collection of epic poetry, wrote on behalf of "the entire people, be they called Croats or Serbs." Filipović further asserted that Kačić's best-known work, *Pleasant Discourses of the Slavic People*, became the most widely read book in the South Slav lands, which, it should be noted, by 1900 had been reprinted thirty times.[162] In the words of one scholar, Kačić's "Slavism was the forerunner of the Yugoslav concept of the nineteenth century not only among the Croats but also among the Serbs."[163]

Thus the authors of the readers focused their primary attention on the early modern period and on the Dalmatian writers, especially those who espoused South Slavic understanding. They also made clear their belief that the writers were Croats and that Dalmatia and Dubrovnik were Croatian. Those facts were brought out not to demonstrate the superiority of the Croats over the other South Slavs, but to explain how, during the dark days of Ottoman rule, one small part of the South Slavic lands, Dubrovnik, remained free.

Having stated the significance of early modern Croatian literature for Croatian nationalism, the readers addressed the specific issue of language. In the nineteenth century there was a widespread conviction that if Magyarization were to succeed, the language and identity of the Croatian nation could be lost. Therefore, beginning with the elementary school readers, textbooks repeatedly drummed into the minds of the students that one's own language was his most precious possession and should be preserved at all costs.

A number of books expressed this concern. The fourth grade reader stated: "Our homeland is surrounded virtually on all sides by the kingdoms and lands over whom rules His Majesty our emperor and king. All these lands together with our homeland are called the Austro-Hungarian Monarchy."[164] The second year reader noted that the difference between the imperial fatherland and the Croatian motherland was that in the latter "one's own sweet language" was spoken.[165] This fact was narrated through a story a son told his father about his extended travels. Wherever he went, he heard: "Greetings, dear fellow countryman!" After listening to his son's adventures, the father remarked: "Now you can definitely say that you know your country and fatherland. But you must also know that you saw many individuals and families of the same language and same blood. All these together comprise a nation." Another reader noted: "You do not feel that you are in a foreign land, but in your home, as long as everywhere you hear your own dear language spoken and you are received everywhere as their own born child. That is why our numerous villages and towns, all our land, streams and rivers, mountains and valleys are known by the beautiful word motherland."[166] In still another account, it was stressed that the motherland "is where there are, with minor exceptions, the same people, who speak the same Croatian or Serbian language that is officially used in the law courts and in the administration. Decrees, announcements, and other official proclamations are published in this language."[167] All these views stemmed directly from the Illyrian movement; thus Illyrianism was inevitably the focus of attention in the readers.

Illyrianism

With the stress placed on language, the readers treated the Illyrian movement as the most important development in the nineteenth century because, first, it produced a new orthography; second, it led to the standardization of the language; and third, it created a common literary language with the Serbs. Just as the Serbian revolution eventually led to the emergence of the modern Serbian state, the Illyrian movement was the linguistic catalyst for the unification of the Croats. All subsequent political, cultural, social, and economic developments came under its influence.[168]

Since Croatian and Serbian understanding and cooperation were cardinal principles of the Illyrian movement, the readers emphasized Croatian-Serbian relations. Thus the intellectual endeavors that linked their two great leaders, Karadžić and Gaj, were constantly stressed, as were those authors and cultural and scholarly organizations that supported Illyrianism and Yugoslavism. It was also assumed that all South Slavic folk poetry, stories, proverbs, and riddles, every one of which was regarded as the true national literature, were a common heritage and could be regarded as either Croatian or Serbian.

In discussing the Illyrian movement, the readers placed great emphasis on Gaj's role in the national revival. The elementary books included three stories Gaj learned as a youth. They were, first, the fable of the three Croatian brothers, Čeh, Leh, and Meh, who, respectively, were believed to have founded Bohemia, Poland, and Russia; second, his account of his mother's admonition on the need for books "in the national language"; and third, his story of his inability to have his first book published in Croatian (it was published only in German).[169] The secondary school readers stressed three points—Gaj's support of the štokavian dialect, the significance of this support for South Slavic unity, and its importance in resisting Hungarian assimilation and Magyarization. The so-called Vukovite authors, in particular, stressed the importance of Gaj's contributions for South Slavic unity. Thus Petračić wrote that "the struggle for the unity of language with its basis upon the vernacular originated with

Vuk";[170] "Gaj followed his example and began to work among the Croats for one literary language and one orthography."[171]

The readers, in addition, reported statements from Serbs—and there were a number of them—who welcomed Gaj's efforts. For example, Petračić cited the case of Petar Jovanović, a Serb from Bačka, who wrote: "United brothers, a Serb extends you his hand. He extends his hand and surrenders his heart. . . . We are all brothers, and we are all Illyrians; we are all brave fighters for our language."[172] In his reader Filipović wrote that as a result of Gaj's work "Croats and Serbs gladly employ the expression Croatian-Serbian or Serbian-Croatian, and at times even Yugoslav, which is understood to include all the Slovenes and Bulgars."[173]

The readers also described the broad scope of the Illyrian movement, which encompassed the printing of books, journals, and newspapers; the opening of museums, theaters, and reading rooms; the performance of music and plays; and the collection of folk poetry. Of these, the greatest attention was placed on folk poetry. Karadžić's collections were praised, and every reader had selections from them. Influenced by Vuk's success, other scholars went through the Croatian-Slavonian Military Frontier, Bosnia, Hercegovina, and Dalmatia, recording what they heard. Students were taught that folk poetry was either male, which was heroic, or female, which was lyric. Heroic poetry was divided into four periods. The first involved early mythology. The second dealt with the era of the medieval Serbian Nemanja dynasty. The third revolved around the battle of Kosovo and the exploits of the legendary Marko Kraljević. The fourth was contemporary and concerned the nineteenth-century exploits of Karadjordje, Miloš, Ban Jelačić, and others. These songs and poems were treated by the readers as the common heritage of the South Slavs, who should all rejoice in the triumphs and share in the tragedies of the Nemanjas, Kosovo, Marko Kraljević, and Karadjordje.[174]

The readers quoted extensively from Croatian writers, for example, Mirko Bogović, Dimitrije Demeter, Antun Nemčić, Ivan Kukuljević-Sakcinski, and Pavao Štoos, not only to demonstrate some of the best contributions of the Illyrian period but also to stress those works which supported South Slavic understanding. However, the two best-known Illyrian writers were Ivan Mažuranić and Petar Preradović, both of whom, it will be recalled, were also cited in the Serbian readers. The Croatian editors chose them precisely because their works extolled South Slavic cooperation. Although Mažuranić was lauded for his completion of Gundulić's "Osman," which provided another example of the link between the Croatian literary tradition of Dubrovnik and that of the Illyrian era, the most frequently found excerpts in the readers came from his major work, "The Death of Smail-Aga Čengić." It dealt with an actual historical event in which a Muslim aga terrorized the Christian population for years before he was killed by the Montenegrins in 1840. The appeal of this poem was that it dramatized all that the Montenegrins, Croats, and Serbs—in fact, all the peoples of the Balkans—had suffered at the hands of the Ottomans. In Petračić's view, Mažuranić was "the greatest advocate of unity among the South Slavs."[175]

There were many more quotations from Preradović than from other writers because of the intensity of his patriotic poems, notwithstanding the fact that he was a general in the Habsburg army. Like Mažuranić, Preradović was an advocate of South Slavic unity, a conviction he expressed in his ode "To Slavdom." Many of his patriotic poems were primarily Illyrian or Yugoslav rather than Croatian and national in spirit, as is evident in two of his best-known poems which dealt with language—"The Language of My People" and "To My People about Language." In the latter, which has nine stanzas, Preradović wrote:

> About the language, kinsmen, let me sing to you
> About the dear language, mine and yours
>
> ―――
>
> Through it the world knows your existence
> On it your future is based
>
> ―――
>
> From Istanbul to Kotor
> From the Black to the Adriatic Sea
>
> . . . .
>
> Through nine regions
> Everywhere mothers teach it to the children
>
> . . . .
>
> Everywhere there is heard singing
> Songs about Marko Kraljević!
>
> . . . .
>
> Love your language above all,
> Live in it, my people, die for it!
> All that you are is on its account:
> Your own body, world's limb,
> A bush of your own flower
> In the vast mix of nations.
> Without it you are nameless,
> Without ancestors, without sons,
> Formerly a people's shadow,
> Henceforth not yet a shadow![176]

The editors of the readers regularly expressed their great admiration of Preradović. For instance, Petračić considered Preradović's drama "Kraljević Marko," which revealed the depth of the author's feelings for South Slavic unity, as an expression of the highest goals of the Croatian and Serbian people.[177] In his reader Pechan wrote: "Preradović is a Croat, who body and soul (Thank God) considers the Serb his identical brother (Croat and Serb) and regards every reciprocal attack folly because Croats and Serbs have one language, one homeland, one common goal! 'We are brothers from the same father and all recognize as equal the heroism of both.'"[178]

After Vienna took steps in 1843 to curb the Illyrian movement, the readers reported, there were only limited gains. Among them was the appointment in 1846 of Vjekoslav Babukić as the first professor of Croatian in the Zagreb Academy or Advanced Gymnasium. Information on the revolution of 1848–49 was sparse, with only the bare facts presented. For example, in his reader Divković observed that in the 1849 attack on Budapest, "the largest number of soldiers killed were Croats."[179]

Notwithstanding these difficult times, the readers reported several advances in the next few years: for instance, in 1850 Ivan Kukuljević-Sakcinski founded the Society for Yugoslav History and Antiquities, and in the following year he launched its publication *Archive for Yugoslav History*. In addition, in the fifties, the *Illyrian Reader*, the first major secondary school reader, appeared.[180]

It will be recalled that in chapter 2 and in the previous section on the Serbian readers, the shift in educational policy after 1878 toward Serbian nationalism and away from a more understanding view of the Croats and their history was described. A similar shift can be detected in the contents of the Croatian readers when events of the sixties were presented. Whereas in Illyrianism the concept of oneness was stressed, now Croatia and Croatianism received more attention. The shift was subtle but nevertheless clear. The Croatian emphasis can be seen from such things as the type of information presented about the formation and function of the Matica Hrvatska, the Croatian Pedagogical Literary Association, the Society of Saint Jerome, the University of Zagreb, and from the excerpts of such authors as August Šenoa, Evgenij Kumičić, and Ksaver Šandor Djalski.[181]

Notwithstanding the appearance of Croatianism, the South Slav orientation in cultural life was still much in evidence in the readers. It was best demonstrated in the formation of the Yugoslav Academy. Its purpose was to foster South Slav linguistic and cultural understanding. Its ultimate goal, however, was to have Zagreb, not Belgrade, become the center of South Slav unification. A step in this direction was the appointment of Djuro Daničić, Karadžić's heir in linguistic research, as the first editor of the Academy's major project, the *Dictionary of the Croatian or Serbian Language*. In other words, a Serb, invited by the Yugoslav Academy in Zagreb, would chart the way for Croatian and Serbian linguistic unity. Or as Filipović told the students in his reader: "Djuro Daničić was the premier linguist among the Croats and Serbs. Thus he is now, after Vuk, the greatest authority about our language." The South Slavs were indebted to the Yugoslav Academy for this development because it had "awakened the senses of all the people and created one common national literary language."[182]

Although Illyrianism and Yugoslavism, which in large measure were based upon the idea of linguistic and literary unity, were presented favorably in the textbooks, Croatia and Croatianism were not subordinated to this wider concept. Rather, South Slav ideas were seen as vehicles through which Croatia's territorial and linguistic unity could be achieved and preserved. Consequently, the importance of South Slavic understanding remained a regular theme in the textbooks. This point is confirmed by the way in which the Serbs were portrayed in the readers.

The Portrayal of the Serbs

The clearest image of the Serbs that Croatian elementary school students would receive came from their readers. By law, it will be recalled, these textbooks were identical to those used in the Serbian schools in Croatia-Slavonia. Hence they contained equally positive portrayals of the Serbs and the Croats. Moreover, since there was no separate history course in the elementary schools, the readers contained the basic facts about the history of the Serbian nation. Therefore, it is important to look carefully at this material when analyzing the readers, because it represented all the information that 95 percent of the Croatian children who attended school would learn about the Serbs.

As noted above, the Croatian reading textbooks assumed that the Croats and Serbs either lived together or as immediate neighbors in their ancestral home. They also taught that the Croats and Serbs came into the Balkans at about the same time, and that they jointly fought the Avars. Thereafter, as the 1909 fourth grade elementary reader commented, "just as in their ancestral home the Serbs were the neighbors of the Croats, so here too they settled the lands to the east and south of the Croats." Like the Croats, the Serbs organized themselves in provinces, the best known of which was Raška (Serbia), which subsequently became "the motherland of the Serbian state." Furthermore, "about the same time that the Croats began to accept Christianity, or shortly after, so did their neighbors the Serbs, who previously had believed in the same gods as the Croats had." Thus these two "brother tribes" who spoke the same language began their new history in the Balkans again as neighbors.[183]

Their histories were also parallel in another respect. Just as it took the Croats considerable time to form their own kingdom, so too did the Serbs have to overcome great obstacles, including internal strife and foreign pressures—Byzantine, Bulgarian, and Hungarian. In the twelfth century Stefan Nemanja united the diverse Serbian lands into a state. Christianity was firmly established, churches and monasteries were built, and the country in general flourished. In 1196 Nemanja abdicated in favor of his son, who was known as Stefan the First Crowned King of Serbia. Meanwhile, the father retreated to Mount Athos, where he became a monk and helped build the Serbian monastery Hilandar.[184]

Although the third and fourth grade readers refer to or discuss many of the Nemanjas, aside from the founder, most of the attention centered on two men, Sava, the patron saint of the Serbs, and Dušan, their greatest ruler. Sava, born Rastko, was Stefan Nemanja's youngest son. The third and fourth grade readers described how Sava initially helped his father rule, but his life changed after he heard a Serbian monk talk about religion and Mount Athos, the holy center for the Orthodox. Rastko informed his parents that he was leaving Serbia for Mount Athos to become a monk. There he took the name Sava and vowed to serve God and the church. Subsequently he returned to Serbia and became the archbishop of Serbia and the spiritual leader of his people. His accomplishments were innumerable. Under his leadership eparchies were created and monasteries, churches, and schools were built. His prestige was so great that when Sava conducted religious services "large crowds of people, including the mighty and the humble, came to church to listen to the wise words and teachings of their great teacher." Thus the grateful Serbian people "even today . . . honor Saint Sava on January 14 of each year."[185] Sava died in Turnovo, Bulgaria, in 1235. Subsequently, his remains were transferred to the monastery of Mileševa in Serbia, where they remained until 1594. Then the Turkish commander had them sent to Belgrade, where they were burned, a telling reminder to the Serbs and Croats of how they were treated under the Ottomans, Filipović emphasized in his reader.[186]

Whereas Sava was significant for developing the spiritual, cultural, and intellectual life of medieval Serbia, Dušan elevated it mili-

tarily, administratively, and politically. In recounting his achievements the readers quoted from the works of the romantic nationalist
historian, Nikola Krstić. He described how Dušan's grandfather
Milutin succumbed to the intrigues of his fourth wife, Simonida, the
daughter of the Byzantine emperor Andronicus II, who was jealous
of Dušan's father, Stefan Dečanski. Consequently, she persuaded
Milutin to have his own son's eyes gouged out. Nevertheless, the
blind Stefan ascended the throne on his father's death, and he in turn
was followed by Dušan in 1335.[187]

Dušan demonstrated his military prowess during his father's
reign when he defeated the Bulgars. Subsequently, as king he fought
successfully against the Hungarians, Bosnians, Bulgars, and Byzantines, and by the time of his death in 1355 he controlled much of the
Balkan peninsula. One of his most notable campaigns, according to
Divković, was against Louis the Great, the king of Hungary, who, it
must be remembered, was also the king of Croatia. Instigated by the
papacy, Louis hoped to return the Serbs to Catholicism, by conquest
if necessary. Thus he requested a meeting with Dušan on the shores
of the Danube, where, without disembarking from his boat, he appealed to Dušan to accept the Catholic faith. But Dušan and his
troops had already taken an oath to defend Orthodoxy, and he rejected Louis's plea. Twice, then, the Hungarians attacked Dušan,
and both times they were decisively defeated. While in the north,
Dušan took the occasion to build the city of Belgrade.[188]

Dušan's military exploits were crowned, the third year elementary reader noted, by his elevation in 1346 to "Stefan, Tsar of the
Serbs, Greeks, and Bulgars." At the time of his death in 1355 he was
marching toward Constantinople, hoping to adorn his reign with the
conquest of the Byzantine capital. The readers were quick to point
out, however, that Dušan's fame did not rest solely on his military
exploits. He elevated the Serbian archbishopric to a patriarchate,
thus freeing Serbia of its dependency on the ecumenical patriarchate
in Constantinople. The tsar endowed the nation with a law code
that provided for the just and efficient administration of his lands.
Churches and monasteries were built. Divković's reader described
him as a ruler who had "a beautiful soul," who was "wise and
strong" but "firm," and who loved "freedom." It was said that "he
was regarded as the tallest, most handsome, and strongest man of his
times." He "enobled Serbian arms, elevated the nation's fame, and
enlightened the Serbian name. In a word, Dušan was the most famous and strongest Serbian ruler of whom the Serbs were proud and
whom foreign rulers respected." These tributes were the equal of
those accorded any Croatian monarch.[189]

Dušan's only failing was that he did not leave his nineteen-year-old son, Uroš, an empire of loyal nobles. As a result, the Ottoman victory at the battle of Kosovo in 1389 ended the Serbian empire. All the readers reiterated that there was a lesson to be learned from what happened when a divided nation was faced by a formidable adversary, and they all described the event in detail. The day before the battle Prince Lazar, the commander of the Serbian forces, assembled his nobles and issued his battle plan. He directed that Miloš Obilić lead one force, which would be supported by troops under the command of Vuk Branković. The latter, who was Obilić's senior, resented his implied demotion. Consequently, in front of Prince Lazar and others, Branković stated that Obilić "was planning a betrayal and would defend the Turks" the next day. That evening Prince Lazar raised his glass to Miloš Obilić, "'who had planned to betray me.'" Stung by this charge, Miloš vowed to reveal who the real traitor would be. The next morning he went secretly to the camp of the Turks, asked to meet their sultan and, when granted an audience, assassinated him. Immediately, the sultan's bodyguards killed Miloš. The second year reader emphasized that whereas Miloš Obilić was "the person who really loved his people," Vuk Branković broke ranks during the battle and exposed himself as the real traitor. Thereafter, the legend had it that every Serbian mother greeted the birth of a son with the words "Hail, young avenger of Kosovo." [190]

The historical account was supplemented in the readers with numerous selections from the Kosovo folk epic, for example, "Kosovo Maiden" and "Empress Milica." In addition, there were many poems about the legendary hero Marko Kraljević, who, astride his horse, singlehandedly fought off the Turks. Such folk-poems as "Kraljević Marko and the Eagle," "Kraljević Marko and the Fifty Turks," "Kraljević Marko and Beg Kostadin," and many others filled the readers. Furthermore, they contained detailed accounts of Marko Kraljević's life, including the four versions of his death. [191] The intent of the elementary readers in citing these poems was to demonstrate the importance of this period in Serbian history and to indicate the central role that the poems played in the evolution of the South Slav oral literary tradition.

The next theme to appear in the Croatian readers dealt with the settlement of the Serbs in Croatia, Slavonia, and Vojvodina in the seventeenth and eighteenth centuries. The second, third, and fourth grade elementary readers provide the basic factual information. They stated the reasons why the Serbs were forced to flee from Kosovo and stressed that Emperor Leopold in 1690 invited Patriarch Arsenije Crnojević and his followers to settle in his domains. In return the Serbs promised to serve in his wars against the Turks, and "they were true to their word." The Serbs were granted religious autonomy, but had to abide by the other laws of the empire. The Croatian readers did not, of course, duplicate the judgment found in the Serbian textbooks: that the Serbian experiences in the Habsburg empire in the eighteenth century represented one of the darkest epochs in their history.[192]

The focus of the readers in the section through the eighteenth century was on Serbian history; for the nineteenth century the emphasis was on language and literature in both Serbia and Croatia. This point was made by Petračić in his second year reader. In his view, Croatian literature could be divided into three epochs, medieval, early modern, and modern, but he maintained that there were only two periods in Serbian literature, the first being from the medieval period through the eighteenth century, the other the nineteenth century. His point was that written literature in the first period was primarily religious in nature, not national. Only the oral tradition was national. In other words, the Serbs were excluded from the literary development associated with Dalmatia and Dubrovnik, which he and the other Croatian writers maintained was only Croatian.[193]

The textbooks also reported in a negative manner on the emergence in the eighteenth century of Slavo-Serbian, which was strongly influenced by Russianisms, as the Serbian literary language. The students were told that the books imported from Russia "brought more harm than good," because they contributed to the archaic Slavo-Serbian. Consequently, in Petračić's view, "Up until just before the end of the last century our brother Serbs did not even know of a literature in the national language, because they employed the church language of the old Slavic Serbian speech." Therefore, he concluded, the first written Serbian national literature did not appear until Karadžić's collection of national folk-poetry.[194] These views were also reiterated by Pechan in his reader; he asserted that only the Serbian clergy welcomed the Slavo-Serbian development because they believed that "the church language was the true language of Cyril and Methodius and thus regarded it as sacred."[195]

The transition from the Slavo-Serbian language and literature began with the writings of Dositej Obradović at the end of the eighteenth century and continued with Vuk Karadžić. Obradović, who originally had entered a monastery, abandoned that calling and became the best-known exponent of the Enlightenment in Serbia. Thus he championed a literature written "in the language of the people." His own writings continued to show traces of his religious training and his orthography was imprecise; nevertheless, the 1895 gymnasium reader exclaimed: "But, oh how far his language had distanced itself from Slavo-Serbian. The nation embraced his work, benefited from it, and is grateful to its first teacher."[196] Not only did he work on behalf of a national language, but he was the first Serbian writer "who was completely aware of the cultural goals of literature. . . . The first in whom the consciousness of national unity was awakened and was clearly expressed; the first who loved and embraced all his people regardless of their religion and who also endeavored to enlighten, enoble, and make happy all the people, not just certain individuals or particular social classes."[197] In other words, Obradović became a spokesman for South Slavic unity, which was expressed in his often-quoted remark, "he is my brother, whatever his religion" (*brat je mio, koje vere bio*), which found its way into the vocabulary of all those who advocated some form of Yugoslavism.

Of all the Serbs discussed in the readers, none received the praise reserved for Karadžić. It is not incorrect to state that he enjoyed as much popularity in the Croatian readers as did any Croat, including Gaj. Karadžić's reaction to the Illyrian movement, his work in standardizing the štokavian literary language, and the role he assumed in the Serbian readers have already been described. Here it is only necessary to cite a few of the many comments about him found in the readers.

In praising Karadžić's first work, a brief collection of folk poems published in 1814, the Petračić-Miler gymnasium reader made clear its importance: "it brought into the open and gave birth to the beautiful contemporary Serbian literature, because its real beginning is found in the first book of national poems, which Vuk St. Karadžić thrust into the world in 1814." With respect to Karadžić's decision to use the ijekavian variant of štokavian, the authors stated that he selected it because he believed "that all national folk poetry was sung in it," and that it was the closest to the Slavic language that "the Dubrovnik writers had used . . . and that only through it could the Serbs unite with their brothers of the Roman [Catholic] rites in one literary language." This folk poetry, which he collected and published in six volumes, was "the source of the living national language, without which the living national literature could not flourish. . . . We are amazed how a poem has preserved for all the Croatian and Serbian people the remembrance of historical events and personalities, especially the battle of Kosovo, which are held to be real miracles and historical truths."[198] Divković, in his fourth grade reader, noted that the poems were not confined to the Christians but were also sung by the South Slavic Muslims of Bosnia, "except that they sang mainly that they had triumphed [that is, over the Christians]."[199]

Given the ultimate success Karadžić achieved, the students

were told that "it seems to us today that from the first moment everyone should have adhered to Vuk's sound principles about language and orthography." Petračić and Miler summed up the sentiments of the Croats, stating that "the Lord knows, Vuk was not well educated, and this was precisely the good fortune of the Serbian people. But he was an extraordinary person, a wise, self-educated man who improved himself so that he has earned a place of honor among Slavic scholars. Of all the educated Serbs, he accomplished the most for his people with his work, and he earned for himself their gratitude for centuries."[200] In his reader Filipović went one step further, stating that Vuk "can be called the father of the national literary language, the father of contemporary Croatian-Serbian literature."[201]

The best proof of Karadžić's great importance is the fact that, of all the readers examined, either Croatian or Serbian, there is not one that does not have selections from Vuk. No other Serbian scholar enjoyed such popularity. The authors of the readers were convinced that through his orthographic and linguistic reforms he had found the link that would establish closer relations between the Croats and Serbs. Thus the readers include excerpts from the historical novels, stories, dramas, and poetry of writers who accepted his reforms. Among these authors were Miloš Cvetić, Vojislav J. Ilić, Djuro Jakšić, Jovan Jovanović-Zmaj, Laza Kostić, Laza Lazarević, Simo Matavulj, Štjepan Mitrov Ljubiša, Milan Miličević, Jovan Sterija Popović, Branko Radičević, Milorad Popović Šapčanin, Jovan Subotić, Jovo Sundečić, and Kosta Trifunović.

Among this group of Serbian writers, three authors in particular—Subotić, Radičević, and Jovanović-Zmaj—are cited in different editions of Petračić's readers to demonstrate their endorsement of closer Croatian and Serbian literary and cultural understanding. Of these, the most active was Jovan Subotić, a better politician and publicist than a writer. In 1848 and 1849 he was Patriarch Rajačić's representative to the Croatian sabor. Later, in the sixties, he was the best-known Serbian representative elected to the sabor. In Zagreb he became the director of the theater, and later held the same position in Novi Sad. There he was elected president of the major Serbian literary organization, Matica Srpska. But he was best remembered for his advocacy of the equality of the Cyrillic and Latin alphabets and his respect for both the Serbian and Croatian names. A champion of Vuk's reforms, he wrote a number of romantic historic dramas from medieval Serbian and Croatian history including "King Dečanski" and "Zvonimir." The latter dealt with the conflict surrounding Zvonimir's accession to the throne as medieval Croatia's last king.[202]

Branko Radičević was one of the best Serbian lyric and epic poets who wrote "in the pure national language" which was "as clear as a tear drop," using Vuk's "štokavian ijekavian" dialect. Of his poems, "The Parting of School Friends" was especially popular. It was written after he left school in Sremski Karlovci for Vienna and it brought back memories, good and bad, of student days, in which he "called upon all brother Serbs and Croats," to express their love and happiness.[203]

Certainly one of the eminent Serbian writers of the second half of the nineteenth century was Jovan Jovanović-Zmaj. An ardent Serbian patriot and champion of the unification of the Serbs, he also encouraged Serbian and Croatian understanding. This feeling was perhaps best expressed in his poem "To Petar Preradović," written to commemorate the Croatian poet when his remains were returned to Zagreb from Vienna. In the poem Jovanović offered a wreath "from the Serbian lands," to show that "the Serbs love you as much as the Croats." Since foreign lands did not welcome remains that were not theirs, Jovanović noted, they must rest among their own. They will not rest in peace until there is "unity of the Serbs and Croats."[204]

From the above it is evident that the Croatian students learned a great deal from their readers about Serbian history, literature, language, and heroes. There was, of course, much more information in the readers about Croatia than about Serbia. Yet it was not any more positive than the information on Serbia. The Serbian students who read these accounts could justifiably be proud of their nation, and the Croatian students could only have respect, even admiration, for the achievements of their Serbian Orthodox brethren. Serbs and Croats were presented as one people with one language, who shared in part a literary tradition inspired by the centuries of Ottoman rule. It is important to state here that this represented the maximum extent to which Croatian and Serbian understanding was evident in the Croatian books. As will be evident in the next chapters, the geography and history books were definitely written more from the Croatian than from the South Slavic point of view.

The South Slavs in Other Lands—Montenegro, Bosnia-Hercegovina, Vojvodina, and Slovenia

As for Montenegro, the other independent Serbian state, the information in the Croatian readers was brief, but it stressed the bravery of the nation and its heroic defiance of the Turks. A typical story concerned a Montenegrin who had been captured by the Turks and whose life was threatened unless he led them to his camp. As they approached it, suddenly he shouted "Turks, Turks!," alerting his comrades. In the ensuing battle the Turks were defeated, but the hero was killed. "Fortunate is the country with such faithful sons as Montenegro," noted the third and fourth grade elementary school readers.[205] This same anti-Turkish theme was found in the writings of Petar Petrović Njegoš, whom many consider to be the most gifted Montenegrin or Serbian poet. His views were best expressed in the secondary readers through his frequently quoted "The Mountain Wreath," an epic historical drama in which Njegoš confronts the issue of how to deal with Montenegrins who converted to Islam and fought their Christian brothers. If they refused to return to Christianity, he decided, the "Turkicized" Montenegrins should be killed in defense of Christianity and the Montenegrin state. Written in language "true to Montenegrin speech," Njegoš's work had a wide appeal in the age of romantic nationalism. The readers also cited him because in his writings he glorified patriotism, extolled Serbdom, and championed South Slavic unity, and he appeared to embody the quintessence of freedom.[206]

Bosnia-Hercegovina, which played a dominant role in the Serbian readers, did not receive similar attention in the Croatian. The information was largely factual. The fourth year reader noted that the two provinces "once partially belonged to the Croatian kingdom, which is the reason why even today the entire region to the river Vrbas is called Turkish Croatia."[207] Yet in describing the Sava River as Croatia's southern boundary, the 1889 third year reader stated that "From the Una River [which was to the west of the Vrbas], only the left bank is ours, whereas the right belongs to Bosnia and Serbia."[208]

Concerning the population of Bosnia-Hercegovina, the fourth grade reader noted that the "vast majority were Croats and Serbs, whereas in religion the Greek Orthodox were the most numerous, then the Muslims and Catholics."[209] In describing Sarajevo, the capital, the reader stated there were 45,000 inhabitants "the majority Croats and Serbs." The city also had "a Catholic archbishopric," "a Greek Orthodox metropolitanate," and "one Catholic, one Greek Orthodox, and several Muslim theological schools." There were public schools. Newspapers were printed in Latin and Cyrillic. From 1878 to 1908 Austria-Hungary administered these lands, but in 1908 Franz Joseph "took them completely under his rule."[210]

There also was a very descriptive portrait of Banja Luka by Ivan Kukuljević-Sakcinski in Petračić's reader. After a brief history of the city, which included the defeat of the Austrian forces by the Turks under Ali Pasha in 1737, Kukuljević described the city as he saw it during an eight-day visit: the one-story houses, the Turkish bazaar, the proverbial merchant sitting cross-legged, the fountains in front of the Feradžija Mosque, and the mosque's interior, all of which gave the students a vivid picture of what it would be like to live in a city inhabited by their South Slavic Muslim brothers.[211]

The secondary readers paid some attention to Bosnian writers if, at times, it was little more than citing the author and some of his works. The Bogomils, the students read, were the first Bosnians to produce a literature, which the Catholic Franciscans destroyed because they regarded it as heretical. After the Turks conquered Bosnia in 1463, "all literary activity died" until another revival began with the Franciscans at the end of the sixteenth century. The literature was primarily of a religious, moral, and educational character. The most prominent authors from this period were Matija Divković and Pavao Posilović. In the eighteenth century, Stjepan Margitić, Lovro Sitović Ljubuščanin, and Tomo Babić were well known. Sitović wrote "in Croatian," and Babić produced a collective work that included a "calendar, religious works, poems, psalms, prayers, and religious essays," and "the truth about the eastern and western churches." "All these men wrote in a beautiful national language that was not much influenced by foreignisms. At first they printed their books in Bosnian Cyrillic letters (*ćirilicom Bosanskom*), which in form and in some letters differed from the basic Cyrillic, which the Orthodox used," Petračić noted in his reader.[212]

As was the case with the other South Slavs, the nineteenth century produced a large number of Bosnian writers, some of whom were discussed in the secondary school readers. Grga Martić, a Franciscan who grew up in the Illyrian era, was best known for his epic poem "The Avengers," whose theme was the Christian resistance to the Ottomans, with special attention to the Montenegrin opposition to the Turks at the battle of Grahovac in 1858. After Austria's occupation of Bosnia, a new generation of South Slavic Christian and Muslim writers emerged. Tugomir Alaupović composed epic poems. Osman Nuri Hadžić wrote stories about Bosnia, as did Edhem Mulabdić, both of whose works were published by Matica Hrvatska. In summary, Bosnia-Hercegovina was presented as part of the South Slavic lands, with inhabitants who were Serbs or Croats of three religious faiths.[213]

The other area inhabited by Croats and Serbs was Vojvodina. Information about Vojvodina in the third and fourth grade readers was primarily factual. Novi Sad was identified as the cultural center of the Serbian nation before 1860. The readers also took note of Novi Sad's theater, newspapers, journals, and its cultural institution, Matica Srpska. There was more information, both factual and descriptive, on the province of Srem. Special attention was devoted to the area's two main attractions, Sremski Karlovci and Fruška Gora. The readers stressed that Karlovci was important because it was "the seat of the Serbian Orthodox patriarchate, metropolitanate, and arch-bishopric, with a beautiful cathedral and a magnificent patriarchal palace." In addition it had a theology school, gymnasiums, and other schools. The sixteen Orthodox monasteries on Fruška Gora were identified and their importance described.[214]

As for the Slovenes, who were included in Gaj's Illyrian plans and in the concept of Yugoslavism, the Croatian readers were only slightly better than their Serbian counterparts. Since the elementary readers, and especially the geography books, described all the lands and peoples of the Habsburg Empire, the Slovenes were included. From them the students learned that the Slovenes lived principally in Styria, Carniola, and Carinthia, that Ljubljana was their capital, that Slovenian was spoken in Maribor and Celje, as was German. In addition, "in the southern part of Carinthia Slovene is spoken, German in the northern and Italian in the west." On the Adriatic littoral, Croatian and Slovene predominated but Italian prevailed in the cities. The elementary school students, thus, obtained a fair idea about the area inhabited by the Slovenes, but not about their history, language, or literature.[215]

What is more revealing is that the gymnasium readers are essentially silent on the Slovenes. The third and fourth year readers, whose purpose was to include writings from the literature of other nations, contained selections from François Andrieux, Hans Christian Andersen, Washington Irving, Albert Rambaud, Leopold von Ranke, Henryk Sienkiewicz, Adolphe Thiers, and Leo Tolstoy, but there was not one selection about Slovenia or a poem attributed to a Slovenian author. Yet there were Slovenian authors, for example, France Prešeren, Antun Aškerc, Josip Jurčič and Fran Levstik, who wrote on the same general themes as did the Serbian, Montenegrin, and Bosnian writers whose works were included in the Croatian readers. Selections from any one of these Slovenian writers could easily have been integrated into the themes found in the Croatian as well as the Serbian readers. The single exception was Stanko Vraz, who was deeply committed to Gaj and the Illyrian cause and whose poems represent some of the best examples of Illyrian poetry. However, Vraz came to be considered more a Croat than a Slovene. In other words, if the Croatian students, as well as their Serbian contemporaries, were to rely solely on their respective readers for knowledge of the South Slavs, they would not be aware of the Slovenes as part of the South Slav movement.

At this point a brief comparison of the Croatian and Serbian readers is instructive. Both stressed two subjects in particular—language and history. The common denominator for Serbs and Croats was their language. Nevertheless, the respective treatments of the subject demonstrate how far apart the two nations were in their understanding of that language's significance. In the Serbian readers, the language was always referred to as Serbian, and written in Cyrillic. In the Croatian, it was called Croatian or Serbian, and written in two alphabets. Both also stressed literature. In the Serbian readers, the literature was identified as Serbian, or Catholic and Western, two euphemisms for Croatian literature. Although the emphasis in the Croatian readers was on Croatian literature, Serbian authors and their writings were also readily discussed.

The same pattern was evident in their presentation of historical subjects. The Serbian books concentrated on Serbian history, ignoring Croatian. Without slighting their own past, the Croatian readers presented Serbian history as positively as they did their own. In other words, in the readers, the most important books for the elementary school students, information that could contribute to South Slav cultural understanding was found in the Croatian books, but not the Serbian. The contrast between the Serbian and the Croatian approaches to this issue was even more pronounced in the geography books, which will be examined next.

4

Geography—The Identification of National Lands

INTRODUCTION

In contrast to the relative ease with which comparisons can be made between Serbian and Croatian readers, where language and literature, with their corresponding readers, represented a common denominator, it is more difficult to compare the geography textbooks. In the 1883 Serbian elementary school curriculum, geography and Serbian history were taught as separate subjects, with separate textbooks for each course. Following the 1899 curriculum revision, they were combined in a course called "geography with history," but they became separate courses again in 1904. However, in the gymnasium and the realka geography and history were taught as separate courses, each with its own textbook. In Croatia geography was not taught as a separate course in the lower elementary school, but information on it was included in the readers. In the upper public schools, the fifth through eighth grades, there was a course entitled "geography and history, with special emphasis on the homeland and its constitution," but the primary textbook dealt with history. Only in the secondary schools were there separate courses and textbooks for geography. Thus in the lower grades, the Serbian students had separate geography books, but the Croatian did not.

Problems also arose because of the political conditions in the respective lands. Half of the area that most Serbs regarded as "Serbian lands" was not included in the Serbian kingdom before 1912. In the case of Croatia, all those lands to which the Croats laid claim were part of the Austro-Hungarian Empire after 1878. Thus when the Serbian students studied about their lands, they learned that the majority of these lands were under Habsburg or Ottoman control. Since the Croatian territories were all part of the Habsburg Empire, the main issue was the lack of a united Croatian administration.

Both the Serbian and Croatian textbooks provided the obvious information not only about their own territories, but also about other countries. However, the Serbian textbooks were more preoccupied with the "Serbian lands." In Croatia the textbooks for the upper elementary grades and especially for the secondary schools stressed the geography of the Austro-Hungarian Empire. Hence the student in Croatia learned a great deal about the various imperial provinces, for example, Carniola, Carinthia, Tyrol, Bohemia, Moravia, Slovakia, Bukovina, Transylvania, Banat, Bosnia, and Hercegovina, as well as about his *domovina* or homeland—Croatia, Slavonia, and Dalmatia. In the Croatian textbooks Serbia, Montenegro, and Macedonia were treated as foreign domains. In contrast the Serbian students read about Croatia, Slavonia, Dalmatia, and Istria as "Serbian lands" under foreign rule. As could be expected, the geography texts, in contrast to the readers, were filled with facts and figures concerning the ethnic, religious, and linguistic background of the people, some of which, as we shall see, were misleading.

SERBIAN GEOGRAPHY TEXTBOOKS

The importance of geography was clearly stated by Mihailo Jović, the author of both an elementary geography textbook and the most popular elementary history textbook. In the preface of his 1882 history book, he wrote that "Geography must precede history." He described his frustration when he began to teach history and learned that "Bojka [a Serbian name for their ancestral homeland], Prizren, Zeta, Bosnia, Constantinople, Mount Athos, Kosovo, and other places were unknown, vague to the children." It was not surprising, continued Jović, to have a student reply that "Thessaloniki was to the north, Bojka to the west, and Kosovo to the east of Serbia."[1] Since it became apparent to the teachers that the students needed solid information, the geography textbooks became veritable encyclopedias, with information about Serbia's form of government, its capital, major cities, citizens, religion, customs, traditions, dress, natural resources, commerce, and trade. The books also identified the Serbian lands and the criteria used to determine who was a Serb.

The Authors

In contrast to the readers and history textbooks, which were often prepared by prominent scholars, the geography textbooks, atlases, and supplementary geography readings were all written by elementary or secondary school teachers. One author, Vladimir Karić, was the dominant influence among them. Karić began his career as a lawyer and then became a gymnasium teacher in Šabac, Požarevac, and Belgrade. He also served as the Serbian consul general in Skopje in the 1880s, the time when Serbia was developing her policies and strategies against the Bulgarians and Greeks in Macedonia. His reputation, however, rests on his major work, *Serbia—A Description of the Land, People, and State* (1887), a work of 935 pages. His other publications include *Geography for the Lower Grades of the Secondary Schools* (1883), *Map of the Serbian Land and the Balkan Peninsula* (1884), *Geography of the Kingdom of Serbia for the Third Grade of the Elementary Schools* (1885), and *Geography of the Serbian Land and the Balkan Peninsula for the Fourth Grade of the Elementary Schools* (1887). He also wrote on education in Serbia.[2] Karić died in 1893, but he continued to exert an influence on the authors of the textbooks to 1914.[3]

The textbooks and atlases for the elementary schools were written or co-authored by a dozen teachers: S. Antonović, Mihailo Jović, Raša Mitrović, Petar M. Niketić, St. J. Nikolić, D. J. Putniković, T. Radivojević, D. J. Sokolović, Mihailo M. Stanojević, Mih. M. Stevanović, and Milan Ubavkić. The atlases were prepared by Milan Hrabrenović, Raša Mitrović, Petar K. Šreplović, Mihailo Stanojević, and Vladimir Simić. The authors of textbooks for the secondary schools were S. Antonović, N. Lazić, Srećko Miletić, T. Radivojević, and Radovan Vasović. Among the authors who gained the most prominence were Mihailo Jović and D. J. Putniković, whose co-authored book became the center of a controversy between Austria and Serbia when the Habsburg government demanded that the authors delete all references to South Slavic lands within the empire as "Serbian lands." A shift in emphasis from a strictly Serbian orientation toward some understanding of the Croatian issues was evident only in the books by Antonović, Lazić, and Radivojević published in 1912 and 1914. The others wrote books that reflected Karić's point of view.[4]

Criteria for Identifying the Serbian Lands and People

In 1883, Karić, in his *Geography for the Lower Grades of the Secondary Schools*, defined the Serbian lands in the following terms. "The land in which the Serbian people have lived from antiquity, in which even today they are either the exclusive inhabitants or in the majority is the Serbian land." He then described the precise boundaries of this territory, using mountains, watersheds, rivers, lakes, and cities as landmarks. Thus, according to his view, the boundary started at the Danube in the east and extended southward following the western watershed of the Timok, Morava and Vardar rivers, south of the city of Strumica, then along the southern watershed of the Crna River to south of Lake Prespa, northward to Lake Ohrid, on to the Black Drim River, following its course to the Adriatic Sea and up the Adriatic to near Trieste. It went from here eastward to the source of the Kupa River, east and north to the Sutla River, along the eastern boundaries of Carniola (Kranjska) and Styria to the Drava River, then eastward along the Drava and northeast toward Pécs (Pečuh), and onward to Mohács, across the Danube to Baja and Senta, south of Szeged, up the Maros River (Mureş) toward Arad, and then south to Temišvar, Vršac, Bela Crkva, and back to the Danube.[5] Within these boundaries were included all the lands of present-day Yugoslavia, except Slovenia, as well as extensive territory in northern Albania and parts of northern Greece, southern Hungary, and western Romania. Collectively, his claims covered 240,000 square kilometers. Moreover, Karić claimed that "there are Serbs outside these boundaries, but they are neither in large numbers nor do they occupy large areas, but live isolated, dispersed as small islands."[6]

In his major work, *Serbia—A Description of the Land, People, and State,* Karić made his point more explicit by illustrating his argument with a multicolored map that identified the inhabitants of all the lands of southeastern Europe. The color legend included the Serbs, Slovenes, Slovaks, Germans, Hungarians, Romanians, Albanians, Greeks, Turks, Bulgars, and Italians, but not the Croats. Croatia, Slavonia, Istria, and Dalmatia, as well as Bosnia, Hercegovina, Bačka, and Banat were represented as inhabited exclusively by Serbs. Zagreb, Varaždin, Bjelovar, Osijek, Rijeka, Rovinj, Pula, Zadar, Šibenik, Split, and Dubrovnik were shown as Serbian cities.[7] In his "political description of the Serbian land," he wrote:

> All the Serbian lands do not comprise one complete state, but are divided in different ways among a number of states. Based upon the present political situation, parts of the Serbian land comprise three categories. In the first belong the independent Serbian states—the Kingdom of *Serbia* and the Principality of *Montenegro.* In the second category are the Serbian lands (under Austria-Hungary)—the Margravate of *Istria,* the Kingdom of *Dalmatia,* the Kingdom of *Croatia* and *Slavonia,* as well as lands under Turkey—*Bosnia, Hercegovina, Old Serbia, and Macedonia.*[8]

Repeating the view advanced by Karadžić in his article "Serbs All and Everywhere," in which he had stated that "at one time all the Slavic peoples were called Serbs," Karić wrote:

> It is claimed that all the people whom we today call Slavs once were called Serbs and that the Slavs were only one Serbian tribe. In

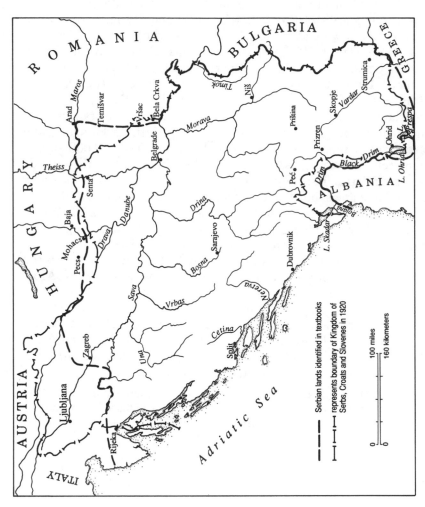

Serbian Lands Identified in the Textbooks

the course of time [the name Slavs] became most prominent and supplanted the common name [Serbs] with its tribal name [Slavs]. Subsequently, they imposed it [the name Slavs] on all the other tribes, except for one, that is, on the name of our [Serbian] people, who . . . even later retained their old name.[9]

This theme, that the Slavs at one time were all called Serbs, was repeated in many of the Serbian geography, history, and literature textbooks.

Karić further asserted that the Serbs had settled in "their present lands" in the first half of the seventh century and had continued to occupy them to the present. In time other peoples had migrated into the lands, mainly along the periphery, but they comprised only "one sixth of the total population, which numbers about 8,600,000 persons. . . . Of this number 7,200,000 are *Serbs*, 300,000 *Magyars*, and about the same number *Romanians* and *Germans*, 140,000 *Italians*, 100,000 *Albanians*, a similar number of *Osmanli Turks*, and the remainder are *Slovaks, Bulgars, Jews, Cincars, Gypsies,* and *Greeks.*"[10] Again, there was no mention of the Croats.

Using language as the proof that the inhabitants were Serbs, he argued further that

the Serbian language was a branch of the great Slavic family. It is spoken by seven and one half million people. . . . It belongs to the southeastern group of Slavic languages, where are found the Russian and Bulgarian languages. . . . Among the Slavic languages, the Serbian language was the most pleasant to the ear—the most melodious. . . . Among the languages of the Slavic family, therefore, the Serbian language has assumed that place which Italian has among the languages of the Latin family, and for the same reasons.[11]

In other statements he asserted that "in Serbian there were three principal dialects—štokavian, čakavian, and kajkavian." He described čakavian as the remnant of the original Croatian dialect; it was spoken mainly in the Croatian littoral but had been supplanted by štokavian "the real Serbian dialect." He identified kajkavian as being related to Slovenian, which was spoken "in those regions of the Serbian land—[that is] in Croatia [u onim krajevima Srpske Zemlje—u Hrvatskoj]," and had also been displaced by štokavian. "All the remaining Serbian people, about 6,300,000," spoke štokavian, "which all the Serbs" had taken as "as their literary language."[12]

There are a number of points to note from his statement on language. By referring to čakavian as the old Croatian dialect, he was repeating Karadžić's point. He rejected Daničić's statement that the Croats spoke all three dialects. By noting that "all the Serbs" had taken the štokavian dialect for their literary language, he was reiterating the information that Hristić, Novaković, and others had presented in their readers, namely, that the Croats had adopted the Serbian literary language. For Karić, thus, not only were the štoka-vian speakers in Croatia, Slavonia, Istria, and Dalmatia Serbs, but so were the čakavians and kajkavians.

In addition to language, Karić stressed the importance of religion:

> Of our people, the only ones who are called Serbs are those of the eastern Orthodox faith. The great majority of those of the western-Orthodox Catholic faith are called Croats. The same is the case with the Serbian Muslims in Bosnia and Hercegovina, as well as those in Old Serbia and Macedonia, who are called Turks, even if they do not speak any other language except Serbian. These religious differences, which terribly torment our national organism, will be straightened out only with more education.[13]

> The Christian faith is the most sacred thing for the Serb. He takes great pride in the fact that he is called a Christian, and, in particular, an Orthodox. He goes so far that he does not separate religion from his nationality, that he calls it the Serbian religion. Consequently he wants to call every person a Serb no matter what his nationality, if only he is an Orthodox, whereas he calls the Serbian Catholic a Šokac or Latin, the Mohammedan [Serb] a Turk. . . .[14]

> The Serbian nation is divided into three religions—*Orthodox*, *Catholic*, and *Mohammedan*. Numerically the Mohammedans are about 600,000, the Catholics about 2,400,000, and the Orthodox almost 4,200,000. Among the Christians there are also some *Uniates*. The Catholics are concentrated in the northwestern parts of the Serbian land, where the population belongs almost exclusively to this church. On the other hand, the Orthodox faith is almost exclusively [found] in the southeastern regions. The strongest roots of Islam are in Bosnia and Hercegovina, that is, in the middle of the Serbian lands, where Orthodoxy and Catholicism meet and compete.[15]

With respect to the other inhabitants of the Serbian lands, Karić wrote, "the Romanians, Bulgarians, Greeks, and Cincars were Orthodox. The Germans and Magyars were Catholics and Protestants, with the latter also having some Calvinists. The Slovaks were Protestants, the Italians Catholics, and the Turks and Albanians Mohammedans, although there were also some Catholics among the Albanians."[16] From the above statements it is evident that Karić saw the Croats as Serbs of the "western-Orthodox Catholic faith," who did not enjoy the same status as those who were of the "Serbian nationality" and the "Serbian religion."

In addition to describing the Serbian lands, language, and religion, the geography books pointed to various national customs, such as the *slava*, a pre-Christian practice carried over into the Christian era of having a protecting saint for each household, and the special celebrations for Christmas Eve, Easter, Saint George's Day and Saint John's Day. They also took careful note of famous sites in Serbian history—Peć, the seat of the patriarchate, Skopje, Dušan's capital, and Prilep, the birthplace of Marko Kraljević.[17]

Among all the issues discussed, the lands were the key factor. Serbia had to control them if the nation was to be strong. The emphasis that was placed on this issue can be demonstrated by quoting authors of later geography textbooks whom Karić influenced. For instance, Sokolović in his 1890 fourth grade reader stated that "those lands in which Serbs live are called Serbian lands." He traced the boundaries, which, in an abbreviated form, paralleled Karić's presentation. There was a separate subsection in his book for each land—Bosnia-Hercegovina, Montenegro, Dalmatia, Istria, Croatia, Slavonia and Srem, Banat and Bačka, Macedonia, and Old Serbia—each with a map and accompanying text. The text described their boundaries, mountains, valleys, rivers, lakes, climate, flora, fauna, the occupations of the inhabitants, their nationality, religion and language, the schools, and the form of government for each province. "In these Serbian lands," Sokolović asserted,

> there are 7,000,000 Serbs, but in addition to the Serbs in these lands there are also some other nationalities, but they are not large numerically. There are also 300,000 Serbs in Bulgaria and about another 300,000 in Hungary, Albania, and lower Macedonia. Therefore the total [number] of Serbs in the Serbian and other lands is 7,600,000.
>
> By religion there are Orthodox, Catholic and Mohammedan Serbs. The Orthodox are in the majority, followed by Catholics, and the fewest are the Mohammedans. These Serbs of the Mohammedan faith even today speak a beautiful Serbian dialect [because] they do not know any other. They accepted the Mohammedan religion at the time when the Serbian empire fell at Kosovo in order to retain their property and their rule.
>
> Among us Serbs there is one great shortcoming: namely, we are not of the same faith; we call one another Vlach [a Serb], Šokac [a Croat], Turk [any South Slav—Bosnian, Montenegrin, Macedonian—who accepted Islam], etc., and that is not good. We are all Serbs. Whatever religion we worship, we must agree and behave like brothers, which is what we are. We must not call one another by various vulgar names.
>
> In the Serbian lands the Serbs speak the eastern, southern, and western dialects. Mostly they speak the eastern, then the southern, and the fewest the western dialect.[18]

Sokolović's comments typified the viewpoint found in other textbooks. For instance, in 1891 Petar K. Šreplović wrote that "all these lands that we have hitherto studied are called Serbian lands. They are called this name because Serbs live in them."[19] In 1900 Raša Mitrović wrote, "All those lands in which Serbs live are Serbian lands"; he identified them by name and then described them. However, he added two areas Karić had not designated—the Vidin and Sredac (Sofia) provinces of Bulgaria. Subsequently, a number of other authors also included them.[20]

In 1902 and 1906 Mitrović collaborated with Mihailo M. Stanojević in a new textbook. In the 1906 edition, instead of repeating their statement of 1902 that "all the lands in which Serbs lived were Serbian," the authors wrote that "Serbian people live in these lands."[21] However, as Karić and the other authors had done, Mitrović and Stanojević identified these lands as being "Serbian lands under Austria-Hungary," "Serbian lands under the Turks," and "Serbian lands under Bulgaria." The explanatory text left no doubt that these lands were considered Serbian.

In 1905 Mihailo Jović and D. J. Putniković wrote that "in the Serbian lands live about 12 million people, of whom 9 million are Serbs. In Serbia and Montenegro live only Serbs; in Bačka and Banat about one-third are Serbs and the remainder are Romanians, Germans, and Magyars; in Croatia and Slavonia there are also Germans and Magyars; in Istria and Dalmatia there are Italians; in Old Serbia Albanians and Turks; in Macedonia there are Turks, Greeks, Cincars, and Bulgars. But in each of these lands the Serbs are the largest number [of inhabitants], which is why these lands are called Serbian."[22] In 1912 Mihailo Stanojević in his fourth grade elementary textbook stated that "Of these Serbian lands only the kingdoms of Serbia and Montenegro are free," whereas the others were under Austro-Hungarian, Turkish, and Bulgarian administrations.[23]

Whereas Karić's influence was paramount in all the textbooks, shortly before the war the same modification was made that has been discussed with reference to the readers. In 1912, Antonović and Lazić continued to use the description "Serbian Lands under Austria-Hungary," but now the inhabitants of Croatia-Slavonia were called "Croats and Serbs," a term that Jović and Putniković had already used in the 1908 sixth edition of their fourth grade textbook.[24] Antonović and Lazić, however, continued to refer to the population of Dalmatia as being "all exclusively Serbs of whom the great majority are Catholics; aside from the Serbs, there are also some Italians."[25] This was the same distinction between Croatia-Slavonia and Dalmatia, it will be recalled, that Jovanović and Ivković had made in their 1913 reader. In 1913 Antonović and Todor Radivojević in their secondary school textbook wrote in a section entitled "Serbian or Croatian Lands" that

> The Serbs or Croats are one people with two names and three religions (Orthodox, Catholic, and Mohammedan). The greatest part of the Serbian or Croatian lands is found in the Balkan peninsula, but, in addition, they extend across the Danube and Sava into Central Europe. Collectively they encompass an area larger than 270,000 square kilometers, with approximately 15 million inhabitants, among whom the Serbs or Croats are about 11.5 million. Only two Kingdoms—*Serbia* and *Montenegro*—are free and independent. With the exception of northern Albania, all the other lands are under Austro-Hungarian rule, that is, *Croatia, Slavonia, Srem, Bosnia, Hercegovina, Dalmatia, Primorije, Istria, Banat, Bačka,* and *Baranja.* . . .
>
> The capital [of Serbia] is the city of *Belgrade.* . . . In it live 100,000 inhabitants. Numerically Belgrade is the second largest city of the Serbian or Croatian lands. Ahead of it there is only the port of *Trieste.* It is accepted that [Belgrade] is . . . the spiritual and political center of all the Serbs or Croats.[26]

Of all the textbooks examined, including the readers and history books, the one by Antonović and Radivojević was the most effective in providing information to promote understanding between the Serbs and Croats, as the minister of education had directed in 1912. It should be noted that in their presentation even Serbia, Macedonia, Old Serbia, and Montenegro were described under the rubric "Serbian or Croatian lands," a description that would have been inconceivable a few years earlier. The extent to which the South Slav orientation had entered into the book can be seen by the claim that Trieste, which some Croats included in their territorial designs, was designated the largest Serbian or Croatian city. Their volume, however, became only available for the academic year 1913–14, and it was for the first grade of the secondary schools. The elementary grade textbooks, which were the only geography books 95 percent of the students ever read, continued to refer to the South Slav lands under Austria-Hungary as "Serbian lands."

South Slav Lands under Austria-Hungary

For this study the most important lands are those under Habsburg administration, in particular Croatia-Slavonia, because here the question of South Slav cooperation was an immediate issue. Hence, in order to make the issues clearer, the Habsburg census figures for

1910, which proportionately did not vary from those for 1880, 1890, and 1900, will be cited for each province, beginning with Croatia-Slavonia.

In the 1910 census, the population of Croatia-Slavonia was 2,621,954, of whom 1,630,354 or 62.6 percent were Croats and 644,955 or 24.6 percent were Serbs. The other inhabitants were mainly Hungarians and Germans. In other words, there were two and one-half Croats for every Serb.[27] The Serbs, as discussed earlier, lived primarily in the former Military Frontier region; in parts of it they comprised an overwhelming majority.

Karić, as we have seen, included Croatia-Slavonia within the rubric "Serbian lands under Austria-Hungary." In his description of these two provinces, he wrote:

> In both kingdoms there are 1,910,400 inhabitants. They are all (96 percent), with minor exceptions, only Serbs, who in some places are called Croats. The remainder are Germans (80,000), Magyars (40,000), Czechs, Slovenes, and some others. The population is, in the majority, of the Catholic faith (1,330,000); next are the Orthodox (550,000). Going from west to east there are more Orthodox, so that in Srem the majority are Orthodox.[28]

In 1891 Šreplović wrote that Croatia, Slavonia, and Srem "are Serbian lands, because real Serbs live in them. Seven-eighths are real Serbs, who speak Serbian just as we do. The Serbs who live around Zagreb are still called Croats. The Serbs who live in the Triune Kingdom are enthusiastic about everything that is Serbian"; this enthusiasm was shown by the fact that many individuals in their wills left their wealth to Serbian schools and churches.[29] Fifteen years later, the 1906 Mitrović and Stanojević fourth grade textbook stated that "the land that is called the Triune Kingdom is composed of the three Serbian kingdoms: Croatia, Slavonia, and Srem" [incorrectly listing Srem, not Dalmatia, as the third part of the Triune Kingdom].[30] In 1909 Simić and Hrabrenović wrote about "these Serbian lands . . . in which about two million Serbs live. . . ."[31]

Some authors made a point of stressing the fact that the Croats were Serbs regardless of their name. Thus, Sokolović stated that there were 1,950,000 inhabitants in Croatia, "who are almost exclusively Serbs. In the northwestern parts of Croatia, these Serbs are called Croats."[32] Nikolić wrote that there were "over 2,000,000 pure Serbs" and that "the Serbs who live in Croatia call themselves Croats."[33] In 1902 Mitrović and Stanojević asserted that the Serbs "in the west are Catholics, who call themselves *Croats*."[34] In that same year Antonović and Lazić published the identical view: "The great majority of the population is composed of Serbs, who in north-western Croatia are called Croats."[35] In their 1905 edition, Jović and Putniković affirmed that the inhabitants were Serbs, Orthodox, and Catholic and added, "The Catholics are two thirds [of the population] and are called Croats." Subsequently the authors wrote "the Catholics are two-thirds [of the population] and are called Croats. The Orthodox are called Serbs and live mostly in Srem and Lika. They are one-third of the entire population."[36] In 1909 Simić and Hrabrenović added that "the Catholics are called *Croats*. However, even if they are of another faith and even are called Croats, neverthe-less they are real Serbs, because with minor exceptions they speak the same way we do." Nevertheless, the authors reminded the students: "However, we and the Croats must understand that 'only unity saves the Serb' and that even a rod, too, is strong in a bundle."[37] The call to the Croats for unity was to "save the Serbs," not the "Serbs *and* Croats," which was how Antonović and Lazić described these two nations in the fifth edition (1912) of their secondary school reader. Or the terms "Serbs *or* Croats" and the "Serbo-Croatian lands," which Antonović, with his other co-author Radivojević, em-ployed in the ninth, or 1913, edition of their textbook.[38] There was no fundamental deviation in the elementary textbooks from Karić's views on the religion and language of the population in Croatia-Slavonia. The inhabitants were Serbs of the Catholic and Orthodox faiths, with the former predominating; the language was Serbian.

Although all the textbooks had information about the cities, historical sites, the birthplaces of prominent Serbs, and descriptions of local institutions, the quantity and quality of this information varied widely from book to book. Nevertheless, they contained a great deal of data. For instance, concerning Zagreb, the reader was typically informed that the Croatian ban resided in the city, the sabor met there, the Yugoslav Academy, the university, and a museum were located in it, as were the Matica Hrvatska and the Society of Saint Jerome. Zagreb was the major publishing center, where "books were printed in Latin." There was a large Catholic cathedral and many beautiful churches, but "the most beautiful was the Orthodox church." Similar information was provided about Rijeka, Slavonski Brod, Osijek, Varaždin, and other cities. However, the books paid especial attention to those areas in which Serbs lived, such as the Lika region and Srem. They stressed that in Karlovac, south of Zagreb, there was a Serbian bishopric, and it was here that Bishop Lukijan Musički, who distinguished himself in the early nineteenth century as a writer of odes to Serbdom, died. Pakrac too had a Serbian bishopric. The well-known Serbian poet, Branko Radičević, was born in Slavonski Brod. Zemun was the birthplace of Dimitrije Davidović, the first Serbian journalist. Jovan Rajić, the eighteenth-century Serbian historian, was from Sremski Karlovci. In Sremski Karlovci one also found the Serbian patriarchate and an Orthodox theological seminary and gymnasium. On Fruška Gora there were many monasteries, the names of which were all listed, and the students were reminded that Dositej Obradović began his career as a monk at the monastery of Hopovo. Fruška Gora was also the burial site of many prominent Serbs.[39]

Although the information about Croatia-Slavonia was by and large factually correct, the emphasis given conveyed the impression that these two provinces were part of the greater Serbian lands. This impression is understandable given the interpretation made about the lands, language, and religion. Thus, with the exception of the two immediately prewar high school volumes by Antonović and Lazić and Antonović and Radivojević, the students had no way of knowing that actually the Croats were a separate nation.

The information about Dalmatia, the third member of the Croatian Triune Kingdom, also raised questions. Two issues were at stake—the nationality of the inhabitants and the ethnic composition of the city of Dubrovnik. In the 1910 census, language, not nationality, was the criterion used to identify the inhabitants of Dalmatia. There were 610,000 Serbo-Croatian speakers, of whom 505,000 were Catholic and 105,000 Orthodox. Thus the Croats represented 83 percent and the Serbs 17. Once again Karić set the guidelines, by referring to Dalmatia as "this Serbian land," a view repeated by other authors.[40] For example, Sokolović wrote, "this is a Serbian land"; Mitrović and Stojanović stated, "this is a very narrow Serbian land alongside the Adriatic coast"; Antonović and Lazić commented, "Dalmatia is a narrow Serbian littoral"; and Simić and Hrabrenović added, "Austria administers this Serbian land."[41] The islands of Brač, Hvar, Korčula, Lastovo, Mljet, Lopud, and Koločep were all presented as Serbian. The city of Split was described as the largest city in Dalmatia, in which "there is found the palace of an emperor, which was built more than 1,400 years ago, that is, before the Serbs migrated to this area."[42]

The South Slavic inhabitants of Dalmatia were always identified as Serbian. In his secondary school textbook published in 1883, Karić wrote that the population in Dalmatia was 480,000, "which is all only Serbs," except for 20,000 Italians. However, Karić added, "only one-fifth are Orthodox and the remainder are Catholic."[43] Šreplović wrote, "real Serbs live in Dalmatia. . . . The Serbs in Dalmatia, who are called Dalmatians, are in the majority Roman Catholics; there are also those of the Orthodox faith."[44] Mitrović and Stanojević stated that "the people are Serbs mixed with some Italians."[45] In the 1905 textbook Jović and Putniković noted that there were 600,000 inhabitants, "in effect only Serbs," except for some Italians. "The Serbs were of two faiths, Catholic and Orthodox," but there were twice as many Catholics as Orthodox. Three years later, in their sixth edition, the authors qualified their remarks. Now they added there were 600,000 inhabitants "in effect only Serbs and Croats. . . . The Serbs and Croats are of two faiths: Catholics and Orthodox. There are twice as many Catholics as Orthodox."[46] However, in that same year, 1908, Miletić commented that "the inhabitants are *Serbs*, next *Italians*, mainly in the cities, and *Germans*, *Albanians*, and *Jews*. The Serbs are *Orthodox* and *Catholic* and the Italians and Albanians are of the *Catholic faith*. The Serbs of the Catholic faith are called *Croats*."[47] In 1912 Antonović and Lazić reported the population as 640,000, "all of whom are only Serbs, the great majority of whom are Catholics."[48] In addition to the Serbs there were some Italians. The authors agreed that the inhabitants spoke "the southern dialect," with some describing it as "a beautiful Serbian southern dialect."[49]

The controversy that centered on Dubronik was the most sensitive. All the authors stressed its Serbian character, with an emphasis not applied to any other city. Karić wrote that "here, in the ninth century, Dubrovnik, a Serbian trading republic, originated, which maintained itself up to the beginning of this [19th] century."[50] In addition to its trade and commerce, Dubrovnik was also well-known for its literary, cultural, and scientific achievements. Concerning these, Karić noted that "in the sixteenth and seventeenth centuries Serbian poetry and science blossomed in it [Dubrovnik]. Many prominent men saw the light of day there—the poet Gundulić, the well-known mathematician and astronomer Bošković, and many others."[51] Sokolović described Dubrovnik as "our oldest Serbian city," in which "the famous Serbian poet Gundulić was born."[52] Nikolić added that in it were born "the well-known Serbian poets *Ivan Gundulić*, [Stijepo] *Djordjić*, and [Djono] *Palmotić*, and the scientist *Rudjer Bošković*."[53] Stanojević reminded the readers that in Dubrovnik there was "a beautiful statue to the famous Serbian poet *Ivan Gundulić*."[54] Note again that the views concerning the Serbian character of Dubrovnik, as well as Dalmatia, did not deviate from those expressed in the readers, including the 1913 Jovanović and Ivković volume.

Of all the South Slavic lands claimed by the Serbs, Istria was the farthest from the kingdom of Serbia. The textbooks gave two basic descriptions: either "Istria is the largest Serbian peninsula" or "this is the smallest Serbian land."[55] According to the 1910 census Istria's population was 403,566, with the Croats being the largest ethnic group, 168,143 or 36.6 percent of the inhabitants. They were followed by 147,417 Italians, 55,134 Slovenes, 12,735 Germans, and less than 2,000 Serbs. Yet the textbooks described the population as being composed of Serbs, Italians, Slovenes, Germans, and Czechs "of whom two-thirds are Serbs."[56] A typical presentation stated that "in this land there is a majority of Serbs, of whom there are more than 200,000. They speak the Serbian western dialect. Most are of the Catholic faith, but there are some who use the Serbian language in church."[57] Antonović and Lazić mentioned that the Serbs were called Croats, a view repeated by Miletić in 1908. He wrote that "the inhabitants were *Serbs* (two-thirds), who are called *Croats*, next came the *Slovenes*, *Italians*, *Germans*, and *Jews*."[58] What is important about these statements is that the Slovenes were recognized as a separate nationality and as "being very closely related to us," whereas the Croats were simply identified as Serbs of the Catholic faith.[59]

Two authors, Jović and Putniković, at first subscribed to the above interpretations but then modified their views. In their 1905 textbook, they wrote that in Istria "the Serbs are called Croats," but three years later they declared that Istria had 300,000 inhabitants "of whom two-thirds are Croats and one-third Italians." Although there was no mention of any Serbs, the authors nevertheless continued to define Istria as part of "the Serbian lands" and as "our largest peninsula." The students also were told that in the elementary schools the language of instruction was "the Serbian language," whereas in the secondary schools it was Italian and German. On the other hand, some authors admitted that in Istria the "dress" of the Serbs was "more foreign than Serbian."[60] This was in contrast to their claim that in Dalmatia and Bosnia-Hercegovina the dress was similar to that in Serbia.

The evidence presented above indicates the firmly held conviction of the authors that the lands of the Triune Kingdom and Istria were "Serbian lands," inhabited by Serbs, either of the Orthodox or Catholic faiths, who spoke "Serbian." Yet the intensity of feeling expressed in presenting the Serbian rights to these lands did not match that employed to justify Serbia's claims to Bosnia-Hercegovina. From the point of view of the authors studied, not one conceded in any manner that Bosnia and Hercegovina were not as Serbian as Serbia or Montenegro was. For them it was an article of faith; without equivocation, every author categorically referred to the South Slavic inhabitants as Serbs. Not one indicated that there were any Croats in these two provinces, despite the fact that they all acknowledged that there were indeed other inhabitants, such as Turks, Germans, Magyars, Czechs, Jews, Albanians, and Gypsies. The Slavs were described by Karić as "all only Serbs," and other authors wrote "the inhabitants of Bosnia and Hercegovina are all pure Serbs," "there live pure Serbs," and "pure Serbs of three faiths."[61]

The authors were equally categorical with respect to religion. In 1883 Karić wrote that "there are 210,000 [18 percent] Catholics, 450,000 [38.8 percent] Mohammedans, and about 500,000 [43 percent] Orthodox."[62] In 1902 Antonović and Lazić reported that "the Serbs are divided by religion into Orthodox (675,000) [43 percent], Muslims (550,000) [35 percent], and Catholics (340,000) [22 percent]," percentages that approximated those of the 1910 census.[63] Other authors cited precise figures or reported the percentages, noting, nevertheless, that the inhabitants were "pure Serbs of three faiths," or "in Bosnia lived Serbs. They are of three faiths, Orthodox, Muslim, and Catholic."[64] A number of authors pointed out that the Habsburg authorities were using the religious divisions to grant preferential treatment especially to the Catholics as well as the Muslims, with the intent of turning the three religious bodies against one another. The students were cautioned, however, not to let this policy of divide and rule affect their feelings for their brethren of another faith. In particular, they were admonished not to scorn the Muslims, "who after all are Serbs and it was wrong to call them Turks because of [their religion]."[65] The same tolerant attitude was not displayed toward Catholics, who were viewed with grave suspicion. Thus Karić wrote that Catholics preferred "the crescent rather than the rule of the Orthodox, whose church was referred to as 'heretical.'"[66] Simić and Hrabrenović contended that "those Serbs of the Catholic faith changed their faith because those lands were now ruled by Austria-Hungary, which does not tolerate the Orthodox and Muslim Serbs, and helps the Catholics." Nevertheless they added, "he is my brother, regardless of his religion."[67]

The authors made a point of saying that the inhabitants of Bosnia-Hercegovina spoke "a beautiful Serbian," the southern dialect. Stanojević described it as "the purest Serbian language." To establish the fact that the Muslim Serbs were not Turks, it was stressed that these people "do not know any other language except Serbian."[68] Jović and Putniković put it more forcefully—the Serbian Muslims "had preserved the beautiful Serbian language and many customs." Yet the authors were concerned because Austrian authorities were trying to suppress Serbian by fostering "a Bosnian lan-

guage," whereas in Bosnia one had "the purest Serbian language."[69]
There was unanimity among the authors that Serbian was the language spoken in Bosnia, and most described it as "the most beautiful Serbian."

As regards the Habsburg administration of Bosnia-Hercegovina, the authors charged that there was discrimination against the Orthodox. In particular, they contended that insufficient funds were provided for Orthodox schools there. They stated that this policy had been introduced by the Ottoman authorities and was being continued by the Habsburg government. In contrast, they said, "the Serbs of the Catholic faith have the most schools."[70] By emphasizing this discrepancy in education and by insisting that all the Slavic inhabitants of Bosnia-Hercegovina were Serbs, even if by religion they were Muslim or Catholic, the authors were thus contending that one group of Serbs, the Orthodox, was being oppressed by another group of Serbs, the Catholics. Although stern words were written against the "Catholic Serbs" in Bosnia, no author called these Serbs Croats, as a number had in reference to the population in Croatia-Slavonia, Dalmatia, and Istria. The authors also took pains to point out that many of the customs practiced in Bosnia were identical to those of Serbia. They acknowledged, however, there were some differences in dress among the inhabitants in these two lands.[71]

The single clear impression about Bosnia-Hercegovina that a student obtained from the geography books was that they were "Serbian lands, because Serbs live in them." In "these beautiful Serbian lands" the Slavic inhabitants were "pure Serbs," some of whom, however, had gone astray in religion. Nevertheless, the students saw the two provinces as Serbian lands to be liberated from Austro-Hungarian rule and united to Serbia. The future of these lands was an issue to be settled exclusively between the Serbs and Austro-Hungarians.

The last two South Slavic lands under Austro-Hungarian rule to be examined were Bačka and Banat. In one respect they differed from the other provinces studied because there the South Slavic population was not in the majority. Both the Serbs and Croats advanced claims to these provinces, although collectively these two peoples represented about 33 percent of the population, with an equal number of Magyars. The other third consisted of Germans, Slovaks, Jews, and Romanians. Nevertheless, the authors of the Serbian textbooks were firm in their belief that Bačka and Banat were Serbian lands. Unable to claim a population majority, they based their case on cultural, religious, and, in particular, historical arguments.[72] The textbooks stressed that after leaving their ancestral home in the sixth century, the Serbs moved southward into Bačka and Banat, where

they lived for a period before crossing the Danube into their permanent home in the Balkans. However, not all Serbs migrated south.
Consequently, a point emphasized by Karić and others was that the
Serbs' descendants had lived continuously in Bačka and Banat for
three centuries before the arrival of the Magyars. All the scholars
agreed, however, that the major influx of Serbs came in the seventeenth and eighteenth centuries, when many fled Ottoman rule and
gained sanctuary in the Habsburg empire.[73]

It should be noted that when stating that there were 450,000
Serbs in Vojvodina, the Serbian authors included the Croats, as well
as the 93,000 Catholic Bunjevci and Šokci, who Croatian authors
claimed were Croats. Thus Nikolić wrote that "a part of the Serbs
are called Bunjevci and they are all of the Catholic faith." Miletić
reiterated this point, stating that "the Serbs are of the *Orthodox* and
Catholic faiths. The Catholic Serbs are called Bunjevci."[74]

The authors also placed great emphasis on the importance of
cultural and educational developments in these lands. The area held
a special place in Serbian history because of the dominating role of
Novi Sad as the cultural center for all the Serbs through much of the
nineteenth century. In particular, the textbooks praised the presence
in Novi Sad of the Matica Srpska, the oldest and most influential
cultural and literary organization, which subsidized many Serbian
writers. The authors were also proud of the strength of Serbian elementary education in the region. Šreplović wrote, "there is hardly
a village in which there is not a Serbian school and Serbian teachers."[75] The authors emphasized the fact that the population spoke
"pure Serbian" or the eastern dialect, that common to the independent Serbian kingdom.[76]

All the textbooks made it clear that the most serious threat to
the integrity and unity of the Serbian nation came from the Habsburg government. Consequently, the greatest attention was paid to
the Serbs in these lands. Whereas the Austro-Hungarian government
was clearly a more formidable adversary, the geography books did
not let the students forget about Serbia's historic lands still under
Ottoman rule, Macedonia and Old Serbia or Kosovo, which included
the center of Dušan's empire and the patriarchal seat of Peć.

South Slavic Lands under Ottoman Rule

In any discussion of Serbian claims to Ottoman as compared to
Habsburg lands certain differences should be pointed out. First, in
the Habsburg lands it was generally accepted that the Orthodox
were all Serbs, as were the Uniate Catholics. In the Ottoman re-

gions, the Slavic Orthodox could be Macedonians or Bulgarians. Second, emphasis was placed on the Serbian slava, a uniquely Serbian custom, which substantiated the premise that "where there is a slava, there is a Serb." Since the slava was not practiced by the Bulgarians, it was used to identify Serbs; but, paradoxically, although the Croats did not practice the custom, they were still considered Serbs. Third, the textbooks were forced to recognize that there were Orthodox of other nationalities—Bulgarians and Greeks—in the Old Serbian and Macedonian lands of the Ottoman empire.

Although the Serbs were deeply attached to both Old Serbia and Macedonia, the former aroused the greatest emotion because this once "sacred land," in which, as Simić and Hranilović wrote: "our kings and emperors reigned" was now also inhabited by Albanian Muslims.[77] Since the Serbian population of Old Serbia was cited as being between 400,000 and 1,000,000, Sokolović attributed an apparent decline to the fact that "many Serbs were forced to become Albanians and to become Turkicized, because of the great pressure of the Albanians." Although compelled to accept Islam, learn Albanian, and adopt other customs, nevertheless "all [Serbs] even up to the present have retained, some more, some less, the real Serbian customs from the Christian era."[78] Other authors agreed that the majority of the inhabitants were Serbs who spoke "a pure Serbian language, celebrated the slava, and had the same customs" as did the other Serbs. They too were certain that the Albanians, Turks, and Gypsies were a minority in Kosovo.[79]

Karić, who knew the area well, having served in Skopje as the Serbian consul general, defined its importance when he wrote that "the largest part of Old Serbia, going back to the oldest period, was called Raška, but that name slowly lost usage after the fall of the Serbian state and it was replaced by this new name. It is one of the best-known Serbian areas for the history of the great idea, the union of all the Serbian lands."[80] Other authors emphasized this theme and reminded the students that the patriarchate of Peć was located there; Priština had been Stevan Nemanja's capital, and Dušan had reigned for a time in Prizren. Once Djakovo had been inhabited exclusively by Serbs.[81]

The books emphasized that their religion and language enabled the Serbs to endure hardships in these areas. The majority of the inhabitants were Orthodox, but there were also "80,000 Serbs of the Mohammedan faith," in an area which had "the most beautiful churches and monasteries" and the largest and richest Serbian cities. As in the other areas, the authors claimed that "the Serbs speak a pure Serbian language. . . . they speak a beautiful Serbian," or "they speak a beautiful Serbian, especially from Kosovo westward." Yet they acknowledged that it was difficult to preserve the language, because Turkish policy did not encourage education. Thus, whereas at the time of the Nemanjas this area had the best educational system, now it had "the worst."[82] The image conveyed by the textbooks was that the civilized Serbs had fallen prey to the uncivilized Albanians. It was incumbent upon the Serbs to liberate the patriarchate of Peć and the lands over which the Nemanjas and Dušan once ruled. From the Serbian point of view, the main issue in Old Serbia was the struggle between Christian, Orthodox Serbs and Muslim Albanians who were supported by the Ottoman Turks.

In Macedonia the problem was more complex because here the principal adversary was not the Albanian Muslims, but the Bulgarian Christians. In the Habsburg lands the Croats were regarded as Slavs who were Serbs, who spoke Serbian, and who had become Catholic. In Macedonia the Bulgars were seen as both Slavic and Orthodox, but not Serbian. The problem was further complicated by the Greek and Albanian claims.

As was the case with Old Serbia, the authors cited varying population figures for Macedonia, in part because there was no common agreement on its boundaries and also because some authors combined the populations of Macedonia and Old Serbia. Consequently, the total population was estimated as from 600,000 to 2,000,000. All the authors recognized the polyglot character of the area. Karić cited these figures: Serbs 500,000, Turks 70,000, Cincars 24,000, Gypsies 5,000, Jews 3,500, and Greeks only 500. He did not acknowledge any Bulgars or Albanians. Sokolović reported 600,000 inhabitants, "virtually all Serbs." Subsequently, Nikolić, Antonović and Lazić, Mitrović and Stanojević, Simić and Hrabrenović, and Stanojević all noted that there were Bulgars in Macedonia, but they listed them as an insignificant minority, along with the other ethnic groups.[83]

To buttress the ethnic claim to Macedonia, which the textbooks variously described as "the largest Serbian land," "the southernmost Serbian land," or "southern Serbia or Macedonia," the Serbian populations of the principal cities were given. With the exception of Thessaloniki, which was recognized as predominantly Jewish, all the other cities were described as having substantial Serbian populations. Although there were discrepancies in the exact number of Serbs in each city, there was unanimity that the Serbs predominated in them. Thus Bitola had 30,000 inhabitants, of whom two-thirds were Serbs and the others were Turks, Jews, and Cincars. In Ohrid, Prilep, and Bitola the population was judged three-fourths Serbian, whereas in Veles it was only two-thirds. In addition to these major cities, Florina and Seres, in present-day Greece, and Melnik, in Bulgaria, were described as being Serbian, as were many of the villages surrounding Thessaloniki.[84]

The Serbian authors also sought to prove that the Slavic inhabitants spoke Serbian. Thus Sokolović wrote that the Serbs "speak Serbian as we do." However, subsequent authors were not so positive. Nikolić wrote, "the Macedonian Serbs speak the eastern dialect, which is a little different from ours." Mitrović commented: "They do not speak accurate Serbian. They make mistakes in cases and in the accents in the pronunciation of words." Mitrović and Stanojević added: "their speech differs from ours in the accenting of words and the declension of words."[85] Notwithstanding the ambiguity in the spoken language, the authors emphasized that every Slavic household that practiced the slava was Serbian because the slava was not a Bulgarian custom.[86]

The textbooks also dealt with the western regions of Bulgaria, that is, the Vidin and Sofia (Sredac) provinces, which were identified as "Serbian lands." Technically these lands remained under Ottoman suzerainty until Bulgaria became independent in 1908, even though Sofia exercised full control over them after 1878. Nevertheless, the textbooks asserted their Serbian character. However, when Karić, in his secondary school geography book published in 1883, described the political, territorial, and educational organization of Bulgaria and Eastern Rumelia, he identified the different nationalities living in the Bulgarian lands, but did not mention any Serbs. In his major work on Serbia, published in 1887, after the 1885 Serbo-Bulgarian War, which Serbia lost, he listed 200,000 Serbs in "western Bulgaria" in a table identifying the lands in which Serbs lived.[87] In 1890 Sokolović noted that there were "Serbs who live in the western parts of Bulgaria."[88] In the following year Sreplović set forth views that a number of other authors would repeat. He wrote, "The western part of Bulgaria, from Lom directly south through Sofia and Rila, once was an integral part of the Serbian state. Pure Serbs live there, who speak Serbian, and each celebrates his name day as we do. The Vidin and Sredac provinces are Serbian lands because the people who live in them speak Serbian and once were united with us in one entity." Sofia, which had a population of 21,000, "was once a Serbian town and was called Sredac." In fact, Serbia's medieval ruler, King Milutin, was buried in Sofia, in a church that he built.[89] In 1899 Nikolić was more explicit. "Even now pure Serbs live there, who speak a beautiful Serbian language, celebrate the slava, are proud of our heroes, sing our songs and have the same customs as we do." He too noted that Milutin was buried in Sofia. The population of the two provinces was 450,000, "of whom over 400,000 were pure Serbs. They speak the eastern dialect. They all are of the Orthodox faith."[90]

In 1900 Mitrović, and then in 1902 Mitrović and Stanojević, added a new element. They reiterated that these were pure Serbs, who spoke the eastern dialect, but added a qualification: after every noun these people use an article, for example, "*kučata, praseto,* etc. There are over 400,000 Serbs here." The noun to which an article is added, of course, is a Bulgarian grammatical form.[91]

The authors were particularly concerned with the plight of the Serbs in Bulgaria. Šreplović asserted that the Bulgars were trying to Bulgarianize the Serbian children, despite the fact that if not for the war effort of the Serbs and Russians in 1876–78, the Bulgars would still be Turkish subjects. Instead of showing gratitude, the Bulgars aimed at seizing Serbian lands, especially Macedonia. In 1899 Nikolić claimed that Serbian children were compelled to attend Bulgarian schools "in order to have them forget they were Serbs." In 1900 Mitrović stressed that "the Bulgars prohibited the Serbs the most beautiful Serbian custom, the slava."[92]

A few years later the statements about the Serbs in Bulgaria became less strident. Thus in 1906 Mitrović and Stanojević remarked that "these [Vidin and Sredac] are two Serbian provinces east of Serbia across the Timok [River] and Stara Planina," without indicating the number of Serbian inhabitants or their dialect. They did, however, reiterate that King Milutin had built a church in Sofia and was buried there. Six years later, in 1912, Stanojević, in a section entitled "Serbian Lands under Bulgaria," described the "Vidin and Sredac provinces" as being "east of Serbia across the Timok River and Stara Planina." The principal cities in the provinces were "*Vidin* and *Sredac* [Sofia]. . . . In Sofia there is a beautiful church built by King Milutin. Even today the remains of King Milutin rest there." In that same year Antonović and Lazić in their textbook for the secondary schools simply noted that Serbs lived in the Vidin and Sofia regions.[93]

The Serbian claims to lands under Bulgarian authority were not given the same weight in the textbooks as assigned to those lands under the authority of Austria-Hungary or the Ottoman Empire. It appears that the reason for including them was to exert pressure on Bulgaria in the contest over Macedonia rather than to pursue a determined effort to acquire these provinces, as was the case with Bosnia, Hercegovina, Old Serbia, and Macedonia.

In conclusion, it can be seen that the Serbian geography books left no doubt about which lands under foreign rule were Serbian.

Each province was identified and declared to be "Serbian lands under Austria-Hungary" or "Serbian lands under the Turks." There was nothing in the geography books that would indicate that these lands were "Serbian or Croatian" and inhabited by "Serbs and Croats" as two separate nations. This matter was first raised when Antonović and Radivojević wrote about the "Serbs or Croats" and "Serbian or Croatian lands" in their secondary school textbooks in 1913. The revised terminology was not introduced into the elementary school textbooks until after the war, so generations of students who had gone only through elementary school would view these lands as Serbian.

CROATIAN GEOGRAPHY TEXTBOOKS

The purpose of the study of geography in Croatia-Slavonia was, among other things, "to awaken one's love for the fatherland and people."[94] Since here geography was not taught as a separate course in the lower or upper grades of the public schools, but was taught through readers in the former and in conjunction with history in the latter, the information was not as precise as it was for the study of Serbian geography. Nevertheless, an examination of all the textbooks over four decades reveals a general pattern. First, the students studied the physical geography of their immediate vicinity. Next, they learned about their province, its principal features, the form of government, its inhabitants, their occupations, historic landmarks, and birthplaces of prominent individuals. Subsequently the students studied the lands of their kingdom—Croatia, Slavonia, and Dalmatia. Finally, they learned about the Austro-Hungarian empire, and about other European countries, including Serbia, Montenegro, and the Slavic lands of the Ottoman empire. In the secondary schools the students were provided with detailed information about the Triune Kingdom and the lands of the Habsburg empire, based on the voluminous statistical data published regularly by the Habsburg government. There was also extensive information on the European countries and other continents.

Although the emphasis was clearly on the Croats and their lands, the political and national stress found in the Serbian books was not evident in the Croatian textbooks, since all the lands to which the Croats laid claim were within the monarchy. Nevertheless, because of the large Serbian population within the empire, the students learned about their fellow Serbs as well as the Serbian lands outside the monarchy.

Vuk Stefanović Karadžić

Frontispiece from Karadžić's *Treasury of the History, Language, and Customs of the Serbs of All Three Faiths* (Vienna, 1849)

Vuk Stefanović Karadžić

В. С. К.

ковчежић

КОВЧЕЖИЋ

З А

ИСТОРИЈУ, ЈЕЗИК И ОБИЧАЈЕ

СРБА СВА ТРИ ЗАКОНА.

I.

У БЕЧУ

У ШТАМПАРИЈИ ЈЕРМЕНСКОГА МАНАСТИРА

1849.

Title page of Karadžić's *Treasury*

Stojan Novaković

СРПСКА ГРАМАТИКА

Srpska gramatika

САСТАВИО

СТОЈАН НОВАКОВИЋ.

Stojan Novakovic

ПРВО ЦЕЛОКУПНО ИЗДАЊЕ.

У БЕОГРАДУ

ИЗДАЊЕ И ШТАМПА ДРЖАВНЕ ШТАМПАРИЈЕ

1894.

Title page of Novaković's *Serbian Grammar* (Belgrade, 1894)

Ljudevit Gaj

Bishop Josip Juraj Strossmayer

I.

Ima naših knjiga, koje niesu tiskane onakovimi pismeni, koja ste učili u „Početnici“, i koja se zovu latinska.

Naše se knjige tiskaju i ćirilskimi pismeni.

Evo ovdje malih ćirilskih pismena, koja glase kao i natiskana pod njimi pismena latinska:

Ćirilska: а, б, в, г, д, ђ, е, ж, з, и, ј,
Latinska: a, b, v, g, d, dj, e, ž, z, i, j,

Ćirilska: к, л, љ, м, н, њ, о, п, р, с, т,
Latinska: k, l, lj, m, n, nj, o, p, r, s, t,

Ćirilska: ћ, у, ф, х, ц, ч, џ, ш.
Latinska: ć, u, f, h, c, č, dž, š.

Ćirilska pismena tako poredjana zovu se az-buka.

Koja su ćirilska pismena sa latinskimi pismeni oblikom i glasom jednaka, koja su samo oblikom jednaka, a koja su oblikom nejednaka?

Vježbe u čitanju.

ако кore, не моrе. — без муке не има науке. — вода све носи изван срамоте. — гладну сит не вјерује. — другому на вољу, а себи на невољу. — ђумбир се треба у љекарству. — ево моје главе. — жут је као восак. — зрело воће само опада. — иде вријеме, носи бреме. — језик горе може посјећи

From a *Reader for the Second Grade of the General Public Schools* (Zagreb, 1891)

I.

Има наших књига, које нијесу тискане онако-
вими писмени, која сте учили у „Буквару“, и која
се зову ћирилска.

Наше се књиге тискају и латинскими писмени.

Ево овдје м а л и х латинских писмена, која гласе
као и натискана под њими писмена ћирилска:

Латинска:	a,	b,	c,	ć,	č,	d,	dj,	e,	f,	g,
Ћирилска:	а,	б,	ц,	ћ,	ч,	д,	ђ,	е,	ф,	г,
Латинска:	gj,	h,	i,	j,	k,	l,	lj,	m,	n,	nj,
Ћирилска:	ђ,	х,	и,	ј,	к,	л,	љ,	м,	н,	њ,
Латинска:	o,	p,	r,	s,	š,	t,	u,	v,	z,	ž.
Ћирилска:	о,	п,	р,	с,	ш,	т,	у,	в,	з,	ж.

Латинска писмена тако поређана зову се а б е-
ц е д а.

Која су латинска писмена са ћирилскими писмени обликом и гласом једнака, која су само
обликом једнака, а која су обликом неједнака?

Вјежбе у читању.

angjeli su u nebu. — bez zdravlja ne ima bo-
gatstva. — criepom se kuće pokrivaju. — ćilim se
zove drugčije sag. — častna haljina sramote ne po-
kriva. — dva lješnika orahu vojska. — djaci ne
smiju biti pospanci. — frtalj je četvrtina. — gradi
ražanj a zec u šumi. — gjurgjic cvjeta u proljeće. —

Šta ćemo čekat? Ajdemo dalje!
S vragom ne ću imati posla,
130   Ti me Hrváti drže za osla."

    Tatarin ode. Slobodno sada
Padoše vrata Kalnika grada,
Iz njèga Bela vĕselo šeta,
S njime c'jela jùnâčkâ četa.
135   Kralj će pòkôrno tada reći:
„Oj, vi ljudi iz sela Vìsoka,
Ljùdine vi ste, momci òd oka,
Hvala na hrani, hvala nà sreći;
Vašim da n'jesam postao gostom,
140   Mučih se i sad nemilim postom.
Plemstvo nek' svim je harnosti plaća,
Vi ste òd sad králjeva braća!"
„Hvala ti, krâlju!" vĕsela oka
Rekoše ljudi iz sela Visoka:
145   Malo je bilo, šačica šljîvâ,
Al' ti je zato glava sad živa,
No ne zabòravi svojega brata,
Čednog šljîvâra, plĕmića Hrváta."

    Tako, reče sl'jepac mi stari,
150   Postaše prvi naši šljivari.

78. Три хајдука.

Од. З. Ј. Јовановића.

Ӳ пô бурне, црне ноћи
Феруз-паша из снâ скочи.
Жѝжак [1] дршће, кô да чита
Стр̏ву сâнка с бл'једа дица.
5   Феруз-паша кȁду [2] пита:
„Камо кључи òд тамнѝцâ . . .

---

[1] Жѝжак (жишка), проста лампица. [2] Кȁда или кȁдуна, ӳдȃтȃ жена ӳ Турȃкȃ.

From Kušar's *Reader for the Third Grade of the Secondary Schools* in Dalmatia (Vienna, 1910)

Три године како трухну,
Ох, хàјдỳчкū пепел клети,
Па још нū сад мира нема,
У̀ сан дође, па ми пр'јети!“   10
„„Немој, аго, немој ноћу
Сūлазити у тамнūне;
Сутра ћемо послат Муја,
Да покòпā̂ кости њине!““
„Хахахаха, бабо моја!   15
Ни живих се н'јесам бòја',
Док су били зā̆ ужā̆са,
А камо ли мртвих паса!
Морам ићи, да их видим,
Како леже нà трухлūшту,   20
Да их питам, што ме зову,
Што ме траже, што ме ишту!“ —
Узе жижак — зрā̆̀ка дршће
Нà пашину бл'једом лицу,
Зā̆рђā̆лā̂ брава шкрипну,   25
Он се спусти у тàмницу. —
У тамници, ледној страви,
Гдје   јàкрепе [1] мèмла [2] дā̆вū̂,
Гдје се грозе хладне гује,
Кад се сјете неких мȳкā̂,   30
Ондје· сједе три костỳра,
Три костура од хајду́кā̂.
Или сједе, ил' се сȃмо
Феруз-паши тако ствара,
Прȇд њима су на камèну,   35
Кȏ на стòлу, три пехáра.
Прогòвā̆рā̂ хàјдȳк први:
„Ево, пашо, пèхȃр крви;
Имао сам вјерну љубу,
Кад ме покри ова тама,   40
Òстала је јадна сама,

---

1) Јакреп, штипавац (шкорпија). 2) Мèмла (турски), влага.

skoj i Slavoniji cvali su gradovi: *Sirmium (Sriem,* gdje je danas Mitrovica); *Taurunum* (današnji Zemun), *Cunctium* (Kunkcium, Ilok), *Mursa* (Osiek). *Siscia* (današnji Sisak) i *Sirmium* pak bijahu medju svimi starimi gradovi najznamenitiji, jer je tu stolovao namjestnik rimskoga cara i kovao se rimski novac.

Rimljani niesu samo gradove dizali, nego su uredjivali i toplice (Topuske, Varaždinske i Daruvarske), gradili su vodovode i sadili vinograde (u Moslavini i Sriemu).

Rimsko je carstvo tako naraslo, da se je moralo razdvojiti: na zapadno rimsko carstvo s priestolnim gradom *Rimom* i iztočno rimsko carstvo s priestolnim gradom *Carigradom.* Svakom polovinom vladaše poseban car. Naša je domovina pripadala iztočnomu rimskomu carstvu.

Tako su Rimljani širili prosvjetu po svih osvojenih zemljah, te su nastojavali, da se i ostali narodi uljude. Još danas imade u našoj domovini mnogo spomenika iz rimskoga doba, koji nam svjedoče, kako su Rimljani bili mogući i slavni.

80. Стари Славени.

Наши прадједови, стари Славени, становаху у старо доба јоште прије Исуса далеко горе на сјеверу. У четвртом вијеку послије Исуса почели су се разни народи селити од сјевера и изтока прама западу и југу, а међу њими и *Славени*, те су тако населили готово све земље данашње Аустро-угарске државе.

Славени иду међу највеће народе на зем-

From a *Reader for the Third Grade of the Public Schools* (Zagreb, 1884)

љи. Славеном припадају данас на сјеверу живући: *Руси, Пољаци, Чеси, Словаци,* па на југу: *Хрвати, Срби, Словенци* и *Чугари.*

Стари Славени бијаху врло миропубив и радин народ, но када би тко на њих навалио, они би га храбро сузбили. Највише су се бавили пољодјелством и трговином, те су живјели врло поштено и савјестно. Стари писци разних народа не могу доста нахвалити њихова простодушја, искрене срдачности, а особито њихове гостољубивости, која се је у нас још данас уздржала. Они су живјели у задрузи, т. ј. цијела породица заједно, а свака таакова задруга имала је свога старјешину или домаћина. Више задруга сачињавало је род, а више родова племе. Што је био старјешина или домаћин задрузи, то је био жупан племену или жупанији. За жупане бираху си обћине људе одличније и богатије или бољаре, који су се могли боље бринути за обће добро свога народа.

Стари Славени вјероваху у једнога бога, који је створио сав овај свијет, но узањ се клањаху и. другим мањим боговом и богињам; били су дакле кривобожци. Својим боговом жртвоваху овце, звјерад и плодове земаљске. Такођер вјероваху, да је душа неумрла и да ће у будућем животу сваки примити плаћу за добра, а казан за зла дјела.

Осим у богове вјероваху још у добре и зле духове, виле, вјештице и вукодлаке.

81. Hrvati dolaze na jug, te si osnivaju državu.

Za prvih vjekova kršćanstva nastala je obćenita vreža i seoba narodâ. Jedni potiskivahu druge. Ni

IV. Opisi i orisi.

From Kušar's *Reader for the Third Grade of the Secondary Schools in Dalmatia* (Vienna, 1910)

GRAMATIKA

I STILISTIKA

HRVATSKOGA ili SRPSKOGA

KNJIZEVNOG JEZIKA.

NAPISAO

Dr T. MARETIĆ

KR. SVEUČ. PROFESOR.

1899

Title page of Maretić's *Grammar and Stylistics of the Croatian or Serbian Literary Language* (Zagreb, 1899)

Authors

In contrast to Serbia, no single geographer exerted as much influence in Croatia as Karić did over the Serbian authors. Croatian geographers studied with German specialists, who had gained an international reputation as being the leaders in their field. In some cases Croatian scholars translated German works, or significant portions of them, into Croatian. As a result, the secondary students in particular were kept abreast of the latest developments in the field.

There were five principal Croatian geographers—Petar Matković, Vjenceslav Mařik, Ivan Hoić, Josip Modestin, and Vjekoslav Klaić. Of these Petar Matković was the best scholar. He studied in Vienna, Prague, and Berlin, where he attended the lectures of Theodor Mommsen, the historian, and Eduard Ritter, the geographer. He became a gymnasium teacher first in Varaždin and then in Zagreb, and in 1883 he was appointed the first professor of geography at the University of Zagreb. He wrote on physical and statistical geography as well as on historical geography, and he published travel accounts of the Balkans from the early modern period. He was a corresponding member of the Russian Academy, the Russian Geographic Society, and the Natural Science and Anthropological-Ethnographic Society of the University of Moscow, the Royal Archeological Institutes in Berlin, Rome, and Athens, and the Serbian Scholarly Society. In Zagreb he was called upon by the government to review publications in his field and to prepare a number of books on geography for the secondary schools. In 1866 he published *Statistics of the Austrian Empire for the Upper Schools*; in 1874 *Geographical-Statistical Outline of the Austro-Hungarian Monarchy*, a book which went through a number of editions; and in 1875 *Geography for the Lower Grades of the Secondary Schools*, his most influential textbook, which appeared in several editions. His works were praised for their accuracy.[95]

Matković's contemporary was Vjenceslav Mařik, a Czech. As was the case with many of his countrymen who could not find positions at home, he went to Croatia, which lacked qualified teachers. After holding several posts, in 1858 he was appointed an instructor in the Zagreb Teachers' College. He became very active in various teachers' organizations, was a close collaborator of Ivan Filipović, and helped prepare the third grade reader after the 1874 educational reform. Disappointed by the poor quality of the textbooks, he wrote books on various subjects, including arithmetic, dictation, natural science, history, and folktales. He also prepared two geography books—*Geography of the Triune Kingdom* (1865) and *Geography and History of the Austrian Lands* (1866). Both works were used in the schools into the 1880s.[96]

The most widely read geographer was Ivan Hoić, who studied geography and history in Innsbruck, Vienna, and Heidelberg. He then became a gymnasium teacher. He published travel accounts, but more important he wrote a number of geography and history books that were used extensively in the years before the war. Among his geography books were *Geography for Public Schools* (1882), which was a general work; *Geography of the Austro-Hungarian Monarchy for the Public Schools* (1882); *Geography for the Upper Schools* (1883); *Geography for the Seventh Grade of the Upper Public Schools* (1886); *Geography for the Seventh Grade of the Upper Girls' School* (1886); *Geography for the First Grade of the Lycée*; and *Geography for the Second–Eighth Grades of the Girls' Lycée* (1909). All of his works appeared in multiple editions.[97]

Josip Modestin also studied in Germany, and he too was a gymnasium teacher. He is best known for his *Geography and Statistics of the Austro-Hungarian Monarchy* (1905) and *Geography for the Secondary Schools* (1905), which was based upon the work of Eduard Richter. Both works were reprinted. The former contained detailed information and even today is valuable for its general understanding of the organization and administration of the Triune Kingdom, as well as of the Austro-Hungarian empire.[98]

The fifth author was Vjekoslav Klaić. Best known as an historian, not a geographer, he studied in Vienna and became a gymnasium teacher in Varaždin. In 1893 he was appointed a professor of general history at the University of Zagreb, where he was recognized as one of the principal historians. In 1896 he was elected to the Yugoslav Academy.[99] Despite later works on medieval history, he began his career with two books about geography—*Bosnia—A Geography* (1878) and the three volumes of *Geography of the Lands in Which the Croats Live* (1880–83). Both of these works were published by the Matica Hrvatska, which played a major role in developing patriotism and Croatian national unity. Although neither of these works was a textbook, they both were used as supplementary reading by teachers, and they were found in the school libraries.[100]

The Lands of the Triune Kingdom and Bosnia-Hercegovina

This analysis will emphasize the contents of the secondary school books, because much of the information available in the readers on geography was already presented in chapter 3. The material found in the history books for the joint course "Geography and History" will be discussed in the next chapter. Here only a few general observations will be made. As noted before, the readers emphasized Croatian subjects—history, geography, literature, stories, folk-poetry, proverbs, fables, riddles, and so forth—all for the purpose of providing examples of the best language and literature in the štokavian "Croatian or Serbian" language written in both the Latin and Cyrillic alphabets.

Croatia and the People. All secondary school geography books covered the same basic topics for Croatia, Slavonia, Dalmatia, Bosnia, and Hercegovina: the geography and physical features of the provinces, followed by a discussion of the economy of the area, mineral resources, industries and crafts, trade and commerce, population and religious affiliation, education and culture, constitutional and administrative structure, and descriptions of the major cities and towns. The early volumes by Matković and Mařik were less detailed than those by Modestin, whose books in some respects resembled minor Baedekers, especially in their descriptions of the cities.

The volumes usually began with a description of Zagreb, the capital. They discussed the sabor, the ban's residence, the cathedral, the various public buildings, and gave the names of the streets and squares honoring national heroes, for example, Frankopan, Jurišić, Zrinski, and Jelačić. Although the same amount of detail was not provided by each author for all the cities, the principal ones in each county were usually identified, together with their most significant features. Among the most important were Varaždin, Pakrac, Osijek, Brod, Sremski Karlovci, Karlovac, Nin, Zadar, Split, Makarska, Metković, Dubrovnik, Hercegnovi, Mostar, Sarajevo, Tuzla, and Banja Luka.[101]

As was the case in the Serbian geographies, the Croatian textbooks discussed the character of the population. The authors emphasized the virtues of the Croats. Hoić, for example, offered a profile of the Croats. He described the men as strong, sturdy, and handsome; the women were beautiful, but they aged quickly because of the hard work they had to perform. The Croats were an honest, law-abiding, God-fearing people who would never betray their word and who were loyal and devoted to their monarch. They had shed their blood throughout Europe in defense of the empire. Croatia also had been a Christian barrier against Islam, thus providing the other nations of Europe with the opportunity to develop their civilizations and cultures. Historical forces had divided the Croatian nation, and only in the recent period was it in the process of being reunited. This romanticized view, of course, did not differ essentially from that which all the peoples of eastern Europe held of their own nations.[102]

Population and Religious Affiliations. In a discussion of the Croatian lands, Klaić, whose books were used only as supplementary readings, was the most explicit. He regarded as Croatian not only the Triune Kingdom, but Istria, Bosnia, and Hercegovina as well. The other authors confined the lands claimed as Croatian to those of the Triune Kingdom, although they all pointed out that Bosnia and Hercegovina had once been a part of the Croatian domains. By implication, at least, they considered them Croatian. None of the authors, including Klaić, laid claim to Serbia, Montenegro, Old Serbia, or Macedonia as Croatian lands, as had Starčević in his political program. Disagreements did, however, arise among the authors over the terms used to identify the South Slavic populations and their religions and relative strengths in the monarchy.

It will be recalled that according to the 1910 census, the Croatian population of Croatia-Slavonia was 62.5 percent and the Serbian 25. In 1871 Mařik, using the 1869 census, reported that the population of Croatia was 633,173, Slavonia 383,733, and the Military Frontier, which had not yet been incorporated, 825,113. He did not, however, identify the inhabitants, although he did indicate that there were more than one million Catholics and over one-half million Orthodox.[103] He repeated the same information in his 1878 edition. Matković, however, was more explicit in his book, which had been commissioned by the government. He wrote that "by nationality the inhabitants [of Croatia-Slavonia] are almost exclusively Croats and Serbs (96 percent)," with two-thirds of the inhabitants Catholic and one-fourth Orthodox, percentages which corresponded to those in the 1910 census.[104]

In 1880, Hoić, in his *Geography for the Public Schools*, wrote that "the inhabitants of Croatia and Slavonia and the [Military] Frontier are Croats." The other inhabitants were Germans, Hungarians, Italians, Gypsies, Albanians, Czechs, and Slovaks; the Serbs were not mentioned. As for the religion of the inhabitants: "The majority were Roman Catholic, next were those of the Greek Orthodox faith (in the Frontier almost half of the population), Greek-Catholics [Uniates], Jews, and Protestants."[105] However, two years later, in 1882, in his *Geography of the Austro-Hungarian Monarchy for the Public Schools*, he listed the Serbs, noting that "the inhabitants of Croatia and Slavonia are in the largest majority Croats and Serbs (90 percent)." Moreover, he added, "the inhabitants of Croatia and Slavonia are differentiated more by religion than by nationality." The

Catholics represented 71 percent of the population and the Orthodox 26 percent.[106] In 1883, in his *Geography for the Higher Girls' Schools—First Grade*, Hoić again indicated that "the inhabitants by nationality are Croats and Serbs (90 percent)" whereas in religion the majority were Roman Catholic, and there were many Greek Orthodox, followed by the Greek-Catholics [Uniates].[107] In 1891 he cited the 1890 census and reported the population of Croatia-Slavonia as 2,184,414, 90 percent of whom were "Croats and Serbs," with the Catholics comprising 71 percent and the Orthodox 26. Yet in 1894, during the height of the conflict between Croats and Serbs during the administration of Khuen-Héderváry, Hoić, in his *Geography for the Seventh Grade of the Higher Girls' School*, made one significant departure from his previous identification of "Croats and Serbs." Now he wrote that "the inhabitants of Croatia and Slavonia in the majority are Croats (Serbs)—namely 90 percent." The word Serbs was put in parenthesis after Croats, which one could interpret to mean that the Serbs were Croats. He used the same identification for Dalmatia. Nevertheless, with respect to religion, he repeated his previous statement that "the inhabitants in Croatia and Slavonia are differentiated more by religion than by nationality," citing again the ratio of 71 percent Catholics and 26 percent Orthodox.[108] Fourteen years later, in 1908, in the era of the Croatian-Serbian Coalition, in his *Geography for the First Grade of the Lyceum* he reiterated his original statements that the population was "Croats and Serbs (88 percent)," whose religion was 72 percent Catholic and 26 percent Orthodox.[109]

In 1905 Modestin, in his *Geography for the Secondary Schools* and *Geography and Statistics for the Austro-Hungarian Monarchy for the Secondary Schools*, agreed that the population was "Croatian and Serbian." In the 1905 and 1912 editions of his textbook on geography and statistics, he wrote that the inhabitants were "by nationality Croats and Serbs . . . with 71 percent Catholics and 25.5 percent Orthodox."[110] Thus, with the exception of Hoić's deviation, the geography books were basically consistent. Yet Klaić's works, which were popular and were used as supplementary reference works in the earlier years, should be emphasized, because his views were fundamentally different from those of the other authors.

In his book *Geography of the Lands in Which the Croats Live* (1880–83), Klaić maintained that when these lands were initially settled by the Croats, the entire area was called Croatia. In time, different regions took on the various names of Dalmatia, Istria, Bosnia, and Slavonia with only Croatia proper retaining the original designation. The population of these lands numbered 3,726,388, but Klaić noted that "the inhabitants of the Croatian lands are not all by origin Croats. There are 3,486,351 Croats, and the remaining 240,037 inhabitants are of different nationality and language, namely Italian, Slovene, German, Magyar, Turkish, etc. The Italians are the most numerous and live mainly in Istria and Dalmatia. The Slovenes are found in Istria, the Germans (32,000) and also Magyars (15,000) reside for the most part in Slavonia. There are a few Osmanlis, and they live in Bosnia-Hercegovina." Thus, continued Klaić, "it is evident that there are not many foreign people in the Croatian lands. It is most difficult for the Croats in Istria where they comprise about half the population; whereas Bosnia and Hercegovina are the purest Croatian lands." Missing from this list, of course, are the Serbs.[111]

In his other volume, *Bosnia—A Geography*, Klaić stated that the Croats were distinguished from the other inhabitants by their language, since "the national language [was] the sole criterion of nationality."[112] The Croats spoke three dialects—kajkavian, čakavian and štokavian—with the latter the youngest but "also the most beautiful Croatian dialect." It was spoken by the majority of the Croats whose "literary language . . . was the ijekavian or Hercegovinian variant of the štokavian dialect."[113]

Klaić also wrote that the Croats were divided by religion—"Roman Catholic, Greek Orthodox, and Muslim." The difference between the Catholic Croats and "the Croats of the Greek Orthodox rite (Orthodox Serbs)" was, according to Klaić, that the latter did not recognize the pope. Instead they had their own "patriarch [Serbian], who resided in lower Karlovac [in Srem]." Their Bible was in Cyrillic, they followed the Julian, not the Gregorian, calendar, and their religious customs were akin to those of the Greeks, Russians, Bulgarians, and Romanians. There also were Croats who were "Greek Catholics or Uniates." Klaić's explanation of why the "Croats of the Muslim faith (Turks)" accepted Islam was the same as that in the Serbian textbooks, namely, that they wished to protect their property and status following the Ottoman conquest.[114]

To clarify why many of the Croats called themselves Serbs, Klaić stated:

> Many Croats of the Greek Orthodox rite today call themselves *Serbs*, in fact many (especially peasants) say *that they are of the Serbian faith*. The reason that so many Orthodox Croats call themselves Serbs comes from these facts—first, many of them indeed come from Serbian areas, from which they fled before the Turks (Ottomans) into Croatian lands, and, second, because they are of the same faith or rite with the Serbs in the present independent

principalities of Serbia and Montenegro. Yet notwithstanding this, they are one and the same people with the other Croats because they speak *one and the same Croatian language.*[115]

Anticipating the question why he did not use the terms "Croats and Serbs" or "Croat-Serbs," Klaić, in the preface to his volume on Bosnia, wrote: "In this book I exclusively employ the name Croatian and that is because I do not like the name Croatian-Serbian. If some Croat, to whom the name Serbian is preferable, reads this book, let him remember that Croat and Serb are two names for one and the same people, and he should not reproach me [because I], who was born a Croat, [find] the name Croatian more precious."[116]

Given these reasons, it is understandable why Klaić, in describing the population of Croatia-Slavonia, would write that the people were "in the greatest majority *Croats.* Of every 100 inhabitants 96 are Croats and only 4 are of another origin. In truth it is well known to us that a large number of the Croats in Croatia and Slavonia are called *Serbs*, especially those who are of the Greek Orthodox faith."[117] Yet they were all Croats, because the only peoples in Croatia-Slavonia, aside from the Croats, were Germans, Magyars, and Italians. He used the same explanation when he wrote about Dalmatia, Bosnia, and Hercegovina. In Istria, however, he readily acknowledged the Slovenes, whom he considered a separate Slavic nation with their own language.

Dalmatia was the third land in the historic Triune Kingdom. The Croatian geographers took it as an article of faith that Dalmatia was Croatian. The information in the textbooks was largely factual. Hence the geographers did not stray far from the percentages given in the 1910 census, which reported South Slavs as being 82.5 percent Catholic and 16.3 percent Orthodox. In 1875 Matković wrote that the inhabitants were "almost exclusively of Croatian-Serbian origin [*plemena*], 89 percent," with 10 percent of the population Italian. Catholics were 82 percent and 18 percent were Orthodox.[118] For the next year, 1876, Mařik stated that the population was 475,000, "almost all Croats and Serbs," with 45,000 Italians in the cities and islands. Most of the Dalmatians were Catholics and the "Orthodox were not one-fifth" of the total.[119] In 1880, Hoić, however, did not mention the Serbs, indicating instead only that "the inhabitants were Croats with about 10 percent Italians," but he acknowledged that "one-sixth, 16.5 percent," were Orthodox. He repeated these views in 1882. In subsequent editions of his book, he stated that the population was "by nationality almost all Croats and Serbs (97 percent)."[120] Finally, Modestin noted that "the inhabitants by nationality are almost totally only Croats and Serbs (97 percent), and by religion a majority Catholic of the Latin and Uniate faith (84 percent), whereas the remainder are Greek Orthodox (16 percent)."[121]

After presenting a report on the development of elementary and secondary education in Dalmatia, Modestin in his 1905 textbook stated that "Croatian was the language of instruction in all the secondary schools," with Italian only in the gymnasium and realka in Zadar. In his 1912 edition he modified this statement to read "Croatian is the language of instruction" in both elementary and secondary schools. It is not clear why he made these statements, since the language for the schools was listed as "Croatian or Serbian."[122] Nor had Modestin used the term Croatian to identify the language of instruction when he discussed education in Croatia, Slavonia, Bosnia, and Hercegovina. Instead he used the authorized identification, "Croatian or Serbian."

The geographers paid just as much attention to Dubrovnik as the authors of the readers had. None of the geographers, however, cited any population figures for Dubrovnik, satisfied that it was understood the city was Croatian, a view substantiated by the 1910 census. It listed the population for the entire Dubrovnik district as 37,252, of whom 36,202 or 97.1 percent were Croats and 1,043 or 2.8 percent were Serbs.[123] However, the geographers cited the same evidence found in the readers to support the Croatian claims. Thus Matković wrote in 1875 that "Croatian poetry blossomed in the sixteenth and seventeenth centuries" in Dubrovnik. Mařik noted that "Dubrovnik can be called the cradle of Croatian poetry, literature, and art" as represented in the works of Gundulić, Palmotić, Djordjić, and Bošković. Hoić referred to the city as "the Slavic Athens." Modestin proudly proclaimed that "Dubrovnik was in the sixteenth and seventeenth centuries 'the queen of the Croatian cities,' 'the Slavic Athens,' where Croatian poetry blossomed forth most beautifully."[124]

Again Klaić was the most positive in his statements. "The inhabitants of Dalmatia are in the largest majority *Croats.* Of every 100 inhabitants 89 are Croats, and only 11 are of another origin. In addition to the Croats there are in the land . . . up to 46,000 *Italians,* and after that some Germans and other nationalities." He did not mention Serbs. He did, however, state that 82 percent of the inhabitants were Catholics and 18 percent were of "the Greek-Eastern or Orthodox" faith.[125] Concerning Dubrovnik, Klaić provided a detailed history of the city and specified its numerous contributions to Croatian history, adding that "it would be difficult simply to enumerate all the individuals who saw the light of day in Dubrovnik."[126]

Similarly in their discussion of the peninsula of Istria, the Croatian geographers omitted any mention of the Serbs. As noted earlier, there were less than 2,000 Serbs or Orthodox in Istria in a total population of 403,566, of whom 168,143 were Croats, 147,417 Italians, and 55,134 Slovenes. Consequently, in the textbooks the issue was not whether the land was Croatian or Serbian, but Croatian or Italian. Among the authors, Mařik wrote that the inhabitants were Italians and Slavs, the latter being Slovenes and Croats. Hoić noted that "in Istria the Croats are in the majority." Modestin added that in the Austrian littoral two-thirds of the population were "Croats and Slovenes, one-third Italians. . . . The Croats comprise the majority of inhabitants in Istria, the Slovenes in Gorica-Gradiska, the Italians in Trieste." Klaić's more detailed views need not be cited, except to say that he made a point of emphasizing that both Croats and Slovenes lived in Istria. He recognized the Slovenes as a separate nation, as did the other geographers.[127]

Whereas in their discussion of Croatia, Slavonia, Dalmatia, and Istria the authors had simply presented evidence that to them seemed obvious and needed no justification, such was not the case with Bosnia-Hercegovina. Here it was apparent that they had to defend Croatian claims, which they did in different ways—for example, through the organization and presentation in their books, the selective use of adjectives, and other means. Their position was understandable because the 1910 census listed only 22 percent of the population as Catholics, not all of whom were Croats, whereas the Orthodox numbered about 44 percent and the Muslims 33 percent.[128]

In 1880, Hoić, who recognized his debt to Klaić's book on Bosnia, wrote that the population in Bosnia-Hercegovina "was in the largest part Croats (Serbs)," plus some Albanians, Gypsies, Jews, and Turks. In 1883 in his geography for the girls' schools he again used the unique nomenclature "Croats (Serbs)" to identify the inhabitants. Yet, in both these books he acknowledged that there were "about one-half million Greek Orthodox, somewhat fewer Muslims, and not quite one-fourth million Catholics."[129] However, in 1882 in his geography of the Habsburg empire, he wrote that the inhabitants of Bosnia-Hercegovina by nationality were "almost exclusively Croats and Serbs." In fact, all of his subsequent textbooks through 1909 used the same terminology, "Croats and Serbs." In addition, he used the correct percentages for the religious division.[130]

Both in 1905 and in 1912, Josip Modestin noted that "the inhabitants by nationality were almost totally Croats and Serbs (97 percent)." He also concluded "that as was generally the case in the East, so it was in Bosnia: the religious divisions were more important" than nationality.[131]

In their discussion and description of the cities in the two provinces the authors sought to strengthen the impression of Croatia's influence there. As a result, one read about "the Gothic Catholic Cathedral" in Sarajevo, "the famous Franciscan monastery" in Sutjeska, "the well-known Franciscan monastery" in Kruševo, "the Trappist monastery" in Delibasino, "the seat of the Catholic bishopric" in Banja Luka, "the Jesuit gymnasium" in Travnik, and "the seat of the Catholic bishop" in Mostar. Since Catholicism was regarded as synonymous with Croatianism in these regions, from the enumeration of these institutions the reader gained the impression that the Croats were more important in these provinces than the Serbs or Slavic Muslims. The books also included information on the Croatian schools as well as on the number of Croatian representatives in the Bosnian assembly.[132]

In contrast to the majority of authors, Klaić presented an extreme case. He described Bosnia and Hercegovina as the "largest" Croatian land, "somewhat smaller that the principality of Serbia." He regarded "the inhabitants of Bosnia and Hercegovina, excluding a few individuals of other nationalities, exclusively Croats." Yet, he added "that in honesty this name [Croats] is not heard much because national consciousness had disappeared among the people, consequently the regional name (Bosnian, Hercegovian) or the religious name (Turk, Serb, Latin) is mentioned. However, the national language, the sole determinant of nationality, demonstrates and proves that these people are of Croatian origin." Nevertheless, he admitted that the "Bosnian Croats themselves called their language 'Bosnian' or 'naški' [our language], and less often Croatian or Serbian."[133]

Klaić was disturbed by the various epithets used by representatives of the three religious bodies to identify one another. The Muslims called the Catholics and Orthodox "Vlasi," a derogatory term for those of another faith, and the Christians labeled the Muslims "Turks or Bosnians." The Orthodox referred to the Catholics as "Šokci or Latins," and they in turn were derided by the Catholics as "Šijaci or Kudrovi." Still others called the Orthodox "Serbs, because they were of the same rite as the neighboring Serbs; and the Catholics [were labeled] Latins, because they followed the Latin (Roman) rites. How many names there are for one and the same Croatian people!" Klaić lamented.[134]

Their religious divisions notwithstanding, Klaić claimed that the Orthodox, Muslims, and Catholics were all Croats; historical events had produced the division and modern developments had accentuated the problem. His explanation was clear. Unable to free themselves of Ottoman rule, "the Orthodox Croats, who best of all preserved the old Croatian character with all its virtues and faults" turned to "Russia, the defender of all the Orthodox Slavs," as well as to Serbia and Montenegro, for assistance. "Seeing that they were of the same faith as the Serbs," many Orthodox Croats "began to call their own religion 'Serbian' and themselves Serbs. However, this was a great mistake, which the Muslims also make, when, because of their religion, they are called Turks. In the same way that the Muslim Croats are in no way Turks, even though they have the same faith as the Turks, so too are the Orthodox Croats not 'Serbs,' even though they are of the same faith as the Serbs in Serbia." Hence, Klaić added, "all the Bosnians, regardless of their religion, are sons of a Croatian mother and . . . Bosnia is the proud and most beautiful pearl in the ancient crown of Croatia, which will be able, with the united cooperation of all its sons, to glisten once again in its former glory."[135]

There is no precise way to judge the extent to which the views in Klaić's reference books influenced the students. Yet they cannot be dismissed for several reasons. First, his books were published by the very influential Matica Hrvatska and the Society of Saint Jerome. Second, Klaić was a member of the Party of Right, which, as described previously, did not recognize the existence of Serbs in the Croatian lands. Furthermore, since the party found great support among the young intellectuals, teachers, and clergy in the 1880s and 1890s, precisely during the era when the Serbian leadership in Croatia-Slavonia was cooperating closely with Khuen-Héderváry's regime, one can conclude that Klaić's views were in all probability introduced into the classroom. Moreover, since "geography and history" were a joint course in the upper grades of the public schools and since Klaić wrote several authorized history textbooks for the secondary schools (which will be discussed in the next chapter), it is safe to assume that his general views were known to many students. However, it should be stressed that Matković, Mařik, Hoić, and Modestin, the authors of the authorized geography books, did not incorporate Klaić's beliefs into their works. At the same time, these authors put forth historical and ethnic arguments to substantiate the Croatian interests in Bosnia-Hercegovina. The difference between them and Klaić was that they acknowledged that in Austria-Hungary there was a "Croatian and Serbian" population, not one exclusively Croatian.

Here it is instructive to note the similarity of Klaić's and Karić's views in the geography books. Both used language as the criterion to identify their nation. Neither used the terms "Croatian or Serbian" or "Serbian and Croatian" to identify the language and people. Religious differences were attributed to historical factors. The one major difference between the two scholars was that Klaić did not assert that Serbia, Montenegro, Old Serbia, and Macedonia were Croatian lands, whereas Karić claimed Croatia, Slavonia, Dalmatia, and Istria as Serbian.

Serbs within the Austro-Hungarian Empire. For all the provinces discussed, the geography books had detailed information on the presence of Serbs in these lands. Beginning with Croatia-Slavonia, they noted that in Zagreb there was an Orthodox church and pointed out that Karlovac and Pakrac each had an Orthodox bishopric, with the latter also having an Orthodox teachers' college. The most information, however, was about Srem, the eastern district of Slavonia, which had a predominantly Serbian population. Mařik and Matković noted that the Serbian patriarch had his residence in Sremski Karlovci. Both Hoić and Modestin wrote about the patriarchate and the Orthodox theological seminary and gymnasium in Karlovci. They mentioned the monasteries, listing most of them by name, that were located on Fruška Gora. Krušedol was described as "the mausoleum of Serbian despots, patriarchs, metropolitans, and kings." They associated Hopovo with Dositej Obradović and noted that "the remains of Prince Lazar" rested in Ravanica. In Dalmatia the Orthodox bishoprics in Zadar and Kotor were identified, as was the fact that their bishop was a member of the Dalmatian sabor. They also named the counties where Serbs resided in large numbers.[136]

The main Orthodox religious centers and institutions were identified in Bosnia and Hercegovina; for example, the three metropolitanates in Sarajevo, Banja Luka, and Tuzla, as well as the bishopric in Mostar. The Serbian gymnasiums in Sarajevo, Tuzla, and Mostar were singled out. The students learned that the metropolitans and the "vice-president of the administrative and educational council of the Serbian Orthodox church" were members of the Bosnian sabor. The textbooks reported that of the seventy-two elected members of the sabor, the law prescribed that thirty-one were to represent the Orthodox curia, twenty-four the Muslim, and eighteen the Catholic.[137]

Serbia, Montenegro, and the Serbs in the Ottoman Empire

Much of the information in the geography books about the Serbs living outside of Austria-Hungary repeated that found in the reading or history textbooks, but not in the same detail. In other words, the geography books reaffirmed what the students learned in other courses, but with added statistical data.

In 1875 Matković wrote that Serbia was 43,555 square kilometers in size, with a population of 1,340,000. Since 1815 Serbia had
been autonomous and had made considerable progress. It had seven
hundred elementary schools, a university with three faculties, a
theological seminary, a teachers' college and a military academy.[138]
In 1876 Mařik was more explicit. Serbia, he wrote, "was just about
as large as the Triune Kingdom." It still paid tribute to the Ottoman
empire, but "otherwise it enjoyed complete autonomy, which it
gained after extended warfare in 1815." To explain how this had
come about, Mařik added that "Serbia was once a powerful, influential, and wealthy empire. However the wild Turks destroyed her in
1389 on the battlefield of Kosovo. Since then the Serbian nation had
been under the Turkish yoke and had endured unbearable slavery
until finally the opportunity arose to create an autonomous state.
Serbia, especially in the most recent period, had progressed in education, crafts, and trade." Belgrade was "the center of the spiritual development of the Serbian nation."[139]

In the 1880s and 1890s Hoić, in his various textbooks, repeated
much of the same information and added other facts. He described
the physical geography of Serbia and noted that "since the beginning
of this century when it freed itself of the Turkish yoke, the young
principality has progressed very well. Elementary education is advancing well and there are a good number of secondary schools.
Higher education is promoted by the Serbian Literary Society, the
university with three faculties, the military academy, a theology
school, etc."[140]

In the next decade Hoić repeated what he had written earlier,
but added that Serbia was a constitutional monarchy ruled by the
Karadjordjević dynasty. Ninety percent of the population was Serbian and Orthodox, with two minorities, Romanians in the northeast and Bulgarians in the southeast. Scholarship and cultural development were fostered by the Serbian Academy, as well as by the
resources of the national library, which had 40,000 volumes and
manuscripts. Information was provided about many cities, including
Belgrade, Smederovo, Kragujevac, Šabac, Požarevac, Negotin, Kruševac and Niš.[141]

All the volumes praised the legendary heroism of the Montenegrins. Students were told that the Ottomans never succeeded in totally subduing them and that in the "battles the Montenegrin
women also acquitted themselves very bravely." Until 1851 Montenegro had been ruled by bishops, thereafter it was a secular state
under the Petrović dynasty. The country was divided into districts
and clans. In 1909 Hoić added that "the population was, except for

some Albanians and Turks, of Serbian or Croatian tribes" with the religion overwhelmingly Orthodox. Tribute was paid to Petar Petrović Njegoš, the poet, for his epic "The Mountain Wreath." There were brief descriptions of Cetinje, Nikšić, and Podgorica, as well as of the tomb of Njegoš on the top of Mount Lovćen.[142]

Concerning Macedonia and Old Serbia, which were still under Ottoman rule, the authors gave essentially factual information. Thessaloniki was the birthplace of Cyril and Methodius, the Slavic apostles. Skopje had at one time served as the capital of the Serbian rulers, and it was here that Dušan had issued his law code. Marko Kraljević called Prilep his home; Prizren had once been the capital of the Serbian rulers; Peć was the former seat of the Serbian patriarchs. To the south of Priština, one found the famous monastery of Gračanica; Kosovo was located in Old Serbia.[143]

All the information about the Serbs in these lands was basically correct, with the exception of Hoić's comment in 1909 that the inhabitants of Montenegro were "Serbs or Croats." There may have been a few Croats living in Montenegro, but most certainly the Slavic population was Montenegrin or Serbian. The books left no doubt that the Serbian nation was comprised of the Serbs in the two independent states together with those still under Austro-Hungarian and Ottoman rule.

Before we conclude our study of the geography books, we should note what was written about the Slovenes. Although they were largely ignored in the readers and history books, the geography texts included much material about them, since students were required to learn the geography of the Habsburg empire, including the lands inhabited by the Slovenians. Very little information, however, was given in the elementary school books, where the empire was studied in very general terms. Detailed information about the Slovenes was found only in the secondary school geography books; thus, only about 5 percent of the students read about the Slovenes, or, put another way, about 95 percent learned very little. In other words, the exception was the Croatian secondary school geography, which, in contrast to the other Croatian and Serbian textbooks, did present information on the Slovenes.

All the geographers—Mařik, Matković, Hoić, and Modestin—gave information on the Slovenes, with the best discussion found in the books by Hoić and Modestin. It is not necessary to cite what each author wrote about the Slovenes. It is sufficient to note that they provided detailed information on the Slovenian population in all the provinces in which it was found. They described Ljubljana in considerable detail, and there was adequate information on other

Slovenian centers—Maribor (Marburg), Celje (Cilli), Celovec (Klagenfurt), Velikovec (Völkermarkt), and Beljak (Villach). In addition, factual information was provided on the history of the provinces and their current economic development. On balance, advanced students learned as much about these lands as they did about the other provinces of the Habsburg monarchy or about the Serbs within the South Slav lands.[144]

To summarize, then, the primary emphasis in the Croatian geography books was on population and religion. This information was largely factual, aimed at demonstrating the strength of the Croats and of their institutions within the Dual Monarchy and, at the same time, acknowledging the role of the Serbs and their institutions. For most of the authors, language was not an issue, as it was for Klaić and the Serbian geographers, or for the authors of the Croatian or Serbian readers. Only if the Croatian geographers had insisted that all štokavian speakers were Croats, could they have advanced territorial claims beyond the frontiers of the Habsburg empire, that is, into Serbia, Old Serbia, Montenegro, and Macedonia. Even Klaić did not advocate that.

The contrast in the contents of the Serbian and Croatian geography books, how each influenced the students, and what they tell us about prospects for South Slav understanding and unification is apparent. The Serbian books laid claim to all the Croatian lands—Croatia, Slavonia, and Dalmatia. They based their case primarily on a linguistic argument. In addition, they used facts, figures, and historical arguments to support their claims to these lands. The Croatian books concentrated on describing the lands of the Triune Kingdom, and they made it clear that other peoples, including Serbs, lived here. Bosnia-Hercegovina did, however, pose questions for the authors. Although not claiming these lands outright, except for Klaić, their books made it clear that Croats did live in these provinces and that Croatia did have an obligation to defend their interests. None of the Croatian books, however, advanced any claims to Serbia, Montenegro, Old Serbia, or Macedonia, which were regarded as Serbian domains.

Certainly if a student relied on the information in the geography books, he would not have been given a strong case for Yugoslav unity. The Serbian authors saw the South Slav lands as part of their unique heritage; their Croatian counterparts emphasized their own history and their leading role among the South Slavs of the Habsburg Empire.

5

History—National or South Slavic

INTRODUCTION

Of the three categories of books here examined—literature, geography, and history—the history books in one respect were the most important. They presented in narrative form a broad sweep of each nation's history, whereas the readers and geography books provided selective information on specific subjects. In the history textbooks the student read about the notable achievements of his nation, the prominent rulers and individuals and their accomplishments, the hardships the nation endured, the sacrifices his ancestors had made, individual acts of heroism, and the nation's adversaries. In their specialized monographs some of the textbook authors produced works that met the criteria of impartiality expected of scholars, but in their school textbooks, their writings followed their national flag. This characteristic was common to all the nations of Europe, and to the United States, in the nineteenth century, when the goal of education was, as in the South Slav lands, to instill the principles of citizenship, patriotism, and loyalty.

As was the case with the geography books, the textbooks available for history in the Serbian elementary schools were not comparable with those in the Croatian. From 1883 to 1899 Serbian history was taught as a separate course in the Serbian fourth grade. Following the curriculum change in 1899 a new course was introduced entitled "Geography with Serbian History," which was taught in the third and fourth grades. Nevertheless, under both curriculums there were separate textbooks for history and geography. In Croatia, history was not a separate course in the elementary schools, but was always taught in conjunction with geography, physics, and natural science from a common reader. On the other hand, there were separate textbooks for history in both the Serbian and Croatian secondary schools.

SERBIAN HISTORY TEXTBOOKS

The history textbooks were indeed effective in presenting and interpreting the history of the Serbian nation. They gave information on the major events, including the arrival of the Serbs in the Balkans; their conversion to Christianity; the achievements of the Nemanjas, especially Saint Sava and Dušan; life under Ottoman rule; the history of the Serbian revolution, including the internal strife among its leaders; and the main developments of the nineteenth century. On essential questions, there was no fundamental disagreement between the readers and the geography and history books, although on some problems there was a shift in emphasis, in part because the history books presented events in greater detail.

The Authors

The authors of the elementary history books were primarily school teachers. The most important author was Mihailo Jović. His *Serbian History Adapted for the Present-day Elementary Schools* was published in 1882; its title was subsequently changed to *Serbian History for the Fourth Grade of the Elementary Schools*. By 1913 it had reached its thirty-fifth edition. Its principal competitors were Joksim St. Marković's *Serbian History for the Fourth Grade of the Elementary Schools* and *Biographies from the Most Recent Serbian History for the Youth in the Lower Elementary Schools* and Mihailo M. Stanojević's *History of the Serbian People for the Fourth Grade of the Elementary Schools*. Other books were written by S. Antonović and Petar M. Niketić; L. Lazarević and P. K. Šreplović; A. Milojković; Petar Niketić; and Milan S. Ubavkić.[1]

There were five prominent authors of secondary school textbooks—Jovan Djordjević, Ljubomir Jovanović, Ljubomir Kovačević, Stanoje Stanojević, and Milenko Vukičević. Three of these men— Djordjević, Jovanović, and Kovačević—served as ministers of education. Jovan Djordjević was first a gymnasium teacher in Novi Sad, and subsequently a professor in and then principal of the Šabac and Belgrade gymnasiums and the Belgrade Teachers' College. In 1888 he was appointed professor of general history at the University in Belgrade, and in 1891 he became minister of education. He wrote two books, *General History for the Second Grades* and *History of the Serbian People from the Oldest to the Most Recent Period for the Secondary Schools and the Public.*[2]

Kovačević and Jovanović were the authors of the well-known two-volume *History of the Serbian People for the Secondary Schools in the Kingdom of Serbia*, which, however, covered only the period through the battle of Kosovo. Kovačević taught in various schools in Serbia, first as a botany and mathematics instructor. In 1877 he was appointed to the Serbian Academy, and later, in 1894, he became a professor of history at the university. Twice he was minister of education, initially serving in the Stojan Novaković cabinet, 1895–97 and again in 1901. In 1906 he became the secretary of the Serbian Academy. Kovačević belonged to the critical school of historians who "fought against the traditional understanding and romantic patriotism in Serbian scholarship." He worked extensively with historical documents and published many texts.[3]

His co-author, Ljubomir Jovanović, was born in Kotor, Montenegro, completed his education in Belgrade and was a volunteer in the Serbo-Bulgarian War of 1885. Subsequently, he was a professor in the Belgrade gymnasium, served as director of the National Library, and in 1903 was appointed professor at the university. In 1905 he began his political career, first as a representative in the skupština, subsequently serving as its vice-president and president. In 1909 and 1910 he was minister of interior, and then served as minister of education from June 1911 to November 1914, in which capacity he issued the directive in 1912 that more information should be included in the textbooks about Croatia. His scholarly contributions to Serbian historiography were not extensive and were largely limited to the medieval period of Serbian history.[4]

The most distinguished of the group was Stanoje Stanojević. With the exception of Djordjević, who briefly studied medicine in Budapest, he was the only one of the five who was educated abroad. He received his doctorate from the University of Vienna, working with Vatroslav Jagić and Konstantin Jiriček. He also studied with two prominent Byzantinists, F. I. Uspenskii in Russia and Karl Krumbacher in Munich. He was most influenced, however, by the works of Edward Gibbon. Because of his caustic reviews of the works of senior scholars, his appointment to the university was delayed until 1900 when he became a docent and in 1905 an associate professor. However, he was not promoted to full professor until 1919. After the war he was made editor of *The National Serbian-Croatian-Slovenian Encyclopedia*, and he also edited the interwar publication *History of the Serbian People in the Nineteenth Century*, of which only fifteen of the projected twenty volumes were published. The author of many notable scholarly works, in 1908 he and his colleague L. Zrnić published *The History of the Serbian People for the Secondary Schools*, which initially served as supplementary reading, in part because it did not reflect the romantic nationalist spirit found in so many of the other history books. Stanojević was also highly critical of Milenko Vukičević's authorized volumes, a view that could be interpreted as a criticism of the Education Council and the minister of education for approving them.[5]

Of the five authors, Vukičević's books were most widely used. Denied an appointment at the university, he served as a professor of history in the Belgrade gymnasium. A supporter of the Socialists in his youth, he later joined Pašić's ruling Radical Party. He was a member of King Peter's inner circle when, in 1906, he published Garašanin's *Načertanije*. A member of the romantic school of Serbian historians, he is best known for his two-volume biography of Karadjordje and other works on the Serbian revolution. In 1902 he published one part of a two-volume *History of the Serbian People for the Secondary Schools*, which remained an approved textbook into the interwar years.[6]

This analysis of the Serbian history books will begin with a discussion of the information found in all the history books published prior to 1912. It will be followed by an examination of the major differences in content between Vukičević's 1914 edition and his previous volumes.

The Serbs: Their Nation, Religion, and Lands

In the centuries between the arrival of the Serbs in the Balkans and the Serbian revolution, the character of the Serbian nation was affected by its conversion to Christianity, the creation of the medieval state, and subsequent Ottoman rule. The theme that held these developments together in the history books concerned the lands where the Serbs settled. Almost without exception every general survey of Serbian history began with a discussion of the Serbs and the Slavs, including their origin, their particular characteristics, and the lands they settled in the Balkans. As was the case in the readers and geography books, the importance of language, religion, and customs was stressed. All the history books especially emphasized that the original Slavs were all Serbs. In 1882 Jović, in describing the Slavs and their ancestral homeland, wrote: "they [the Slavs] were then still called Serbs."[7] In 1891 Ubavkić added that "at the beginning they [the Slavs] were one people and therefore they were called by one name, Serbs."[8] It was left to Vukičević to make this point most explicitly in 1904.

> All the Slavs at one time were called *Serbs*, and only from the sixth century after Christ did they begin to be called *Slavs*. In the beginning they were one people, who were composed of a number of tribes. Subsequently these tribes increased and then each was called by its own name. Thus from the Slavs an entire people emerged. Of all the Slavs only we and the Lusatian Sorbs retain our old national name *Serb*.[9]

These statements had a direct bearing on the other authors' perception of the Croats. As noted in the discussion of the readers and geography books, the Catholic Slavs in Croatia who spoke štokavian were identified as Serbs, not Croats. In 1900 Djordjević reiterated this point. "All the Serbian tribes (the best known . . . Lusatian, Serbian, Croatian . . .) were the same in language and custom and comprised one large entity—the Serbian nation. . . . Among these Serbian tribes the largest and the best known, it seems, was the Serbian tribe and after them their neighbors the Croats."[10] It was unfortunate, Djordjević continued, that the other Slavs did not retain the name Serb but adopted the name of their own tribe. Previously Ubavkić had written: "To the west of the Serbs, across the river Una, the Serbian tribe [called] the Croats settled." However, he added, "to the east of the Serbs, across the river Iskra [that is, in Bulgaria] some Slavic tribes had settled."[11] This distinction made it clear that the Croats were a Serbian tribe, not a separate nation as were the Bulgars. Jović emphasized this point in the 1896 and 1902 editions of his book by referring to their common language when he stated that "we Serbs and Croats speak the same language, which is why it is said about them that we are one people."[12] Mihailo Stanojević reiterated this view when he wrote: "The Croats speak essentially the same language as we do."[13] Hence, it must be strongly stressed that within the context of the textbooks the historians saw the Serbs and Croats as two tribes of the Serbian nation with different names for the same people. Their historic origin and their language identified them as Serbs, notwithstanding their religious differences and the historical experiences over the preceding millennium. Thus the references to the Croats in the textbooks are not to be construed as though they referred to a separate nation.

As was the case with the geography books, the history textbooks emphasized the issue of the identification of the Serbian lands. Both historic rights and the ethnic principle were stressed, with a greater emphasis on the former. The textbooks also devoted considerable attention to the Serbian ancestral homeland, variously described as beyond the Carpathians, (that is, in the western parts of what is now the Soviet Union). The Asiatic invasions destroyed this center and one group of Slavs moved southward, with the Serbs finally settling in the Balkans in the seventh century.

What happened thereafter was important because without exception the authors looked back to the medieval era to justify the Serbian claims to the South Slav lands. The books identified the lands by their medieval as well as their contemporary names, for example, Hum-Hercegovina, Zeta-Montenegro, Raška-Old Serbia; they also gave their present-day boundaries. Using this information, together with that learned in the geography books, the student could immediately recognize the extent of the Serbian *otadžbina* or fatherland. In these descriptions, it should be noted, Banat, Bačka, Bosnia-Hercegovina, Dalmatia, Old Serbia, Montenegro, and Macedonia, and some even added Slavonia, were described as Serbian territory. For example, Jović wrote in his elementary textbook that in the seventh century the Byzantine Emperor Heraclius approved the settlement of the Serbs in Macedonia and, in fact, "gave them the Macedonian lands." They established their city Srpčiste (Srbica) near Thessaloniki. Eventually, however, they withdrew to the north and "settled near their brothers the *Croats* and the other *Slavs* who had settled in the Greek [Byzantine] lands even before the Serbs." The Serbs thus settled "in the west to the Adriatic Sea, in the north somewhat beyond the Sava and Danube, in the east to the Timok [River] and in the south up to Lake Ohrid." In another elementary textbook published in 1908 M. M. Stanojević wrote that the Serbs settled between the Una, Timok, Danube, and Thessaloniki.[14]

Djordjević in his secondary school textbook stated that the Serbs had seized and settled Banat, Bačka, Srem, Slavonia, Croatia, Istria, Dalmatia, Bosnia, Hercegovina, Montenegro, Serbia, Old Serbia (Serbia under the Turks), Macedonia, and the western parts of present-day Bulgaria and Romania. He added, "Here, as in the ancestral home, the Serbian tribe the Croats (Brdjani), who settled on the spurs of the Alps, retained their old name."[15]

Vukičević provided more details. He stated that in the seventh century "the Serbs arrived with the Croats. . . . The Serbs took the opportunity to settle between the Una and Timok, the Danube and Thessaloniki and the Croats [settled] northwest of the Serbs." A few pages later Vukičević elaborated on this.

The new fatherland of the Serbs extended from the Drava and Tamiš southward across the Sava and Danube and reached to the plains of Thessaloniki and to Mount Olympus and the Pindus Mountains, and in present-day Albania to the city of Durrës. In the

> west the boundaries of the Serbian fatherland extended to the river Una, Cetina and the Adriatic Sea and in the east beyond the Sredac (Sofia) province and the Rhodope Mountains. The provinces that comprised the land on which the Serbian tribe was dispersed when they settled in their new fatherland were *Serbia, Old Serbia with Macedonia, Bosnia, Hercegovina, Dalmatia, Montenegro with northern Albania, Slavonia, Srem, Banat, and the Vidin and Sredac provinces.*[16]

He did not include Croatia and Istria.

Stanoje Stanojević with his co-author Zrnić wrote that the Slavs had settled in the Balkans "as . . . tribes," whose numbers and size were not known. Two tribes, the Serbs and Croats, were the strongest, and soon others joined them. The Croats settled "in the northwestern regions of the Balkan peninsula and some land outside the peninsula"; the Serbs "essentially settled in the present-day Serbian lands: *Serbia, Montenegro, Dalmatia, Srem, Bačka, Banat, Bosnia, Hercegovina, Old Serbia,* and one part of *Macedonia.*" The authors thus omitted Croatia as well as Slavonia from their list of Serbian provinces. From the beginning, they asserted, the boundary between the Serbs and Croats was "the Cetina and Una [rivers] but later the Serbs settled also one part of Croatia."[17]

Vukičević summarized what others had written about the *otadžbina* or fatherland. It included the lands in which the people "speak the Serbian language and . . . are of Serbian origin." They lived in Bosnia, Hercegovina, Croatia, Slavonia, Dalmatia, Banat, Bačka, and Montenegro, as well as in Old Serbia and Macedonia. "All these lands in which the people speak the Serbian language are *the fatherland of the Serbian people.*"[18]

The reference by Jović and Vukičević to the Serbian lands as extending southward from the Drava and Tamiš or as being somewhat north of the Sava and Danube included Slavonia, which encompassed much of the Military Frontier, as well as Srem, Bačka, and Banat. The reference to the Una-Cetina river boundary by M. M. Stanojević, S. Stanojević and Zrnić, and Vukičević roughly corresponded to the western boundary of Bosnia, implying that the province was Serbian. Or as one author put it, the lands beyond were Croatian. The reference to the Cetina River also meant that Dalmatia south of the city of Omiš, near Split, was regarded as historic Serbian territory. This area included Dubrovnik. Thereafter throughout the different time periods—medieval, Ottoman, and modern—when discussing developments in the various provinces, the histories repeated the historical arguments and new criteria, such as religion and the ethnic principle, were introduced in support of territorial claims.

The importance that was attached to the conversion to Christianity and, in particular, to Orthodoxy is understandable. Much attention was paid to the missionary role of Cyril and Methodius, their translation of the Bible into Slavic, and the introduction of the Cyrillic alphabet. The books emphasized that these "Slavic apostles" had come to save all the South Slavs. They were successful among the Serbs, but the "Serbian Croats" were lost to the nation and to Orthodoxy. Discussing the implications, Djordjević wrote that under the influence of Cyril and Methodius and their followers, the Croats "had become Orthodox, because up until that time the propagation of the Catholic faith by the Pope's priests did not have great success." After the deaths of Cyril (869) and Methodius (885), the Croatian rulers and nobles quickly rejected Orthodoxy. Then, in a church council convened in Split in 925, during the reign of King Tomislav, the rulers "decided, against the wishes of the nation, that they would eliminate from the Croatian churches books in the national, Slavic (old Serbian) language and that in [the churches] only the Latin language would be used." Thereafter the country was "inundated" with Catholic priests and "in the eleventh century the nation was forced to accept the Catholic faith."[19]

This action took place when Croatia "was at the height of her power," and when "virtually all of Dalmatia and Slavonia" were under her rule. The consequence of these developments was that the two Serbian tribes, Serbs and Croats, became separated, but "only by religion because their language was the same," although they wrote it with different alphabets. The real issue for the Serbs was that "those [Serbs] who accepted the Latin (Catholic) faith were in danger of losing their nationality."[20] The same general argument was stressed in connection with the conversion to Islam of the Slavs in Bosnia.

Hereafter, for all practical purposes, any discussion of the Catholic Croats and Croatia disappeared from the Serbian textbooks until the sixteenth century. Instead, for the period from the eleventh to the fifteenth centuries, the major attention was devoted to Byzantium, the Bulgars, the establishment and rule of the Nemanja dynasty, the reign of Tsar Dušan, the battle of Kosovo, Tvrtko's Bosnian kingdom, and the final subjugation of Serbia and Bosnia by the Turks. The complete Ottoman conquest of the Balkans by the sixteenth century again brought the Croats into the Serbian history books. Three main points were made concerning this period. First, the advance of the Ottoman forces into Serbia and Bosnia caused many Catholic Croats to flee from parts of Dalmatia, Croatia, and Slavonia in the sixteenth century, and it was primarily in these abandoned lands, part of which would be designated the Military

Frontier, that the Orthodox Serbs would settle. Second, from 1690 through the eighteenth century there were Serbian migrations into Srem, Bačka, and Banat, most often at the invitation or with the approval of the Habsburg emperor, who promised the new settlers political, economic, and religious rights and privileges. Third, the lot of the Orthodox Serbs did not improve in the Austrian empire because the population came under intense political pressure from the Hungarians and Croatians. In addition, there were persistent attempts by the clergy—Croatian and Hungarian—of various faiths to convert the Serbs to Catholicism, to the Uniate church, and even to Calvinism.

All the history books stressed that the Serbs who had settled in the Military Frontier had been promised freedom of religion, local administrative autonomy, a plot of land, the right to wear their native dress, and exemption from paying a 10 percent tithe to the Catholic clergy in return for military service. The Serbs fulfilled their obligations: they fought bravely and loyally against the Turks, they helped defend Vienna in 1683, they assisted in supressing Rákóczi's rebellion of 1703–11, and they took part in other eighteenth-century Habsburg military operations. On the other hand, the Habsburg rulers failed to honor their promises.[21]

According to Djordjević the Serbs were persecuted "because of [their] religion. In Croatia, Slavonia, and Hungary [they were pressed] to become Catholics."[22] Serbs were imprisoned, "their only crime being that they were Orthodox." Soon they even were forced to pay the 10 percent tithe to the Catholic priests. Later they were denied the right to own land in Croatia-Slavonia.[23] "The unfriendly attitude that the Hungarian and Croatian state authorities adopted, with respect to the Serbian privileges and the Serbs themselves, was strengthened by the fact that immediately following the arrival of the Serbs there developed a bitter hostility between them and the old inhabitants, the Magyars and Croats."[24] Other authors commented that the hardships of the Serbs were more severe under the Catholics than under the Muslims.

The same general arguments were advanced with respect to Vojvodina, that is, Bačka and Banat. In the last decade of the seventeenth century thousands of Serbian families fled the southern Serbian lands and settled north of the Danube. Here also, the students were told, the emperor granted their ancestors political and religious privileges in return for their loyalty and support; they responded dutifully. They worked hard, cleared much of the arable land, and made it productive. When called upon, they rallied to the empire's defense. Soon, however, they found themselves at odds with the Magyars, who resented the fact that they had taken over much of the fertile land in the Danube-Tisza (Theiss) plain. More important, the Serbs were persecuted by the Catholic and Calvinist clergy. Even though "the Serbs remained faithful to the Orthodox religion," by mid-century the pressure had become unbearable, causing 100,000 Serbs to migrate to southern Russia.[25]

In 1912 Vukičević repeated most of the points made above, but he especially stressed the religious persecution at the hands of the Jesuits. However, the leaders of the Orthodox church and the Serbian merchants and traders, many of whom had become prosperous, led the Serbian opposition to the Catholics. They encouraged the Serbian children to attend Protestant schools, "which were not as dangerous as the Catholic." Notwithstanding these difficulties, by the end of the eighteenth century "virtually every village in Hungary in which there were a large number of Serbs had its own [Serbian] school, in which qualified teachers worked to bring education to the people." Soon some secondary and vocational schools were also opened. Serbian books and newspapers were printed. By the time of the Serbian revolution, the Vojvodina had become the cultural center of the Serbian nation.[26]

Yet the resistance of the Serbs merely intensified the Hungarian opposition. They now condemned the Serbs as intruders and interlopers in the Magyar lands, a charge rejected by Vukičević as well as by Stanojević and Zrnić. Vukičević asserted that "there were Serbs in these lands even before the ninth century, although the largest number settled after the fall of Serbia and Bosnia,"[27] the implication of his statement being that Serbian rights, both on historical and ethnic principles, predated the arrival of the Hungarians by three centuries. Stanojević and Zrnić concurred that the Serbs had inhabited the region continuously since the sixth century. At the end of the ninth century, when the Magyars appeared in the Danubian plain, the Serbs had established a small state in Vojvodina. Eventually it succumbed to the Hungarian forces, but the Serbian population did not totally disappear. Instead, in the eleventh century, during the joint Hungarian-Raška (Serbian) war against Byzantium, the Serbian population increased. It was augmented further in the fourteenth and fifteenth centuries, especially after the Turks attacked Serbia and Bosnia. At the beginning of the sixteenth century, "the Serbs in great masses settled in Dalmatia, Croatia, and southern Hungary."[28] Thus Stanojević and Zrnić joined Vukičević in defending the Serbian claims to the Vojvodina upon historical and ethnic grounds.

The student was left with the impression that the Serbs had

been forced to fight for their very survival in Croatia, Slavonia, Bačka, and Banat. They did not live in these lands as intruders: either they had occupied them for a millennium, or they had moved there when these territories were abandoned, or they came as settlers at the invitation of the Habsburg authorities. Now the Croatian and Hungarian rulers and the Catholic church sought to deny the Serbs their national heritage. Therefore, in the early modern period the student encountered Croatia and the Croats in the textbooks only when they were in opposition to or were threatening the Serbian nation.

In some respects the textbooks were more dogmatic in their comments involving Dalmatia. Here the enemy was again the Catholic church, but the secular state was Venice, not Austria or Hungary. The geography books, it will be recalled, gave population statistics for Dalmatia. The Slavic inhabitants, Orthodox as well as Catholic, were regarded as Serbs. The history textbooks did not quote statistics. They simply stated that the original Serbian settlements in Dalmatia had extended to the Cetina River. Hence the islands of Brač, Hvar, Korčula, and Mljet were identified as Serbian.[29] After the fall of Bosnia and Serbia to the Ottoman empire in the fifteenth century, it was claimed, "the Catholics left their homeland and abandoned their churches. And thus the Croats migrated from the areas that the Turks occupied, and the lands from the Cetina to the Zrmanja [River] were immediately settled by the Serbian people from Bosnia, Hercegovina, and Serbia. That was the largest migration of Serbs into Dalmatia (it occurred between 1523 and 1527). The settlement of the Serbs in Dalmatia was aided by the Turkish authorities, especially the Sanjak bey of Knin, who wished to have someone cultivate the abandoned land that the Croats left when they migrated."[30] The area between the Cetina and Zrmanja extended up the Adriatic beyond Split and Zadar to Obrovac near Novigradsko More. Later Serbian refugees moved farther into northern Dalmatia and occupied Otočac, Senj, and Vinodol, reaching almost to the port city of Rijeka (Fiume).[31] In other words, the textbooks left the impression that all of Dalmatia and the Croatian littoral was inhabited by Serbs and was Serbian territory. As Jović phrased it: "Dalmatia, a land in which Serbs live and which extends along the sea."[32]

For the Serbs in Dalmatia, the eighteenth century was the "dark age," as it had been for them in Croatia, Slavonia, and Vojvodina. At that time the Venetians again established control, to the detriment of the Orthodox population. Vukičević was especially strong in his comments about these developments. He wrote that "the Dalmatian bishops employed all that the worst religious fanaticism could invent. . . . The Serbian clergy was persecuted from all sides." The people became "inundated in barbarian religious wars that the Catholic agitators provoked." In addition, he stressed that the "Serbian clergy was persecuted from all sides so that no one dared say he was an Orthodox. He who would say that he was an Orthodox was looked upon as a traitor to the state, he was fined, thrown into jail, or expelled from the country." Yet the church and clergy remained firm and "fought off the Latin assault" in which "the Latins called the Serbian monks 'the blind leaders of a blind people.'"[33]

The history books, like the readers and geography books, maintained that the center of Serbian hopes in Dalmatia was Dubrovnik. Originally it had been a Roman city. Then, "little by little, the Serbs began to colonize it and later they settled it."[34] Subsequently "only Serbs lived in Dubrovnik."[35] By the fourteenth century Dubrovnik ruled all of Dalmatia from Boka Kotorska to the Neretva river.[36] The textbooks also stressed that Dubrovnik was the only Serbian "republic," whereas "all the other Serbian states had a monarchy."[37] When Serbia, Bosnia, and Hercegovina fell to the Turks, "in the whole peninsula only Dubrovnik remained as the reflection of the once-independent Serbian life."[38] And "of all the medieval creations of the Serbian people, the *republic of Dubrovnik* lasted the longest."[39] Even Napoleon, who eventually abolished the republic, "sought a loan of one million dinars from our Dubrovnik."[40]

The city became a great trading center, whose merchants were known throughout the Balkans and in the Serbian lands. When the Turks conquered the Balkans, Dubrovnik was forced to pay a yearly tribute, in return for which it received the protection of the sultan. Through skillful diplomacy, "Dubrovnik gained great respect with the Porte so that the representatives used their own Serbian language when the Sultan received them officially." As a result of its prestige and authority, "Dubrovnik protected, as much as it could, not only the Catholics from Turkish oppression, but also the Orthodox." It also "defended refugees from the Turks and paid [the ransom] of Catholic and also Orthodox slaves."[41]

Dubrovnik, however, was best known for its literary and scientific achievements. Thus, like the readers and geography books, the history volumes stressed this part of its history. Hence Dubrovnik was described as being "the most enlightened city in all of Slavdom."[42] There poets "sang in the Serbian and Latin language."[43] To support this opinion, the textbooks identified all the prominent writers from Dubrovnik and Dalmatia as Serbs.[44]

Concerning Bosnia and Hercegovina, the historians were emphatic about their Serbian character. Accepting the Una and Cetina

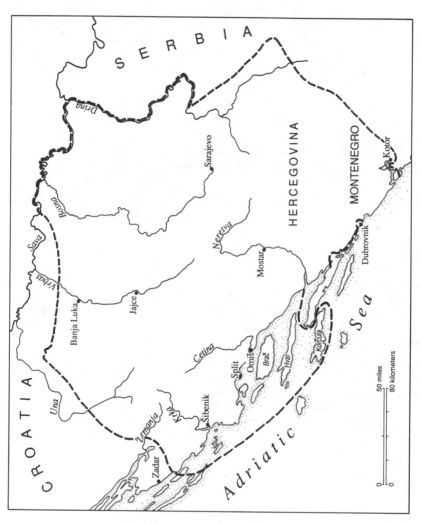

The Bosnian Kingdom in the Fourteenth Century

rivers as the western boundaries of the territory settled by the Serbs, they naturally claimed that the provinces were part of the original Serbian lands, although they recognized that the population was of three faiths. From Jović the elementary school children learned that "in Bosnia there were many Serbs of the Latin faith and their senior priest was the pope in Rome."[45] As for the Muslims, Jović added, "even today their grandchildren speak beautiful Serbian, except that they pray to God as do other Turks. For the Serbs that is a great misfortune, because today they do not say they are Serbs, but that they are Turks even though they cannot speak Turkish."[46]

Considerable attention was also paid to Tvrtko, the king of Bosnia (1377–91), who the students were reminded was one of the great Serbian rulers. Tvrtko's domains were extensive, and for three years (1388–91) he succeeded in uniting Serbian, Croatian, and Bosnian territories. Doing so permitted him to take the title "Stefan Tvrtko, by God's Grace, King of Raška (Serbia), Bosnia, Dalmatia, Croatia, and the Littoral." Kovačević and Jovanović wrote that Tvrtko's "idea had been a union of Serbia and Croatia." In 1388 "Croatia from the sea to Velebit" fell under Tvrtko's rule.[47] In 1390 all of Dalmatia "from Velebit to Kotor," including the islands of Brač, Hvar, and Korčula, but excluding Dubrovnik and Zadar, became part of his domain.[48] His kingdom, however, could not survive his death. "Never did the Serbian people need a ruler like Tvrtko more than" after his reign. They required someone "again to bring together and unite the Serbs. . . . This was felt especially in Croatia and Dalmatia, where the Serbian role was undermined" by Hungary.[49] King Sigmund of Hungary had attacked Bosnia "and defeated two Serbian armies," an event that resulted in the loss of "Croatia and Dalmatia" to the Hungarians in 1395. A half-century later, when the Turks attacked in force, "the cities, which were unprepared, surrendered without fear; at least part of the reason for this was that the Bogomils, who had been terribly persecuted by the Catholics because of their faith, gladly welcomed the Turks."[50] Thereafter, Bosnia became a major Turkish province in the Balkans. From 1463 to approximately 1800, the textbooks were mainly concerned with Ottoman administration in Bosnia, the inferior status of the Christian inhabitants, and their difficulties under Ottoman rule.

The major institutional development in the early modern period emphasized in the texts was the restoration of the patriarchate of Peć in the sixteenth century. At that time Mehmed Sokolović, a Serb from Lim who converted to Islam, rose to become the grand vizier for Suleiman the Magnificent. He used his influence to restore the patriarchate of Peć in 1557, with his brother, the monk Makarija,

appointed patriarch.[51] Stanojević and Zrnić noted that by this action the Serbs abandoned their previous religious jurisdiction over
Thessaly, Aeolia, "and other foreign provinces" and concentrated on
"Bosnia, Srem, Lika, and other provinces that were taken over, either partly or completely, only after the arrival of the Turks." In the
opinion of these authors the patriarchate was stronger than in the
period of Tsar Dušan, because it included "only ethnically pure Serbian areas and virtually the entire Serbian nation."[52]

Vukičević shared these views. He wrote that the "patriarchate
of Peć included virtually all the Serbian lands, which were under the
Turks. . . . Excluding the Catholic and Muslim Serbs, the patriarchate of Peć had united religiously all the Serbs in one unit, because it encompassed all the Serbian provinces from Sentandrija
[Szent Endre, north of Budapest] to the great Drim [River in northern
Albania] and to Veles; from Gomirje [in Lika] and the Adriatic Sea to
the middle of the river Maros [Mureş], to Miroč [in northeast Serbia]
and Niš and Tatar-Pazardžik."[53] The Peć patriarchate was subsequently abolished, but nevertheless, during two difficult centuries
in the nation's history (1557–1766), it provided not only spiritual
guidance to the Serbs but, through its territorial jurisdiction, the
semblance of political unity for the nation.

The Serbian State and Its Achievements
in the Nineteenth Century

The focus of all the textbooks was directed to one event, the Serbian
revolution of 1804. The presentation and interpretation of the developments of the medieval and early modern periods served primarily
as background to the revolt and the revival of the Serbian nation-
state in the nineteenth century. The accounts are both informative
and detailed. The importance played by the revolution in the narration of Serbian history can be demonstrated by the space devoted to
it. For instance, in Jović's elementary textbooks, which ranged over
the entire course of Serbian history, 29 of 121 pages (24 percent) in
the 1896 edition and 28 of 125 pages (22 percent) in the 1902 edition
were allocated to it. In other words, almost one-fourth of the volume, which covered thirteen centuries of Serbian history, concerned
an event that lasted eleven years. Even more revealing are the statistics for the book by Vukičević. In his second volume for the secondary schools, which narrated the years after 1450, 66 of 144 pages
(46 percent) in the 1906 edition and 41 of 126 pages (35 percent) in the
1914 edition dealt with eleven of 450 years of Serbian history.

The students in both the elementary and secondary schools thus obtained a detailed description of the single major occurrence in their recent history. The events were presented with the suspense of a historical drama and in a manner that could easily influence the young mind. The lesson that was taught was that a divided nation would continue to suffer foreign domination, whereas unity would lead to its independence. Just as Karadjordje and Miloš had created the territorial nucleus for the modern Serbian state and Karadžić had created its linguistic-literary unity, the young generation was directed toward completing the task of reconstituting the divided Serbian nation.

The most important event in this period that is relevant to the study of South Slav unity concerns Napoleon's formation of the Illyrian Provinces. In discussing this subject Djordjević wrote that Napoleon created "the Illyrian kingdom: (Illyrians—Serbs)." Under his rule the Catholics could not interfere in Orthodox affairs and "he introduced the Serbian language in the national schools instead of Italian."[54] Stanojević and Zrnić added that in 1809 Napoleon organized the Illyrian kingdom, which included "Dalmatia and the western parts of the Triune Kingdom. Thereby one part of the Serbian people came directly under French administration." French rule "in these Serbian lands," contributed to the development of commerce and trade with the building of roads. In education, "Serbian schools were opened and assisted." In addition, the Serbs enjoyed "complete freedom in religious and national development." They were also influenced by the concepts of freedom and equality of the French revolution.[55] Aside from "Dalmatia and the Triune Kingdom," none of the other provinces were mentioned by any of the authors as being part of the Illyrian kingdom. Yet it is important to identify them to appreciate the full implications of what the students were taught. The Illyrian kingdom included Carinthia, Carniola, Goricia, Istria, Dalmatia, including Dubrovnik, part of Civil Croatia, Tirol, and the Military Frontier from the Sava and Una rivers to the Adriatic. Of the 1,556,000 inhabitants in the Illyrian provinces, the Slovenes and Croats were the overwhelming majority, followed by the Italians, the Austrians, and then the Serbs.[56]

In the period after the conclusion of the revolution, the main emphasis in the textbooks centered on internal developments within the autonomous Serbian state and on those international events in which Serbs were involved, including the impact of the revolution of 1848–49 on the Serbs of the Habsburg empire, the foreign policy goals of Prince Michael (1860–68), the significance of the treaties of San Stefano and Berlin for Serbia, and the evolution of Serbian-Croatian relations before the war. Of these, only the developments involving the South Slavs of the Habsburg empire, Bulgaria, and Macedonia will be discussed.

The importance of the 1848–49 revolution for the Serbs was perhaps best summarized by Vukičević:

> Sometimes the battle for the language was sidetracked but it quickly returned to the proper course and it repelled foreign attacks on the Serbian name and language. The stronger the pressure was from the Hungarians, the greater the resistance grew. When the Poszony [Pressburg, Bratislava] parliament in 1847 introduced a law that Hungarian was the official language and that officials would not receive any communication which was not written in Hungarian, the Serbs and Croats rose up against this illegal decision. The Magyars began to threaten that they would use force. The tension and bitterness grew stronger until finally in 1848 it led to bloody battles.[57]

The other textbooks similarly placed the emphasis on events that affected the Serbs. They described how Serbian representatives met, formulated their demands, and sent them to the emperor. They elected Metropolitan Josif Rajačić as their patriarch and Stevan Šupljikac as their military commander. The texts depicted the destruction and burning of Serbian villages by the Magyars as well as the atrocities they committed against women and children. They emphasized the resistance of the Serbian forces and their great victory at Srbobran. They stressed in particular their loyal support of Vienna and the sacrifices they made in behalf of the empire. They paid close attention to the 10,000 volunteers from Serbia who fought under the command of Stevan Knićanin. The purpose of the authors was to describe the close ties between Serbs who lived on either side of the Danube and Sava rivers.[58]

In addition, the textbooks discussed the relations between the Serbs and Croats in almost identical terms. Jović in his 1906 and 1913 editions wrote that following the Hungarian political successes, the Serbs and Croats "came to an understanding to separate from the Magyars." "First the Croats separated" and elected Jelačić as their leader. Then they appealed to the emperor to confirm him as *ban* and approve the use of Croatian in the schools. "Immediately after this the Serbs met in their assembly and elected Josip Rajačić as patriarch and Stevan Šupljikac as the military commander of Bačka, Banat, and Srem."[59] Djordjević wrote that in 1848 "the Serbs rose up [as did] also their brothers the Croats." Then the Serbs "entered into an alliance with Slavonia, Croatia, and Dalmatia—called a kingdom—on the basis of mutual freedom and complete equality. . . . The leader of the Serbs (Croats) (Vodja Srba (Hrvati)) in Slavonia,

Croatia, and Dalmatia was Jelačić, who was confirmed in this role by the emperor."[60] In his 1902, 1906, 1909, and 1912 editions, Vukičević did not vary his account of the events. His main point was that the Serbs "sent a national delegation to Croatia to effect an alliance and friendship with the Croats through the Croatian sabor."[61]

All the authors expressed disappointment at the results of the revolution. The hopes of the Serbs for autonomous rule were not realized because Vienna imposed a strong centralized administration after the revolution. Stanojević and Zrnić concluded that the revolt had not been successful, "even though [the Serbs] had been allied with the Croats."[62] Vukičević perceived "moral gains" because common action had strengthened the ties "between the Serbs from one side and the other side of the Sava," and it had demonstrated "Serbian heroism, about which nothing had been heard of since 1815." In addition, as a result of the revolt, "the Serbian name now was recognized in official relations, whereas hitherto Vienna and Rome called the Serbs in Austria 'Rascians, Illyrians, Vlachs, Greek Orthodox, etc.'"[63]

Given the considerable political and military cooperation between the Serbs and Croats in 1848, the information presented in these books was meager. For instance, the accounts omit the most significant event, certainly the most dramatic, which occurred when Patriarch Rajačić journeyed to Zagreb and bestowed his blessing on Jelačić as the ban of Croatia. In a sense this act represented the symbolic reconciliation of the Orthodox Serbs and Catholic Croats in the Habsburg Empire.

The next event involving the South Slavs took place during the reign of Prince Michael, 1860–68. Vukičević praised Michael as "the most enthusiastic champion of the national idea. . . . He worked the most for the liberation of the Serbian people and the creation of a large independent Serbian state,"[64] including "the Serbian people in all the Serbian lands."[65] Similarly, M. M. Stanojević noted that Michael had "prepared the country for the liberation and unification of the remaining Serbian regions that were under foreign slavery."[66] S. Stanojević and Zrnić added that "the idea of Serbdom and the unity of the Serbian people at that time had permeated all groups and helped the drive for political and cultural unity." These authors also described Michael's negotiations with the various Balkan peoples, including the "Muslims" in Bosnia-Hercegovina and "with the Croats."[67] Yet "regretfully" his opponents "among the Serbs" were envious of his success. "Consequently, when the prince was working the hardest for the liberation of the Serbian people and the formation of a large independent Serbian state," he was shot. With-

out exception, all the history books presented Michael's endeavors
as aiming toward the liberation and unification of the Serbian nation, not of the South Slavs.[68]

As we have seen, one of the most volatile problems in the nineteenth century concerned the status of Bosnia and Hercegovina. In
every textbook, reader, geography, and history, these two provinces
were presented as being Serbian. Vukičević in the 1902, 1906, 1909,
and 1912 editions of his book restated the same points: that "these
two provinces had been settled by the Serbs since the seventh century. . . . The population was divided by three faiths—Muslim, Orthodox, and Roman Catholic. The adherents of all three faiths speak
the Serbian language and are of the same origin." At the beginning of
the nineteenth century, "there was great inequality between the
Serbian Muslims and the Christians." Most important, Vukičević asserted that the Catholic religious rites resembled the Orthodox here
more than in any other South Slav area. They observed the same
fasts as the Orthodox and each family had a slava according to the
Serbian national custom. As for the Muslims, they "retained their
maternal (Serbian) language and many customs of their ancestors.
They shared the Christian calendar with the Christians. Many Muslim families have retained the old saints of their ancestors and celebrate Saint Elijah and Saint George's day." Vukičević thus used
historic rights, language, religion, and customs to affirm that the
Slavic-speaking Catholics and Muslims of Bosnia and Hercegovina
were Serbs.[69] Stanojević and Zrnić shared his views, writing that the
population was of three religions, but "they are all of the same Serbian origin, and they speak the Serbian langauge."[70]

Given these strongly held opinions, the intensity of the Serbian
reaction to the Habsburg occupation in 1878 was understandable.
Jović told the elementary school children that "even if Serbia enlarged her homeland [in 1878], at the same time this war brought
much harm because Austria gained two of the most beautiful Serbian lands—Bosnia and Hercegovina."[71] Djordjević wrote that these
lands were seized against "the resistance of the people, both Orthodox and Muslim." Subsequently Austria-Hungary used the Catholic
church, and by implication the Catholic Croats, in Bosnia "to work
to assimilate the Serbs into the empire. The Serbs were forbidden to
call themselves by their own Serbian name, and their language was
referred to as 'the regional [i.e. Bosnian] language.'" In exchanging
the Ottoman overlord for the Habsburg, "the conditions [in Bosnia
and Hercegovina] had not improved in any manner."[72] Vukičević
echoed this precise sentiment when he wrote that "a worse fate than
they had had under the Turks" awaited the Bosnians and Hercegovi-

nians.[73] Stanojević and Zrnić added that Austria-Hungary, afraid of the Serbs, "began to create Croats in Bosnia out of the existing Catholic population and to help them [Croats] in their battle against the Serbs." This meant that "Serbdom, especially Orthodox Serbdom and the Serbian church, was persecuted and oppressed."[74] The comments by Stanojević and Zrnić were especially relevant because they point up the dilemma facing those who supported closer cooperation with the Croats, as Stanojević did, and the conflicting claims about Bosnia and Hercegovina.

For the years between the Congress of Berlin and the Balkan Wars, the information in the history books on matters affecting Serbs and Croats is sparse, notwithstanding the fact that these three decades witnessed major developments, such as the deterioration of relations between the Serbs and Croats during the administration of Khuen-Héderváry, and then the unprecedented cooperation that emerged with the formation of the Croatian-Serbian Coalition in 1905. The omissions can be partially explained by the reluctance of the historians to deal with current topics. Several decades or more usually separated an event from its appearance in a textbook. Nevertheless, the history books did contain at least brief outlines of what occurred in these years.

Jović devoted slightly more than a page to the events between 1878 and 1894. He mentioned that Milan had been proclaimed king, "thus, after 511 years Serbia had again become a kingdom after so much pain and misfortune, slavery and suffering." King Milan sought to develop the country, improve the army, build railroads, and strengthen education. In 1885 Serbia went to war with Bulgaria, but in the ensuing battles "the Serbs were driven out of Bulgaria, and they were forced to make peace." In part because of this defeat, Milan decided to abdicate. First, he convened the *skupština* and had it promulgate a new constitution, and then in 1889 he entrusted the kingdom to his thirteen-year-old son. He advised the future monarch "*to look after and defend his people, and not believe the notables, who would deceive him and estrange him from his people.*" King Alexander was crowned in June 1889—"five hundred years after the battle of Kosovo." When his regency began to violate the laws, Alexander assumed the reins of government in 1893 at the age of sixteen. Jović concluded this brief summary by emphasizing "*that every Serb must be proud of the goodness, wisdom, and bravery of his young king, that he be proud of the beautiful Serbian name, and that he be always prepared to sacrifice himself for his king and his fatherland. And the Serbian fatherland is every Serbian land.*"[75]

Vukičević in his 1909 edition, which was published thirteen

years after Jović's elementary history book, had even less information on this period. Two brief paragraphs repeated some of the same points; Alexander's assassination was dealt with in one sentence: "having lost the confidence of his people with his unstable regime, he [Alexander] lost his life on May 29, 1903." This statement was followed by a single, short paragraph on the first years of King Peter's reign that did no more than mention that the skupština had elected the grandson of Karadjordje as monarch, that he took the oath to uphold the constitution, and that he was crowned in 1904, the hundredth anniversary of the Serbian revolution.[76] It is well to note that Vukičević, who was a member of the king's inner circle, did not mention the political, economic, cultural, and foreign policy issues that arose during these years of Peter's reign. Nor did he make any mention of the developments affecting Serbs and Croats that were taking place in Croatia-Slavonia at this time.

Croatian History and Yugoslavism in Vukičević's 1914 Textbook

In sharp contrast to the Serbian orientation found in Vukičević's editions published through 1912, the volumes in 1914 introduced a different approach to Serbian and Croatian relations and to Croatian history, in conformity with the directive of the minister of education in 1912 that more information about the Croats be included. The shift in emphasis, it will be recalled, was made in order to strengthen the pro-Serbian sentiments in Croatia-Slavonia and to heed the increasing calls for South Slav understanding and cooperation found throughout the South Slav lands of the Dual Monarchy. On certain basic issues, however, no changes were apparent. Thus Vukičević repeated in the 1914 edition the same statements previously made about the Serbian nation, language, and territorial claims.

> Where is our fatherland located? Is it only the kingdom of Serbia?
> No. Our fatherland is not only the kingdom of Serbia, because when one goes across the Sava and Danube through the villages and towns of Slavonia, Srem, Bačka, and Banat, people are found who speak the Serbian language, who sing Serbian songs, who recall the Serbian kings and emperors, and who are proud of the Serbian heroes. The same people are found when one crosses the Drina [River] into Bosnia, Croatia, Dalmatia, Hercegovina, and Montenegro. Such people are found also in Old Serbia and Macedonia. In all these areas the people speak the Serbian language, are proud of the Nemanjas, Tsar Dušan, Prince Lazar, Marko Kraljević, Miloš

Obilić, and honor Saint Sava, the first Serbian archbishop and teacher. In all these regions a people live who speak the Serbian language. Therefore all the provinces that have been mentioned are *the fatherland of the Serbian people.*[77]

These statements, appearing on the first two pages of his book, could not fail to impress the students.

In describing the lands that were initially settled by the Serbs, Vukičević placed the Croats west of the rivers "Una and Cetina," which meant that Bosnia, Hercegovina, and Dalmatia, south of Omiš, were claimed as Serbian domains. When the Croats, seeking to escape Ottoman rule, abandoned the lands in northern Dalmatia and the future Military Frontier zone, the Serbs, fleeing Ottoman domination, moved into these regions as well as into southern Hungary or Vojvodina.[78]

Concerning Dubrovnik, Vukičević declared "that of all the medieval creations of the Serbian people the *republic of Dubrovnik* maintained itself the longest." He added that "during the sixteenth century Dubrovnik was the most enlightened city in all of Slavdom," but he made no mention of the prominent individuals whose names were associated with the city.[79]

Although many of the key arguments found in the early editions were restated, any student who compared the 1902, 1906, 1909, 1912, and 1914 editions of Vukičević's textbooks would have easily recognized the major changes in the last edition. They were evident in the table of contents. Whereas in Vukičević's earlier editions, there were no chapters or subheadings devoted to the Croats, the 1914 edition included them. In the first volume, in the chapter entitled "The Slavs," there was a subsection entitled "Serbs and Croats in the New Fatherland." Other subsections were "What Were the Lands Called that the Serbs and Croats Settled?"; and "Byzantine Dominance over the Serbs, Frankish Dominance over the Croats." There was a chapter called "The Liberation of Zeta (Montenegro) and the Strengthening of Croatia in the Second Half of the Eleventh Century," which had subsections entitled "Croats during the Reign of Krešimir the Great (1058–1075)" and "The Fall of Croatia (1102)." Another subsection was on "The Croats at the End of the Fifteenth Century." The second volume included a subsection "Croats under Austrian Habsburg Rule." However, the most significant information was contained in two separate chapters entitled "The Croats until 1848" and "The Croats since 1848."[80]

The first change of importance in the new edition was that Vukičević did not reiterate the claim that at one time all the Slavs

were called Serbs. Instead he wrote: "how they [the Slavs] called
themselves in ancient times is unknown, but other people called
them by various names—Sarmartians, Wends, and later Slavs." Moreover, he added that the Serbs had kinsmen "who today are called
by the common name *Slavs*, in which are included, together with
the Serbo-Croats, the Slovenes, Bulgars, Czechs with the Moravians, Poles, Slovaks, Russians with the Little Russians and Lusatian Sorbs." This was the first occasion in which the term Serbo-
Croats was used. Hitherto when both peoples were mentioned they
were identified either as Serbs or as Serbs or Croats, but with the
understanding that the Croats were Catholic Serbs.[81]

Parenthetically in 1913 Jović, in his elementary book, met the
same issue, writing that all the Slavic people "at one time spoke one
Slavic language," but in the course of time different Slavic languages
evolved. Now "only the Serbs and Croats speak the same language."
When the Slavs moved into the Balkans, they came as a number of
small tribes, each with its own name. Eventually the smaller tribes
joined neighboring tribes and adopted their name, that is, Slovenes,
Croats, or Serbs. Of these "the Serbs were the strongest and largest
tribe, thus the largest number of tribes accepted the Serbian name."
As for the Croats, Jović added "that one of the larger tribes was
called *Croats*. It settled between the Sava and Drava [rivers] and the
Adriatic Sea. The *Slovene* tribe settled to the northwest of them
and the *Serbs* to the southeast. . . . Thus in the south three Slavic
peoples emerged: Serbs, Croats, and Slovenes. The Serbs and Croats
speak the same language and that is why it is said that they are *one
people*. The Slovenes speak virtually as do the Serbs and Croats, consequently they too can be regarded as one people."[82] This statement
was most characteristic of the views being expressed by the supporters of South Slav unity. It could have been taken almost verbatim from the writings of any number of prominent supporters of
Yugoslavism.

Whereas on pages one and two of his textbook, as quoted above,
Vukičević had defined the Serbian fatherland as including Bačka,
Banat, Srem, Slavonia, Croatia, Dalmatia, Bosnia, Hercegovina, Montenegro, Old Serbia, and Macedonia, on page three he made a significant qualification. Here he stated that "the Serbian fatherland
encompassed the western half of the Balkan peninsula, the part between the Sava and Danube to near the plain of Thessaloniki, from
the Timok and Struma [rivers] to the Adriatic Sea. The nucleus of
the Serbo-Croatian fatherland is found in the area from Kotor and
Dubrovnik on the Adriatic to the Drava in the north to the Morava
in the east and to the southern spurs of the Šar Mountains in the

south."[83] There are two points to note here. First, by using the Sava-Danube as the northern boundary of the Serbian fatherland, Vuki-čević excluded Croatia and Slavonia. Second, by identifying the Drava as the northern boundary of "the Serbo-Croatian fatherland," he tacitly acknowledged these two provinces of the Triune Kingdom as Croatian.

The students also learned that "there were no differences between Serbs and Croats either in name or in speech or in the shape of their head or body. They arrived [in the Balkans] as kinsmen and established themselves as neighbors. Moreover, for three hundred years after their arrival in the new fatherland, they did not differentiate themselves by name, but in some areas they were called by one and the other name." In this early period the Serbs and the Croats carried out joint military operations against the Bulgarians, who were seeking control over Serbian lands.[84]

In the earlier editions, as we have seen, considerable attention was devoted to the acceptance of Christianity by the South Slavs. The reader was left with the clear impression that from the initial contacts with Christianity the Serbs and Croats had found themselves in opposite camps. Now Vukičević wrote that

> when the Serbs and Croats arrived in their new fatherland, they were not differentiated either by language or by customs or by faith. Even when they accepted Christianity they were not differentiated, nor were they divided into *Orthodox* and *Catholic*, because they were one and the same people. Only when the Christian church was divided into West and East, into Rome and Constantinople, when a struggle emerged between the Church leaders in Rome (Popes) and in Constantinople (Patriarchs), as to who would have primacy and seniority, it was then that the Christian church turned brother against brother, split and alienated them, and from one people with two names it created two separate peoples, *Serbs* and *Croats*, who even today cannot reconcile themselves. Hence, as a result of their quarrels, the foreigner benefits at their expense. The quarrels and factionalism, the aspirations, one toward Rome, the other toward Constantinople, meant that the Serbs and Croats could not advance in education as much as they could have had both belonged to one or the other church. Instead hatred and fighting flared up between them on account of Rome and Constantinople, in behalf of Orthodoxy and Catholicism, so that they became estranged from one another for centuries.[85]

Most significant in this statement is Vukičević's observation that it would have been better for both the Serbs and the Croats if they all had belonged either to the Orthodox or to the Catholic church, a view that must have struck many as being sacrilegious or blasphemous. Hitherto the emphasis had been on the danger posed by Catholicism to the Orthodox Serbs. Vukičević's new analysis was in the spirit of those intellectuals and students championing South Slav unity in 1914.

The new edition also provided the Serbian students with their first information about the medieval Croatian kingdom. Here Vukičević concentrated on the reign of "Krešimir the Great (1058–73), the restorer of the Croatian state." His mother was Venetian, and gave him a "Latin-Italian education," which made him "one of the best educated men of his times." As monarch, he brought the nobles under his control and he annexed "Dalmatian towns, islands, and the Neretva province to his state, again seeking to develop Croatian power on the Adriatic Sea." After these great successes Krešimir was called "*the illustrious and saintly King of Croatia and Dalmatia.*" His reign, however, involved Croatia in religious controversies over the use of Slavic or Latin in the Church liturgy and the question of celibacy. As a result of his own background and his mother's influence, he sided with the Latin faction.[86]

Next Vukičević described the events that brought an end to Croatian rule in their kingdom. Following Krešimir's death, the country was plunged into a bitter struggle over succession. The nobles reasserted their authority and King Zvonimir could not control them. Following his death, the queen, supported by some nobles, invited her brother Ladislav, the Hungarian king, to rule over Croatia. He was able to establish his control over only part of the Croatian kingdom. Koloman, who succeeded Ladislav, defeated the last Croatian king, Peter II, and subdued the country in 1099. In 1102 Koloman was crowned king of Croatia. Vukičević explained Croatia's loss of independence as due to disunity and jealousy among the nobles, the resistance of the Dalmatian cities, and the religious-language controversy. He added: "Separated from the Serbs, under the strong influence of Rome and Hungary, the Croats were constantly represented as being a separate nation, [a view] that even today is supported by those who do not wish to see the Serbs and Croats as one people."[87]

The information about Croatia for the early modern period was equally instructive. Whereas previously the textbooks had concentrated on presenting only the Serbian role in resisting Ottoman rule, now the Croats were also given credit for opposing Ottoman domination. The text, for instance, stated that in 1440 Ivan Tagovac, the brother of the Croatian ban, Matko Tagovac, fought with the Hungarians against the Turks in defense of Belgrade. "Similarly the

Croats fought alongside John Hunyadi at Kosovo (1448), where the Croatian army together with the Hungarian was defeated and where the Croatian Ban Tagovac was killed." In addition, "after the defeat on the field of Krbava [1493] the Croatian nation was exposed to constant attacks by the Turks. It [the Croatian nation] carried on desperate battles for the defense of its homeland, as did those Serbs who had migrated to Hungary."[88] After the Ottoman victory of Mohács (1526), "the same fate awaited a large part of the Croats as awaited their brothers the Serbs. Thereafter the history of the Serbs and Croats is filled with long and difficult battles that they constantly fought together with the western states against Islam and the Turks. With their breasts they defended central Europe against the Turkish invasions."[89]

In the description of the resistance to Ottoman rule, the Serbian students were introduced for the first time to three Croatian heroes. They learned that Nikola Zrinski fought the Turks at Siget (1566), that Matija Gubec had led a peasant revolt against the nobility in 1573, and that Petar Zrinski was executed in 1671 for his role in a conspiracy against the Habsburg emperor. The Croats had also "served together with the Serbs" in the Thirty Years' War in support of Habsburg interests. After the second siege of Vienna (1683), the Croats fought against the Ottoman Empire (1683–99) "as did the Serbs."[90]

Vukićević presented a similar approach to the events of the eighteenth century, stressing the common destiny of the Serbs and Croats and that the century was not a "dark era" for the Serbs alone. The vast lands of the Military Frontier had been detached from Croatia-Slavonia, organized militarily, and placed under the direct political-military control of Vienna. Under Maria Theresa and Joseph II, the Military Frontier had become one "large military barracks, which was maintained at a minimum cost. For several centuries it provided military strength for the Viennese court. Its [troops] were the terror of the European states, serving the interests of the Viennese court. Both the Serbs and the Croats perished for centuries on behalf of foreign interests, shedding their blood on all the battlefields to which they were led by German generals." In addition, the peasants suffered economically at the hands of Croatian, Hungarian, and German nobles. The situation became most difficult when Joseph II sought to create "one strong state, in which there would be one constitution, one nation, one language (German), and one law." His policy was resisted jointly by the Magyars and Croats. Eventually Joseph had to retreat, and the rights of the Croats and Magyars were restored. Again this account certainly corresponded more to the facts than had the earlier versions, which had presented a solitary picture of oppression and persecution of the Serbs alone.[91]

Although Vukičević still regarded Dubrovnik as a Serbian city, its literature now was declared to have been written "in the Serbo-Croatian language."[92] Similarly the text stated that when Napoleon created the Illyrian kingdom, schools were opened and children were taught in "the national language," not Serbian as previously stated. Nor were books published in Serbian but in "the national language." In Croatia, General Marmont introduced Croatian as the official language, "which was the first time since the existence of Croatia that the national language was the official one." In other words, earlier Vukičević had called the language Serbian; now he identified it as Croatian. In addition, he stressed that this era brought in a new legal system and trade associations; roads were built and rivers were made navigable. "In this manner for the first time since the fall of the Croatian kingdom, the Serbs, Croats, and Slovenes in the newly formed Illyrian kingdom were able to breathe a sigh of relief from the violence and oppression that they suffered for centuries under either the Venetian Republic or the Magyars or the Germans."[93]

The Illyrian movement, which hitherto had been ignored, was discussed in the chapter "The Croats to 1848." The students learned that after the French revolution, the Magyars sought to impose the Hungarian language in the Croatian as well as the Serbian schools. To counteract this pressure, "a literary and political movement [developed], which was called *Illyrianism*, at the head of which was *Ljudevit Gaj* with his newspapers." With the collaboration of others, Gaj set as his goal

> to awaken the national conscience and to foster the national language. However, seeing that the language that they had hitherto written was spoken only in some parts of Croatia, they, therefore, accepted the Serbian dialect, the one in which Vuk Stefanović Karadžić wrote. Thus they merged the Serbian and Croatian languages and called it *Illyrian* and Ljudevit Gaj named his newspaper *Illyrian News*. Later Croatian and Serbian scholars called this language by its real name—the *Serbo-Croatian language*. Thus, today, the Serbs and Croats, as one people with two names, write the same language. The only difference is that one writes in *Latin* and the other in *Cyrillic* script.[94]

These developments frightened the Habsburg authorities who, in order to forestall the unification of the Serbs and Croats, "forbade the terms *Illyrianism, Illyrian,* and *Illyria.*" Croatian youth were also prohibited from engaging in politics. All these measures contributed to the "bloody battles between the Croats and Magyars in

1848. . . . . The fusion of the Serbian and Croatian languages into one immediately produced good results, because the Serbs and Croats, in the battle against the Magyars, emerged as one people and their armies joined forces in order to fight together." This unity was best symbolized by Ban Jelačić and Patriarch Rajačić, who said "*We are all one people . . . therefore let there be unity and brotherhood between us without regard to religion; no longer let brother be estranged from brother.*"[95]

Although scholars will take issue with Vukičević's assertion that the Croats had "accepted the Serbian dialect," the students did learn that the goal of the Illyrian movement was the cultural and political union of the Serbs and Croats. This fact had not been discussed previously in the Serbian textbooks. Nor had the call for unity and brotherhood by Jelačić and Rajačić been reported.

Vukičević was equally forthright about developments in Croatia in the chapter entitled "The Croats after 1848." When the Habsburg government sought to impose a centralized authority over the empire in 1861, the "Croatian sabor, convened on the basis of the Constitution of 1861, would not agree to it. In it [the sabor] there was a very strong party that sought to have a Yugoslav state (*Jugoslavensku državu*) formed, which would be in union with Austria only to the extent that the Austrian emperor would at the same time be the king of the Yugoslav state." Vienna rejected the Croatian demands, the sabor was disbanded, then reconvened in 1865 and dissolved again in 1867. This information was followed by brief comments on the three Croatian political parties—the Strossmayer-Mažuranić National Liberal Party, Starčević's Party of Right, and the Magyarones.[96]

On the significance of the Austro-Hungarian Ausgleich of 1867, Vukičević wrote: "the interests of the Croatian-Serbian peoples in the empire were sacrificed to the Germans and Hungarians." Thereafter there were political persecution and electoral fraud in Croatia as shown in the 1867 elections won by the Magyarone party. The terms of the Nagodba were also given: namely, that the Croats could independently administer education, the judiciary, and internal affairs.[97]

Next, in a subsection entitled "The Croats from 1868 to 1912," Vukičević described the consequences of the Ausgleich and the Nagodba for the Croats and Serbs and the emergence of Serbian and Croatian understanding and cooperation in the twentieth century. The Nagodba had contributed to popular dissatisfaction, the press was controlled, and prominent men were harassed. In 1883 the Habsburg government appointed Khuen-Héderváry as ban and ordered him "to crush every national movement." He was not immediately successful, because the Serbs and Croats renewed the unity that Ban Jelačić and Patriarch Rajačić had forged in 1848. Eventually, however, a pro-Hungarian majority was achieved in the sabor through "the use of gendarmes, bayonets, and forged documents." Thereafter, Khuen-Héderváry ruled Croatia by means of "the fist and gendarmes' bayonets, seeking to create even greater hatred and disunity between the Serbs and Croats."[98]

"The regime of the fist and bayonet," continued Vukičević, "stifled any free expression, suppressed the Croatian aspirations for independence, constantly fostered strife between the Serbs and Croats, weakened the power of resistance of the people in the Triune Kingdom, and sought thereby to subjugate these Serbo-Croatian lands more strongly to Hungary." Although the Serbian and Croatian leaders recognized the tactics being employed against them, "it was difficult to bring about closer ties between brothers of one nation with two names and two faiths" because of Vienna's policy of "divide and rule." Finally in 1895 and 1902 Austria's policy led to clashes between Serbs and Croats in Zagreb. In 1903, however, "an uprising occurred throughout all parts of Croatia. The Serbs and Croats united together to oust the oppressors." Vienna used force, killing eleven peasants and imprisoning many individuals in the cities. Nevertheless, they "could not suppress the uprising and Ban Khuen was forced to flee Croatia."[99]

This success led to the electoral victory in the sabor of the "united Serbian and Croatian parties" (the Croatian-Serbian Coalition) in 1906, which was repeated in 1908. In Vienna the Serbs were seen as those responsible for these victories. Consequently, "all the most prominent Serbs in Croatia and Slavonia were accused as traitors and charged with working in agreement with Serbia against the emperor and Austria."[100] The charges were proven false and the Serbs released. Vukičević concluded his account on a positive note by stating: "Even today the united Serbs and Croats in the Triune Kingdom are carrying on a sharp and stubborn battle against the foreigners, hoping that the day will dawn when they will be freed of oppression, persecution, and abuse because the goal for which they are fighting is just and in the end justice must triumph."[101]

Vukičević's account of the Khuen-Héderváry years was a romanticized version, not always factual, which glossed over the hostility of the era. The purpose of the section was, however, to emphasize South Slavic understanding as evidenced by the successes of the Croatian-Serbian Coalition. The Croats were not portrayed as Serbia's adversaries, as had been the case in the earlier editions; instead, they were depicted as allies against the common enemy, the Austro-

Hungarian Empire. Notwithstanding the more favorable impression students now gained of the Croats and their history, the Croats still were not portrayed as a separate nation, as were the Albanians, Bulgars, and Hungarians.

Notably absent from Vukičević's textbook, as well as from all the others examined, were the Slovenes. Aside from their enumeration as members of the Slavic family, the only significant reference to them was the comment in Jović's elementary history book in 1913 that since the Serbs and Croats spoke the same language, they were "one people," and since the Slovenes also "speak virtually as the Serbs and Croats do . . . [they too] can be regarded as one people."[102] The students had to take this statement on faith; there was no information in the history books that would justify the assertion.

Macedonia and Old Serbia

The conflict with Bulgaria over Macedonia was in many respects as emotional for the Serbs and their historians as was their dispute with the Croats over Bosnia and Hercegovina. The latter was an "intra-family" dispute, involving "Serbs" who had gone astray in the medieval period, but who eventually, through their common literary language, would be reunited with their Orthodox brothers. The Bulgars, by contrast, were regarded as foreigners who sought to annex Macedonia, a historic Serbian land. Hence, the historians portrayed Bulgaria in the same light as they did Hungary, Austria, Venice, and the Ottoman Empire—that is, as an enemy state.

In defense of their claims to Macedonia, the Serbian historians concentrated on historical arguments. Macedonia was considered a Serbian province because Serbs had settled it in the seventh century at the invitation of Emperor Heraclius, who, according to Jović, "gave them the Macedonian lands." Thereafter the Serbs inhabited Macedonia continuously. However, their control was challenged by the rulers of both the First and the Second Bulgarian empires, that is, through the ninth and tenth and the twelfth through fourteenth centuries. Both Serbs and Bulgars had control of the province at different times, but finally Dušan gained undisputable mastery over it. From this center he established Serbia's dominance in the Balkans.[103]

After the victory at Kosovo in 1389, the Ottoman Empire, not Bulgaria, became Serbia's principal adversary in Macedonia. At the same time the Greeks too joined the ranks of the national enemies because of the role of the Ecumenical Patriarchate, which consistently opposed the existence of a separate Serbian Orthodox church authority. Vukičević stressed: "The Greeks were more unbearable for the Serbs and Bulgars than the Turks had been because they tormented one's soul and conscience, whereas the Turks broke one's body."[104] Consequently, he continued, "a struggle began between the Greek bishops and the Serbian clergy that lasted until the appearance of the Bulgarian Exarchate. The Greek bishops carried on a campaign not only against the Serbian clergy but also against the Serbian people and against the Serbian liturgical language in church services, disregarding the means and methods [used] in this conflict."[105]

The establishment of the Bulgarian Exarchate in 1870 and the creation of an autonomous Bulgarian state in 1878, as well as Russia's support of the Greater Bulgaria in the Treaty of San Stefano, were a direct challenge to Serbia's claims to Macedonia. Serbian historians, as could be expected, reacted strongly to these events and to their repercussions in Macedonia. Stanojević and Zrnić contended that Russia's intention had been "to create a Slavic exarchate."[106] Vukičević maintained that the Exarchate was created "with the help of the Serbian government and Russian intervention."[107] But then, continued Vukičević, what had been gained through the joint efforts of the Serbs and Bulgars "the Bulgars were to use for their own interests." The Bulgars sought to develop Bulgarian sympathies among the population by opening schools, where students were taught in Bulgarian using Bulgarian books.[108] Djordjević commented that some Serbs joined the Exarchate in order to escape the jurisdiction of the Greek Ecumenical Patriarchate. "These Serbs are called *Bulgars*, but they are not Bulgars but Serbs, who were enticed by promises and money to join the Bulgars," Djordjević wrote. "That is why these Serbs, who joined the Bulgars, are called 'Bugaraši'."[109] Bulgaria's propaganda campaign had become so brazen that "they even proclaimed Marko Kraljević, the son of King Vukašin, a Bulgar and a Bulgarian king," noted Vukičević.[110]

Russia's role in the Bulgarian national advancement was also discussed. The historians particularly resented the Treaty of San Stefano, which awarded Macedonia to Bulgaria. Vukičević stressed that "Russia sacrificed Serbian interests" at San Stefano.[111] Had the treaty been implemented, "the most important places in the old Serbian state would have come under Bulgaria."[112] Stanojević and Zrnić wrote that San Stefano took all of Macedonia, part of Old Serbia, and one part of the present Serbian kingdom and awarded them to the Bulgars.[113]

Although the Congress of Berlin dismembered the Greater Bulgaria of San Stefano and returned Macedonia to Ottoman control, the nation had been alerted to the Bulgarian threat. King Milan was praised for focusing the nation's attention on this problem in the

1880s. Even Serbia's defeat in the Serbo-Bulgarian War of 1885 had a salutary effect, because it demonstrated how a united Bulgaria might seize Macedonia. In fact, Vukičević wrote that it was only "after the Serbo-Bulgarian War that the Serbian statesmen began to think about the Serbs in Old Serbia and Macedonia, and through schools and churches they began to work to strengthen the national consciousness and to educate the people for a more favorable time."[114] The culmination of these efforts came during the Balkan Wars.

Notwithstanding the fact that the history books normally did not discuss current events, the acquisition of Macedonia and Old Serbia in the Balkan Wars represented a major victory in modern Serbian history, in some respects equivalent to the achievements of the Serbian revolution. Hence Jović (1913) and Vukičević (1914) rushed into print their accounts and interpretations of the wars. Each told essentially the same story. The Bulgars and Serbs had agreed beforehand to liberate Old Serbia and Macedonia through joint military operations. Instead the Bulgarians advanced toward Adrianople and Constantinople, leaving the Serbs with the burden of freeing the two provinces. The Serbs scored quick military victories and gained control of them. The Bulgarian operations stalled around Adrianople, and the Serbs had to send troops in support of their ally. Yet when the First Balkan War ended, the Bulgars demanded that the Serbs surrender "all of Macedonia and half of Old Serbia." The Serbs were ready to let Tsar Nicholas II settle this dispute, but the Bulgars instead carried out a surprise attack on the Serbs. Quickly the Greeks, Montenegrins, Romanians, and even the Turks turned against the Bulgars, thus leading to a decisive Bulgarian defeat. With this victory Serbia had established her control in Macedonia. Serbia's pride in her triumph was expressed in Jović's declaration: "Everywhere Serbs were hero knights. All nations marveled at the heroism and speed of the Serbian army. We must be proud that we are the sons of such heroes, that we are the daughters and brothers of Serbian falcons, that we are Serbian men and Serbian women."[115]

The claims that the historians made to Old Serbia and northern Albania were based on arguments similar to those used against the Bulgars in Macedonia. Disregarding the Albanian national movement, some Serbian historians sought to justify Serbia's pretensions to northern Albania territory by noting that Tsar Dušan had defeated the Albanians and "had himself proclaimed *King of the Serbs and Albanians.*" Some contended that Skenderbeg, the great Albanian medieval leader and hero, was of Serbian origin—Djuradj Kastriotić. Certainly the textbooks cultivated the feeling that Old

Serbia with the patriarchate of Peć and the battlefield of Kosovo were sacred regions for every Serb, and that the nation would not be complete or fully united without them. Although Serbia regained Old Serbia in 1913, she was denied northern Albania by Austria-Hungary and Italy, both of whom supported the formation of the Albanian national state. Vukičević summarized the feelings of his countrymen when he wrote that Vienna and Rome had succeeded in "creating a new state in the Balkans out of Albania and the barbarian Albanians." None of the textbooks had employed this language in describing any of their other neighbors. He also condemned Vienna for having "sought to extend the boundaries of the new Albanian state," a reference to Austria's attempt to include Old Serbia within Albania.[116]

The history books provide the best illustration of the extent to which Serbianism and Yugoslavism were a part of Serbian education. Until 1912, it would be difficult to draw any conclusion but that the historians were exclusively concerned with the Serbs and their lands. A Croatian nation, in the sense in which the Serbs conceived their own nation or the Greek, Bulgarian, Romanian, and Hungarian nations, did not exist. Only in 1913–14 was this approach altered; Vukičević and Jović in their respective textbooks modified their previous definitions of the Serbian *otadzbina*, now calling it "the Serbo-Croatian fatherland." This redefinition represented the first admission of the possible existence of a joint South Slav nation, an assertion made even more apparent when the common language was termed "Serbo-Croatian." Notwithstanding the new information about the Croats, the predominant role given Serbia, the Serbian nation, and Serbia's unique characteristics remained unchanged in the Vukičević and Jović textbooks.

CROATIAN HISTORY TEXTBOOKS

As was the case with the Serbian history textbooks, the Croatian books forcefully presented their nation's history. In the best national and romantic tradition, the focus was on Croatia, her people, and her lands. The main aim was to present Croatian national history, identify the heroes, and describe the nation's relations with Vienna and Budapest within the Habsburg Empire. The books described vividly the nation's history from the days of the Croatians' settlement in the Balkans to the establishment of the medieval kingdom. Major attention was devoted to the centuries of Venetian, Hungarian, Ottoman, and Habsburg influence and, in particular, to the national revival of the nineteenth century.

Like the Croatian readers, the Croatian history books contained considerable information on the Serbs. Yet there was a noticeable difference in their presentation of Serbian affairs. Whereas the readers emphasized—their critics said overemphasized—the close linguistic and literary ties between the Serbs and Croats, the historians were more cautious. As will be seen below, they presented a broad sweep of Serbian history, but at the same time they focused on the contributions and sacrifices that the Croats had made on behalf of the Serbs. Often the reader was left with the impression that the Serbian nation would have had an even more difficult history, especially in its relations with the Bulgarians and Ottoman Empire, had it not been for the fraternal assistance of the Croats.

As noted previously, history was taught in the Croatian elementary schools from readers that included geography and the natural sciences. A comparison of the subjects discussed in the readers and secondary school history textbooks indicates that the same basic questions were covered in both. Whereas the reader might contain only several paragraphs on the medieval Croatian and Serbian kingdoms, the secondary books had a number of pages or sections in chapters. The basic facts in each were essentially identical, but the high school textbooks elaborated on events in a way that could leave students with a different impression than they might derive from the brief comments found in the elementary school readers. Although more information will be cited from the secondary books, in part because much of the material on history has already been covered in the chapter on readers, reference nevertheless will be made to both the readers and the secondary school books.

The Authors

There were five principal authors of Croatian history textbooks—Ivan Hoić, Vjekoslav Klaić, Franjo Kořinek, Stjepan Srkulj, and Ljudevit Tomšić. Of these, two, Hoić and Klaić, had written geography books as well. Both wrote successful textbooks, with Hoić perhaps being the most influential among the students. His history books included *General History for the Public Schools*; *General History for the Lower Grades of the Secondary Schools*, which by 1912 had reached its seventh edition; *History of the Modern Period for the Lower Grades of the Secondary Schools*; and *Croatian History for the Eighth Grade of the Gymnasium*.[117] Whereas Hoić wrote primarily for the lower grades of the secondary schools, Klaić's textbooks were directed more toward the higher grades, although his first book was *History of the Medieval Centuries for the Lower Grades of the Secondary Schools*. Since Klaić's own speciality was the medieval period, he wrote *History of the Medieval Centuries for the Upper Grades of the Secondary Schools*, which was reprinted often. His other book was *Croatian History for the Upper Girls' Schools and Lycées*. He was also entrusted with revising and republishing the well-known book by Franjo B. Kořinek that appeared under the title *Fr. B. Kořinek's History of the Modern Period for the Higher Grades of the Secondary Schools*. Klaić's *Atlas for Croatian History* did not go beyond the medieval period. In addition, Klaić published several histories of the ancient period for the secondary schools that were based upon works by the German scholar Anton Gindely and the Czech Emanuel Hannak.[118]

Of the other historians, Kořinek completed his studies in geography and history in Prague and then became a gymnasium teacher first in Varaždin, subsequently in Zagreb. He wrote a three-volume general history for the secondary schools; the first volume (1866) covered the ancient period and was based upon the work of the German scholar Wilhelm Putz; the second surveyed the medieval centuries (1874); the third, which Klaić revised, examined the modern era (1867).[119] Stjepan Srkulj received his doctorate in Vienna, taught in the Zagreb gymnasium for two decades, was an active member of the Croatian-Serbian Coalition, and from 1917 to 1919 served as mayor of Zagreb. He also played a role in the formation of the South Slav kingdom in 1918. His *History of the Medieval Period for the Higher Grades of the Secondary Schools* was well received, as was his three-volume *Sources for History for the Higher Grades of the Secondary Schools*.[120] The last author, Ljudevit Tomšić, was a teacher in the public schools first in Karlovac and then in Zagreb. He wrote children's stories, essays on geography, biographies of Cyril and Methodius, and *A Primer of Croatian History for the Youth in the Public Schools*. In the preface to his first edition (1872), he stated that his purpose was not to intrude on the field of scholars, but to relate what he, as a teacher, believed students should know about Croatian history.[121] His book was used primarily as a reference work.

The Croats and the Lands They Settled

The critical issue for every Croatian historian was to identify the Croatian lands. There were two arguments used—the historical and the ethnic. The historical argument was employed to support the contention that certain lands had been settled first by Croatians. Where their historical claims were challenged by another nation, as for example in Bosnia and Hercegovina, the historians contended that Croats had lived continuously in these lands, notwithstanding their current numerical inferiority. Hence the ethnic argument was used to buttress the historical, which, for the Croats, was the vital one.

To establish the historical argument, it was important to describe precisely what occurred when the Slavs arrived in the Balkans. All the authors agreed that the original home of the Slavs had been somewhere north of the Carpathian Mountains, in lands at present a part of Poland and the Soviet Union. Tomšić implied that the Croats originally lived in an area called White Croatia or, as some called it, Greater Croatia, which was separate from the area inhabited by the other Slavs. Klaić wrote that "Greater or White Croatia [was the land] from which all the Slavic tribes and nations emigrated," an argument somewhat analogous to the Serbian claim that at one time all the Slavs had been Serbs. On the other hand, Srkulj wrote that there were only a "few meager sources" on the original homeland of the Slavs, a view shared by the other historians. Accepting the general belief that the Slavs had emigrated from north of the Carpathians, he concentrated his attention mainly on the Slavic settlements in the Balkans.[122]

All the historians agreed that sometime in the fifth century the South Slavs started their trek southward and by the sixth century had reached the Danube and into parts of the Balkans. It was a most difficult era for the Slavs because they were conquered by the Avars, who forced them to fight in their wars against Byzantium. Hoić commented that the Avars had subdued so many Slavs "that they [the Avars] could boast to the Byzantines that there were so many of them [the Slavs], they could drink up all the water in the empire and their thirst would not be quenched." At different times during the seventh century both the Avars and the Byzantine Empire enlisted the Slavs in campaigns against one another. Eventually the Avars were defeated. By the end of the century the Slavs had populated much of the Balkan peninsula, and, as Hoić stated, "the Croats were the masters of these lands that they now inhabit."[123]

All the authors agreed that the Croats had settled mainly the western portions of the Balkan peninsula and that Dalmatia became the nucleus of the future Croatian kingdom. However, two basic questions emerged: one, the identity of the Slavs in this area, the other, the exact lands that they occupied. Klaić, Srkulj, Hoić, and Tomšić all relied on Constantine Porphyrogenitus, who reported that the Croats had been led into their new homeland by five brothers named Hrvat, Klukas, Lovel, Kosenjec, and Muhlo and two sisters, Tuga and Buga. They acknowledged that not all the original Slavs in the future Croatian lands were Croats.[124] Tomšić wrote that

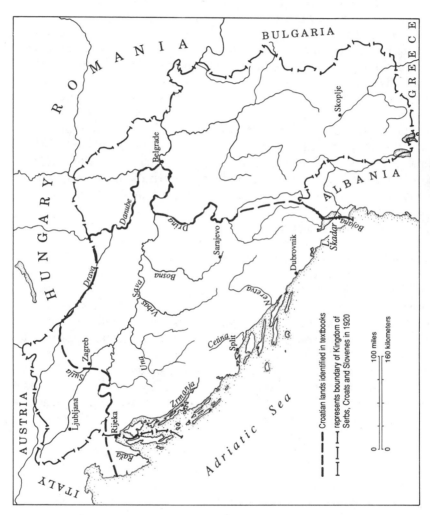

Croatian Lands Identified in the Textbooks

in "their new homeland, our ancestors lived happily . . . with a number of related tribes."[125] Klaić admitted that many Slavic tribes had settled in Dalmatia and Pannonia. In addition to the Croatians, he noted, there were the "Neretljani, Humljani, Travunjci, Dukljani, Gračani, and others." In time, however, they all were to be called Croats.[126] Srkulj noted that "during the seventh and eighth centuries these tribes united into one people to be called Croats, it seems because of the chief tribe, Croats, which had settled between the rivers Zrmanja and Cetina."[127]

The second point concerned the historic Croatian lands. Srkulj provided the best description when he wrote that

> The land where the Croats settled extended from the Adriatic Sea and the Raša [River] in Istria all the way to the Bosna [River] in the east; on the north from the Danube and Drava to the Bojana [River] in the south. The land, which first extended from the Cetina to Zrmanja, and then to the Raša in Istria—the old Liburnia—is called in the Chronicle of Father Dukljanin (from the twelfth century) *White Croatia* and the area from the Cetina to the Bojana *Red Croatia*. In the latter the following tribes lived: *Neretljani* from the Cetina to the Neretva, *Zahumljani* between the Neretva and Dubrovnik, *Travunjani* from Dubrovnik to Kotor, and *Dukljani* from Kotor to the Bojana in Duklja, present-day Montenegro. . . . The Croats also seized southern Pannonia—land to the south of the Drava and Danube and southwest all the way to Kapela or Gvozd in the southwest.[128]

Hoić included in the same basic area lands extending eastward to the Drina River, that is, areas corresponding to present-day eastern Istria, Croatia, Slavonia, Dalmatia, Bosnia, Hercegovina (excluding Novi Pazar), and parts of Montenegro.[129] In other words, Bosnia, Hercegovina, and Montenegro, which the Serbian authors considered an integral part of their territory, were identified as historic Croatian lands.

The enumeration of which lands were Croatian and which were Serbian became more precise when the Serbian settlements were discussed. Hoić wrote that "soon a Serbian tribe having different names began to expand to the southeast of these [Croatian] lands." Quoting Franjo Rački, Hoić stated that their "brother Serbs arrived under the leadership of two brothers, who conquered and settled the land next to the Croats. . . . The Croats and Serbs are simply two tribes of the same nation."[130] Hoić identified the Serbian boundaries, within which he included most of Serbia, the eastern halves of Bosnia, Hercegovina, and Montenegro, northern Albania to the Drim River and northern Macedonia to the Šar Mountains.[131] These same lands were included in Srkulj's textbook. However, he added that from these lands "the Serbian name slowly began to extend into the province of Red Croatia," that is, in southern Dalmatia.[132] Klaić was less specific. He merely noted that "from the north, immediately following the Croats, another Slavic tribe arrived, Serbs by name, and the closest relatives of the Croats, and settled in the Byzantine lands to the east of the Croats."[133] According to these historians the Serbs lived approximately to the east of a line that extended from the Bosna River south to Mount Durmitor in Montenegro and southward to the Morača River, which flowed into Lake Skadar (Scutari), then into northern Albania as far as the Drim River, then eastward to the Šar Mountains in Macedonia, with the Morava River as the eastern boundary of Serbia. The Serbs, thus, were excluded from all of Dalmatia and from the western parts of Bosnia, Hercegovina, and Montenegro. However, none of the textbooks claimed that present-day Serbia, Old Serbia, Macedonia, and Vojvodina were Croatian lands. They also conceded that the Serbs had settled in the eastern parts of Bosnia, Hercegovina, and Montenegro, although the area had originally belonged to the Croatian nation.

Medieval Croatia—Christianity, the Kingdom, and Hungary

Having defined their original settlements and historic lands, the historians then turned their attention to the three major events in Croatian medieval history—the conversion to Christianity, the formation of the Croatian kingdom, and relations with Hungary. In regard to the conversion to Christianity the textbooks made two important points. First, the students learned that in 640 the pope sent missionaries among some of the Croats in Dalmatia. "How many Croats, if any, were converted by Abbot Martin" is not known, "because he did not know Croatian." A decade later the priest Ivan Ravenjanin was more successful and "christened many Croats."[134] It was not, however, until 678, according to Constantine Porphyrogenitus, whom the textbooks quoted often, that the "Croats accepted the cross" and the primacy of the pope. Thus the student read that the Croats "were the first among all the Slavic nations to become Christians, becoming thereby a recognized member of the European Christian community."[135] The books pointed out, however, that not all the Croats were converted at that time; this goal was reached only in the ninth century.

The second point concerned the use of the Slavic language, not Latin, in the church liturgy. The books recorded the prolonged struggle between Rome and Constantinople for primacy in the Christian world, and, in particular, its effect on the Croats. Some Croatian rulers and Dalmatian bishops followed Byzantium; others took the side of Rome. The discord largely ended in the reign of Prince Branimir (879–90), who chose Rome, as a result of which "in 880 Pope John VIII approved the use of Slavic in the church." Thus, "of all the nations belonging to the Catholic Church, the Croats were the only ones to gain and preserve the right to have the church service in their national language."[136] Subsequently, these two claims, that the Croats were the first Slavs to become Christians and that they were the only nation in the Catholic world to whom the pope granted the right to use their own language in church services, were impressed upon the students as unique achievements of their forefathers.

Hoić took note of the fact that Croatia's involvement in the conflict between Rome and Constantinople meant that her relations with the Serbs had suffered. He asserted that the results of the church schism "are felt even today by the Croatian and Serbian people. This split between the Latin and Greek worlds also separated these two tribes from one another, so that the Serbian tribe became a part of the Greek [Byzantine] cultural sphere and the Croats the Latin. Each developed its own history;" the Croats were to live "under rulers of their own blood and their own language."[137]

Although the period of the medieval Croatian kingdom was to provide inspiration for nineteenth-century nationalist politicians, scholars, and writers, it was hardly a tranquil era for their ancestors. Between 600 and 1102, they fought against or were ruled by Avars, Byzantines, Franks, Venetians, Bulgarians, and Hungarians. The success of the foreigners in large measure was facilitated by the lack of unity among the Croats themselves, a problem, the textbooks made clear, that would plague them throughout their history. Nevertheless, there were bright periods to which the student could look with pride.

At the time when Charlemagne ruled over much of Europe, including Croatian lands, there were three Croatian political units—White Croatia, Red Croatia, and Pannonian or Posavska Croatia. The first two roughly represented northern and southern Dalmatia and adjacent areas, whereas Pannonian Croatia, or the more familiar Posavska Croatia, referred to Croatia between the Sava and Drava rivers, or what is largely present-day Croatia-Slavonia. The textbooks reported with great pride the Croatian successes against Charlemagne. Again quoting Constantine Porphyrogenitus, they stressed that when the Franks came into the Croatian lands, their soldiers "tore away" Croatian babies from their mothers and fed them to the dogs. Ljudevit, the leader of Posavska Croatia, protested to Charlemagne, but to no avail. Thereupon Ljudevit led a successful Slavic revolt against the emperor, which was "the first to so stagger the Frankish state that the other nations now began to break away from it, so that eventually it [Charlemagne's empire] was dismembered into its natural parts. Then each nation created and solidified its own kingdom."[138] Moreover, "even the Timočani, a Serbian tribe in the east, came under the banner of the Posavian Croatian ruler" at this time.[139]

A half-century later "one of the best-known rulers of White Croatia," that is, the northern Dalmatian region, Trpimir, referred to his state as "regnum Chroatorum." It extended "from the Raša River [of Istria] to the Neretva in the south and somewhat beyond the Drina in the east to the Danube near Belgrade." As "dux Chroatorum," Srkulj and Tomšić reported, Trpimir commanded "100,000 infantry soldiers, 60,000 cavalry, and on the sea he had eighty large ships, each with forty men, and a hundred smaller ships manned by ten to twenty men." Although these figures were attributed to Porphyrogenitus, in all probability they were an exaggeration. Nevertheless, they strengthened the impression of Croatia's power in the Balkans.[140]

The most famous ruler, however, was Tomislav (910–28), who finally united the Croatian nation after defeating the Hungarians and Bulgarians. In 925 he was crowned king of Croatia. The textbooks made a special point of his wars with the Bulgarians, because the issue concerned the fate of the Serbs. Caught in the middle of the struggle between Bulgaria and Byzantium, Prince Zaharija, the Serbian ruler of Raška, who had initially sided with Tsar Simeon of Bulgaria, subsequently cast his lot with the Byzantine emperor. Consequently, in 925 Simeon sent his army against Zaharija, who was forced to flee to Croatia, where Tomislav "received him in his court hospitably and in a brotherly manner." The Bulgars pursued Zaharija into Croatia, but were defeated by the Croats. Subsequently, Tomislav was able to lead the great župan Zaharija and many of his people back into Serbia.[141] Two years later, in 927, Simeon attacked the Croats, "and once more he was beaten to his knees. He died of grief on the day of the battle." Peace was established between the Croats and Bulgars; thus, "Serbia was freed from Bulgarian control and came under the protectorship of the Croatian king."[142] Throughout the textbooks, as will be seen below, the students would read of similar assistance to or cooperation with the Serbs. The clear impression given was that the Croats had contributed much to the well-being and success of the medieval Serbian nation.

Given his achievements, it is understandable that the textbooks would praise Tomislav's reign. In describing his kingdom, Klaić wrote that Tomislav had "united all the large and small Croatian and Serbian provinces in one large state, which included the entire Croatian and Serbian people and all the Latin cities along the seacoast (Dalmatia)."[143] Hoić observed that "Red Croatia and the Serbian provinces recognized Tomislav as their ruler. His authority extended to the Drina, the field of Kosovo, and the Bojana River. Under his banner the heroes of Duklja, Serbia, Bosnia, and all of Croatia assembled." Consequently, when Pope John X crowned Tomislav as king of Croatia and Dalmatia, "this was the most important event in the earliest history of Croatia, because Croatia had now become a kingdom and she gained a ruler of her own blood and language. . . . Thus Tomislav, the first king of the Croats, united the nation, regulated church and state relations, and elevated Croatia [to a position] as no other king was able to do either before or after him." Hence "a grateful national tradition bestows on him the title 'saint,' that is, a great king."[144]

The kingdom of Croatia, which lasted until the union with Hungary in 1102, experienced difficulties immediately after Tomislav's death. Hoić attributed the decline to the struggle for power within the royal family, the opposition of princes to centralized rule, the Venetian danger, and the threat to Red Croatia or to southern Dalmatia from the emerging Serbian state, aided by Byzantium.[145] Of these factors, the one which runs like a red thread throughout the textbooks in describing all of Croatian history was the harm done to the nation by the dissension and lack of unity among the Croats themselves. There always seemed to be nobles who, for selfish reasons, would side with a foreign power to undermine Croatian national authority.

Of the other medieval rulers, the books singled out Krešimir (1058–74), who reunited most of the former Croatian land. His title was "By God's grace, King of Croatia and Dalmatia"; in his court "Croatian was spoken."[146] The last prominent monarch was Zvonimir (1075–89), who was crowned by Pope Gregory VII. Zvonimir sided with the papacy in its wars with the Holy Roman Empire, but after some initial successes the Croatian forces were defeated. In time Zvonimir restored peace and prosperity to his lands. Eventually, however, he lost some of his southern lands to the principality of Zeta or Montenegro.[147]

When Zvonimir died without an heir, a scramble for power ensued among the nobility, who had become more powerful than the king.[148] Four political factions emerged. One, composed of several Dalmatian cities, cast its lot with Venice. The second was led by a number of nobles who cooperated with the Serbian leaders and sought the protectorship of the Byzantine emperor Alexis. The third group preferred to follow Ban Peter, who believed that the Croats should rule themselves. The fourth faction was pro-Hungarian, in part at least because Zvonimir's widow, Queen Helen, was the sister of Ladislav, king of Hungary. The clergy also favored Ladislav because of his support of the church. More important, many Croatian nobles favored the link with the Magyars because of the rights and privileges enjoyed by the aristocracy in Hungary. As a result of their support Ladislav was able to gain control of those Croatian lands between the Drava and Sava before he died in 1095.[149]

In 1102, Koloman, the new king, signed the famous Pacta Conventa, which united the Croatian and Hungarian kingdoms and brought him, in addition to the title "King of Hungary," that of "King of Croatia and Dalmatia." This accord was reached with twelve nobles representing the Croatian nation. Every textbook was emphatic that the agreement was between two equal political entities— Croatia and Hungary. It was a personal union in which Koloman swore "that he would faithfully abide by all the rights of the [Croatian] kingdom" and "that he would defend the privileges of the nobles and cities. He would administer royal matters only in conjunction with the magnates and nobles of the kingdom. He would not permit any foreigner to settle in any city; he would defend all the authority of the church."[150] Yet the significance of the union was clearly expressed by Hoić when he admitted that Croatia was no longer its own master, but had "to live in union with the lands of the Hungarian crown. The center of this union was not Croatia, but Hungary."[151]

For the next four centuries, from 1102 to 1526, when the battle of Mohács took place, the Croats and their domains were involved, directly or indirectly, in the politics of the Hungarian kingdom. There were wars with Venice, Byzantium, and the Ottoman Empire, dynastic controversies with Poland and Bohemia, threats from the Germans and Habsburgs, and even conflicts with Serbia and Bosnia. Perhaps the most serious issues revolved around the almost constant strife between the dynasty and the nobles and the quarrels among the nobles. Croatia shared in the fortunes and misfortunes of the Magyars, but the Croats were not in a position to determine their own destiny in these centuries, notwithstanding the assumed equality of the kingdoms envisaged by the Pacta Conventa. Thus, for example, the Croatian lands were not administered as one political unit, but organized into two *banovine* or provinces—one Croatia-Dalmatia, the other Slavonia. It was not until the sixteenth century that Croatia, Slavonia, and Dalmatia were constituted as a single political entity, the Triune Kingdom.

Srkulj made the point that between 1102 and 1235 each Hungarian ruler was crowned separately as the "King of Hungary" and the "King of Croatia." Beginning with Bela IV (1235–70), the ruler was crowned as the "King of Hungary and Croatia," which meant that the former "personal union began to be transformed into a real union."[152] The textbooks often used the hyphenated term "King of Hungary-Croatia" when discussing relations involving the South Slavic lands, especially Serbia and Bosnia. Therefore, the student could gain two impressions from this development. First, that it was the king of Croatia who was dealing with Serbia and Bosnia, which gave credence to the idea of the historical continuity of the Croatian kingdom. The second impression related to Bosnia. Since Hungarian rule was maintained almost without interruption for several centuries, one could infer that the monarch of Croatia, that is, "the King of Hungary-Croatia," ruled over Bosnia until the Ottoman conquest.

Medieval Serbia and Bosnia

The Croatian historians, although concentrating on national events, devoted considerable attention to the Serbs and their role in Balkan affairs. It should be emphasized that the historians recognized the Serbs as belonging to a separate nation, unlike their Serbian colleagues, who, it will be remembered, considered the Croats as part of the Serbian nation. As noted above, the Croatian textbooks described the Serbian settlement in southeastern Europe, the assistance that King Tomislav rendered to Prince Zaharija in his conflict with the Bulgarians, and some of the religious controversies. All the authors took note of the fact that Serbian rulers negotiated with Rome and Constantinople over the course of centuries and appeared to waver in their religious allegiance. The intent was to prove that the Croatians had become Christians before the Serbs, and that they were steadfast in their loyalty to Rome.

The Serbs, as had been the case with the Croats, had to overcome adversity over many decades before they became independent. Citing Constantine Porphyrogenitus, Srkulj wrote that the first ruler of Raška, "the original center of the Serbian lands," was Višeslav, who ruled at the end of the eighth century, but it was not until Časlav's reign in the tenth century that Serbia became more united.[153] Soon thereafter, according to Hoić, the Serbs, under Bulgarian pressure from the east, began to penetrate into Red Croatia. The consequence of this was that in a later period both Croatian and Serbian names prevailed in these regions.[154] Furthermore, by the eleventh century, parts of Red Croatia joined Zeta (Montenegro) and later Serbia. Thus by the time of Stefan Nemanja, in 1159, "the Serbian name was being heard more and more in these regions [Red Croatia] and was superseding the old Croatian name."[155]

Although the history books covered the medieval period in considerable detail, the impression that they wished to convey can best be seen through the honor and respect they accorded to three prominent Serbs—Stefan Nemanja, Saint Sava, and Dušan—and the attention devoted to the battle of Kosovo. Stefan Nemanja's (1169–96) fame rested upon three principal facts—one, his founding the dynasty, two, his unifying the small and previously warring Serbian provinces, and, three, his devotion to Orthodoxy, as demonstrated by the churches and monasteries he built. All authors praised Nemanja's contributions to Serbian history. Srkulj summarized their sentiments when he wrote that "with Nemanja begins the great period in Serbian history. . . . Nemanja is numbered among the most famous Serbian rulers. His personality is so deeply ingrained in the mind and soul of the Serbian people that they have completely forgotten the predecessors of Nemanja. When his heirs mention him, it is done as though there had been no one before him. In fact, even his father is not mentioned. It is as though Serbian history began with him."[156] Only his son Sava and Tsar Dušan could rival him in popularity and importance.

The books nevertheless took note of the fact that his reign had not begun auspiciously. He had joined Venice against Byzantium, he was captured, and then, "barefooted and bareheaded, with a rope around his neck, he threw himself at the feet of the emperor." Pardoned, he was sent back to rule in his province. When disorder erupted in the Byzantine empire following the death of Emperor Manuel, Nemanja made an alliance "with the Hungarian-Croatian king," which enabled him to expand the Serbian domains in the east, south, and west at the expense of the Byzantine empire.[157] As a result, Hoić observed, "the power of Serbia was now unleashed so that in a brief period Stefan Nemanja created a united Raška, or Serbia, and he began to penetrate into the poorly defended southern Croatian lands."[158] But, as Srkulj added, "it is interesting that Nemanja sought to bring Dubrovnik under his rule, but he did not succeed."[159]

Not only had Nemanja united the Serbian lands, but he also was the father of Sava, the patron saint of the Serbs. The history books were just as attentive in reporting Sava's importance in Serbian history as the readers had been. After the Serbian church was declared autonomous in 1219, Sava was appointed archbishop, which meant that "henceforth it was not necessary for the Serbian archbishops and bishops to go to the [ecumenical] patriarch for their consecration." He organized the Serbian church and created bishoprics. He worked for the welfare of priests and helped build schools. He "laid the foundations for national education. For this a grateful nation proclaimed him 'The Teacher.'" In addition, Sava reconciled the conflict between his two brothers, Stefan the First Crowned, "one of the most gifted" Nemanjas, and Vukan, over the succession to their father's throne, thereby preserving the unity of the state.[160]

Other Nemanjas made their contributions also, but none rivaled the most famous medieval Serbian ruler, Dušan (1331–55). "Neither before nor after was Serbia so powerful and famous" as in his reign. He defeated the Albanians, Bosnians, Bulgarians, Greeks, and Hungarians. He "remained an unyielding foe of the Catholic Church."[161] He elevated the Serbian metropolitan to patriarch and then had himself crowned as tsar of "the Serbs, Greeks, and Bulgars" in 1346. He endowed the nation with a law code; he built schools and developed trade. The "Serbian empire flourished" under Dušan, "a man of tall stature, a handsome face, resolute and brave." The German emperor, Karl IV, addressed him as "Dear Brother."[162] Although the students were thus taught that Tsar Dušan had truly been a great man and that Serbia was the dominant power in the Balkans when he died in 1355, the books stressed that notwithstanding his successes Dušan failed to leave a viable empire. He son and successor, Uroš, could not command the allegiance of the provincial rulers. His death in 1371 was a multiple blow to the nation. First, it brought an end to the Nemanja dynasty. Second, the struggle for primacy among the nobles, which plagued Uroš, became more intense. No noble would accept another as the nation's leader. Third, the Hungarians exploited the situation by extending their influence among the Serbs. Fourth, and most significant, Serbia's misfortunes coincided with the establishment of the Ottoman Empire as the major force in the Balkans.[163]

Although the defeat of the Serbs at the battle of Kosovo is generally associated exclusively with Serbian history, the Croatian textbooks portrayed it as a major event in their medieval history also; it was depicted as a disaster for the Croats as well as for the Serbs. For over five centuries, from 1389 to 1913, the Ottoman Turks would be, in the textbooks' view, the principal obstacle to the well-being and progress of the South Slavs and the other Balkan nations. The books contained the generally accepted popular account of what happened at Kosovo. In summary, Miloš killed Sultan Murad; the Turks won the battle and captured and killed Prince Lazar, the leader of the Serbian forces; their defeat, in part, was attributed to the betrayal of Vuk Branković, who broke ranks. His actions doomed not only the Serbs, but also all the Christian forces who fought alongside the Serbs. Thus the students learned that the Turks had overwhelmed the Serbian army, which was reinforced by Albanian, Bosnian, Croatian, and Wallachian units. The immediate consequence was "the ruin of the Serbian state" and its subjugation to Ottoman rule.[164] For the Serbs it meant that they would have to pay a tribute to the Turks and help them militarily; the widow of Prince Lazar was even forced to send her own daughter to Sultan Bayezid's harem.[165] These developments did not bring unity to the nation as Serbian leaders vied for power or curried Ottoman favor. Consequently, a century after Dušan had elevated his empire to the dominant state in the Balkans, Serbia in 1459 was relegated to the role of an Ottoman *pashaluk* or province. It was clear that the moral which the textbooks wished to convey to the students was that when self-interest was placed above that of the nation, the people would suffer the fate of the Serbs. It was the same message the textbooks drew from the collapse of the Croatian kingdom after Zvonimir. What the significance of Kosovo would be for the Croats was precisely stated by Hoić: "The mournful impression which this defeat had on the Serbian and also on the Croatian nation is clearly demonstrated in the national folk songs, which fathers have passed on to their sons. Henceforth, Croatia would be the first to bear the brunt of the Turkish attack."[166]

As can be seen, the overall impression given of medieval Serbia was highly positive. In addition to the information on the Serbian lands and the various Nemanja rulers, the students read about the structure of the Serbian state, its commerce and trade, and the famous Serbian monasteries—Studenica, Žiča, Mileševa, Sopoćani, Dečani, and Ravanica. They also learned that the Serbs had written extensively about the lives of their rulers. Any student in the age of romantic nationalism, Croat or Serb, who read the detailed accounts of medieval Serbia would easily be moved by them.

In addition to Serbia the textbooks devoted considerable space to Bosnian affairs, in part because of Croatia's interest in the area and also because of the success of the Bosnians in the second half of the fourteenth century. In connection with Bosnia four main topics were examined—the land, its relations with Croatia and Hungary, the Bogomils, and the reign of Stjepan Tvrtko.

As we know, both Croatia and Serbia claimed Bosnia. In 1875 Klaić wrote that "Bosnia . . . once was a Croatian land," but in 1903 he was to amend this statement when he indicated that "Bosnia was composed of a number of Croatian and Serbian provinces."[167] In 1898 Hoić averred that Bosnia "was once a part of the Croatian kingdom."[168] In 1912 Srkulj asserted that Bosnia had "expanded at the expense of Croatian and Serbian provinces."[169] It was thus made clear to the students that Croatia's claims to Bosnia could be substantiated. This fact was strengthened by the second point, namely, the frequent references to Bosnia's subordination to the rule of "the Hungarian-Croatian ruler" during the twelfth and thirteenth centuries. Other information was cited to show Croatia's ties with Bosnia, such as the fact that Pavao Šubić, a Croatian nobleman, ruled over Bosnia in the thirteenth century and that the daughter of Stjepan Kotromanić, a fourteenth-century Bosnian ruler, gave his daughter in marriage to King Louis, which made her the queen of "Hungary-Croatia."[170]

With regard to the third point, the religion of the Bosnians, the textbooks explained that the Bosnians had become Bogomils, an heretical sect, stemming from the Manichaeism of the east and related to the Albigensian and Waldensian sects in the west. Notwithstanding repeated attempts by both Catholic and Orthodox rulers to suppress the Bogomils, they defended their faith. After the Ottoman conquest many Bogomils converted to Islam and formed the basis for the large Slavic Muslim population.[171]

The books placed particular emphasis on the reign of Stjepan Tvrtko (1377–91), who was able to conquer part of Raška and was crowned "by the Grace of God, King of Serbia, Bosnia, and the Littoral" in 1377.[172] He exploited the internal strife among the Croatian nobles and, as a result, was able to conquer "all the Croatian lands up to the coastal cities," at which point he was forced to abandon his campaign because of an alliance with Prince Lazar in 1389 against the Ottomans.[173] After Serbia's defeat at Kosovo, Tvrtko renewed his campaign against the Croats and acquired "all of Croatia and the Dalmatian coastal cities south of Velebit, except Zadar."[174] His subsequent conversion to Catholicism endeared him to his Croatian subjects.[175] His achievements were rewarded in 1390 when he was crowned "King of Croatia and Dalmatia." Klaić characterized his reign as "fortunate and glorious."[176]

All the readers and textbooks stressed that Tvrtko had achieved a special place in South Slav history because he succeeded in uniting the Bosnians, Croats, and Serbs in one state, even if its duration was only two years. He died in 1391, two years after Kosovo and one year after being crowned "King of Croatia and Dalmatia," a title that he had added to his previous one of King of Bosnia and Serbia.[177] No more successful than Zvonimir in Croatia or Dušan in Serbia, Tvrtko did not leave a strong kingdom to his successors. At his death the nobles quarreled, and soon the kingdom broke apart. By 1463 Bosnia was firmly in the Ottoman grip.

Croatia and the Ottoman Threat

The Ottoman ascendancy colored the presentation of Croatian history in the textbooks, even affecting the accounts of Croatian relations with the Hungarians and Austrians. If only the latter two nations had listened to the Croats, the readers and textbooks seemed to say, they all would have suffered less at Ottoman hands. When confronted by disaster, the Croats remained loyal and defended Christianity against Islam. Hoić exulted that "after the greatest defeats the genius of our people remained unbroken, as our national folk songs bear witness."[178] Even the vocabulary in the history books became more eloquent in describing Croatian encounters with the Ottoman forces.

Of the more notable events of the fifteenth century, the students learned that Venice exploited the weakness of the Hungarians and Croats so that "the Croatian nation now definitely lost its primacy on the Adriatic Sea, for which it had fought bloody battles for centuries. Henceforth, the Croatian coastal inhabitants would [man the ships that] spread the glory and greatness of arrogant Venice."[179] At the same time the Ottoman forces raided and plundered the Slavic lands and Transylvania. Then in 1453 the Ottomans achieved their supreme triumph when Constantinople, the seat of Christian Orthodoxy, fell to Mohammed the Conqueror. The only respite came in 1456 when the Hungarian forces of John Hunyadi, supported by units composed of Slavic citizens, whom the Catholic friar John of Capistrano (Ivan Kapistran) had rallied to battle, beat back the Turks at Belgrade, an event that was hailed as a brilliant victory for the Christians. Yet three years later Serbia finally succumbed, and four years thereafter, in 1463, Bosnia shared the same fate. Subsequently the Turks "attacked Croatia more strongly every year."[180] In part the Ottoman success was due to the fact that the Hungarian nobles had weakened the power of the king for their own selfish interests, so that Croatia was "left to defend herself." Consequently, "while the Croatian nation, with its nobility, was, so to speak, on guard against the Turks day and night, the great nobles of Hungary were curbing the royal power, more and more."[181]

Croatian resistance was demonstrated dramatically in 1493 when the Bosnian pasha, Yakub, invaded Slovenia and Styria. The Croatians made their stand against him on the battlefield of Krbava

(Udbina). In Hoić's words: "In a bitter battle, the Croats fell to a stronger Turkish force. Seven thousand Croats covered the field of battle, and six thousand of them, including Ban Derečin, fell into Turkish hands. The Turks subsequently devastated Croatia far and wide. A contemporary author wrote that 'The destruction of the Croatian kingdom took place on the field of Udbina.'" [182] Klaić asserted that the "flower of the Croatian nobility" perished in 1493, after which the "desperate" struggle of the Croats began. Much blood would be shed, but for their efforts the Croats would earn "the glorious name—'the strongest shield and bulwark of Christianity." [183] The theme that the Croats were left to defend their nation alone, notwithstanding their ties with the Hungarians and subsequently the Austrians, was to recur throughout the textbooks, as was the contention that Croatia defended Catholicism, sometimes almost single-handedly.

When the papacy and the Hungarian and Polish rulers could not present a united front against the Ottoman danger, a greater burden was thrust on the Croatian leaders. Thus when the Ottoman empire threatened Central Europe, Croatia became the defender of Christianity. In this endeavor, the books emphasized the actions of Petar Berislavić, who was appointed ban in 1513. He erected strategic fortifications, which temporarily repulsed the invader. In 1520 "the Turks, as usual, raided the Croatian lands," but Berislavić routed them: in the pursuit, he was killed in an ambush. Yet his successes against the Turks had become so well known that the pope and the emperor praised "the bravery and the sacrifices of the Croats ('the strongest shield and rampart of Christendom')." Subsequently, Berislavić was immortalized in national folk songs. [184]

Following Suleiman's conquest of Belgrade in 1521, "'the golden key' to the Kingdom of the Croats and the Hungarians," where "ten thousand of the bravest soldiers" fell, Krsto Frankopan emerged as the next Croatian hero. [185] In 1525 he defeated a major Turkish force at Jajce. "With this victory Krsto became famous as the leading Croatian hero and father of his homeland. Even King Louis awarded him the title 'Defender of the Croatian kingdom.'" [186] The efforts of the Croats were to no avail, however, for the next year the Ottoman forces triumphed over the Hungarians at the battle of Mohács.

The textbooks did not dwell on the battle itself, which has been described before. The authors did, however, stress one point, namely, that both John Zapolya and Krsto Frankopan had strongly advised King Louis to avoid battle until his forces had been reinforced by troops from Transylvania and Croatia. He ignored this counsel and suffered the consequences. Once again, the books implied, association with the Hungarians had led to disaster. In Klaić's opinion the best parts of the Croatian lands now came under Ottoman domination. The regions that escaped Turkish rule represented "the pitiful remains of the kingdom of Dalmatia, Croatia, and Slavonia."[187] Hereafter, the fate of the Croats would be tied to the Habsburg dynasty.

King Louis's death precipitated a struggle over his succession. The vast majority of Hungarian nobles supported John Zapolya and elected him their monarch, but a minority chose Ferdinand, archduke of Austria and brother of Emperor Charles V. More important was the fact that he was the brother of Louis's widow, Queen Marie, and husband of Louis's sister, which strengthened his claim to the Hungarian throne. The issue of succession also divided the Croats. Initially Krsto Frankopan and most of the Slavonian nobles supported Zapolya, but eventually they gave allegiance to Ferdinand. As Hoić wrote, "the Croats turned to the House of Habsburg, which, at the time, was so strong that the sun never set on her domains," a reference to the global Spanish empire.[188] Each student, thus, could feel that Croatia had once been a part of the mightiest empire in the world.

Whereas the Croats chose Vienna, the majority of the Hungarian nobles resisted. Zapolya concluded an alliance with the Turks, which, in effect, made him their vassal. With their aid, he proceeded to rule most of Hungary, with his principal base in Transylvania. Ferdinand, on the other hand, in control of only a small area of the Hungarian kingdom, held the title of both king of Croatia and king of Hungary.

Croatia and the Habsburg Empire

Since four centuries (1526–1918) of Croatian history were directly linked to the Habsburg Empire, it is understandable that considerable attention would be devoted to this relationship and to the role that the Croatian nation and its national heroes played in defense of the monarchy. The first major test for Croatia as part of the Habsburg realm came in 1529 when Suleiman lay siege to Vienna. Surprisingly, the textbooks did not dwell on this battle, although it is generally regarded as a turning point in Ottoman-European relations. The books simply took note of the fact that 15,000 Habsburg soldiers were able to hold off Suleiman's assaults. After losing more than a third of his troops and short of supplies, the sultan withdrew. What role the Croats played in the siege is not mentioned. However, every reader and textbook regaled the students with the subsequent exploits of two Croats, Nikola Jurišić (1532) and Nikola Zrinski (1566), who resisted Suleiman's forces, in contrast to Zapolya and his Hungarian supporters, who collaborated with the enemy of Christendom.

In 1532 Suleiman renewed his campaign against the Habsburg Empire. One of his units, led by Ibrahim, lay siege to the fortress city of Kiseg (Köszeg), which was defended for a month by Jurišić. The textbooks, as had the readers previously, emphasized how Jurišić, with only 700 soldiers, was able to hold off a Turkish force that some authors claimed numbered over 100,000, certainly an exaggeration. Unable to defeat Jurišić, Ibrahim planted the Ottoman flag on the fortress wall and withdrew. Jurišić's "victory" became known far and wide, because no one expected that he would triumph. In the opinion of a contemporary: "Neither the representatives of the Holy Roman Empire nor the emperor himself believed that it was possible to overcome the forces besieging Kiseg, and yet what they considered impossible, the Croats made possible." The Turks vented their frustration on other parts of Croatia, but the Croats "did not despair. They were, in fact, dubbed 'the remnants of the remainder of the former Croatian kingdom,' and their motto was: 'We do not surrender alive to the Turks.'"[189]

Throughout the rest of Suleiman's reign, Croatia, which was on the frontier of the Habsburg Empire, remained under constant Ottoman attack. The individual who best symbolized Croatian resistance was Nikola Zrinski, the ban since 1542. Until his death in 1566, he seemed to thrive, according to the textbooks, on fighting the Turks. He, more than any other member of the Zrinski clan, made his family name a household word in Croatian history.

In 1566, when Suleiman prepared for his final campaign against the Habsburg Empire, Zrinski defeated an advancing Turkish force. The sultan, according to the books, was determined to punish Zrinski, who had been a constant thorn in his side. His army tracked Zrinski to the fortress city of Siget (Szigetvar) in August of 1566. What happened subsequently has been described in the readers, but because of the interpretation placed upon the event by the Croatian historians, it is well to repeat briefly what they reported, because Zrinski was a major figure in Croatian historical mythology.

Zrinski's goal was to stall the Ottoman army until the major Habsburg forces arrived. When they failed to appear, Zrinski, with a contingent of about 2,500 "brave Croatian heroes," was left to face alone an Ottoman army of over 100,000. Even though the outcome was inevitable, Zrinski and his supporters inflicted huge losses on the Ottoman troops. According to the textbooks, Suleiman tried to bribe Zrinski into surrendering by offering him rule over all Croatia and the release of his son, who had been captured earlier. Zrinski would not hear of it. He "remained loyal to Emperor Maximilian, knowing well that there was no more disgraceful sin than the betrayal of one's homeland."[190] When, after a month, the end was apparent, Zrinski dressed himself in his finest uniform, put 100 ducats in his pockets so that the Turkish soldiers who found his body would be rewarded, and prepared for his last stand. There also was a woman of noble birth in the fort. Zrinski was going to strangle her to spare her disgrace at Ottoman hands. Instead she persuaded him to allow her to dress as a man, and she too joined the battle. He assembled the remaining forces and said, "Let's finish this task for our faith, homeland, and king."[191] He invoked the name of Jesus three times, then led an attack on the Ottoman forces. He was shot in the head and chest. The Turks stormed into the fort, and, as if in a final act of Christian retribution, a powder magazine exploded, killing another 3,000 Turks. In all, over 30,000 Turks had fallen. Zrinski's head was "mounted on a stake."[192] Suleiman had died several days earlier, but the event had been concealed from the Ottoman troops by the grand vizier, Mehmed Sokolović, whom Klaić described as a "Turkicized Croat."[193]

From the above description, it is understandable how Zrinski became one of the major heroic figures in the accounts written by the nationalistically minded historians. Tomšić wrote: "the unparalleled bravery of Nikola Zrinski is known far and wide, and our masses even today honor it. They proudly recall the name of Nikola Zrinski. . . . There is hardly any greater example in history of heroism than that of Nikola Zrinski."[194] Hoić noted that "contemporary Europe was astonished by such heroism and world history gained its second Leonidas." Furthermore, he added, "the death of Nikola Zrinski and Suleiman concludes this period of Turkish history, when it was at the zenith of its power. With the death of Suleiman, the crescent paled; it no longer had the brilliance of Suleiman. With the death of Zrinski, the morning star of the Christian world shown brightly."[195] The symbolism evoked is clear. The Croats, under Zrinski, turned the tide of battle in favor of the Christians against the Ottoman Muslims, who, since they first set foot on the European continent in 1354, more than two centuries earlier, were a constant threat to the well-being of European civilization. Siget was for the Croats what Kosovo was for the Serbs. Each battle in its own way provided the historical inspiration of the nationalistic revival of the nineteenth century. For the Croats, it also was proof that they had carried more than their fair share of the burden of protecting the Habsburg Empire.

Although the exploits of Jurišić and Zrinski could bolster the pride of the students, the authors did not conceal the grim conditions of the sixteenth and seventeenth centuries. As Hoić wrote, "the picture of what remained of the Croatian kingdom in these two centuries was sad."[196] The defeat at Mohács changed everything for the worse. Much of the Croatian land—Slavonia, Lika, Krbava, and parts of Dalmatia—was now under Ottoman control. Moreover, the demography of the Croatian lands would be changed because "there never was a war between the Turks and Croats in which the Christians, caught between two fires, did not flee to our lands." Thus, during the reign of Emperor Leopold (1657–1705), the population "under the Turkish yoke was enticed into our lands by the imperial government's proclamation promising to all 'golden freedom under the Christian king.'"[197] At this time also, territory was created out of the Croatian lands to serve as a military buffer zone between the Ottoman and the Habsburg empires. Initially the ban of Croatia ruled over this territory, but in time it came under the immediate control of Vienna and its inhabitants were directly responsible to the emperor, not to the Croatian ban. Thus more than one-half of Croatia-Slavonia was either under Ottoman domination or part of the Habsburg Military Frontier.

The difficult life of the students' ancestors in this period received much attention. The Ottoman forces pillaged the land, terrorized the population, and exacted heavy taxes. The fate of the Croats who were under Habsburg control was not much better, because German officers and military units were sent into the Military Frontier, where they "often raided and plundered worse than the Turks, in addition to which they also trampled the old laws of the kingdom."[198] Furthermore, under Habsburg rule the Croats "were almost constantly under arms, so that many times all of Croatia was transformed into one camp." What made matters worse was that there was no unity within the Croatian leadership. At times members of the aristocracy found common cause with their Hungarian counterparts, and thus Croatian national interests were not defended.[199] The era was one in which, "as our national folk songs bear witness, the genius of the people remained unbroken after the greatest defeats."[200]

During this difficult period the Catholic church provided the guiding light for the Croats. Although the Turks closed bishoprics, churches, and monasteries, converted some churches to mosques, and forced some priests to leave their flocks, "the Croats, despite all their troubles, remained true to the faith of their fathers; religion was their holy shield and most ennobling banner in the battle for survival."[201] Not only did the Croats remain steadfast in their loyalty to Catholicism when faced with the Islamic danger, but they were equally resolute in their defiance of Protestantism, which was seeking to gain converts.[202] In the popular mind Croatianism and Catholicism were synonymous concepts.

There were two attempts to alleviate the plight of the Croats within the Habsburg domains—one, the peasant revolt led by Matija Gubec, the other, a conspiracy of two noble families, Zrinski and Frankopan. The peasant revolt has already been described and will only be briefly summarized here. As a result of the unbearable economic conditions and the misrule of the nobles, one of the largest peasant revolts in Croatian history broke out in 1573 north of Zagreb, with its center in Stubica. It was crushed, and Gubec was seized, tried, and quartered. The moral that the textbooks wished to convey was that this was how the peasants were rewarded for their contributions to the empire, including their defense against the Ottomans.[203]

In the Zrinski-Frankopan conspiracy of the seventeenth century, the nobles fared no better than had the peasant Gubec. They were considerably upset by the peace terms Emperor Leopold accepted in 1664 following the first major Habsburg victory over the Ottoman Empire in more than a century. The peace settlement did not provide for the retention of Croatian lands conquered, and thus it appeared to make the Croatians' valiant military contributions meaningless. In addition, the nobles objected to excessive state taxation and the violation of the ban's authority in Croatia by German officials.[204] Another grievance was the appointment of a German general to command the strategic Karlovac garrison instead of Petar Zrinski, the ban, who had a distinguished military career. Thus, in 1671 Zrinski, together with his brother-in-law Franjo Krsto Frankopan, joined Hungarian conspirators, among whom was the Palatine, Ferenc Wesselényi, in a plan to detach the kingdoms of Croatia and Hungary from the empire. They appealed to the French, Poles, Turks, and Venetians for aid. When their scheme was discovered, Zrinski and Frankopan were tried and executed, and their possessions were confiscated.

The Zrinski and Frankopan families were the most illustrious in Croatian history. They had rendered faithful and loyal support to the Hungarians before 1526 and to the Habsburgs subsequently. They were always in the forefront of the campaigns against the Ottomans. Although the punishment for conspiracy and treason was identical in all states, "the Croatian nation was petrified at this horrible catastrophe. . . . It was as though Croatia had also died with the death of Zrinski and Frankopan," lamented Hoić.[205]

By the end of the seventeenth century, Croatia's fortunes had changed dramatically, as all the history books noted. In 1683 a Turkish army was stopped at Vienna for the second time, in large measure due to the assistance of the Polish king, John Sobieski. "Now the entire Croatian nation, from the Danube up to Montenegro, rose up in arms to put an end to Turkish rule in the Croatian lands."[206] By the peace of Sremski Karlovci (Karlowitz) in 1699, Slavonia to the Sava and Croatia to the river Una came under Habsburg rule, while most of Dalmatia was awarded to Venice.

As we have already seen, the fate of Dalmatia and Dubrovnik had preoccupied the authors of the readers and geography books. The historians were even more attentive to the question. They described in considerable detail the role and influence that the Byzantines, Venetians, Hungarians, Ottomans, and Habsburgs had there. They noted how European intellectual concepts influenced Dalmatian writers and scholars. Dubrovnik's success in commerce and trade was lauded as well as the skillful diplomacy the city pursued, which enabled it to maintain a degree of independence when the Ottomans dominated the Balkans. Although Dalmatia suffered heavily at the hands of foreigners, it nevertheless had been more fortunate than the other Croatian lands.

As was the case with their colleagues in literature and geography, the historians offered no concessions to the Serbs on the issue of Dalmatia, and especially Dubrovnik. Dalmatia and Dubrovnik were Croatian. Evidence of various kinds was produced to support this assertion. Srkulj noted that in the thirteenth and fourteenth centuries, during the period of Venetian control, "the Serbian rulers tried in vain to bring [Dubrovnik] under their rule, but, fortunately, it always withstood them and in fact gained land from them." Nevertheless, at the same time, "many Serbian and Croatian families, seeking refuge, settled in Dubrovnik."[207] Hoić made it clear that with the exception of Zadar, where the Italians predominated, the nobility was mainly "of old Croatian stock." Furthermore, he added, "throughout all of Dalmatia, Croatian customs and language prevailed."[208] The Croats made Dubrovnik "the Croatian (Slavic) Athens."[209]

Great emphasis was placed by the textbooks on the importance of humanism in the development of Croatian learning and society. While readily admitting their debt to Italian influence, they also stressed the Croatian contributions. Hoić wrote that "the universal rays of humanism illuminated the cradle of Croatian literature on the shores of the Adriatic Sea";[210] it was the inspiration for the flowering of culture in Dalmatia. The Croats, in fact, had achieved so much success that even Matthias Corvinius, the Hungarian king (1458–90), invited Dalmatians to teach at the university in Pozsony and the academy in Buda.[211]

Humanism, the texts emphasized, brought Croatia into the mainstream of Western European civilization, and equally important, it led to the first national Croatian literature. The movement ended a period of religious dominance in which books were written in Glagolitic, Latin, and Cyrillic. Now, Kořinek stated, the Croats wrote in "a pure national language (if one excludes the liturgical books), whereas the Serbs still for a long, long time held to the inferior, so-called Church Slavic language." Leading the way, Dubrovnik produced many poets, historians, theologians, and mathematicians, whose contributions made the "place of their birth famous." For example, "in Dubrovnik Croatian poetry rose to the pinnacle of its renown at the beginning of the seventeenth century," as exemplified by Gundulic's Osman.[212] Hoić stated that "there was not a city in the world which at that time could contribute as much, relatively speaking, to the general culture of humanity as Dubrovnik (the Slavic Athens) could." Hoić acknowledged that in poetry the writers in Dubrovnik were equaled by their "Croatian brothers in Split and Hvar. These three cities created an entire literature, which was very rich and interesting."[213] Finally, the authors repeated the names of many of the best-known authors, for example, Držić, Gundulić, Marulić, Palmotić, and Zlatarić. Most significant, the students were reminded that the writings of the Dalmatian authors also found their way to Croatia and Slavonia, thus strengthening the link among the Croats. This condition was important in the eighteenth century, when, once the Ottoman threat had been contained, the Croatian leadership endeavored to restore its authority throughout the nation. Dalmatia was the intellectual springboard for this revival.

Although in the eighteenth century the nobles and the sabor wished to assert control over the liberated Croatian lands, they were not successful. Thus, notwithstanding the hopes of the Croatian leaders, the function of the Croatian nation continued to be to serve the imperial interests, as, for example, when Austria fought the Ottomans in 1716–18 and 1736–39, or in the War of Austrian Succession, (1740–48) and the Seven Years' War (1756–63). In the latter two wars, "over 80,000 men from the Croatian Military Frontier fought."[214]

Since Croatia and Slavonia were part of the Habsburg Empire, it is understandable that the textbooks gave particular attention to its rulers. Among them Maria Theresa was the most popular with the historians. All approved of the reforms she introduced. Tomšić noted that Maria Theresa had appointed a Croatian military commander as ban and had reunited the port of Rijeka (Fiume) to Croatia-Slavonia. An academy and gymnasium were opened in Zagreb. The empress modified the laws on serfdom, making it easier for some serfs to move, "make brandy (rakija), cut wood, and pick acorns."[215] In Hoić's view, "the peasants now saw that there was a master above the nobles and aristocracy." In 1767 she established "a council of the Kingdom of Croatia, Slavonia, and Dalmatia for political-economic and military matters." However, thirteen years later, in 1779, the council was abolished and Croatia was incorporated into the Hungarian administration.[216] Klaić, who was the most sympathetic to Maria Theresa, let the students know that "the prosperity and happiness of her downtrodden people were constantly before her eyes. . . . Her rule was glorious. She hated war, yet she had to wage difficult wars that unintentionally burdened her people. Even though her times were turbulent, they are called golden because of her solicitude and goodness."[217]

Maria Theresa's son Joseph II, whose reign was discussed by every author, received a mixed reception. The authors appreciated his efforts to learn the views of his subjects during his travels throughout the empire, including a trip to Croatia in 1775. They endorsed the measures he took to improve the lot of the serfs and the steps he made to revise the civil and criminal law codes. His reforms in taxation were also lauded, as were the patents on religious toleration for Orthodox, Protestants, and Jews. However, they rejected his efforts to create "*from his various lands and kingdoms a unitary, powerful state in which there would be one constitution, one nation, and one law.*" Had his program succeeded, the Croats would have been Germanized.[218]

Although the history books had a great deal of information on the Serbs in the medieval period, there was by comparison relatively little about them in the years between the battle of Kosovo in 1389 and the beginning of the eighteenth century, a time when thousands of refugees settled in the Habsburg Military Frontier. As we have seen, the Ottoman conquest had caused a great exodus of Slavic Christians from south of the Sava-Danube river into the Croatian-Hungarian lands. Although most historians believed that each war brought in more refugees, Klaić made a distinction between the Christians who fled in the fifteenth and sixteenth centuries and those who followed in the seventeenth and eighteenth. In the earlier period, he contended, the newcomers, called Uskoks, were "Christian refugees from Croatian provinces that groaned under the Turkish yoke." They sought a sanctuary from which to carry on their battle against the Turks. In contrast, those who followed in the seventeenth and eighteenth centuries were "'Vlachs,'—in the majority they were of the Greek-Eastern religion; hence under no condition did they wish to submit to the royal [Croatian] laws, or to the authority of the ban, but only to the [German] generals and emperor. It was [for this reason] that the Frontier slowly was completely detached from the motherland."[219] Klaić thus attributed the "loss" of the Military Frontier region, in part at least, to the Serbian refugees, whom he called by the pejorative term "Vlach."

None of the other textbooks made similar judgments. In their accounts the refugees were both Croats and Serbs. The largest influx of Serbs arrived after 1690 and settled "in our regions," that is, in the Military Frontier and southern Hungary. They came at the invitation of Emperor Leopold, who granted them political and religious rights. These rights were reaffirmed by Maria Theresa in 1743 "as long as the rights of others were not violated."[220] Both Kořinek and Hoić remarked that the religious unity enjoyed by the Serbs through their national church and patriarchate in Peć was in part retained in the Habsburg Empire under the Serbian metropolitanate in Sremski Karlovci and their bishoprics.[221] They also pointed out to the students several problems the Serbs encountered. For example the Uniates actively proselytized among them, and in 1777 Maria Theresa approved a Uniate bishopric in Križevac for "the whole Croatian kingdom." Klaić made clear the intent of her act. The empress "began to contemplate how she could bring the Orthodox Greek-Eastern inhabitants in Croatia under the wing of the Catholic church." Joseph II thwarted her plans, however, affirming that "it is immaterial to us what the religion of our subjects is, just as long as they are loyal."[222]

The historians also discussed the Slavo-Serbian literary language used by the Serbs in Vojvodina. While Croatia had its own "pure national language" which was developed by the Dalmatian writers, the authors claimed that the Serbs did not have one of their own: "In the Serbian land a deathly silence prevailed for a long, long time in the realm of literary work. Only when the Serbs began to settle in large numbers in the Croatian and Hungarian lands did their literature revive again," a viewpoint somewhat analogous to the statements which Hristić, Novaković and others had made in their readers that the Croatian literary language began when the Croats adopted the Serbian language.[223]

The initial centuries of Habsburg rule were depicted by the historians as a mixed blessing. Whereas Croatia's association with Vienna shielded it from the Ottoman Empire and preserved its ties with Western civilization, the textbooks also stressed that the Croats had carried their full share in the military defense of the empire. In addition, they lost control of half of Croatia-Slavonia when the Military Frontier was created and placed under the direct control of Vienna. With the influx of Serbian refugees into the frontier zone, Croatia's demographic composition changed drastically. Notwithstanding these problems, this era also produced men like Zrinski, whose careers and exploits were described in detail in the textbooks because they raised Croatia's self-esteem and served as heroic figures in the era of romantic nationalism.

Croatian Political Developments in the Nineteenth Century

In contrast to the textbooks by Jović and Vukičević, in which 25 to 35 percent of their contents were devoted to the Serbian revolution, the Croatian historians slighted the Illyrian movement, a similar event for Croatian national development. It was perceived as being primarily a literary-cultural movement and, as such, it was discussed extensively in both the elementary and secondary school readers, with only the essential facts presented in the history books. In fact, the treatment of the nineteenth century in general was limited when compared to the discussion of previous centuries. For the same reason that the Serbian textbooks did not have information about current events, the Croatian historians avoided subjects that might have a political significance. Thus the coverage in the textbooks ended either with the Nagodba of 1868, or with Austria's occupation of Bosnia and Hercegovina in 1878 and its significance for Croatia. There is thus little information on, for instance, the era of Khuen-Héderváry or the Croatian-Serbian Coalition. Nevertheless, when the information found in the history books was combined with what the students learned from their readers and geography books, they could gain a clear understanding of the development of Croatian nationalism, at least for the first three-quarters of the nineteenth century.

In describing the events of that century, the history textbooks emphasized two themes—the political goals of the nation and Croatian relations with the Serbs. The principal aim was the unification of Croatia-Slavonia and Dalmatia under a single administration. In discussing the issue, the historians described the political situation at the beginning of the century and pointed out that the nobles, who had been the spokesmen for the nation in the preceding centuries, were no longer effective in defending the nation's interests. They had, for instance, yielded to Hungarian demands that Magyar be taught in the Croatian schools. As a result a new generation of young men, headed by Ljudevit Gaj, with the assistance of some nobles, had assumed the national leadership. The Illyrian movement, founded in the 1830s, had as its purpose the uniting of the nation, first linguistically and then politically.

The textbooks pointed out that the first calls for linguistic unity had been made even earlier. For example, in 1813 Bishop Vrhovac called on the Croatian clergy to collect "national folk songs, proverbs, and vocabulary." Two years later Antun Mihanović wrote "about the benefits of writing in one's native language." In 1823 Djuro Šporer published the *Illyrian Almanac*, which stressed Croatian themes. In Hoić's view, "All these developments preserved the love of the national language among the Croats," and had great influence on the youth.[224]

The decisive step toward political unification, however, came when Gaj rallied the leadership of the nation behind the štokavian dialect. In Klaić's opinion Gaj thus started "the revival of the Croatian nation."[225] In choosing this dialect Gaj aimed, in Tomšić's view, at purifying the languge "in order that the people could defend themselves more resolutely against all foreign influences." As a result of his achievement, within a few years the Croatian language and literature reached "a very high pinnacle."[226] The proof of Gaj's success was the fact that in 1843 the Hungarian government and its supporters in Croatia persuaded the Habsburg authorities to suppress the Illyrian movement and to support Magyar at the expense of Croatian. Notwithstanding this result, by 1847 Croatian became the official language in the nation.[227]

Whereas the principal goal of the Illyrian movement was the unification of the Croatian nation, Gaj, as discussed previously, also believed that it would be more easily achieved if the Croats cooperated with the Serbs, given their common štokavian dialect. Nothing in the textbooks indicated that the historians believed that the primacy of the Croatian nation was compromised by association with the Serbs. In their view, language was merely the link between two separate but related nations. Or as Kořinek wrote: "there was no difference [in the literary language] between them [the Croats] and the Serbs except for the alphabets."[228] As viewed by the historians, Croatian-Serbian cooperation served to strengthen the Croatian nation.

The textbooks also discussed political cooperation between the Serbs and Croats. The first concrete example of it occurred during the revolution of 1848–49, when together they took up arms against Kossuth's Magyarization policies. Thus Kořinek wrote that when it became clear that the Lands of Saint Stephen (the Kingdom of Hungary) had become in effect an independent unitary state retaining its link to Vienna solely through the personal union of the monarch, "Neither the Croats in Croatia and Slavonia, nor the Serbs and Romanians in Hungary, would hear of a new unitary state, which would only be of benefit to the Magyars. Thus they took up arms to defend their old rights and own language."[229] None of these nations was ready to become Magyarized or to have its lands become merely Hungarian provinces.[230] Soon, however, the course of events compelled the emperor to yield to Croatian demands for self-rule. He appointed Jelačić as ban—"a brave man . . . full of enthusiasm and unusual eloquence." He was loyal to the emperor and supported the integrity of his domains, but he also was committed to protecting Croatia's historic rights and language. When Kossuth rejected the demands of the Serbs in the Vojvodina for greater autonomy, they let it be known that they would cooperate with "the Croatian nation as brother with brother."[231] In Hoić's opinion the prime example of cooperation with the Serbs was that "no one ever was received in Croatia with such rejoicing and enthusiasm as was Jelačić, when Rajačić, the Serbian patriarch, blessed him as ban in Zagreb."[232] Aside from these comments, little more was said about the extensive cooperation that in fact did develop between the Croats and Serbs. The Serbian textbooks, it will be recalled, had also had only sparse information on this cooperation.

As if to reiterate the point made about the loyalty and support that the Croats had given the empire in previous centuries, the historians focused on the Croats' role in the military defeat of the Hungarians in 1849. At the same time, however, Hoić sharply criticized Field Marshal Haynau's order directing that the commanding officers of the Hungarian army be executed. Haynau's action was "cruel. . . . Virtually everyone whom misfortune brought before his tribunal perished."[233]

More as a lament than as a criticism, the textbooks noted that Croatia's contributions to the monarchy were not rewarded. Emperor Franz Joseph and his ministers, first Schwarzenberg and then Bach, instead sought to impose a centralized regime on the empire. Although administrative, judicial, and educational reforms were introduced and roads and railroads built, Croatia's constitution and historic rights were disregarded. Jelačić continued to serve as "ban under this German government until 1859, when grief and illness cut short his life."[234]

Croatia, as noted before, was deeply affected by the emperor's decision to reorganize the empire in the 1860s. Neither the October Diploma of 1860 nor the February Patent of 1861 produced stability in the monarchy. Hence, after its defeat by Prussia in 1866, the monarchy was forced to come to terms with the Hungarians in the Ausgleich, or compromise, of 1867. The importance of these developments for Croatia and the subsequent Croatian-Hungarian Nagodba of 1868 have already been discussed. Although the Nagodba recognized the symbolic unity of the lands of the Triune Kingdom of Croatia, Slavonia, and Dalmatia, as long as Croatia-Slavonia was associated with Hungary but Dalmatia remained a province of Austria, this provision was meaningless. Nevertheless, Hoić was able to offer an optimistic assessment of these political developments when he commented that the Nagodba "guaranteed our homeland, in union with Hungary, a peaceful development, and all progress."[235]

On a more positive note, in his textbook Hoić described the rapid expansion of Croatian cultural and intellectual activity in the sixties in contrast to the sterile decade of the fifties. In all fields the nation flourished—sculpture, painting, music, theology, philosophy, law, history, natural sciences, medicine, and mathematics. This revival was led by Bishop Strossmayer, "who through his great intellect and ardent love of country built for the Croatian people various cultural institutions (academy, university, gallery, pictures, etc.)," as a result of which the Croatian nation had proclaimed him "the father of his country." His motto was "everything for one's faith and fatherland."[236] Other famous Croats were also active in this period—Rački, Kukuljević, Jagić, Preradović, Mažuranić, and Šenoa, as well as the Serbian linguist Djuro Daničić and the author Jovan Jovanović-Zmaj.[237] The students were left with the impression that despite the setbacks of the revolution of 1848, the decade of Bach, the Ausgleich of 1867, and the Nagodba, the position of the Croatian nation had been strengthened as a result of the Illyrian movement.

Serbia and Montenegro in the Nineteenth Century

Information about Serbia was reported in the Croatian histories in the same approving tones as were the positive events in Croatian history. Since the major developments have already been discussed, only a straight factual account of the contents of the history books will be offered here. Concerning the Serbian revolution, the students learned that "after the battle of Kosovo, centuries passed and the Serbian people groaned under the Turkish yoke. As soon as it became unbearable, then the desire for freedom grew stronger in the Serbian nation."[238] The first signs of success came in the eighteenth century. The wars against the Ottoman Empire, fought by Austria as well as Russia, and the internal struggles between the sultans and their unruly janissaries and *dahije* (the leaders of the janissaries), weakened the central authority. It was precisely the failure of Constantinople to restrain these local units, which had "tyrannized the people," that precipitated the Serbian revolution.[239] Hence the entire Serbian nation rose up in arms, elected Karadjordje as the leader, and forced the marauding janissaries to flee. This action was supported by the sultan, who had sent Turkish Bosnian troops to assist the Serbs in driving out the dahije and janissaries.[240] With Serbia freed of the undisciplined units, Karadjordje demanded guarantees against their return. Instead the sultan ordered the Serbs to disarm and renew their pledge of loyalty to him. When Karadjordje refused, the sultan "ordered two armies into Serbia." They were beaten back by the Serbs, who went on to liberate Belgrade and to drive the Turks from the Belgrade pashaluk. Subsequently, Karadjordje carried the campaign into Bosnia and sought an arrangement with Montenegro. From 1806 to 1812 Serbia held its own against the Ottomans.

In part Serbia's success was attributed to the military and diplomatic support it received from Russia. Kořinek, in fact, commented that no nation had done more for the liberation of all the Balkan Christians than Russia had.[241] When the Russian forces in the Balkans were withdrawn in 1812 to meet Napoleon's invasion, however, the fortunes of Serbia suffered. The Ottoman offensive in 1813 forced Karadjordje and Metropolitan Leontije to flee across the Danube into Austria, leaving the Serbs at the mercy of the Turks. The "unbelievable barbarism" of the Turks led to the killing of "150 prominent Serbs . . . 50 of whom were impaled."[242] This cruelty brought on the second Serbian revolt, under "the brave Miloš," who, with Russia's support, restrained the Turks and secured Serbia's autonomy under Ottoman sovereignty.[243]

Although Miloš had emerged as the new Serbian leader, his position was not secure as long as Karadjordje remained a rival. Thus, when Karadjordje secretly returned to Serbia in 1817, Miloš had him killed, "on orders of the Turkish pasha." Thereupon, the Serbian notables acknowledged Miloš as their prince, and gave his family hereditary rights of succession.[244] However, it was not until 1829, in the Treaty of Adrianople that followed Russia's defeat of the Turks in the Greek revolution, that the sultan officially recognized the hereditary succession of the Obrenović family. Meanwhile Miloš had unified his principality through reforms. He collected taxes, developed an army, built schools and churches, and succeeded in gaining a metropolitanate for his nation.[245] Notwithstanding his achievements, Miloš ruled as an "autocrat," causing dissatisfaction among the notables and leading to his ouster as prince in 1839. His son Michael ruled for three years before he in turn was ousted in favor of

Alexander Karadjordjević, Karadjordje's son. In 1858 Miloš, by now an octogenarian, was returned to power, to be succeeded a second time by his son Michael in 1860–68. Michael modernized the Serbian army, forced the evacuation of the Turkish garrisons in Serbia, and, "in addition, worked to unite around himself all the Slavs in the Balkan peninsula."[246] He fell to an assassin's bullet in 1868. The histories presented the political history of Serbia from the revolution through Michael's reign in positive terms, notwithstanding the difficulties the nation experienced in the forties and fifties. Serbia still was under Ottoman sovereignty, the students were reminded, but there was progress throughout the principality.

The textbooks also discussed Serbian cultural accomplishments. They noted that Gaj and Karadžić had worked essentially in tandem to create the basis for a common language, so that "there was no difference between the two except for the alphabets."[247] In Serbia an educational system was developed, with schools built and books printed. In their discussion of literature, the textbooks often linked the Serbian authors Njegoš and Jovanović-Zmaj with the Croats Mažuranić and Preradović.

Whereas most of the information in the Croatian books about Serbia in the nineteenth century coincided factually with that presented in the Serbian history books, the accounts differed over the events of 1875–78. The Croatian students, like the Serbian, learned that the revolt began for social and economic reasons, that the Serbian and Montenegrin governments aided the rebels, that volunteers from Croatia participated, and that Russia went to war against the Turks "to liberate the Christian peoples from the Turkish yoke."[248] The basic provisions of the treaties of San Stefano and Berlin were also given. However, as regards the Habsburg occupation of Bosnia-Hercegovina, the Croatian books said little more than that "Austria-Hungary was entrusted to occupy Bosnia and Hercegovina and to reestablish law and order."[249] Although the history textbooks did not discuss the national composition of the provinces, it will be recalled that Klaić and Hoić dealt with the issue in their respective geography books. Klaić was emphatic that Bosnia and Hercegovina were historically Croatian domains and were inhabited exclusively by Croats. Hoić did not share this view, but he was firm that Croatians lived in Bosnia and Hercegovina, a condition that justified Croatia's interest in the provinces. Thus, tacitly or explicitly, the historians were defending the interests of the Croatian nation. The Serbian textbooks, in strong contrast, emphasized that these provinces were and always had been ethnically Serbian, with the clear implication that they should be part of Serbia.

Concerning the subsequent periods of Serbian history, the textbooks did little more than take note of certain facts, namely, that there had been a Serbo-Bulgarian War in 1885 in which Serbia was defeated, that King Milan abdicated in 1889, that his son Alexander was assassinated in a military conspiracy in 1903, and that the skupština elected Peter Karadjordjević as his successor.[250] In fact, the Croatian students learned more about Serbian and Croatian affairs in the years after 1878 from their readers than they did from their history books.

The other South Slav state, Montenegro, was described in the history books in the same positive, heroic terms that had been used in the readers. The Montenegrins' love of country and bravery were praised as models of true patriotism. Their resolute opposition to the Ottomans was extolled. Although many incidents in Montenegrin history were described, only one from the eighteenth century will be mentioned here. When Stephen the Small, an imposter who claimed to be Peter III of Russia (who in fact had died in 1762), established himself in Montenegro, the Ottomans ordered 100,000 troops against the province. "The Montenegrins were in great trouble," Kořinek wrote, because the Venetians had cut off their supply of gunpowder. "Notwithstanding all of this, the brave Brdjani defeated the Turkish forces in a bloody battle at Čevo." During the reign of Bishop Peter I Petrović (1782–1830), the Ottomans several times attempted to impose a tribute on Montenegro. In 1787 Montenegro joined Austria and Russia in the war against the Ottoman empire, but when the great powers were compelled to accept peace in 1791, the Ottomans sought to subdue Montenegro. Their first assault having failed, the Turks attacked again and "were defeated even more thoroughly." The pasha who led the Ottoman forces, together with twenty-six of his commanders, fell in battle. "This brilliant victory secured the freedom of Montenegro and Brda and proclaimed to the whole world the bravery of the Montenegrin people."[251] Concerning the crucial question of whether the Montenegrins were Serbs, as many believed, some of the Croatian history books simply referred to them as Montenegrins and others called them Serbs, leaving the impression that they were fellow South Slavs.

The Slovenes

Whereas the information in the history books about the Serbs was instructive, the textbooks had only fragmentary information about the Slovenes, and, with one or two exceptions, there was no attempt to integrate them into a general South Slav concept. The principal material that the books presented concerned the medieval and early modern periods and religion. Klaić wrote that in the seventh century, pressed by the Avars, the Slovenes settled in Styria, Carinthia, Carniola, and part of the Adriatic littoral, that is, the lands that they now inhabited.[252] Srkulj added that their "oldest city was Ljubljana, the old [Roman] city of Emona."[253] Unlike the Croats, who largely had been able to chart their own course in religious matters, the writers noted that the Slovenes were not so fortunate and did not control the church in their lands. Beginning with Charlemagne, they were under the jurisdiction of religious authorities in Bavaria or Salzburg, and thus Slovenia was under constant threat of "Germanization."[254]

The other information about the Slovenes was fragmentary. Students who read Hoić's textbook learned that when Matija Gubec led the Croatian peasant revolt in 1573, he received support from Slovenian peasants in Styria and Carniola.[255] Upon retirement, Baron Hans Ungnad, who had been in command of the royal forces in Croatia during the Reformation, went to Württemberg, where he founded a printing press "with Latin, Glagolitic, and Cyrillic letters in order to print religious books based upon Protestantism for Slovenes and Croats." Primož Trubar, the father of Slovene literature, joined Ungnad. With the support of Emperor Maximilian (1564–76) and some German princes, their goal was "to spread Protestantism in Croatia and from there even among the Turks, 'because the Croatian language was spoken up to Constantinople.'" Ungnad worked "ceaselessly" at his goal, and in a brief time "about a thousand new books appeared among the Croats and Slovenes."[256] For the nineteenth century there were brief comments about the Slovenes in Napoleon's Illyrian province and Stanko Vraz's contribution to Gaj's Illyrianism. On the whole, however, the Slovenes were not of major interest to Croatian historians.

In contrast to the readers, which, because of their emphasis on language and its role in literature, sought to convey a close affinity between the Croats and Serbs, the history books presented a traditional nationalistic interpretation of their history, with the focus on Croatia and not the South Slavs. Hence the history of Croatia presented in the textbooks was that of a noble Christian nation, that once had its own kingdom but then because of a combination of factors—geography, domestic political disunity, and external forces—found itself under foreign domination for the next eight centuries. It endured hardships during these eight hundred years, but it demonstrated honorable qualities. It never wavered in its support of and loyalty to its monarch, first the Hungarian king, then the Habsburg emperor. This fact was demonstrated through the nation's contributions in warding off the Ottoman advance, which helped save Christianity and Western civilization from the Islamic Ottoman state. The nation remained steadfast in its adherence to its Christian Catholic faith.

Furthermore, the Croatian nation regularly came to the assistance and defense of the Serbs, first against the Bulgarians and later against the Ottomans. In discussing the nineteenth-century Illyrian movement, historians stressed its significance for the revival of the Croatian nation rather than its South Slavic implications, although they noted these. The historians were charitable toward their Serbian Orthodox brothers, but they did not convey the idea that the Serbs were equal to the Croats.

The differences between the Serbian and Croatian accounts of one another's history are obvious. In the Serbian books, Croats lived in lands that were considered Serbian; no Croatian history of the period before the Balkan Wars was discussed. In contrast, Serbian affairs were well covered in the Croatian readers and textbooks. Moreover, the Serbs were presented in a favorable light in the history books, but as a separate South Slavic nation. As for the Slovenes, both the Croatian and Serbian historians basically ignored them in their presentations.

6

Slovenian Textbooks

INTRODUCTION

In contrast to the Serbian and Croatian readers and geography and history books, which have been discussed separately, the Slovenian texts will be analyzed together. There were three themes found in all these books. First, most striking was the extent to which the books fostered loyalty not only toward Slovenia, but just as strongly toward the Habsburg empire and the Catholic church. In fact the readers left the impression that the concepts of nation, empire, and church were inseparable. Undoubtedly, the accounts were influenced by the fact that Slovenia, unlike Serbia and Croatia, did not have an independent educational program, but was part of the Habsburg system, in which loyalty to the dynasty and church were taught as cardinal tenets. However, the manner in which the subjects were presented indicates that the authors also wrote from conviction. Second, whereas the Serbian and Croatian authors discounted Slovenia in their presentations, the Slovenian texts, in relative terms, contained a considerable amount of factual information about the other South Slavs. It was, however, not presented in a manner indicating support for any form of South Slav unity or Yugoslavism. Finally, well aware of the importance of nationalism, the authors used every opportunity to develop the self-esteem and national self-awareness of the Slovene students.

SLOVENIAN TEXTBOOKS
Authors

Beginning in the 1830s, both Serbia and Croatia made concerted efforts to produce their own textbooks. Previously both nations had relied heavily on works published in the Habsburg Empire for their format and content. Now the authors in each nation were encouraged, even prodded, to become more independent and write their own volumes. By the 1870s Serbs and Croats were publishing their own books on all subjects. In Slovenia's case, however, aside from the grammars and readers there was a greater dependency on the Austrian textbooks. It was not until the 1860s that the first texts from a Slovenian perspective became available; even then, the Austrian influence was still evident. By the beginning of the twentieth century the readers, which were veritable encyclopedias, were clearly Slovenian productions. Nevertheless, the geography books remained under the influence of German scholarship. In the secondary schools, especially in Carinthia and Styria, where Slovene students attended German schools, the instruction and textbooks were in German, except for the course on the Slovenian language and literature. In other words, the Slovenes had a more difficult time in projecting their national self-identity than did the Serbs and Croats.

In the elementary field, there were three pairs of authors who dominated the preparation of readers before 1914: Fran Močnik and Andrej Praprotnik, M. Josin and Engelbert Gangl, and Heinrich Schreiner and Fran Hubad. Močnik and Praprotnik were especially important because they were the first to publish primers and elementary readers in which the previous emphasis on religious themes was slowly abandoned and more secular topics introduced. They also were more selective in the literary quality of the excerpts cited in the readers. Močnik was a teacher, trained in Ljubljana, who taught at several different schools, became a principal, and used his position to champion Slovenian education in the elementary schools. Praprotnik completed the teachers' college and taught in various cities before being assigned to Ljubljana in 1858, where he became principal in 1864. He was very active in the teachers' associations and founded *Učiteljski tovariš* (Teachers' Companion) (1861), which became the leading Slovenian pedagogical journal. Together with Močnik, he produced the excellent *First Reader for the Slovenian Schools* (1862) and *Second Reader for the Slovenian Schools* (1864). Subsequently, Močnik wrote readers for the second, third, and fourth grades (1878–83). The volumes by Močnik and Praprotnik, thus, represented the initial break with the strong German influence and the emergence of a Slovenian orientation in the readers.[1]

Their books were followed by those of M. Josin and Engelbert Gangl, whose readers paid close attention to Slovenian history and literature. Of the two, Gangl was the more prominent author. He attended the teachers' college in Ljubljana and taught in the secondary

schools in Idrija, Trieste, and Ljubljana, where he became superintendent of schools. An author of children's books, he stressed morality.
In later years he served as the editor of *Učiteljski tovariš* (1903–19),
which Praprotnik had founded. Together with Josin, he produced the
Second Reader and Grammar for the General Public Schools (1897)
and *Third Reader and Grammar for the General Public Schools*
(1897).[2]

The last pair of writers, Fran Hubad and Heinrich Schreiner,
wrote both elementary and secondary school readers and were best
known for the latter. Hubad attended the gymnasiums in Trieste
and Ljubljana and studied Slavistics and classical philology at the
University of Graz. He taught in Graz and Ptuj. For a time he served
as a consultant to the ministry of education in Vienna. He was a prolific writer who was especially interested in folklore and folk customs. His research centered on Montenegro, Bosnia-Hercegovina,
Serbia, and Bulgaria; many of his writings about these areas were
quoted extensively in the Slovenian readers. Schreiner completed
his gymnasium studies in Maribor and concentrated on natural science and physics at the University of Vienna. After a brief teaching
career in a Viennese gymnasium, he moved to Bolzano, where he
taught before becoming a school superintendent. He served on various educational commissions and, because of his exemplary professional achievements, was elected an honorary member of the
Croatian Pedagogical Society. His interest in education was primarily in the theory and practice of teaching, about which he wrote extensively in German. Of their many works, he and Hubad were
especially known for their *Reader for the General Public Schools*,
which appeared in four parts between 1900 and 1906.[3]

The initial lower secondary school readers in Slovenian, prepared in the early 1850s by the prominent politician and publicist
Janez Bleiweis in collaboration with F. Cegnar, K. Dežman, and
I. Navratil, had a few poems, some translations, and selections in
history and the natural sciences. In the early 1860s the distinguished
linguist Fran Miklošič, together with M. Cigale and I. Navratil, produced the upper gymnasium readers, which contained considerable
poetry as well as translations, mainly from other Slavic languages.
The two dominant authors of secondary school textbooks, however,
were Anton Janežič and Jakob Sket.[4]

Janežič, a product of the early Slavic revival associated with the
Illyrian movement, attended the gymnasium in Klagenfurt and studied Slavistics with Miklošič at the University of Vienna. He was a
teacher in Klagenfurt, where he introduced the teaching of Slovenian into the gymnasium and also taught Slavistics, German, his-

tory, and geography. He was associated with many of the leading Slovenian journals, founding three of them. The most prominent of his secondary school readers were *Anthology Reader for the Slovene Youth* (1865, 1867) for the lower grades; *Anthology for Slovenian Poetry* (1861) for the fifth and sixth grades; and *Anthology for Slovenian Literature—Reader for the Upper Gymnasium and Realschule* (1868). These volumes were the basis for those subsequently published by Jakob Sket.[5]

Sket completed the gymnasium in Maribor and studied Slavistics as well as Greek, German, and philology at the University of Graz. Subsequently, he received a fellowship to continue his work in philology in Berlin. Later he taught in the Klagenfurt gymnasium. He had extensive research interests; however, his most popular works were historical novels with Ottoman themes, which were frequently quoted in the readers. Between 1889 and 1912, he produced readers for all eight grades of the secondary schools, although the second and fourth grade readers were done in collaboration with J. Wester. It is in these readers that one can discern the emergence of an obvious Slovenian orientation.[6]

Another author was Peter Končnik, who finished the gymnasium in Klagenfurt and studied Slavistics in Vienna. He taught in Celje, Ptuj, and Graz before becoming the gymnasium principal in Celje. From 1900 to 1906 he served as superintendent of the elementary and secondary schools in Carniola and then became superintendent of all the Slavic and some German schools in Styria. He wrote three readers—*Second Reader for the Public Schools* (1878), *Third Reader for the Public Schools* (1880), and *Fourth Reader for the Public and Continuation Schools* (1883).[7]

Among the historians and geographers, three stand out: Janez Jesenko, Fran Orožen, and Janez Trdina. Jesenko completed the gymnasium in Ljubljana and the University of Vienna, where he was trained as a geographer and historian. Among his works are *Beginning Geography for the Gymnasium and Realka*; *General History for the Lower Grades of the Secondary Schools* (1871, 1878, 1881), with revisions appearing in 1883 and 1896; *A Short General Geography* (1876); *Geography for the First Grade of the Secondary Schools* (1882), which other authors revised; and *Geography for the Second and Third Grades of the Secondary Schools* (1883).[8]

Fran Orožen graduated from the Celje gymnasium and also studied geography and history at the University of Vienna. He taught in the gymnasiums in Koper, Novo Mesto, and Ljubljana. His primary interest in geography was in methodology, about which he wrote numerous articles. Intrigued by travel accounts, he translated a num-

ber of them, including some of Stanley's works on Africa. He was the
author of *Geography for the Public Schools* for three grades—I (1891,
1903), II (1894), and III (1896). In addition, he published a *Geography
of the Austro-Hungarian State* (1907) for the fourth grade of the secondary schools.[9]

As was the case with so many others, Janez Trdina completed
the gymnasium in Ljubljana and then studied history, geography,
and Slavistics in Vienna. He taught in the Varaždin gymnasium until he was dismissed in 1867 for espousing Masonic ideas. He was the
author of *History of the Slovenian Nation* (1866). In addition, influenced by the nationalistic developments of the revolution of
1848–49, he became a collector of Slovenian folktales, fables and
proverbs.[10]

Mention should also be made of a number of non-Slovenian
scholars whose works were either regularly employed in the Slovenian schools or frequently cited in the Slovenian works. There were
three Austrian authors—Franz Heiderich, geographer and cartographer; Franz Martin Mayer, teacher and historian; and Anton Gindely, historian. Blasius Kozenn, geographer and cartographer, was a
Slovene who grew up in a German environment and wrote in German, but in time became keenly interested in the Slovene cause.
The works of Emanuel Hannak, Czech by origin and teacher and historian by profession, were cited by not only the Slovenes, but the
Croats and Serbs as well.[11]

Slovenian Lands

The textbooks presented a straightforward account of the settlement of the Slovenian lands in the early medieval period and the
brief period of local self-rule. The invasions, wars, and domination
by Charlemagne and the Franks, Germans, Venetians, Magyars, and
others were treated thoroughly. The Slovenes' conversion to Christianity and the conflict over religious jurisdiction in the Slovenian
territories were described in detail, including the maneuvers of the
German and Italian ecclesiastical authorities to expand their jurisdiction in the Slovenian domains. The conflict persisted for centuries with a clear decision reached only when Carniola, Styria, and
Carinthia came under Habsburg rule in the thirteenth and fourteenth centuries.[12]

Whereas the Serbs and Croats claimed some of the same lands,
Slovenia did not have any serious territorial conflicts with her Cro-
atian neighbor. Her disputes were with the Germans in Styria and
Carinthia, the Italians in the Littoral regions, and the Hungarians in

southwestern Hungary. The readers and geography and history books gave the Slovenian population figures for Styria, Carinthia, and the Littoral either in absolute figures or in percentages. Beginning with the textbooks in the 1870s, the relative figures remained consistent with each new census report. Carniola, the most homogeneous province, regularly was cited as having about 94 to 95 percent Slovenians, which, in 1910, meant about 491,000, with 30,000 Germans and others. In Styria the Slovenians numbered about 410,000 or one-third the population, with the Germans being about 983,000. In Carinthia, the Slovenes were 82,000 or 20 percent, with 304,000 Germans. In Styria and Carinthia the Slovenian population lived in the southern regions contiguous to Carniola. It was in these areas where the most serious conflicts in regard to education occurred. The rural areas were heavily Slovenian; the towns and cities were German centers.

Following the pattern seen throughout the entire Habsburg Empire in the nineteenth century, ethnic conflicts erupted over education.[13] The Austrian education law called for the language of instruction in elementary schools to be decided by provincial and local authorities. The provision was ambiguous, however, in that it did not state clearly whether the final decision rested with the province or with the locality. The goal of the Slovenians was to gain control over education in localities where they had a majority, and then to work for the political and administrative unification of all Slovenian regions in a single province. If they were successful, it would mean that Styria and Carinthia would be partitioned. Understandably the Germans, whose population in these provinces was twice that of the Slovenes (ca. 1,287,000 Germans to 491,000 Slovenes) rejected measures that might lead to the dismemberment of their historic lands.

The same principles were involved in the conflict with the Italians in the Littoral. Here, however, the Italians and Germans joined forces against the Slovenes, who were supported by the Croats in Istria and its neighboring Slavic islands. The percentage of the population that was Slavic varied between 50 and 60 percent. Numerically the South Slavs were superior, but they did not act or vote as one bloc. Here, also, the issues centered on schools and local administration.[14]

In the readers and geography books, extensive information was presented on the physical features of the provinces, their cities, industries, and resources to substantiate Slovenian claims to them. These points were made especially clearly with respect to the regions in dispute in Carinthia and Styria. Consequently, the books

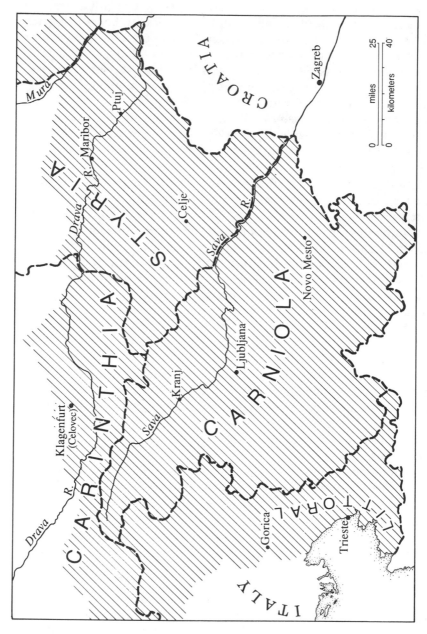

Slovenian Lands Identified in the Textbooks

took great pains to emphasize that Slovenian secondary schools and other cultural institutions were found in Maribor, Celje, Klagenfurt, Villach, Gorica, and Trieste. In addition, the names of former Roman centers, now Slovenian cities, such as Ptuj-Petovium and Celje-Celeja, also received considerable attention.[15]

As was the case in Serbia and Croatia, the Slovenian textbooks stressed the importance of language. The purpose was to strengthen not only national identity, but love for one's language. This sentiment was best expressed in Sket's fourth grade secondary school reader in an excerpt from France Zakrajšek, entitled "Patriotic Thoughts": "Always speak your mother tongue gladly. . . . He who disdains his mother tongue is more stupid than an animal. . . . Each language is God's gift. . . . Before all the world defend the mother tongue. . . . Look that you do honor to your homeland. . . . Love your homeland and remain faithful to it as long as you live."[16] The students were told that when Franz Joseph visited Ljubljana in 1883 to commemorate the six hundredth anniversary of Habsburg rule over Styria and Carniola, he declared that "he loved the Slovenian language."[17] They also took special note of the fact that when Napoleon created the Illyrian kingdom, he authorized the language of instruction to be the mother tongue, which meant Slovenian.[18]

Slovenia and the Habsburg Empire

While the textbooks sought to generate a deep sense of Slovenian identity, they also stressed the Slovenes' keen affinity to the Habsburg dynasty and empire. This fact was demonstrated in the stories told of the benevolence of the rulers and the loyalty that the Slovenians rendered the empire at all times, and especially in its wars against the Ottomans. Thus, the six hundredth anniversary of Habsburg rule in Carniola and Styria understandably was an occasion for celebration. The fourth and fifth grade Schreiner-Hubad reader, citing an account by Hubad, stated that "from that time [1283], the Slovenes never forgot their loyalty to the Habsburg family. In 1883 we renewed, each in his own heart, our oath to Franz Joseph I and his heirs." When the emperor set foot on Slovenian soil, all shouted "Long Live the Emperor," which was repeated wherever he traveled. "All paid homage to him. No one will ever forget that moment when he stood before the emperor. His kindness was so great that it embraced everyone." Peasants throughout the lands greeted him. "Nowhere were there any disorders, nor were there any guards." The most elaborate occasion was in Ljubljana. "In Tivoli [the city park], there were great festivities where the emperor observed Slovenian national costumes and customs. There he saw and heard of the progress we made." He laid the cornerstone for the museum and asked that the building be named in honor of his son Rudolf. "If one could look into each Austrian's heart (*vsakemu Avstrijcu v srce*), he would see that in it is no one else but the emperor." This account was followed by a long poem commemorating the emperor's next visit to Ljubljana in 1895. Hubad's reader ended with the imperial hymn, which was found in every reader.[19]

In the same textbook there was another excerpt from Fran Hubad in which he described Franz Joseph's student days, paying attention especially to his knowledge of languages. Not only did he study Latin, Greek, French, and English, but also almost "all the languages of Austria."[20] Another story, by Josef Apih, a prominent Slovenian historian, reported how the Archduchess Sophie asked Marshal Radetzky to look after her son during the campaigns against the Italians in 1848. Subsequently, it was reported that at the battle of Santa Lucia, Franz Joseph behaved as though he were "not aware of any danger, nor did he care about it." Nor did he flinch when cannon shots fell nearby. Furthermore, his assistance to his troops led his subjects to admire his gallantry.[21]

These simple, sentimental tales about Franz Joseph symbolized the respect and reverence that all the Slovenian textbooks expressed for the Habsburg dynasty. Other accounts followed a similar pattern. Citing an episode from the reign of Emperor Albrecht I (1298–1308), in a story entitled "Brotherly Love," the second year reader reported that the emperor had many enemies, so, in order to protect himself, he had a fierce watchdog. One day when Leopold, his younger son, wished to see his father, the dog attacked him, whereupon Leopold accidentally killed it. When the emperor learned that his dog was dead, he assembled the entire court and demanded to know who was responsible. Knowing his father's temperament, Leopold trembled with fear. However, his older brother, Frederick, aware of what had occurred, stepped forward and assumed responsibility. He knelt before the emperor and pleaded that he had to defend himself from the dog. The emperor raised his hand to strike Frederick when Leopold interjected to say that he, not Frederick, was guilty, whereupon he embraced his brother and began to cry. Seeing their affection and loyalty, the emperor rejoiced that with such sons he need not be concerned about defending himself from his enemies.[22]

Some of the same stories found in the Croatian textbooks were repeated in the Slovenian, as, for example, the account of how Maria Theresa granted a pension to a destitute retired Dalmatian lieutenant, whose son Vukasović was the best swordsman in the empire; or the two stories about Joseph II, one in which he gave money to a girl whose father had died and mother was ill, and another in which, incognito, he helped a peasant plow. These and other stories were designed to create a positive impression of the dynasty in the minds of the youth.[23]

The importance of the theme of loyalty in the Slovenian history books can also be demonstrated by comparing accounts of the same events in the Slovenian and Croatian textbooks. There are four good illustrations. The first concerns the battle of Mohács. While not denying that King Louis should have been better prepared for the battle and should have awaited the support of auxiliary units before engaging the superior Ottoman forces, the Slovenian textbooks nevertheless extolled his bravery. They also lamented his accidental death by drowning in a swamp, but welcomed the news that his body had been recovered several months later and given a proper burial. They also applauded the addition of the Hungarian lands to the Habsburg realm.[24] The Croatian textbooks, on the other hand, attributed Hungary's defeat to the fact that Louis and his advisers ignored the counsel of the Croatian military strategists. As for King Louis's death, the Croatian authors left the impression that he had brought it upon himself. They also attributed much of the misfortune that subsequently befell Hungary and Croatia to the divisions in the Hungarian political ranks.

In their account of the Thirty Years' War, the Slovenian books praised the dynasty for saving Catholicism. They also attributed the defeat of Gustavus Adolphus to the imperial army. In contrast, the Croatian books emphasized the role of the troops from the Croatian Military Frontier who, it was asserted, were mainly responsible for the defeat and death of the Swedish king.[25]

In regard to the second siege of Vienna in 1683, the Slovenian books attributed the Habsburg success chiefly to Prince Starhemberg, who led the imperial forces. The role of Jan Sobieski and the Poles was acknowledged, but not emphasized. The Croatian books ascribed the victory to the imperial forces, meaning the various nationalities, and the invaluable assistance of the Polish king and his troops.[26]

Finally, in discussing the reforms of Joseph II, the Slovenian books stated that the Hungarians did not understand that his real intent was the betterment of the empire. They cited his often-quoted epitaph: "Here rests a prince whose intentions were most noble, but had the misfortune that all of his plans failed."[27] The Croatian textbooks welcomed the measures he took on behalf of the peasantry and schools, but they criticized those steps that they believed would have led to the centralization, or Germanization, of the empire. Whereas the Slovenian textbooks basically could find no fault with any of the Habsburg actions, the Croatian books criticized those measures that they believed caused harm to their nation.

Reaction to the Ottoman Empire

Slovenia's loyalty to the empire was perhaps most strongly emphasized in the accounts concerning the struggle with the Ottoman empire. As was the case in the Serbian and Croatian textbooks, here too the Ottoman empire was portrayed as a cruel and implacable foe. This opinion was made clear in the Schreiner-Hubad reader in an excerpt entitled "Janissaries" by Ivan Verhovec, the Slovenian historian, in which he assailed the devshirme system, by which young Christians were recruited, forcibly converted to Islam, and then became the elite troops who fought against their fellow Christians. In Verhovec's view the first task of the Ottoman conquerors was to suppress any

> remembrance of Christianity [in the recruited Christians], to stifle in the heart every better feeling . . . and to erase from their soul all remembrances of their homeland, its customs, and its habits, and to tear asunder all ties that so sweetly bind a person to his fatherland and his birth. In place of it they implanted blind obedience to their Turkish masters, the greatest passion for the Islamic faith, and the most cruel hatred of everything that had any links to Christianity. It is no wonder that the janissaries, Christian children, became the greatest foe of the Christian.[28]

Consequently, the janissary plundered his forgotten homeland and shed the blood of his relatives and co-nationals.

The havoc wrought by the Ottoman forces was described by Verhovec in the third year reader for the secondary schools edited by Jacob Sket. In particular, he paid attention to Ottoman actions in the fifteenth century when Ottoman armies plundered Slovenian regions such as Crnomelj, Metlika and Novo Mesto. As a result of these raids, the peasants developed an elaborate communication system to warn of the approach of Ottoman troops and alert the defensive installations. Although the Slovenians contributed to some of the victories over the Ottomans, for example, in killing a pasha in 1483, in Verhovec's view Slovenia in the fifteenth century could only be described as a land bathed in "blood and fire."[29]

The Ottoman attacks in the sixteenth century were even more devastating, but, at the same time, the Slovenians were better prepared to meet them. This fact was demonstrated by the successes of prominent Slovenian commanders. Ivan Kacijanar, who distinguished himself at the first siege of Vienna in 1529, was one example. Following the battle, Kacijanar pursued the Ottoman troops and was successful in rescuing many Christian prisoners and seizing a great quantity of Ottoman livestock. As a result of his accomplishments, King Ferdinand appointed him commander of all the troops in Styria, Carinthia, and Carniola. In 1532 Kacijanar's troops cut off a large Turkish force that was on its way to aid the Ottoman forces besieging Kiseg, which, as will be recalled, was being defended by the Croatian commander Nikola Jurišić. As a result of Kacijanar's action, the sultan was determined to punish the Slovenes, according to Verhovec.[30]

In the next engagement, however, Kacijanar disgraced himself, his nation, and his empire. In 1536 he was placed in command of all the allied forces—German, Czech, Polish, and Hungarian—at Osijek with the mission of halting another Ottoman attack on the empire. When he was not able to establish his authority over some of his feuding commanders, who retreated with their units, Kacijanar also abandoned Osijek. After being imprisoned, Kacijanar escaped and then further disgraced himself by conspiring with the Ottoman forces.[31] Zrinski ordered him seized and executed. The lesson to be drawn from this story was to demonstrate how two men under somewhat similar circumstances responded. Having taken an oath to defend his nation and emperor, Zrinski sacrificed himself, thus becoming a national hero, whereas Kacijanar betrayed his trust, his nation, and his ruler, and became a traitor and a disgrace to the Slovenian nation.

Not all Slovenian military men behaved as dishonorably as Kacijanar. Thus the students read about Ivan Kenkovič and Herbert Turjaski, and the less well-known Blaž Gjurak, Matija Fintič, Josip Lamberg, Baron Ravbar, Andrej Turjaski, and Jost Turn, all of whom were cited for their military exploits. Their contributions eventually helped turn the tide of battle against the Ottoman Empire. This was demonstrated best in 1578 in Karlovac, the strategic fortress south of Zagreb, where Croatian troops, reinforced by Slovenian units, halted Turkish attacks into Croatia and Slovenia. Thus the Slovenes were able to show the Croats that they were truly brothers and that the disasters and misfortunes that befell Croatia affected the Slovenes as well. Slovenia's fate finally changed in 1606 when Emperor Rudolph secured peace with the Ottoman government. For the Slovenes it meant the end of the "bloody and unfortunate" invasions, although there continued to be sporadic Ottoman attacks. Yet the Islamic Ottoman threat served to bind together not only the Slovenes and Croats but the Serbs as well, as will be shown below. It also strengthened the loyalty of the Catholic Slovenes to the Catholic Habsburg empire.[32]

The Croatians

Whereas the Serbian textbooks and the Croatian readers and history books largely ignored the Slovenes, the Slovenian books contained a great deal of information about the Croats and Serbs and the lands in which they lived. By 1914 the Slovenian students had good factual knowledge about the other two South Slavic nations. The explanation for this is that the Austrian educational system was remarkably thorough in presenting information about all the people within the empire and in neighboring states.

The first point to emphasize is that the Serbs and Croats were presented in the Slovenian textbooks as one people, who spoke the same language, which some books called "Serbo-Croatian" (*Serbohrvatje*) or "Serbian or Croatian," which was written using two alphabets. In the 1911 reader for the sixth, seventh, and eighth grades compiled by Schreiner, he quoted an excerpt from Izidor Kršnjavi, who wrote that in

> Lika and Slavonia there were many Serbs who spoke the same language, loved the same national fables and listened to the same heroic songs as the Croats. Since almost half of the people, especially in Lika, do not know how to read, as a result one can hardly differentiate the Serbs from the Croats by means of handwriting (Cyrillic). Thus one easily considers religion as the decisive factor. The Serbs are exclusively of the Orthodox faith, while the Croats belong to the Catholic faith. Consequently, it is religion that divides the Serbs and Croats, who speak the same language.[33]

Even the Slavic Bosnian Muslims were depicted as one with the Serbs and Croats.

Although the textbooks assumed that the Serbs and Croats were one people, they contained more information on the Croats than on the Serbs. Both the Croats and Slovenes were part of the Habsburg Empire, and thus the books contained extensive descriptions of and factual information about the Croatian lands, and their shared common experiences in the empire—for example, their relations with the Ottoman Empire. In addition, the textbooks cited events from Croatian history that demonstrated the loyalty of the Croats to the Habsburg Empire, the same theme emphasized by the Slovenes. The descriptions of the Croatian lands were thorough, based mainly on Habsburg statistical handbooks. Thus one found information on the regions, resources, cities, population, education, trade, and commerce. The students were also provided with similarly reliable information about the cities in Dalmatia and Bosnia-Hercegovina.

In addition to information about Croatia and its history, the textbooks devoted considerable attention to Croatian heroes and cooperation between the Slovenes and Croats. As one example, Končnik's fourth grade reader narrated the bravery of Zrinski, that "famous Croatian hero," who with "his brave soldiers live in fond memory of their descendants as a beautiful example of loyalty to their monarch and fatherland."[34] Whereas the legend of Siget belonged to Zrinski, the books wished to establish the fact that the Slovenes contributed to the Croatian victory over Hasan Pasha at Sisak in 1593. Not only was the city a major Croatian outpost, but its fall to the Turks would have exposed Austria and the Slovenian lands to Ottoman attacks. For several years it was known that Hasan Pasha was preparing to storm the fortress, located at the juncture of the Sava and Kupa rivers. A contingent of 10,000 allied troops— Croatian, German and Hungarian, of whom 4,000 were Slovenian— led by Baron Ravbar and Andrej Turjaski were able to defeat the Ottoman army of 30,000. The Christian victory, in which Hasan Pasha and a number of his commanders were killed, included the capture of 2,000 horses, about forty cannon, and twelve large boats, as well as Hasan Pasha's tent and all his jewelry. The significance of this victory was expressed in a Slovenian folk-poem that stated that if the Turks had taken Sisak, the result would have been disastrous.[35]

The bravery of the Croats was also lauded in a selection by Apih about the Napoleonic Wars that was published in Schreiner's upper grade reader for the public schools. The French attacked two strongholds manned by Croats—one at Naborjet, commanded by Hensel, the other at Predel, defended by Hermann. For three days, three hundred Croats from Ogulin fought off the strong French assaults. When the French called upon Hensel to surrender and spare his outnumbered men, he replied: "My duty is to defend the fortress and not to negotiate." When he was mortally wounded, he shouted to his men, "I am dying, comrades," but they fought on until finally the French overran the fortress. They killed its defenders, who, however, had fulfilled Hensel's prophecy that "this fortress will be my grave and that of my comrades, a grave as noble as that which Leonidas and the Spartans had at Thermopylae."[36]

At the same time Hermann and a smaller force of 250 Croats fought the French at Predel. When Hermann learned from the French that Naborjet had fallen and that he too was doomed, he replied: "My orders are to defend the fortress by all means; I have given my word and I am not afraid to die for my fatherland." A bitter battle ensued in which Hermann was wounded, but he called on each soldier to fight on. Only eight wounded Croats survived. "At Predel and Naborjet there is," wrote Apih, a bronze memorial lion to the heroes "who went to their death for their fatherland and emperor."[37]

Finally the reader included an excerpt entitled "The Heroic Croatian Ban Jelačić," by Fran Ilešič, the Slovenian literary historian. Lacking funds to equip his army, Ban Jelačić held a meeting in the sabor in Zagreb on July 4, 1848, at which voluntary contributions for the defense of the fatherland were made by individuals. When Archimandrite Ilić's turn came, he had no money, but took the gold chain and cross from his neck and offered it as his contribution on behalf of the fatherland. Ban Jelačić stepped forward and stated that the archimandrite, who was a Serb, had proven that he indeed deserved to wear the Holy Cross, whereupon Jelačić returned it to the archimandrite and donated fifty ducats in the archimandrite's name. With tears in his eyes, the archimandrite remarked that hitherto he had considered it his holy duty to wear the cross, but now he would regard it as his most precious gift from the beloved ban. Many regretted not having been in the sabor that day. Thereafter, contributions came from all of Croatia, "from men and women, old and young, Catholic and Orthodox. . . . The Slovenes also contributed many hundred florins. Thus they too helped the ban save the fatherland and emperor."[38] The impression that the textbooks conveyed of the Croats was that they, like the Slovenes, were loyal, patriotic citizens ready to sacrifice themselves for the empire. Whatever reservations they may have had about Habsburg government policies in regard to the Croats and Slovenes, these two nations would never betray the monarchy.

The information about Dalmatia differed in one fundamental respect from that found in the Croatian and Serbian books. Whereas the Serbs and Croats each considered Dalmatia their own province, the Slovenian textbooks identified it as a Slavic or Serbo-Croatian land. For example, the 1873 geography book stated that the population was composed of Serbo-Croats (*Serbohrvatje*), the 1879 volume declared them to be of Serbo-Croatian nationality (*Serbsko-hervatske narodnosti*), the 1885 book called them "all Slavs Serbs and Croats" (*vsi Slovani—Srbije in Hrvatije*), and the 1905 textbooks noted that they were Serbo-Croats (*Srbo-Hrvati*).[39] Their language was called "Serbo-Croatian" or "Serbian or Croatian." What divided the Serbs and Croats was their religion; they were listed as being about 16 percent Orthodox, with the remainder Catholic. The controversy over whether the literature of Dubrovnik was Croatian or Serbian was avoided by describing it as Yugoslav.[40]

The other information given about Dalmatia was factual. There was a good description of Zadar, its capital, which included an account of the gymnasium, realka, library, and Orthodox archbishopric, as well as data on the composition of the Dalmatian sabor. The significance of Diocletian's palace in Split, and other features of the city were noted. Dubrovnik's role as an independent republic was mentioned. All the major islands were discussed, along with their cities and principal resources. In summary, the students were given a clear picture of the province.[41]

The pro-Habsburg orientation of the textbooks was further demonstrated in the discussion of Bosnia and Hercegovina. The German secondary school textbooks attributed much of the general mid-century unrest among the Orthodox Balkan Slavs to Pan-Slavism. The account of the Balkan crisis of 1875–78, including the origins and the general terms of the treaties of San Stefano and Berlin, was accurate. The books noted that "Austria was commissioned to occupy and administer Bosnia and Hercegovina," and they did not conceal the fact that the two Habsburg commanders, General Filipović in Bosnia and General Jovanović in Hercegovina, met fierce resistance from the Orthodox and Muslim populations before the provinces were subdued. Thereafter, "under Austrian administration began, for these neglected lands, a new period in their development" by an "impartial and friendly reform-minded government."[42]

As was the case for all the Habsburg provinces, the textbooks contained a good deal of information about the newly acquired lands. For example, they gave the correct religious percentages for the population, which was identified as being almost "all Serbo-Croats" (vsi Srbo-Hrvatje). The prominent features of Sarajevo, the capital of Bosnia, which, "except for Constantinople [was] the most attractive city in the Balkan peninsula," were described.[43] Yet the data about the provinces were in part misleading. The textbooks did not make clear the historic role and importance of Sarajevo for either the Muslims or the Serbs. Nor did the books contain any significant information about the Muslims and Serbs in Bihač, Banja Luka, Travnik, Mostar, or any of the other important cities in the region. Consequently, the only impression that the students could obtain was that Bosnia-Hercegovina was now a Habsburg province; it had been liberated from the Islamic Ottoman empire and was now part of the benevolent Christian Habsburg realm. The role of the Serbian Orthodox population was largely discounted.

The Serbs

The facts in the Slovenian textbooks on the Serbian nation, including the Serbs who lived under Ottoman rule and in Montenegro, were detailed and accurate. Thus, for example, in 1873 Janez Jesenko in his geography book provided the basic data on the Serbian principality, that is, a description of its population, government, education, and religion. The textbooks also contained historical information about the country. Although the books stated that the initial Serbian colonists had advanced into Greek territory, they stressed that the main body of the Serbian population was located in the central and western Balkans. Accounts of the medieval Serbian Nemanja dynasty were included, and the importance of Kosovo, the cities of Skopje and Prizren, and other historical landmarks were discussed. The books did not, however, identify Macedonia as Serbian, although they did state that Serbs lived there along with other groups, including Bulgarians, Greeks, Turks, and Albanians. As far as the modern principality was concerned, they noted that Belgrade's fortress was "the key to Hungary," that is, the point from which the Ottomans attacked the Hungarian domains. Smederovo was described as once having been the seat of the Serbian kings, and Kragujevac was mentioned as having been Prince Miloš's capital briefly.[44]

However, it was the heroic resistance of the Serbs against the Ottomans that drew most of the Slovenian attention. The battle of Kosovo, which dominated Serbian medieval history, was also the focus of attention among the Slovenian scholars. Many of the readers thus included excerpts from F. S. Pirec's vivid account of the historic conflict. The basic facts about the battle did not vary from those mentioned in the Serbian or Croatian textbooks, but Pirec's version was more explicit and dramatic.

> Kosovo is that place which penetrates the bones and marrow of every son of brave Serbia. On Kosovo is buried the glory of the once-powerful Serbian empire. On the field of Kosovo lie the heroic ancestors of the oppressed people, who for many years were bound in shackles. The battle on the field of Kosovo demonstrates clearly how selfishness leads to disunity and death.

Pirec also depicted Sultan Murad I as a "bloodthirsty tiger" whose goal was to trample the "Holy Cross," to exterminate Christianity, to devastate countries, and to destroy European civilization.[45]

Pirec also described in detail the quarrel between Miloš Obilić and Vuk Branković, including the role that their wives played in precipitating it. Pirec did, however, go further in describing the immediate consequences of the defeat for Serbia. Thus he wrote that not only did the Turks rejoice at the victory, but so did the traitor Vuk Branković, who assumed that with both Prince Lazar and Miloš dead, Bayezid, Murad's successor, would entrust the rule of the Serbian lands to him. Instead the sultan chose Milica, Lazar's widow, and in turn she gave her daughter in marriage to Bayezid and agreed to pay a tribute. Subsequently, Vuk Branković sought to overthrow Milica and her son, but he was captured, imprisoned, and poisoned. "Thus came to an end the traitor Vuk Branković."[46]

Three years later, Pirec continued, Prince Lazar's remains were discovered in Kosovo and taken to the monastery of Ravanica for burial. In the beautiful Serbian national poems, the Serbian nation honored the heroic Lazar and the brave Miloš Obilić. As for the unfortunate Vuk Branković, people could only say: "How his mother grieves." For four centuries the Serbs endured the Ottoman yoke but then, continued Pirec, at the end of the eighteenth century Ottoman dominance began to wane and the Serbs were on the road to "golden freedom."[47]

These accounts of the battle of Kosovo were supplemented with extensive excerpts, translated into Slovenian, from the various poems of the Kosovo epic, for example, "Kosovo Maiden," "Empress Milica" and "Miloš Obilić." There were also frequent quotations of proverbs, fables, and the like that Vuk Karadžić had published.

The lesson conveyed in this and other accounts of Kosovo in the Slovenian books was that disunity and betrayal of one's homeland and faith lead to national disaster. Notwithstanding this adversity, the Serbs were portrayed as a heroic people whose spirit had not been broken. The clear impression was that anyone would be proud to be a member of the Serbian nation.

As for the Montenegrins, whom the Slovenian textbooks considered Serbs, they were depicted as a brave, noble people whose indomitable spirit would not permit them to be conquered by the Turks. It was in Montenegro, furthermore, that the Serbs could find haven and refuge from the marauding Ottomans.[48]

Within the context of this study of the contribution of the Slovenian textbooks to an understanding of Yugoslavism, several points can be made. First, they took pains to show the identity of interests among the Croats and Slovenes in defending their nation against the Ottoman threat. Second, through their geography books in particular, they taught Slovenian students a great deal about Croatia-Slavonia and Dalmatia. The population was identified as Croatian and Serbian and the language as Croatian or Serbian, or Serbo-Croatian, a fact which was stressed in particular for Dalmatia. Third, aside from religion and alphabet, the books did not mention any other points that divided the Croats and Serbs, for example, culture, civilization, or customs. Fourth, the textbooks stressed the advantage for the population of Austria's occupation of Bosnia-Hercegovina, depicting it as the liberation and salvation of an oppressed people who could now enjoy the benevolence of an enlightened regime. Furthermore, they led the students to believe that the Serbs were not a significant factor in these provinces. Fifth, the works paid tribute to the Serbian nation, its history, and its successes, as reflected in the Serbian and Montenegrin principalities. Sixth, they emphasized Slovenia's loyalty and devotion to the Habsburg Empire at every opportunity, using quotations and excerpts from the works of Slovenian writers. In conclusion, thus, the textbooks did provide information that could lead to an appreciation of the factors that united the South Slavs, but without diminishing the Slovenians' loyalty to their own homeland and to the Habsburg Empire. These views, however, influenced at most the 5 percent of students who attended the secondary schools, whereas the 95 percent who completed only elementary education learned very little about the other South Slavs.

Conclusion

The purpose of this study, as stated in the preface, is to determine to what extent those students who attended elementary and secondary schools in the South Slav lands and later represented the overwhelming majority of the educated public were prepared to accept the kingdom that was created in December 1918. As we know, the basic issues that had divided the Serbs, Croats, and Slovenes previously, and had to be resolved if an amicable union were to be realized, surfaced during the war and the postwar era. Eventually these conflicts plunged the state into the bitter civil war of 1941–45. The importance, therefore, of the study of the textbooks rests not only on what their contents reveal about South Slav issues, but also on their influence on individuals who would hold responsible positions in the new kingdom, for example, ministers, provincial administrators, city officials, teachers, priests, the police, the military cadre, bureaucrats, and others, all of whom were educated under the system previously described. Hence, when controversial questions arose, as they did immediately after World War I, those individuals and the broad, educated electorate based their judgments on their prewar experiences. Thus, the textbooks represent another source for a broader study of Yugoslavism and the problems that continued to confront the South Slavs in the decades after 1918.

The goal of the Serbian nation, starting with the Serbian revolution, was to liberate and unite all the Serbian people living under Ottoman and Habsburg rule into a single independent state. All the textbooks echoed this theme. The role that the textbooks would play in the attainment of this objective was defined in 1881 by Stojan Novaković, who formulated Serbia's first independent educational system, when he stated that the subject matter of textbooks should be directed toward furthering national aims. The political leadership in Belgrade never deviated from this position. Even the 1912 directive by the minister of education that more information should be devoted to the Croats had as its aim to exploit the support for Serbia in the Triune Kingdom that was implicit in the Croatian-Serbian Coalition and among intellectuals and university students. It would also serve to strengthen the position of the Serbs in the Dual Monarchy. This point cannot be minimized when it is remembered that in 1914 there were approximately 1,957,000 Serbs or 30 percent of the Serbian population living under Habsburg rule in Vojvodina, Croatia-Slavonia, Dalmatia, and Bosnia-Hercegovina. There is no convincing evidence before 1914 that the Serbian government had committed itself to anything other than the union of the Serbian nation. The argument made after 1918 that Serbia could not openly profess her support for South Slav unity or Yugoslavism for fear of provoking the Austro-Hungarian government does not seem valid. The repeated calls for the liberation and unification of the Serbian nation made by political parties, military leaders, religious spokesmen, and the press at large, as well as the information found in the textbooks, was perceived in Vienna and Budapest as being just as serious a threat to the empire's survival as the danger emanating from those who championed Yugoslavism. Both programs aimed at the dismemberment of the Habsburg domains.

The Croatian goals were to unite the Croatian lands of the Habsburg Empire into a single political entity, thereby making the Triune Kingdom a reality; to make the štokavian dialect the standard literary language for the Croats; and to integrate the Serbs, who numbered 25 percent of the population, into the Croatian state, where their loyalty would be to Croatia and not to the neighboring Serbian kingdom. These goals were inherent in some form in Gaj's Illyrianism, Strossmayer's Yugoslavism, Starčević's Greater Croatianism, and the program of the Croatian-Serbian Coalition. Consequently, the textbooks stressed the unity of the lands of the Triune Kingdom, but with the clear understanding that these were Croatian lands in which Serbs also lived. Their language was the same, but the only political nation in the Triune Kingdom was the Croatian.

The goal of the Slovene leadership was to unite their nation, which lived in four contiguous provinces, into a single political entity within the Habsburg Empire and to strengthen the national consciousness by ensuring that Slovenian would be the sole language of instruction in its schools. Slovenian political leaders of all major persuasions professed their loyalty to the Habsburg dynasty and empire, as the textbooks made explicit.

The programs of each nation were based on what its leaders conceived to be in the best interest of their people, and not that of the South Slavs as a collective entity. Hence, the fundamental divisions that had existed among them for centuries remained. In language, the Serbs, Montenegrins, and Croats established a closer bond through the štokavian dialect, but the Slovenes retained their own kajkavian speech. The Serbs and Montenegrins defended their Orthodox faith and the Croats and Slovenes their Catholicism. Culturally the Serbs and Montenegrins shared an Orthodox, Byzantine heritage, whereas the Croats and Slovenes stood by their Catholic, Western orientation. By 1914 the influence that the Ottoman Empire had exerted on the lives and habits of the Serbs, Montenegrins, and South Slav Muslims was still evident, as were the ties that bound the Croats to the Habsburg Empire and Hungarian kingdom.

Although the Serbian, Croatian, and Slovenian scholars accepted the idea that a nation was identified by its language, the issue, instead of uniting them, served to divide them. There were two points on which the Serbian and Croatian readers agree: one, that they both spoke the štokavian dialect, and, two, that Slovenian was a separate language. On all other fundamental matters there were disagreements. First, without exception, every Serbian textbook, excluding the few that were published after 1912, referred to their language as Serbian. The Croatian textbooks used the term "Croatian or Serbian" to identify their common language. Second, the authors of the Serbian readers were positive that all štokavian speakers were only Serbs. The Croats, of course, were just as adamant that they spoke štokavian and that they were Croats, not Serbs. Furthermore, they insisted that one nation could speak three dialects, in their case štokavian, kajkavian, and čakavian, a view rejected by the Serbian authors.

These differences carried over into the controversy surrounding literature. Since sixteenth- and seventeenth-century Dalmatian literature, and especially the literature of Dubrovnik, was superior to anything found among the South Slavs at that time, it is understandable that both Serbs and Croats would claim it. The Serbs were categorical in asserting that the literature of Dubrovnik and of its great writers was theirs. In part these views were based upon the pro-Slavic and anti-Ottoman themes of some of the writers, and, in part, upon the evidence advanced by historians that Dalmatia up to the Cetina River had historically been Serbian. Logically, therefore, it was possible to conclude that the literature of the area was Serbian. The Croatian readers countered these arguments by pointing out that the writers were Catholics, most of whom identified themselves as Croats. Furthermore, many also wrote in Latin. Even Croatian textbook authors such as Petračić and Divković, who were avowed Vukovites and who in their own readers referred to their language as "Croatian or Serbian," insisted that the literature of Dubrovnik and Dalmatia was Croatian written in the ijekavian variant of štokavian.

Both the Serbian and Croatian readers emphasized that their modern literary language could be traced to the works of the Dalmatian writers, yet each rejected the other's interpretation. The Serbian readers maintained that the Croatians lacked a modern national literature until they adopted the Serbian štokavian dialect in the nineteenth century. Petračić, representing the Croatian view, stated that the Serbs had only a religiously based literature until Karadžić produced the first national literature with his volumes of oral folk-poetry in the nineteenth century. The Croatian readers, however, insisted that this folk-poetry was a common heritage of the Croats and Serbs, a view which the Serbian readers rejected. In contrast, when the works of nineteenth-century Croatian authors such as Mažuranić and Preradović could be integrated into a presentation of Serbian literature and thus were included in the Serbian readers, the authors were not identified as Croats.

The significance of these disagreements over language and literature can further be appreciated when the importance attached to the name of the nation and its language is considered. If the Serbs and Croats were one people, or if the Slovenes were included, what difference did it make whether these people were called Serbs, Croats, Slovenes, Yugoslavs, or Illyrians? Karadžić had raised precisely this issue when he questioned "the Serbs of the Catholic faith [who] do not wish to be called Serbs. . . . If they [the Catholics] do not want to be Serbs, then they have no national name." In other words, one's national name and his language were synonymous. Notwithstanding the fact that they referred to their language as "Croatian or Serbian" and regularly identified the Croats and Serbs as one people or nation, the Croatian readers never indicated that the Croats were anything but Croats, who, however, spoke the same language as their Slavic brothers, the Serbs, did.

As for the Slovenes, they did not have to contend with any of these issues, because all linguists accepted the fact that they were a separate nation with their own Slovenian language. Some Serbs and Croats hoped that the Slovenes would abandon their kajkavian dialect and adopt štokavian, thereby assimilating themselves into a štokavian-speaking South Slavic nation. As for the language of the Serbs and Croats, the Slovenes called it either Croatian or Serbian or Serbo-Croatian.

Whereas issues concerning language and literature might not be simple for all students to comprehend, geography was a different matter. Maps, of which there were many in the textbooks, as well as excellent wall maps, were easy for a student to understand. He could locate his hometown and determine the relationship of his province to those lands which his textbook and teacher stated belonged to his nation. Consequently, in one sense the geography books, more than the readers and history books, strengthened national sentiments.

The only point on which the Serbian and Croatian geography books could agree was the general date of the arrival of the South Slav tribes in the Balkans; but they disagreed sharply on the lands which they initially inhabited. This issue was critical, because it brought up the question that plagued every East European nation, namely, the matter of historic rights. Overlooking the fact that populations migrated, the principle of historic rights was applied not only to those lands in which the respective nations believed their ancestors had initially settled, but also to many of those regions over which, at one time or another, they had ruled, even if only for a limited duration. In the Middle Ages, throughout Europe, medieval provinces, states, kingdoms, and empires were not single ethnic entities; the situation in the Balkans was no different.

The conflicts caused by the competing issues of historic versus ethnic rights in South Slav history and in Serbian and Croatian relations can be demonstrated by two examples. Without exception, all Serbian geography books, as well as all readers and history books, categorically asserted that the province of Kosovo, where the patriarchate of Peć was located, was irrevocably Serbian. The fact that the province had been largely populated by Albanians ever since the exodus by thousands of Serbs under Patriarch Arsenije at the end of the seventeenth century was irrelevant. Historically it was Serbian and should remain so forever. In addition, Serbian writers also claimed as ethnically theirs the lands to which those Serbs fled, that is, the Military Frontier and Vojvodina. However, the Croats and Hungarians, employing the same arguments that the Serbs had advanced to support their claims to Kosovo, denied the Serbian ethnic pretensions to these regions. Similarly, the Croats defended their historic claims to Bosnia and Hercegovina, where all the nineteenth-century censuses revealed that at most only 22 percent of the population was Catholic, presumably Croatian, with about 44 percent Orthodox or Serbian. On the other hand, the Croatian textbooks scoffed at the Italian claims to Dalmatia, citing the overwhelming 82 percent of the population that was Croatian and disregarding the fact that the same textbooks described Dalmatia, including Diocletian's palace in Split, as part of the Roman Empire before the Croats settled the province.

In advancing Serbia's claims, the Serbian geography books also used other evidence. Employing the linguistic criteria that Karić had stressed, every geography book maintained that the štokavian-speaking South Slavs were Serbs, a standpoint that justified their claim not just to those parts of Croatia, Slavonia, Dalmatia, Bosnia, and Hercegovina where Orthodox Serbs lived, but to the entirety of these provinces. In other words, these were Serbian provinces in which other peoples also resided. The Croatian geography books made no compromise on Croatia, Slavonia, Dalmatia, and Istria, but they did not assert that Bosnia and Hercegovina were Croatian lands in which only Croats lived. In fact, the precise population percentages by religion were always provided, and the inhabitants were identified as Croats and Serbs. Nor did the Croatian books lay claim to the štokavian-speaking areas of Serbia, Montenegro, and Kosovo.

For the Slovenes their conflict in geography was not with the Serbs and Croats, but with the Germans and Italians. The goal of the Slovenian geographers was to provide factual and statistical data to establish the primacy of their nation in those provinces in which its nationals lived.

The historical arguments employed by the geographers were based on the research of the historians, most of whom wrote in the romantic nationalist tradition common in the nineteenth century. Even where standards of impartial scholarship were understood, it was usual to find that historians respected for their objective monographs would produce textbooks laced with nationalistic themes. In other words, scholarly integrity was compromised in order to defend the national flag. As a result, South Slavic students read little, if any, impartial history in the elementary and secondary school textbooks, whose goal, after all, was to instill pride in their nation's past by dramatizing historical events.

As was the case with the readers and geography books, the Serbian, Croatian and Slovenian history books agreed on the approximate date of their migration into the Balkans, and they also shared the same disdain for the Ottoman Empire. On other questions, there was no agreement. The focus of the Serbian history books was the Serbian nation. They emphasized the great achievements of Nemanja, Saint Sava, and Dušan in the medieval period and of Karadjordje, Obradović, and Karadžić in the modern era. The motto "Only unity saves the Serb" was nowhere more apparent than in the history books. It was Serbian, not South Slavic, history that the students studied and in which they took pride.

The Croatian history books also stressed their medieval period, noting the roles of Tomislav and Zvonimir and the nation's adoption of Catholicism, and, in the modern era, they pointed to the contributions of Gaj and Jelačić. In contrast to the animosity that the Serbs had against the Ottoman Empire and the effect that it had on the Serbian nation, the Croats' association with Hungary and the Austrian empire lasted for over nine centuries and, on balance, was seen as a positive influence because of the ties to Western civilization. Union with another state or nation, thus, had become a part of their history. In the same manner, the Croatian textbooks included considerable information on the Serbs, who comprised one-quarter of the population of Croatia-Slavonia and one-sixth of that of Dalmatia. There was no attempt, however, to present the Croatian and Serbian nations as equals within the context of Croatian history. It was a Croatian nation-state in which Serbs lived.

In the Slovenian history books, the theme repeatedly emphasized was the nation's loyalty to the Habsburg Empire. Lacking the kind of political and institutional history that had enabled the Serbian and Croatian nations to maintain a sense of national identity throughout their history, the Slovenian books stressed local or regional issues. This emphasis served to indicate to the student the subordinate role of the Slovenes within the Habsburg Empire. The only information that might conceivably be interpreted as being South Slav in orientation dealt with the wars against the Turks, but this material was presented in the context of the defense of the empire, Christianity, and Western civilization, not of South Slavism.

Throughout the Serbian, Croatian, and Slovenian readers and geography and history textbooks, religion played a prominent role. This fact is understandable since it was a compulsory subject in every grade of the elementary and secondary schools and was always listed as the first subject in the curriculum. Although the schools had been secularized in the three South Slavic lands, the church nevertheless had a privileged position. The church might not endorse the entire contents of each book used in the schools, but the priests were always in a position to criticize views that they held to be inimical to the church. No political party or politician could expect to survive for long after blatantly condemning the church or its tenets. It was one thing to work for the secularization of education, which would bring the nation in step with the modern world, but to do so was not a license to subvert religion and the function it served in the nation. Furthermore, the church was perceived by many as the nation's guardian, and for this reason, the priests often took the lead when issues involving the national interests were at stake. It was especially the case in those areas where Serbs and Croats came into conflict.

In Serbia there was no divergence of opinion on the importance of the church and the role it played in the nation's history. In the textbooks' discussion of the history of Christianity and the history of the Serbian church, the schism between Rome and Constantinople in 1054 was attributed to Rome, or, as one volume described it, "the separation of the Western Church from the Eastern." In other words, Rome was blamed for the rupture in Christian unity. Consequently, in recounting the history of the Serbian church the texts stated that "*Serbian Catholics*" had been led astray by the "enemies of the Serbian faith." They presented the same accounts as found in the textbooks of the persecution of the Serbs in the eighteenth century by the Catholics. The histories of the Serbian church and the textbooks lauded the church for sustaining the nation during the centuries of Ottoman domination and Catholic proselytizing. The textbooks pointed with pride to the fact that priests joined in military campaigns, urging the soldiers forward on behalf of their faith and nation. These general sentiments about the church were shared by the political parties, the military, the intellectuals, and the citizenry at large. In other words, church and state were perceived as one in the popular mind.

At the same time, however, the ecclesiastical and secular leaders in the kingdom assiduously cultivated non-Turkish-speaking Muslims in Bosnia and Hercegovina, trying to persuade them that they were Serbs. Moreover, the Serbian textbooks admonished the students not to refer to those Muslims who knew no Turkish, and spoke only štokavian, as Turks. They were Serbs of the Islamic faith. Although similar claims were made about the štokavian-speaking Catholic Croats, these declarations lacked the same ardor. The mistrust of or reservations about the Catholics expressed by the Orthodox leaders throughout their history were apparent in the Serbian textbooks.

Consequently, it was this belief that caused the Serbian leaders, both ecclesiastical and secular, in Croatia-Slavonia to resist any attempt to secularize education. As long as they controlled their own schools, they could teach Serbianism and thereby defend the identity of their nation within the Catholic Croatian state. Secularization of education and Zagreb's control of the textbooks were seen as a danger to Orthodoxy and the Serbian nation. As a result, the Orthodox church, both in the Triune Kingdom and in Serbia, became the defender and bastion of Serbianism. It did not foster South Slav understanding, much less unity.

The Croatian textbooks were no less vigorous in defense of their religion. Proud of the fact that they were one of the first Slavic peoples to accept Christianity and that the papacy allowed them to use their Slavic speech in the church services, the Croatians believed that they shared a privileged position within the Catholic faith. Since the Croatians had no single national ecclesiastical organization similar to the Serbian church, students learned about the conflict with the Orthodox from the Catholic textbooks' discussion of the history of Christianity. In these accounts, Constantinople was held responsible for the schism. Furthermore, it was emphasized that Stefan Nemanja, "the First Crowned" ruler of Serbia, received his crown from Rome, and that Stefan Dušan had sought an agreement with the papacy before he created the patriarchate of Peć and had had himself proclaimed tsar.

The Croatian books also stressed that in the wars against the Ottoman empire, the Croats fought for not only their state but their faith as well. Zrinski had expressed it best when he said that he was prepared to die for his "fatherland and faith." Furthermore, it was their faith that enabled the nation to endure the innumerable hardships chronicled in the books. Their religion thus served as both a shield against adversity and a source of hope.

In the nineteenth century, however, two different but related issues involving religion in Croatia were raised. First, as we know, the church strongly resisted the secularization of education, charging that it was being stripped of its guardianship of the nation, which it had exercised since the adoption of Christianity. Second, the Croatian-Serbian conflict over education spilled over into the political arena in a manner not evident before 1874. Each Serbian demand or complaint produced a counterdemand or accusation from either Starčević's Party of Right, or the Frankovites, or the Clericalists, or others. The opposition to the Serbs became especially acute during the years when the Croatian-Serbian Coalition gained ascendancy. The attacks by the Frankovites and Clericalists against the Coalition, and against what they perceived was its sacrifice of Croatian interests to appease the Serbs, understandably alarmed the Serbian ecclesiastical leaders in both Croatia-Slavonia and the Serbian kingdom. Whatever sympathy the Coalition may have generated among the Serbs regarding the possibility of better Croatian-Serbian understanding was tempered by these attacks. Nor were the Serbs reassured by the regular attempts in the Croatian sabor to reduce the quantity of material about the Serbian nation in the Croatian textbooks or even to eliminate it entirely. Consequently, it was understandable that Serbian religious and secular leaders would have

doubts about the extent to which Strossmayer's profession of brotherhood between Catholics and Orthodox, Croats and Serbs, had support among the Croatian populace at large. It was a legitimate concern. As in Serbia, the Catholic church leadership in Croatia saw as
its function to defend the nation and its faith, not to sacrifice them
on behalf of unity with the Orthodox Serbs, with whom they had
been at odds for centuries.

In the Slovenian books, religion was even more strongly emphasized. Slovenians' pride in being Catholics and their loyalty to their
faith were proclaimed. The books lauded the role played by Cyril and
Methodius in their religious development. They also emphasized the
leadership taken by the Catholic church in rallying Europe against
the Ottoman empire. The political domination of the nation by the
Clerical Party was evident. In every election it garnered about two-
thirds of the votes. Furthermore, the Liberal Party was reluctant to
advocate extending the franchise, a principle of liberalism throughout Europe, knowing well that it would only increase the electoral
majority of the Clericals. As far as Yugoslavism was concerned,
some Clericals were ready to consider a political union with the
Croats within the Habsburg empire, but only as a means of strengthening Catholicism. It was not construed as a prelude to Yugoslavism. Here again, as in the case of the Serbs and the Croats, religion
acted as a deterrent to South Slav understanding.

An analysis of the textbooks makes one point very clear: none of
the books—Serbian, Croatian, or Slovenian—even remotely conveyed the type of information and enthusiasm about South Slav
unity or Yugoslavism that was being expounded by intellectuals,
university students, and a few politicians in the decade before the
war. The books made professions of brotherhood, cooperation, and
understanding, but not unity or assimilation in the sense that could
be interpreted as jeopardizing the interests of one's own nation. Yugoslavism appealed to idealists, but not to those who had to deal
with the realities of the South Slav world.

At the same time, if the textbooks are evaluated from the point
of view of the amount of information about other nations that they
contained, knowledge that could enable the students to know more
about one another and act as a basis for closer understanding, it is
clear that the Croatian and Slovenian books were most successful.
For example, if all the information about the Serbs found in the
Croatian fourth grade elementary reader had been published separately, or if all that found in the Croatian readers, geographies and
history books for one of the secondary grades had been published as
an individual volume, anyone reading them could have acquired a

good understanding of the basic facts of Serbian history. The Croatian books, however, contained little information about the Slovenes. In relative terms, the Slovenes, in their books, provided considerable material about both the Croats and the Serbs, which could serve their students well. The Serbian books, however, offered no information about the other two South Slavic peoples. Even those few volumes published in 1913 and 1914 gave only meager information about the Croats. Furthermore, they continued to ignore the Slovenes.

The books do not reveal, however, the influence exercised by teachers and families on the issues of South Slavic unity. From articles in the educational journals and letters to the editors, it is apparent that the teachers were devout nationalists and patriots; in the age of nationalism, it could hardly have been otherwise. National issues and unification were their first priority, with social problems a definite second. Articles by teachers deploring the lack of patriotism in the schools were not uncommon. Other articles demanded greater emphasis on the study of history and geography. There is no precise way to determine the influence of families. Yet if we judged by the almanacs to which they subscribed, which were highly nationalistic, patriotic, and religious, we may conclude that the parents shared the sentiments of the teachers and the views about the nation found in the textbooks. South Slav unity or Yugoslavism was, at best, a remote vision.

In the final analysis, however, each government set its own educational policies and the goals it hoped to achieve. In the national question, the overriding issue was to instill, through the schools and textbooks, a sense of pride, patriotism, and loyalty in the nation, its past, and its future. The principal goal of the Serbian, Croatian, and Slovenian leadership, of whatever persuasion, was to unite its own nation. No political party or politician in any of these nations could hope to have any success without having national unification, not South Slav unity, as the first priority. This is clear from an examination of the platforms of the Serbian parties before the war. Even in Croatia, where the Croatian-Serbian Coalition came closest to championing South Slavic unity, the goal of the Serbian representatives in the Coalition was to protect the interests of their nationals within the Triune Kingdom. At the same time, the objective of the Croats was to have the Serbs commit themselves to the integrity of the Croatian state. The lack of trust shown by the Croats and Serbs in one another found justification in the political, religious, educational, social, and economic differences of the past centuries. The suspicions that each harbored surfaced in the war years.

Although South Slav relations up to 1914 have been described and the general history of the kingdom in the interwar years, which was briefly mentioned in the Preface, is known, South Slav developments during the war must also be discussed briefly. They add further evidence in support of the view that the same lack of South Slav understanding, mutual suspicion, and disunity that characterized the pre-1914 era as seen through the textbooks and political developments not only persisted but intensified during the war. In other words, a solid basis on which to create a new state was lacking. Hence, to provide a link between the prewar and postwar eras and underline the significance of the textbooks' failure to create a sense of national identity, a brief outline of the critical developments that occurred during the war will be presented.

Although the war began in August of 1914, not until November did the Serbian government unequivocally commit itself to support a united South Slav state. In the meantime, however, a number of prominent South Slavs—Croats, Slovenes, and Serbs—from the Austro-Hungarian Empire fled abroad and created the Yugoslav Committee. It had two goals: first, to work for the creation of a united Yugoslav state that would include all the South Slav lands of the Dual Monarchy as well as Serbia and Montenegro, and, second, to act as the representative of the South Slavs of the Dual Monarchy. In other words, the Committee regarded itself as an equal partner with the independent kingdom, a premise the Serbian government refused to acknowledge. Consequently, the basic divisions that had characterized the prewar period persisted. In part, this situation was exacerbated by the fact that the Habsburg South Slav soldiers— Croats, Slovenes, and Serbs alike—readily, even enthusiastically, fought the Serbian army, something the Serbian leaders never forgot.

From the beginning of the war to the 1917 collapse of the Tsarist regime, on which Belgrade had relied for diplomatic support, the Serbian government and the Yugoslav Committee remained at odds. Following the March 1917 revolution, and with prodding from the British and French governments, the two sides met on the island of Corfu in July to discuss their future. In the resulting Corfu Declaration, the representatives agreed to form a united state that would be "a constitutional, democratic, and parliamentary monarchy headed by the Karadjordjević dynasty." The agreement called for mutual respect for the individual national names, the acceptance of the respective flags, religious freedom, and the use of both the Cyrillic and Latin alphabets; agreement was not reached, however, on the central issue of the internal structure of the state—that is, would it have a centralized administration, as the Serbs preferred, or be a federal organization, as the Croats and Slovenes desired? This question was instead to be decided by a postwar constituent assembly. Many Croats and Slovenes, however, feared that without a prior understanding, the numerically superior Serbs would impose upon them a centralized regime, which would leave their political status much as it had been under the Austrians and Magyars.

A further difficulty lay in the fact that although the Yugoslav Committee had co-opted for itself the role of spokesman for the South Slavs of the Dual Monarchy, many of the elected representatives in the Croatian sabor did not share its views; nor were they ready to join in any union with Serbia. During the first three years of the war, in fact, the legally elected Croatian leadership was in the majority avowedly pro-Habsburg and anti-Serbian. In May 1917, two months before the Corfu Declaration was adopted, the Yugoslav Club in the Vienna Reichsrat called for the union of the Habsburg South Slavs—Slovenes, Croats and Serbs—in a form of Trialism within the monarchy. Although in the postwar era many have contended that this decision was made under political duress rather than through conviction, the evidence does not fully support this view.

Woodrow Wilson's Fourteen Points further exacerbated South Slav relations. In Point 10, he called for the "autonomous" development of the peoples of the Habsburg Empire, not for its dismemberment. Although this proposal was directly related to the secret negotiations aimed at effecting a separate peace with the Dual Monarchy, it nevertheless upset the Serbian government. Without the support of any great power and believing that the Allies were ready to preserve the empire, Pašić sought to assure that in the peace Serbia would be awarded the contested territories of Bosnia and Hercegovina and an outlet to the Adriatic Sea. When this endeavor was leaked to the Yugoslav Committee by Pašić's own diplomatic representatives abroad, its members were convinced that the Serbian government was committed not to the Yugoslav cause, but to the achievement of exclusively Serbian national aims.

Notwithstanding the shift in Allied policy in the spring of 1918 to support the dismemberment of the empire and the formation of a Yugoslav state, relations between the Serbian government and the Yugoslav Committee, which were never cordial, became even more strained. Moreover, as the war's end approached, each side became more intransigent. Hence, with the failure of the final military action of the Central Powers by the late summer of 1918, it became increasingly clear that the Habsburg Empire would disintegrate. The national leadership thus had to prepare for the new situation. In August, the South Slav leaders of the Habsburg Empire took steps to organize their lands as a separate political entity. In October, representatives of the Croatian, Serbian, and Slovenian political parties met in Zagreb and created a National Council, whose goal was the formation of an independent South Slav state. At the same time, the Croatian sabor, joined by representatives from Dalmatia, proclaimed the union of Croatia, Slavonia, and Dalmatia, that is, the unification of the Triune Kingdom, a goal that the Croatian leaders had long sought. The sabor then voted to join the National Council. In other words, there now were four South Slav political organizations—the Serbian government, the Montenegrin government, the Yugoslav Committee, and the National Council—all with individual constituencies and with definite ideas about the form of any South Slav union.

Of these four centers, the Serbian government was obviously in the strongest position. First, its army was intact and in control of Serbia and Vojvodina. Moreover, when the local authorities in the South Slav lands of the former monarchy were unable to maintain order in the chaotic postwar turmoil, they were compelled to call upon the Serbian forces to help restore it. The Croatian leadership became further dependent on the Serbian army when Italian forces advanced into parts of Istria and Dalmatia. Hence, domestic turmoil and the Italian threat to the South Slav lands meant that the Serbian government was in a stronger position to defend its concepts of a centralized South Slav state.

With little leverage and with little more than the hope that somehow things would work out, the National Council instructed a delegation to proceed to Belgrade to effect the union of the South Slav lands of the former empire with the independent Serbian and Montenegrin kingdoms. The delegation, however, had specific instructions that mandated that the final organization of the state should be determined by a Constituent Assembly, that a provisional government composed of representatives of the principal regional bodies should be constituted under the leadership of the prince regent, and that regional control should remain in the hands of local authorities until a constitution was adopted. In essence, this program was a compromise between Serbian centralism and Croatian and Slovenian federalism.

On December 1, 1918, the Kingdom of the Serbs, Croats, and Slovenes came into being under the leadership of Prince Regent Alexander Karadjordjević. The terms of the union and the provisions of the constitution of 1921 left the Serbs in control of the state. The postwar history of the kingdom has been discussed elsewhere; the consensus of opinion is that it did not live up to the expectations of the South Slav idealists who had dreamed of a Yugoslav nation di-

The Kingdom of the Serbs, Croats, and Slovenes, 1920

vested of the historical, religious, cultural, and economic differences that had for so long divided the Serbs, Croats, and Slovenes. The war had brought a Serbian victory over the Habsburg Empire, but it did not lead to the creation of a Yugoslav nation permeated with this sentiment. Instead, the entire interwar period saw a strengthening of the Serbian, Croatian, and Slovenian nationalism that had characterized the national programs of the nineteenth century and whose fundamental principles had been incorporated in the school textbooks—which, of course, had formed the basis of the education of all of the leaders of interwar Yugoslavia.

Notes

CHAPTER 1

1. The literature on South Slav nationalism and the Yugoslav movement is extensive. Only a few representative works will be cited. A recent study, with the most exhaustive bibliography, is Wolf Dietrich Behschnitt, *Nationalismus bei Serben und Kroaten 1830–1914: Analyse und Typologie der nationalen Ideologie* (Munich: R. Oldenbourg, 1980). For Serbian developments consult the new six-volume *Istorija srpskoga naroda* (Belgrade: Srpska književna zadruga, 1980–83), edited by Radovan Samardžić et al.; Vaso Čubrilović, *Istorija političke misli u Srbiji XIX veka* (Belgrade: Prosveta, 1958); and Michael Boro Petrovich, *A History of Modern Serbia, 1804–1918* (New York: Harcourt Brace Jovanovich, 1976), 2 vols. For Croatia see Ferdo Šišić, *Pregled povijesti hrvatskoga naroda* (Zagreb: Matica hrvatska, 1962); Jaroslav Šidak et al., *Povijest hrvatskog naroda g. 1860–1914* (Zagreb: Školska knjiga, 1968); and Wolfgang Kessler, *Politik, Kultur und Gesellschaft in Kroatien und Slawonien in der ersten Hälfte des 19 Jahrhunderts* (Munich: R. Oldenbourg, 1981). Slovenian developments are discussed in Carole Rogel, *The Slovenes and Yugoslavism 1890–1914* (Boulder, Colo.: East European Quarterly, 1977); and Ferdo Gestrin and Vasilij Melik, *Slovenska zgodovina od konca osemnajstega stoletja do 1918* (Ljubljana: Državna založba Slovenije, 1966). Ivo Banac's *The National Question in Yugoslavia: Origins, History, Politics* (Ithaca, N.Y.: Cornell University Press, 1984), winner of the Vucinich Book Prize of the American Association for the Advancement of Slavic Studies, has been highly praised for the detail with which it presented the national problem in all its complexities. Two interwar works that championed the Yugoslav idea are Viktor Novak, *Antologija jugoslovenske misli i narodnog jedinstva (1390–1930)* (Belgrade: Državna štamparija, 1930); and Ferdo Šišić, *Jugoslovenska misao. Istorija ideje jugoslovenskog narodnog ujedinjenja i oslobodjenja od 1790–1918* (Belgrade: Balkanski institut, 1937).

2. The works available on Karadžić are extensive. The best account of his life and accomplishments in English is Duncan Wilson, *The Life and Times of Vuk Stefanović Karadžić, 1787–1864: Literary, Literature, and National Independence in Serbia* (Oxford: Clarendon Press, 1970). His collected works are found in Vuk Stefanović Karadžić, *Sabrana dela* (Belgrade: Beogradski grafički zavod, 1965–74), 36 vols. The article in question is in

V[uk] S[tefanović] K[aradžić], *Kovčežić za istoriju, jezik i običaje Srba sva tri zakona* (Vienna: U štampariji jeremenskoga manastira, 1849), pp. 1–27. See also "Srbi svi i svuda," *Kalendar matice srpske za 1903* (Novi Sad), pp. 72–73.

Since South Slav dialects will play such an important part in the subsequent pages, a definition of the principal variants of the Serbo-Croatian language is necessary. Serbo-Croatian has three dialects—štokavian, kajkavian, and čakavian. The most important is štokavian, the literary language of the Serbs and Croats. It has three variants—ekavian, ijekavian, and ikavian. The eastern variant is ekavian, spoken primarily by the Serbs; the southern variant is ijekavian, spoken by most Croats; and the western variant is ikavian, heard mainly in Dalmatia. The Croats also speak two other dialects, kajkavian, which is used primarily in northwestern Croatia, and čakavian, the least used, which is spoken in parts of Dalmatia. Further information on this subject is on pages 7–9, 78–81, 105–6, 143–47, 166.

3. A fine biography of Garašanin is by David MacKenzie, *Ilija Garašanin: Balkan Bismarck* (Boulder, Colo.: East European Monographs, 1985). For the controversies surrounding the Načertanije see Mirko Valentić, "Koncepcija Garašaninova 'Načertanije' (1844)," *Historijski pregled* 7 (1961): 128–37; Nikša Stančić, "Problem Načertanije Ilije Garašanina," *Historijski Zbornik* 21–22 (1968–69): 179–96; Behschnitt, *Nationalismus*, pp. 54–65; and Charles Jelavich, "Garašanin's Načertanije und das großserbische Programm," *Südost-Forschungen* 27 (1968): 131–47.

4. A discussion of Gaj's views is found in Wayne S. Vucinich, "Croatian Illyrism: Its Background and Genesis," in *Intellectual and Social Developments in the Habsburg Empire from Maria Theresa to World War I*, ed. Stanley B. Winters and Joseph Held (Boulder, Colo.: East European Quarterly, 1975), pp. 68–73; Kessler, *Politik, Kultur und Gesellschaft*, pp. 79–102, 134–92; Elinor Murray Despalatović, *Ljudevit Gaj and the Illyrian Movement* (Boulder, Colo.: East European Quarterly, 1975), pp. 42–45; Antun Barac, *Hrvatska književnost od preporoda do stvaranja Jugoslavije* (Zagreb: Jugoslavenska akademija znanosti i umjetnosti, 1954), I, pp. 7–50; and Jaroslav Šidak, *Studije iz hrvatske povijesti XIX stoljeća* (Zagreb: Institut za hrvatsku povijest, 1973), pp. 113–24.

5. *Danica Ilirska* (Zagreb: Franjo Suppan, 1835), I (1835), pp. 66–67, 78, 83, 234–35; II (1836), proglas (proclamation).

6. Charles Jelavich, "The Croatian Problem in the Habsburg Monarchy in the Nineteenth Century," *Austrian History Yearbook* 3 (1967): pt. 2, p. 94.

7. Ljudevit Jonke, *Hrvatski književni jezik danas* (Zagreb: Školska knjiga, 1971), pp. 85–87; Wilson, *Life of Karadžić*, pp. 312–13; Pavle Ivić, *Srpski narod i njegov jezik* (Belgrade: Srpska književna zadruga, 1986), 2nd ed., pp. 184–89; Mirjana Gross, *Počeci moderne hrvatske. Neoapsolutizam u civilnoj Hrvatskoj i Slavoniji 1850–1860* (Zagreb: Globus, 1985), pp. 418–24.

8. Vojislav J. Vučković, *Politička akcija Srbije u južnoslovenskim pokrajinama habsburške monarhije 1859–1874* (Belgrade: Naučno delo, 1965), pp. 223–24, 240–41.

9. Ibid., pp. 260–83, 318; Čubrilović, *Istorija političke misli*, pp. 225–36; Šidak, *Povijest hrvatskog naroda*, pp. 34–37; Vasilije Dj. Krestić, *Srpsko-hrvatski odnosi i jugoslovenska ideja* (Belgrade: Narodna knjiga, 1983), pp. 119–52; and Gale Stokes, *Legitimacy through Liberalism: Vladimir Jovanović and the Transformation of Serbian Politics* (Seattle: University of Washington Press, 1975), pp. 101, 119.

10. Jovan Skerlić, *Eseji o srpsko-hrvatskom pitanju* (Zagreb: Jugoslavensko nakladno dioničarsko društvo, 1918), p. 47; Behschnitt, *Nationalismus*, pp. 98–108; Woodford D. McClellan, *Svetozar Marković and the Origins of Balkan Socialism* (Princeton: Princeton University Press, 1964), pp. 184–86; Svetozar Marković, *Sabrani spisi* (Belgrade: Kultura, 1960–65), IV, p. 422.

11. Mirjana Gross, *Povijest pravaške ideologije* (Zagreb: Institut za hrvatsku povijest, 1973), pp. 15–53, 195–251; Ljerka Kuntić, *Kvaternik i njegovo doba (1825–1871)* (Zagreb: Znanje, 1971), pp. 320–408; Vjekoslav Fleiser, "Dr. Ante Starčević," in *Bog i Hrvati-kalendar za 1897* (Zagreb), pp. 65–72; Ante Starčević, *Politički spisi* (Zagreb: Znanje, 1971), pp. 46–50, compiled by Tomislav Ladan; Ante Starčević, *Izabrani spisi* (Zagreb: Hrvatski izdavalički bibliografski zavod, 1943), pp. 246–50, edited by Blaž Jurišić; Ante Starčević, *Misli i pogledi: Pojedinac-Hrvatska-Svijet* (Zagreb: Matica hrvatska, 1971), pp. 57–65, edited by Blaž Jurišić; Behschnitt, *Nationalismus*, pp. 172–86; Ivo Banac, "Main Trends in the Croatian Language Question," in *Aspects of the Slavic Language Question*, ed. Riccardo Picchio and Harvey Goldblatt (New Haven: Yale Concilium on International and Area Studies, 1984), p. 232; and Banac, *National Question*, pp. 85–87.

12. N[ikola] S[tojanović], "Srbi i Hrvati," *Srpski književni glasnik* 4 (1902): 1149–59.

13. "Prosveta u Srpstvu," *Učitelj* 27 (1908): 600–616.

14. Dragoslav Janković, *Srbija i Jugoslovensko pitanje 1914–1915 godine* (Belgrade: Institut za savremenu istoriju, 1973), pp. 42–43.

15. Ibid., p. 43; Djordje Dj. Stanković, *Nikola Pašić: Saveznici i stvaranje Jugoslavije* (Belgrade: Nolit, 1984), pp. 24–26; Banac, *National Question*, pp. 106–07; Čubrilović, *Istorija političke misli*, p. 413.

16. *Vardar - Kalendar za 1908* (Belgrade), p. 94, plus map; ibid., *Kalendar za 1911*, pp. 21–22; and Janković, *Srbija i Jugoslovensko pitanje*, pp. 58–61.

17. Milan Ž. Živanović, *Solunski proces hiljadu devetsto sedamnaeste* (Belgrade: Srpska akademija nauka, 1955), posebna izdanja, vol. 243, pp. 669–70.

18. Janković, *Srbija i Jugoslovensko pitanje*, pp. 36–37; Čubrilović, *Istorija političke misli*, pp. 384–91.

19. *Slovenski Jug* 8, no. 32 (August 6, 1911): 249–50; 8, no. 34 (August 20, 1911): 265–66.

20. Janković, *Srbija i Jugoslovensko pitanje*, pp. 57–58.

21. Ibid., p. 56.

22. Stanković, *Nikola Pašić*, pp. 20–21; Čubrilović, *Istorija političke misli*, pp. 385, 451–74.

23. Stanković, *Nikola Pašić*, pp. 21–23.

24. Ibid., p. 26.

25. Novak, *Antologija*, pp. 453–54.

26. Ibid., p. 469.

27. Ibid., pp. 464–65.

28. Mirjana Gross, "Nacionalne ideje studentske omladine u Hrvatskoj uoči svejtskog rata," *Historijski zbornik* 21–22 (1968–69): 127–28; Banac, *National Question*, pp. 100–102; Čubrilović, *Istorija političke misli*, pp. 435–38; Behschnitt, *Nationalismus*, pp. 201–30.

29. *Starčevićeva hrvatska stranka prava* (Zagreb: Hrvatska radnička tiskara, 1907), pp. 34–37.

30. Rogel, *The Slovenes and Yugoslavism, 1890–1914*, pp. 78–79.

31. Fran Zwitter, "The Slovenes and the Habsburg Monarchy," *Austrian History Yearbook* 3, no. 2 (1967): 183.

CHAPTER 2

1. Vladeta Tešić et al., *Sto godina prosvetnog saveta Srbije, 1880–1980* (Belgrade: Zavod za udžbenike i nastavna sredstva, 1980), pp. 37–38.

2. Ibid., p. 39.

3. Ibid., p. 82.

4. Ibid., pp. 39, 82.

5. Ibid., p. 52.

6. Ibid., pp. 58–59.

7. Ibid., p. 46.

8. Srečko Ćunković, *Školstvo i prosveta u Srbiji u XIX veku* (Belgrade: Pedagoški muzej, 1971), pp. 50–51, 171–93.

9. Tešić, *Sto godina*, pp. 52–57.

10. Ibid., p. 61.

11. Ćunković, *Školstvo*, pp. 134–35.

12. Ibid., pp. 137–140. *Prosvetni Glasnik—Službeni list ministarstva prosvete i crkveni poslova* (Belgrade: Državna štamparija, 1904), XXV, p. 331; *Učitelj*, XXIV (1904/5), p. 465; Tešić, *Sto godina*, p. 74.

13. Ćunković, *Školstvo*, p. 159.

14. Ibid., p. 160, 167–70.

15. Ibid., pp. 176–80.

16. Tešić, *Sto godina*, p. 63.

17. Ibid., p. 69.

18. Ibid., pp. 63–70.

19. Ibid., pp. 70–72. There were three classifications for textbooks: those officially approved by the government for use in the classroom, those that also received the government's endorsement and could be used as supplementary reading and were found in most public and school libraries, and those published independently with the hope that they would be adopted in the future, as was the case with a number of books.

20. Stanoje Stanojević, *Letopis matice srpske* 232 (1905): 99–111; Milenko Vukičević, *Nastavnik* 20, no. 3–4 (1909): 125–32, 214–22.

21. Tešić, *Sto godina*, pp. 70–71.

22. *Prosvetni Glasnik*, XXXIII (1912), p. 11.

23. Ibid., XXXV (1914), pp. 172–74.

24. The relevant Serbian statistical information is found in *Statistički godišnjak Kraljevine Srbije* (Belgrade: Državna štamparija) (1900), V; ibid. (1905), X; and in Franja Kuster, *Glavni demografski podatci o kraljevini Srbiji* (Belgrade: Državna štamparija, 1928), pp. 16–19.

25. James P. Krokar, "Liberal Reform in Croatia, 1872–1875: The Beginnings of Modern Croatia under Ban Ivan Mažuranić" (Ph.D. diss., Indiana University, 1980), p. 124.

26. Ibid., p. 124.

27. Ibid., p. 156.

28. Ibid., p. 147; Antun Cuvaj, *Gradja za povijest školstva Kraljevina Hrvatske i Slavonije od najstarijih vremena do danas* (Zagreb: Kr. zemaljska tiskara, 1911), 2nd rev. and enlarged ed., VI, 362–63.

29. *Saborski dnevnik kraljevinah Hrvatske, Slavonije i Dalmacije godina, 1872–1875* (Zagreb: Lav. Hartman, 1875), II, pp. 1188–93.

30. The complete text of the education law of 1874 is found in Cuvaj, *Gradja*, VI, pp. 435–54.

31. Dragutin Franković, ed., *Povijest školstva i pedagogije u Hrvatskoj* (Zagreb: Pedagoško-književni zbor, 1858), p. 163; *Saborski dnevnik*, II, pp. 1167–70.

32. *Saborski dnevnik*, II, p. 1199.

33. Krokar, "Liberal Reform," pp. 163–66, 179–97; *Saborski dnevnik*, II, pp. 1271–81; Cuvaj, *Gradja*, VI, pp. 222–43.

34. Cuvaj, *Gradja*, VI, p. 453.

35. Krokar, "Liberal Reform," pp. 124, 164.

36. Cuvaj, *Gradja*, VI, pp. 51–58, 62–96, 101–07.

37. Ibid., VII, pp. 273–303; Franković, *Povijest školstva*, pp. 172–76; Šidak, *Povijest hrvatskog naroda*, pp. 132–33.

38. Cuvaj, *Gradja*, VII, pp. 466–78.

39. Ibid., p. 470.

40. Ibid., p. 477.

41. The complete text of the education law of 1888 is in Cuvaj, *Gradja*, VII, pp. 695–719.

42. Franković, *Povijest školstva*, pp. 183–88.

43. Cuvaj, *Gradja*, VI, pp. 440–41, articles 54 and 70.

44. Ibid., VII, pp. 700, 702, articles 50 and 66.

45. Franković, *Povijest školstva*, pp. 179–80, 250.

46. Cuvaj, *Gradja*, V, pp. 440–42.

47. Ibid., VI, p. 442, article 81; ibid., VII, p. 704, article 76.

48. Ibid., IX, p. 302.

49. Ibid., VII, pp. 27–28.

50. Ibid., pp. 28–29.

51. Franković, *Povijest školstva*, pp. 200–202.

52. Cuvaj, *Gradja*, VII, pp. 29–33.

53. Ibid., VIII, p. 199.

54. Ibid., p. 200.

55. Ibid., p. 207.

56. Ibid., pp. 215–16.

57. *Statistički godišnjak Kraljevine Hrvatske i Slavonije* (Zagreb: Kr. zemaljska tiskara, 1913–17) (1905), I; ibid., (1906–10), II. See also *1875–1915 Statistički Atlas Kraljevine Hrvatske i Slavonije* (Zagreb: Kr. zem. tiskara, 1915).

58. Walter Goldinger, "The Nationality Question in Austrian Education," *Austrian History Yearbook* 3, no. 2 (1967), pp. 136–56.

59. Ibid., pp. 151–52.

60. *Enciklopedija Jugoslavije*, VII, pp. 301–02; Vlado Schmidt et al., *Osnovna šola na Slovenskem 1869–1969* (Ljubljana: Slovenski šolski muzej, 1970), pp. 9–63.

61. *Enciklopedija Jugoslavije*, VII, p. 303.

62. Schmidt, *Osnovna šola*, pp. 121–36, 171–210, 413–38, 547–70.

63. *Enciklopedija Jugoslavije*, VII, p. 303.

64. Goldinger, "Nationality Question," p. 154.

65. Bogumil Vosnjak, *A Bulwark against Germany* (London: George Allen & Unwin, 1917), pp. 230–42; Schmidt, *Osnovna šola*, pp. 65–153;

Adam Wandruszka and Peter Urbanitsch, *Die Habsburgermonarchie 1848–1918: Die Völker des Reiches* (Vienna: Verlag der Österreichischen Akademie der Wissenschaft, 1980), III : 2, pp. 818–23.

CHAPTER 3

1. Stojan Novaković, *Srpska gramatika* (Belgrade: Državna štamparija, 1894), 1st complete ed.; Tomislav Maretić, *Hrvatska ili Srpska gramatika za srednje škole* (Zagreb: L. Hartman, 1899).

2. Novaković, *Srpska gramatika*, pp. iii–xi; *Enciklopedija Jugoslavije*, VI, p. 308.

3. *Enciklopedija Jugoslavije*, VI, p. 308.

4. Novaković, *Srpska gramatika*, pp. iv–v.

5. Ibid., pp. v–vi.

6. Ibid., p. vii.

7. Ibid., p. 1.

8. Ibid., pp. 21–22.

9. Ibid., p. 22.

10. Ibid., p. 26.

11. Ibid., p. 26.

12. Ibid., p. 122.

13. Ibid., pp. 156, 160, 163, 166, 172, 177, 190.

14. Ibid., pp. 283, 292, 313, 315.

15. Ibid., p. 390.

16. Ibid., p. vi.

17. Stojan Novaković, *Srpska čitanka za niže gimnazije i realke Kraljevine Srbije* (Belgrade: Državna štamparija, 1895), II.

18. Ibid., p. iii.

19. Ibid., p. v.

20. Ibid., p. vi.

21. Ibid., pp. 271–75.

22. *Enciklopedija Jugoslavije*, VI, pp. 12–13; Ljudevit Jonke, *Hrvatski književni jezik 19 i 20 stoljeća* (Zagreb: Matica hrvatska, 1971), pp. 190–91.

23. *Enciklopedija Jugoslavije*, VI, p. 12.

24. Ibid., p. 13.

25. Maretić, *Hrvatska ili srpska gramatika*, p. 1.

26. Ibid., pp. 29–30.

27. Ibid., pp. 185, 139, 168, 122, 125, 168, 133, 184, 117.

28. Ibid., p. 189.

29. Tomislav Maretić-Ivan Šarić, *Hrvatska čitanka za II razred gimnazijski* (Zagreb: Kraljevska zemaljska tiskara, 1906).

30. Ibid. See table of contents, pp. iii–iv.

31. *Enciklopedija Jugoslavije*, IV, p. 29. Stanoje Stanojević, *Narodna enciklopedija srpsko-hrvatsko-slovenačka* (Zagreb: Bibliografski zavod, 1924–29), I, pp. 841–42.

32. Ibid., VI, p. 632.

33. Ibid., II, p. 617.

34. *Enciklopedija Jugoslavije*, III, p. 204; Stanojević, *Narodna enciklopedija*, I, p. 632.

35. *Enciklopedija Jugoslavije*, VIII, p. 559; Stanojević, *Narodna enciklopedija*, IV, p. 1187.

36. *Enciklopedija Jugoslavije*, VIII, p. 241.

37. Ibid., IV, pp. 546–47.

38. Novaković, *Srpska čitanka*, I (1893), pp. iii–vii.

39. Ibid., pp. vi–vii.

40. Ibid., II (1895), p. vi.

41. Sreten Pašić and Milan Šević, *Srpska čitanka za srednje škole* (Belgrade: Državna štamparija, 1894), I, p. ix.

42. Milan Šević, *Srpska čitanka za srednje škole za III razred* (Belgrade: Državna štamparija, 1909), III, p. ix.

43. Milan Šević, *Srpska čitanka za srednje škole za IV razred* (Belgrade: Državna štamparija, 1903), IV, p. xi.

44. [Filip Hristić], *Treća čitanka za osnovne srpske škole* (Belgrade: Državna štamparija, 1872), p. 89.

45. Miloš Ivković, *Srpska čitanka za prvi razred srednjih škola* (Belgrade: Geca Kon, 1911), p. 63.

46. Milan Šević, *Srpska čitanka za srednje škole za II razred* (Belgrade: Državna štamparija, 1911), II, p. 82.

47. [Hristić], *Treća čitanka* (1872), p. 86.

48. Ibid.

49. Ibid., p. 88.

50. Ibid.

51. Ibid., pp. 86–87.

52. [Filip Hristić], *Treća čitanka za četvrti razred osnovni srbski škola* (Belgrade: U knjigopečatni kniažestva Srbie, 1855), p. 101; [Hristić], *Treca čitanka* (1872), p. 114; [Filip Hristić], *Četvrtka čitanka za osnovne škole* (Belgrade: Državna štamparija, 1885), pp. 119–21.

53. Ljub. M. Protić and Vlad. D. Stojanović, *Srpska čitanka za IV*

razred osnovnih škola u Kraljevini Srbiji (Belgrade: Državna štamparija, 1907), III, 7th rev. ed., p. 223.

54. Šević, *Srpska čitanka*, II (1911), pp. 83–84.

55. Ljub. M. Protić and Vlad. D. Stojanović, *Srpska čitanka za III razred osnovnih škola u Kraljevini Srbiji* (Belgrade: Državna štamparija, 1912), II, 9th ed., pp. 105–07.

56. [Filip Hristić], *Druga čitanka za osnovne škole* (Belgrade: Državna štamparija, 1872), pp. 66–67.

57. Svetislav Vulović, *Srpska čitanka za niže gimnazije i realke* (Belgrade: Državna štamparija, 1874), II, pp. 199–200.

58. Antun Barac, *A History of Yugoslav Literature* (Ann Arbor: University of Michigan Slavic Publications, 1973), p. 164–66, translated by Petar Mijušković; *Enciklopedija Jugoslavije*, IV, pp. 325–26. Ivković, *Srpska čitanka* (1911), p. 25.

59. Ivković, *Srpska čitanka* (1911), pp. 24–25.

60. Vojislav M. Jovanović and Miloš Ivković, *Srpska čitanka za četvrti razred srednjih škola* (Belgrade: Geca Kon, 1913), pp. 260–62.

61. Vojislav M. Jovanović and Miloš Ivković, *Srpska čitanka za treći razred srednjih škola* (Belgrade: Geca Kon, 1913), pp. 251–52.

62. Ivković, *Srpska čitanka* (1911), p. 31–36.

63. Ibid., pp. 48–52. A guslar is a bard who sings with a one-stringed folk instrument called a gusle.

64. Protić and Stojanović, *Srpska čitanka za IV razred* (1907), p. 2.

65. Jovanović and Ivković, *Srpska čitanka za četvrti razred* (1913), pp. 113–17.

66. Protić and Stojanović, *Srpska čitanka za IV razred* (1907), p. 5; Sreten Pašić and Milan Šević, *Srpska čitanka za srednje škole za I razred* (Belgrade: Državna štamparija, 1902), I, p. 21, 3rd rev. edition.

67. Protić and Stojanović, *Srpska čitanka za IV razred* (1907), pp. 77–79.

68. [Hristić], *Treća čitanka za IV razred* (1855), pp. 101–02.

69. [Hristić]. *Četvrta čitanka* (1885), p. 120.

70. Ivković, *Srpska čitanka* (1911), p. 111.

71. Protić and Stojanović, *Srpska čitanka za cetvrti razred* (1907), pp. 218–20.

72. Novaković, *Srpska čitanka*, II (1895), pp. iii–vi, 275, 355–58.

73. Barac, *Yugoslav Literature*, 115–17; *Enciklopedija Jugoslavije*, VI, p. 605.

74. Jovanović and Ivković, *Srpska čitanka za treći razred (1913)*, pp. 250–51.

75. Ibid., pp. 137–45, 236–39; Barac, *Yugoslav Literature*, pp. 137–40.

76. Jovanović and Ivković, *Srpska čitanka za treći razred* (1913), p. 197.

77. Jovanović and Ivković, *Srpska čitanka za četvrti razred* (1913), pp. 71–73.

78. Ibid.

79. Protić and Stojanović, *Srpska čitanka za IV razred* (1907), p. 157.

80. Ibid., pp. 148–49.

81. Ibid., pp. 149–50. "Srbima je u slozi spas," *Kalendar narodnih novina za 1909* (Belgrade), pp. 84–89.

82. Ibid., pp. 154–56.

83. P. P. Djordjević and U. Blagojević, *Srpska čitanka za IV razred osnovnih škola u Kraljevini Srbiji* (Belgrade: Državna štamparija, 1906), 8th ed., pp. 95–100.

84. Protić and Stojanović, *Srpska čitanka za IV razred* (1907), p. 223; Šević, *Srpska čitanka*, II (1911), p. 84; ibid., III (1909), pp. 95–98.

85. Djordjević and Blagojević, *Srpska čitanka za IV razred* (1906), pp. 89–91; Šević, *Srpska čitanka*, III (1909), 54–63, 100–104.

86. Djordjević and Blagojević, *Srpska čitanka za IV razred* (1906), p. 90.

87. Jovanović and Ivković, *Srpska čitanka za četvrti razred* (1913), p. 53.

88. Protić and Stojanović, *Srpska čitanka za IV razred* (1907), pp. 217–18.

89. Djordjević and Blagojević, *Srpska čitanka za IV razred* (1906), pp. 84–85.

90. Ibid., pp. 74–75.

91. Ibid.

92. Protić and Stojanović, *Srpska čitanka za IV razred* (1907), pp. 217–18.

93. Jovanović and Ivković, *Srpska čitanka za treći razred* (1913), pp. 250–51. See also ibid., table of contents, pp. 253–56. Jovanović and Ivković, *Srpska čitanka za četvrti razred* (1913), pp. 265–66.

94. [Hristić], *Treća čitanka za četvrti razred* (1855), pp. 97–98. [Hristić], *Treća čitanka* (1872), pp. 109–10; [Hristić], *Četvrta čitanka* (1885), pp. 115–17.

95. Protić and Stojanović, *Srpska čitanka za IV razred* (1907), p. 223; Šević, *Srpska čitanka*, II (1911), pp. 83–84.

96. Protić and Stojanović, *Srpska čitanka za IV razred* (1907), pp. 214–16.

97. Djordjević and Blagojević, *Srpska čitanka za IV razred* (1906), pp. 86–87.

98. Protić and Stojanović, *Srpska čitanka za IV razred* (1907), pp. 216–17.

99. Djordjević and Blagojević, *Srpska čitanka za IV razred* (1906), pp. 73, 79.

100. Ivković, *Srpska čitanka* (1911), pp. 117–18.

101. *Enciklopedija Jugoslavije*, III, p. 321; Cuvaj, *Gradja*, IV, pp. 5–6.

102. *Enciklopedija Jugoslavije*, III, pp. 283–84; Cuvaj, *Gradja*, VII, p. 29.

103. Cuvaj, *Gradja*, VI, pp. 269–70; ibid., VII, p. 28; *Enciklopedija Jugoslavije*, II, pp. 904.

104. Cuvaj, *Gradja*, VI, pp. 18–20.

105. Ibid., X, pp. 182–83.

106. *Enciklopedija Jugoslavije*, VIII, p. 469: Antun Mažuranić, Matija Mesić, and Adolfo Veber-Tkalčević, *Ilirska čitanka* (Zagreb: Tiskarnica Ljudevita Gaja, 1856); ibid., II, p. iii; Cuvaj, *Gradja*, IV, pp. 235–41.

107. Cuvaj, *Gradja*, VI, p. 17; *Enciklopedija Jugoslavije*, VI, p. 77.

108. Cuvaj, *Gradja*, III, pp. 90–91; *Enciklopedija Jugoslavije*, VI, p. 55; Antun Mažuranić, Matija Mesić, and Adolfo Veber-Tkalčević, *Čitanka za I i II razred* (Vienna: Kraljevska naklada školskih knjigah, 1869); Antun Mažuranić, Matija Mesić, and Adolfo Veber-Tkalčević, *Čitanka za III i IV razred* (Vienna: Kraljevska naklada školskih knjigah, 1857).

109. *Enciklopedija Jugoslavije*, VI, pp. 12–13.

110. Cuvaj, *Gradja*, X, pp. 495–96; *Enciklopedija Jugoslavije*, VII, p. 412.

111. *Enciklopedija Jugoslavije*, II, p. 603; ibid., VI, pp. 477–78.

112. Stanojević, *Narodna enciklopedija*, I, p. 521.

113. *Enciklopedija Jugoslavije*, II, p. 237; Cuvaj, *Gradja*, VIII, pp. 219–21.

114. Cuvaj, *Gradja*, VII, pp. 209–11; *Enciklopedija Jugoslavije*, I, p. 279; ibid., VI, pp. 22–23.

115. *Čitanka za četvrti razred obćih pučkih škola* (Vienna: U carskoj kraljevskoj nakladi školskih knjiga, 1889), p. 88.

116. *Slovnica i pismovnik za obćenite pučke učionice* (Vienna: Kraljevska naklad učioničkih knjiga, 1891), pp. 15, 40.

117. For examples, see *Čitanka za drugi općih razred pučkih škola u Hrvatskoj i Slavoniji* (Zagreb: Kraljevska zemaljska tiskara, 1893), pp. 3–5; as well as *Prva slovnička čitanka za pučke učione* (Vienna: Kraljevska naklada školskih knjigah, 1875), p. 158.

118. Franjo Petračić, *Hrvatska čitanka za više gimnazije i nalike jim škole: Historija literature u primjerah* (Zagreb: Kraljevska zemaljska tiskara, 1880), II, pp. 1–2.

119. Petračić-Miler, *Hrvatska čitanka*, II (1895), p. 4.

120. Antun Pechan, *Povjest hrvatske književnosti za učiteljske pripravnike* (Zagreb: L. Hartman, 1910), p. 7.

121. Mirko Divković, *Hrvatska čitanka za IV razred gimnazijski* (Zagreb: Kraljevska zemaljska tiskara, 1901), 5th ed., pp. 1–3; Novak, *Antologija*, pp. 383–85.

122. *Čitanka za treći razred pučkih škola* (Zagreb: Kraljevska zemaljska tiskara, 1880), p. 88.

123. Ibid. pp. 84–90; (1884), pp. 82–83.

124. Ibid. (1880), pp. 93–94; *Čitanka za treći razred* (1897), pp. 14–15; Cvjetko Rubetić, *Kratka poviest crkve za preparandije i gradjanske škole* (Zagreb: Kraljevska zemaljska tiskara, 1880), 2nd rev. ed., pp. 27–29, 54–58, 114–19; Cvjetko Rubetić, *Kratka povjest crkve Kristove za realne gimnazije, učiteljske i gradjanske škole* (Zagreb: Kraljevska zemaljska tiskara, 1896), 4th ed., pp. 28–30, 55–60, 116–27; Franjo Lasman, *Povijest crkve Hristove za više razrede srednjih škola* (Zagreb: Kraljevska zemaljska tiskara, 1917), 2nd rev. ed., pp. 62–65; 94–97. Glagolitic was the Slavic alphabet composed by Saint Cyril in the ninth century that gained prominence in Dalmatia. The Croats consider it a unique aspect of their medieval religious and literary development.

125. *Čitanka za četvrti razred* (1889), pp. 88–89; Rubetić, *Kratka poviest crkve* (1880), pp. 30, 58–59; ibid. (1896), pp. 30, 53–54; Lasman, *Povijest crkve Hristove* (1917), pp. 69–71, 80–86.

126. *Druga slovnička čitanka za katoličke pučke učione u austrijskoj carevini* (Vienna: Kraljevska naklada školskih knjigah, 1879), p. 44.

127. Ibid., pp. 15–16.

128. Mirko Divković, *Hrvatska čitanka za III razred gimnazijski* (Zagreb: Kraljevska zemaljska tiskara, 1896), pp. 3–6, 64–66.

129. *Druga slovnička čitanka* (1879), p. 132; *Čitanka za treći razred* (1880), pp. 98–99.

130. *Čitanka za treći razred* (1894), pp. 195–96.

131. Ibid., pp. 100–101.

132. Divković, *Hrvatska čitanka za III razred* (1896), p. 54.

133. Divković, *Hrvatska čitanka za IV razred* (1901), pp. 75–79.

134. Ibid., pp. 61–63; *Čitanka za četvrti razred* (1889), p. 104.

135. Divković, *Hrvatska čitanka za IV razred* (1901), pp. 79–81; *Čitanka za treći razred* (1880), p. 105; *Prva slovnička čitanka* (1875), pp. 118–21; *Druga slovnička čitanka* (1879), pp. 135–39; *Čitanka za drugi općih razred* (1893), pp. 130–32; Petračić-Miler, *Hrvatska čitanka*, II (1895), p. 266.

136. *Prva slovnička čitanka* (1875), pp. 118–21.

137. *Enciklopedija Jugoslavije*, VIII, p. 632.

138. Divković, *Hrvatska čitanka za IV razred* (1901), pp. 38–41.

139. Ibid., pp. 87–91; *Čitanka za četvrti razred* (1889), pp. 112–13.

140. *Čitanka za treći razred* (1907), pp. 174–76; *Čitanka za četvrti razred* (1889), pp. 121–25. Divković, *Hrvatska čitanka za IV razred* (1901), pp. 51–54.

141. *Čitanka za treći razred* (1894), p. 198; Divković, *Hrvatska čitanka za IV razred* (1901), pp. 47–50; Petračić-Miler, *Hrvatska čitanka*, II (1895), p. 266.

142. *Druga slovnička čitanka* (1879), pp. 185–86.

143. *Čitanka za treći razred* (1880), pp. 108–09.

144. *Čitanka za četvrti razred* (1889), p. 125.

145. *Prva slovnička čitanka* (1875), pp. 125–26.

146. *Početnica za obće pučke škole* (Zagreb: Kraljevska zemaljska tiskara, 1889), pp. 127–28.

147. *Čitanka za drugi razred nižih pučkih škola* (Zagreb: Kraljevska zemaljska tiskara, 1894), p. 106; *Čitanka za treći razred* (1880), pp. 111–12.

148. *Čitanka za treći razred* (1894), p. 200.

149. Ibid., (1907), pp. 182–84.

150. Petračić, *Hrvatska čitanka*, II (1880), p. 3.

151. Ibid., p. 4.

152. Ibid., pp. 5–9; Petračić-Miler, *Hrvatska čitanka* (1895), pp. 28–29.

153. *Čitanka za četvrti razred* (1889), pp. 80, 120.

154. Petračić, *Hrvatska čitanka*, II (1880), p. 5.

155. Ivan Filipović, *Kratka poviest književnosti hrvatske i srpske za gradjanske i višje djevojačke škole* (Zagreb: Lav Hartman, 1875), p. 29.

156. Divković, *Hrvatska čitanka za IV razred* (1901), pp. 98–103.

157. Ibid. (1891), pp. 110–111.

158. Pechan, *Povjest hrvatske književnosti* (1910), p. 34.

159. *Čitanka za treći razred* (1894), p. 183.

160. Petračić-Miler, *Hrvatska čitanka*, II (1895), pp. 123, 216, 222.

161. Ibid., II (1908), 4th ed., pp. 67–74; Pechan, *Povjest hrvatske književnosti* (1910), pp. 27–30.

162. Filipović, *Kratka poviest književnosti* (1875), p. 47; Petračić-Miler, *Hrvatska čitanka* (1908), pp. 164–67; *Čitanka za četvrti razred* (1889), p. 114.

163. *Enciklopedija Jugoslavije*, V, p. 170.

164. *Čitanka za četvrti razred* (1889), p. 60.

165. *Čitanka za drugi općih razred* (1889), pp. 127–28.

166. Ibid. (1893), p. 127.

167. *Čitanka za treći razred* (1907), p. 131.

168. The Illyrian movement is discussed in all the readers.

169. *Čitanka za treći razred* (1880), p. 69; Tomislav Maretić-Ivan Šarić, *Hrvatska čitanka za II razred gimnazijski* (Zagreb: Kraljevska zemaljska tiskara, 1910), 8th ed., pp. 194–96.

170. Petračić, *Hrvatska čitanka*, II (1880), p. 315.

171. Ibid.

172. Petračić-Miler, *Hrvatska čitanka*, II (1895), p. 508.

173. Filipović, *Kratka poviest književnosti* (1875), p. 68.

174. Petračić, *Hrvatska čitanka*, II (1880), pp. 317–23; "Ljudevit Gaj," *Sveti Sava - Srpski narodni kalendar za 1910* (Novi Sad) p. 84; V. K., "Slava Ljudevitu Gaju!," *Svačić-kalendar za 1910* (Zadar), pp. 119–22.

175. Petračić-Miler, *Hrvatska čitanka*, II (1895), pp. 515–45; Pechan, *Povjest hrvatske književnosti* (1910), pp. 65–69.

176. Divković, *Hrvatska čitanka za IV razred* (1901), pp. 242–45.

177. Petračić-Miler, *Hrvatska čitanka*, II (1895), p. 639.

178. Pechan, *Povjest hrvatske književnosti* (1910), p. 90.

179. Divković, *Hrvatska čitanka za IV razred* (1901), p. 36.

180. Petračić-Miler, *Hrvatska čitanka*, II (1895), pp. 630–35; Filipović, *Kratka poviest književnosti* (1875), p. 75–78.

181. Petračić-Miler, *Hrvatska čitanka*, II (1895), pp. 702–03; ibid., II (1908), pp. 376–78; Pechan, *Povjest hrvatske književnosti* (1910), pp. 94–96; Filipović, *Kratka poviest književnosti* (1875), p. 80.

182. Filipović, *Kratka poviest književnosti* (1875), pp. 83, 89.

183. *Čitanka za četvrti razred* (1909), pp. 123, 125; *Čitanka za treći razred* (1893), p. 101.

184. *Čitanka za treći razred* (1893), pp. 101–02.

185. Ibid., pp. 104–05; *Čitanka za četvrti razred* (1909), pp. 143–44.

186. Filipović, *Kratka poviest književnosti* (1875), p. 22.

187. Divković, *Hrvatska čitanka za III razred* (1896), pp. 149–50.

188. Ibid., pp. 177–79; *Čitanka za treći razred* (1893), pp. 106–07.

189. Ibid., p. 179; *Čitanka za treći razred* (1893), p. 107.

190. *Čitanka za drugi općih razred* (1889), pp. 128–29; ibid., (1893), pp. 128–29.

191. *Čitanka za treći razred* (1894), pp. 127–29; ibid. (1907), pp. 155–62; *Čitanka za četvrti razred* (1909), pp. 23–25; Divković, *Hrvatska čitanka za III razred* (1896), pp. 234–51; Maretić-Šarić, *Hrvatska čitanka za II razred* (1910), p. 11.

192. *Čitanka za treći razred* (1880), p. 106; *Čitanka za četvrti razred* (1909), p. 171.

193. Petračić *Hrvatska čitanka*, II (1880), pp. 1–10; Petračić-Miler, *Hrvatska čitanka*, II (1895), pp. 1–16; 415–16.

194. Petračić-Miler, *Hrvatska čitanka*, II (1895), pp. 416; 440–41.

195. Pechan, *Povjest hrvatske književnosti* (1910), pp. 45–46.

196. Petračić-Miler, *Hrvatska čitanka*, II (1895), pp. 417–20.

197. Filipović, *Kratka poviest književnosti* (1875), p. 55.

198. Petračić-Miler, *Hrvatska čitanka*, II (1895), pp. 441–44, 487–90.

199. Divković, *Hrvatska čitanka za IV razred* (1901), p. 12.

200. Petračić-Miler, *Hrvatska čitanka*, II (1895), pp. 491–94.

201. Filipović, *Kratka poviest književnosti* (1875), p. 61. S. R. "Vuk Stefanović Karadžic," *Narodni koledar za 1890* (Zadar), pp. 75–96.

202. Petračić-Miler, *Hrvatska čitanka*, II (1895), pp. 604–06; ibid., II (1908), pp. 448–49; *Enciklopedija Jugoslavije*, VIII, p. 205.

203. Petračić-Miler, *Hrvatska čitanka*, II (1908), pp. 449–50; ibid., II (1895), pp. 606–07; Pechan, *Povjest hrvatske književnosti* (1910), p. 83.

204. Petračić-Miler, *Hrvatska čitanka*, II (1908), p. 451, 478–79; ibid., II (1895), pp. 774, 780–84.

205. *Čitanka za treći razred* (1880), pp. 42–43; *Čitanka za četvrti razred* (1889), p. 85.

206. Petračić-Miler, *Hrvatska čitanka*, II (1908), pp. 446–48; ibid., II (1895), pp. 601–04.

207. *Čitanka za četvrti razred* (1909), p. 117; ibid. (1889), p. 81.

208. *Čitanka za treći razred* (1907), p. 107.

209. *Čitanka za četvrti razred* (1909), p. 116; ibid. (1889), p. 82.

210. Ibid. (1909), pp. 117–19.

211. Petračić-Miler, *Hrvatska čitanka*, II (1908), pp. 292–94.

212. Ibid., pp. 160–62; ibid., II (1895), p. 259.

213. Ibid.,II (1908), pp. 310–11, 331–33.

214. *Čitanka za treći razred* (1880), p. 81; *Čitanka za četvrti razred* (1907), pp. 101–06; Divković, *Hrvatska čitanka za IV razred* (1901), pp. 142–44.

215. *Čitanka za četvrti razred* (1889), pp. 65–73; ibid. (1909), pp. 99–112.

CHAPTER 4

1. Mihailo Jović, *Srpska istorija udesena za današnju osnovnu školu* (Belgrade: Štamparija zadruge štamparskih radnika, 1882), pp. v–vi.

2. *Enciklopedija Jugoslavije*, V, pp. 213.

3. Ibid.

4. Not as much biographical information is available for the geographers, who were principally secondary school teachers, as for the authors of Serbian readers and history books. The exceptions: for Jovan Dragašević, see *Enciklopedija Jugoslavije*, II, p. 67; for Jovan Gavrilović, see ibid., III, p. 433; for Todor Radivojević, see ibid., VII, p. 15; and for Milovan Spasić, see ibid., VII, p. 499.

5. V. Karić, *Zemljopis za niže razrede srednjih škola po najnovijim izvorima - politički zemljopis - Jevropa* (Belgrade: Štamparija srpske napredne stranke, 1883), I, part 3, pp. 33–34.

6. Ibid., p. 34.

7. V. Karić, *Srbija - Opis zemlje, naroda i države* (Belgrade: Državna štamparija, 1887), pp. 240–41.

8. Karić, *Zemljopis za niže razrede*, p. 72.

9. Ibid., p. 68.

10. Ibid., pp. 68–69.

11. Karić, *Srbija - Opis*, p. 203.

12. Ibid., pp. 203–04.

13. Ibid., p. 244.

14. Ibid., p. 226; Pavle Švabić, *Istorija srpske crkve za učenike i učenice srednjih škola* (Belgrade: S. Horović, 1901), II, pp. 4–17; Grigorije (Nikola) Živković, *Istorija Hriščanske crkve za školsku mladež* (Tuzla: Nikola Pisenberg, 1897), 3rd. enlarged and rev. ed., pp. 93–120; 144–46.

15. Karić, *Zemljopis za niže razrede*, p. 69.

16. Ibid.

17. Karić, *Srbija - Opis*, pp. 168–86; Mih. Jović and D. J. Putniković, *Zemljopis Srbije i srpskih zemalja za IV razred osnovne škole* (Belgrade: Savić, 1905), 3rd ed., p. 61.

18. Dim. J. Sokolović, *Zemljopis srpskih zemalja i balkanskog poluostrva za učenike IV razreda osnovnih škola* (Belgrade: Petar Čurić, 1890), pp. 40–41.

19. Petar K. Šreplović, *Atlas srpskih zemalja i balkanskog poluostrva sa zemljopisom za učenike -ce IV razreda osnovnih škola* (Belgrade: Prosveta, 1891), p. 33.

20. Raša Mitrović, *Zemljopis Kraljevine Srbije sa kratkim opisom sviju srpskih zemalja za učenike i učenice IV razred osnovne škole* (Belgrade: Velimir Valožić, 1900), pp. 114, 128–29.

21. Raša Mitrović and Mih. M. Stanojević, *Zemljopis Kraljevine Srbije sa kratkim opisom sviju srpskih zemalja za učenike i učenice IV razreda osnovne škole* (Belgrade: Velimir Valožić, 1902), p. 76; ibid. (1906), p. 86.

22. Jović and Putniković, *Zemljopis Srbije* (1905), pp. 91–92.

23. Mih. M. Stanojević, *Zemljopis Kraljevine Srbije i srpskih zemalja za učenike i učenice IV razreda osnovne škole* (Belgrade: Velimir Valožić, 1912), p. 49.

24. S. Antonović and I. Lazić, *Zemljopis za II razred srednjih škola* (Belgrade: Geca Kon, 1912), 5th ed., pp. 60–62; Jović and Putniković, *Zemljopis Srbije* (1908), pp. 92, 95.

25. Antonović and Lazić, *Zemljopis za II razred* (1912), p. 65.

26. S. Antonović and I. Radivojević, *Zemlja - Osnovna zemljopisna znanja za prvi razred* (Belgrade: Geca Kon, 1913), pp. 57–59.

27. Josip Lakatoš, *Narodna statistika* (Osijek: Radoslav Bačić, 1914), 2nd ed., p. 3.

28. Karić, *Zemljopis za niže razrede*, p. 117.

29. Šreplović, *Atlas srpskih zemalja za IV razred*, p. 29.

30. Mitrović and Stanojević, *Zemljopis Kraljevine Srbije* (1906), p. 86.

31. Vladimir T. Simić and Milan Hrabrenović, *Atlas Srbije i srpskih zemalja sa zemljopisom za učenike -ce IV razreda osnovne škole* (Belgrade: Mita Stajić, 1909), 2nd rev. ed., p. 66; "Srpstvo - Statistički podaci o narodu i zemljama," *Srbobran kalendar za 1897* (Zagreb), pp. 32–39. "Srbi i srpske zemlje," *Kalendar narodnih novina za 1908* (Belgrade), pp. 6–8. "Koliko ima Srba i gde su," *Kalendar narodnih novina za 1909* (Belgrade), pp. 20–22. "Još se dobro ne poznajemo," *Kalendar narodnih novina za 1912* (Belgrade), pp. 73–76. "Srpske zemlje," *Vardar kalendar za 1911* (Belgrade), pp. 21–38. Rad. M. Grčić, "Srbi pod Austro-Ugarskom," *Vardar-kalendar za 1911* (Belgrade), pp. 88–108.

32. Sokolović, *Zemljopis srpskih zemalja za IV razred* (1890), p. 31.

33. St. J. Nikolić, *Kraljevina Srbija i kratak pregled srpskih zemalja za IV razred narodnih škola* (Belgrade: Sv. Nikolić, 1899), 2nd rev. ed., p. 108.

34. Mitrović and Stanojević, *Zemljopis Kraljevine Srbije* (1902), p. 92.

35. Antonović and Lazić, *Zemljopis za II razred* (1902), p. 90.

36. Jović and Putniković, *Zemljopis Srbije* (1905), p. 88; ibid. (1908), p. 87.

37. Simić and Hrabrenović, *Atlas Srbije za IV razred*, p. 66.

38. Antonović and Lazić, *Zemljopis za II razred* (1912), p. 60; Antonović and Radivojević, *Zemlja - Osnovna zemljopisna znanja*, p. 60.

39. Karić, *Zemljopis za niže razrede*, pp. 119–22; Šreplović, *Atlas srpskih zemalja za IV razred*, pp. 27–29; Mitrović, *Zemljopis Kraljevine Srbije*, p. 137.

40. Karić, *Zemljopis za niže razrede*, p. 112.

41. Sokolović, *Zemljopis srpskih zemalja* (1890), p. 18; Mitrović and Stanojević, *Zemljopis Kraljevine Srbije* (1902), p. 90; Simić and Hrabrenović, *Atlas Srbije za IV razred*, p. 65; Antonović and Lazić, *Zemljopis za II razred* (1912), p. 63.

42. Sokolović, *Zemljopis srpskih zemalja* (1890), p. 18.

43. Karić, *Zemljopis za niže razrede*, p. 112.

44. Šreplović, *Atlas srpskih zemalja za IV razred*, p. 24.

45. Mitrović and Stanojević, *Zemljopis Kraljevine Srbije* (1902), p. 90.

46. Jović and Putniković, *Zemljopis Srbije* (1905), p. 75; ibid. (1908), p. 74.

47. Srećko A. Miletić, *Zemljopis za srednje i stručne škole - Balkansko poluostrvo* (Belgrade: Dositej Obradović, 1908), p. 51.

48. Antonović and Lazić, *Zemljopis za II razred* (1912), p. 65.

49. Nikolić, *Kraljevina Srbija*, pp. 105–06; D. Sokolović and I. Sokolović, *Zemljopis Kraljevine Srbije i srpskih zemalja za učenike IV razreda osnovnih narodnih škola* (Belgrade: Velimir Valožić, 1900), p. 116.

50. Karić, *Zemljopis za niže razrede*, p. 55.

51. Ibid., p. 115.

52. Sokolović, *Zemljopis srpskih zemalja* (1890), p. 18.

53. Nikolić, *Kraljevina Srbija*, p. 106.

54. Stanojević, *Zemljopis Kraljevine Srbije*, p. 55. Sima Lukin Lazić, "Dubrovačka slava - svesrpska slava," *Srbobran kalendar za 1894* (Zagreb), pp. 93–101. "Nešto po nešto o Dubrovniku," *Srbobran kalendar za 1893* (Zagreb), pp. 83–88.

55. Nikolić, *Kraljevina Srbija*, p. 106; Jović and Putniković, *Zemljopis Srbije* (1905), p. 90; Antonović and Radivojević, *Zemlja - Osnovna zemljopisna znanja*, p. 61; Mitrović, *Zemljopis Kraljevine Srbije*, p. 128; Simić and Hrabrenović, *Atlas Srbije za IV razred*, p. 69.

56. Mitrović, *Zemljopis Kraljevine Srbije*, p. 128; Sokolović, *Zemljopis srpskih zemalja* (1894), p. 42; Nikolić, *Kraljevina Srbija*, p. 107; Jović and Putniković, *Zemljopis Srbije* (1905), p. 90; Miletić, *Zemljopis za srednje škole*, p. 54.

57. Mitrović, *Zemljopis Kraljevine Srbije*, p. 128.

58. Antonović and Lazić, *Zemljopis za II razred* (1902), p. 93; Miletić, *Zemljopis za srednje škole*, p. 54.

59. Sokolović, *Zemljopis srpskih zemalja* (1894), p. 42; Nikolić, *Kraljevina Srbija*, p. 107; Antonović and Lazić, *Zemljopis za II razred* (1902), p. 93; Mitrović and Stanojević, *Zemljopis Kraljevine Srbije* (1906), p. 91; Miletić, *Zemljopis za srednje škole*, p. 54.

60. Jović and Putniković, *Zemljopis Srbije* (1905), p. 90; ibid. (1908), p. 89; Miletić, *Zemljopis za srednje škole*, p. 55; Mitrović, *Zemljopis Kraljevine Srbije*, p. 128; Mitrović and Stanojević, *Zemljopis Kraljevine Srbije* (1902), p. 95.

61. Karić, *Zemljopis za niže razrede*, p. 128; Sokolović, *Zemljopis srpskih zemalja* (1890), p. 9; Mitrović, *Zemljopis Kraljevine Srbije*, p. 122; Jović and Putniković, *Zemljopis Srbije* (1905), p. 67.

62. Karić, *Zemljopis za niže razrede*, pp. 128–29.

63. Antonović and Lazić, *Zemljopis za II razred* (1902), p. 74.

64. Jović and Putniković, *Zemljopis Srbije* (1905), p. 67; Mitrović and Stanojević, *Zemljopis Kraljevine Srbije* (1906), p. 89.

65. Šreplović, *Atlas srpskih zemalja za IV razred*, p. 20; Simić and Hrabrenović, *Atlas Srbije za IV razred*, p. 62.

66. Karić, *Zemljopis za niže razrede*, p. 132.

67. Simić and Hrabrenović, *Atlas Srbije za IV razred*, p. 62.

68. Stanojević, *Zemljopis Kraljevine Srbije*, p. 54; Sokolović, *Zemljopis srpskih zemalja* (1890), p. 9; Nikolić, *Kraljevina Srbija*, p. 104; Mitrović, *Zemljopis Kraljevine Srbije*, p. 133.

69. Jović and Putniković, *Zemljopis Srbije* (1905), p. 68. Smailaga Čemalović, "Nacionalizam i Muslimani," *Vardar kalendar za 1914* (Belgrade), pp. 59–66; Stanojević, *Zemljopis Kraljevine Srbije*, p. 54.

70. Antonović and Lazić, *Zemljopis za II razred* (1902), p. 75; ibid. (1912), p. 57; Jović and Putniković, *Zemljopis Srbije* (1905), p. 70; Mitrović and Stanojević, *Zemljopis Kraljevine Srbije* (1906), p. 89; Simić and Hrabrenović, *Atlas Srbije za IV razred*, p. 62.

71. Mitrović, *Zemljopis Kraljevine Srbije*, p. 133; Mitrović and Stanojević, *Zemljopis Kraljevine Srbije* (1902), p. 89; Jović and Putniković, *Zemljopis Srbije* (1905), p. 67.

72. C. A. Macartney, *Hungary and Her Successors: The Treaty of Trianon and Its Consequences, 1919–1937* (London: Oxford University Press, 1937), p. 381; Karić, *Zemljopis za niže razrede*, p. 123–27; Nikolić, *Kraljevina Srbija*, pp. 108–09. Mitrović and Stanojević, *Zemljopis Kraljevine Srbije* (1902), pp. 93–94; Antonović and Lazić, *Zemljopis za II razred* (1902), pp. 97–99; Jović and Putniković, *Zemljopis Srbije* (1905), p. 86; Antonović and Radivojević, *Zemlja - Osnovna zemljopisna znanja*, p. 61; Lakatoš, *Statistika*, pp. 56–57.

73. Karić, *Zemljopis za niže razrede*, pp. 123–25.

74. Nikolić, *Kraljevina Srbija*, p. 109; Miletić, *Zemljopis za srednje škole*, p. 64; Antonović and Lazić, *Zemljopis za II razred* (1902), p. 99; Jović and Putniković, *Zemljopis Srbije* (1905), p. 86; Lakatoš, *Statistika*, p. 59.

75. Sreplović, *Atlas srpskih zemalja za IV razred*, (1891) p. 32.

76. Sokolović, *Zemljopis srpskih zemalja* (1890), p. 35; Mitrović, *Zemljopis Kraljevine Srbije*, p. 138; Stanojević, *Zemljopis Kraljevine Srbije*, p. 52; Karić, *Zemljopis za niže razrede*, p. 125.

77. Simić and Hrabrenović, *Atlas Srbije za IV razred*, pp. 70–73.

78. Sokolović, *Zemljopis srpskih zemalja* (1890), p. 21; Karić, *Zemljopis za niže razrede*, p. 136.

79. Karić, *Zemljopis za niže razrede*, p. 136; Mitrović and Stanojević, *Zemljopis Kraljevine Srbije* (1902), p. 78; Antonović and Lazić, *Zemljopis za II razred* (1902), p. 80; Sokolović, *Zemljopis srpskih zemalja*, p. 136.

80. Karić, *Zemljopis za niže razrede*, p. 135.

81. Sokolović, *Zemljopis srpskih zemalja* (1890), pp. 19–23; Šreplović, *Atlas srpskih zemalja za IV razred*, pp. 7–10.

82. Every geography book contained information about Old Serbia. Representative examples are found in Sokolović, *Zemljopis srpskih zemalja* (1890), p. 21; Mitrović, *Zemljopis Kraljevine Srbije*, p. 114; Mitrović and Stanojević, *Zemljopis Kraljevine Srbije* (1902), pp. 76–79; Karić, *Zemljopis za niže razrede*, pp. 135–40.

83. Karić, *Zemljopis za niže razrede*, p. 140; Sokolović, *Zemljopis srpskih zemalja* (1890), p. 25; Nikolić, *Kraljevina Srbija*, p. 103; Antonović and Lazić, *Zemljopis za II razred* (1902), p. 85; Mitrović and Stanojević, *Zemljopis Kraljevine Srbije* (1906), 92–93; Simić and Hrabrenović, *Atlas Srbije za IV razred*, p. 75; Stanojević, *Zemljopis Kraljevine Srbije*, p. 59.

84. Nikolić, *Kraljevina Srbija*, pp. 102–03; Mitrović and Stanojević, *Zemljopis Kraljevine Srbije* (1902), pp. 80–81; Šreplović, *Atlas srpskih zemalja za IV razred*, pp. 11–14.

85. Sokolović, *Zemljopis srpskih zemalja* (1890), p. 25; Nikolić, *Kraljevina Srbija*, p. 103; Mitrović, *Zemljopis Kraljevine Srbije*, p. 118; Mitrović and Stanojević, *Zemljopis Kraljevine Srbije* (1902), p. 80. "Crkvene prilike u Novoj Srbiji," *Srpska crkva kalendar za 1914* (Belgrade), pp. 32–49.

86. Sokolović, *Zemljopis srpskih zemalja* (1894), p. 38; Simić and Hrabrenović, *Atlas Srbije za IV razred*, p. 75.

87. Karić, *Srbija - Opis*, p. 243.

88. Sokolović, *Zemljopis srpskih zemalja* (1890), p. 43.

89. Šreplović, *Atlas srpskih zemalja za IV razred*, p. 39.

90. Nikolić, *Kraljevina Srbija*, p. 110.

91. Mitrović, *Zemljopis Kraljevine Srbije*, p. 129; Mitrović and Stanojević, *Zemljopis Kraljevine Srbije* (1902), p. 96.

92. Šreplović, *Atlas srpskih zemalja za IV razred*, p. 40; Nikolić, *Kraljevina Srbija*, p. 110; Mitrović, *Zemljopis Kraljevine Srbije*, pp. 128–30.

93. Mitrović and Stanojević, *Zemljopis Kraljevine Srbije* (1906), p. 93; Stanojević, *Zemljopis Kraljevine Srbije* (1912), pp. 59–60; Antonović and Lazić, *Zemljopis za II razred* (1912), pp. 75–76.

94. Cuvaj, *Gradja*, II, p. 719.

95. Ibid., V, pp. 340–41; *Enciklopedija Jugoslavije*, VI, p. 50.

96. Cuvaj, *Gradja*, IV, pp. 215–16.

97. *Enciklopedija Jugoslavije*, IV, p. 22.

98. Josip Modestin, *Zemljopis i statistika Austro-Ugarske monarhije za srednja učilista* (Zagreb: Kraljevska zemaljska tiskara, 1912), 3rd rev. and enlarged ed., p. iv.

99. *Enciklopedija Jugoslavije*, V, pp. 252–53.

100. Ibid.

101. Vjenceslav Zaboj Mařik, *Kratak sveobći zemljopis za mladež narodnih učionah* (Zagreb: Spisatelj, 1891), 4th rev. ed., pp. 3–8; *Zemljopis trojedne kraljevine* (Zagreb: Lav. Hartman, 1873), 3rd rev. and enlarged ed.,

pp. 16–21, 86–91, 102–05; P. Matković, *Zemljopis Austro-Ugarske monarhije za niže razrede srednjih učilišta* (Zagreb: Kraljevska zemaljska tiskara, 1882), pp. 115–33.

102. Ivan Hoić, *Zemljopis za VII razred viših djevojačkih škola* (Zagreb: Kraljevska zemaljska tiskara, 1894), p. 93.

103. Mařik, *Kratak zemljopis* (1873), pp. 23–24; Vjenceslav Zaboj Mařik, *Kratak sveobći zemljopis za mladež narodnih učiona* (Zagreb: Mučnjak & Senftleben, 1878), 8th ed., p. 4; Lakatoš, *Statistika*, p. 12.

104. Petar Matković, *Zemljopis za niže razrede srednjih učilištah* (Zagreb: Lj. Gaj, 1878), p. 197.

105. Ivan Hoić, *Zemljopis za gradjanske škole* (Zagreb: Kraljevska zemaljska tiskara, 1880), p. 73.

106. Ivan Hoić, *Zemljopis austrijsko-ugarske monarkije za gradjanske škole* (Zagreb: Kraljevska zemaljska tiskara, 1882), pp. 96–97.

107. Ivan Hoić, *Zemljopis za više djevojačke škole prvi stupanj* (Zagreb: Kraljevska zemaljska tiskara, 1883), pp. 35–36.

108. Ivan Hoić, *Zemljopis za više pučke škole* (Zagreb: Kraljevska zemaljska tiskara, 1891), pp. 43–44; Hoić, *Zemljopis za VII razred* (1894), pp. 91–92.

109. Ivan Hoić, *Zemljopis za I licejski razred* (Zagreb: Kraljevska zemaljska tiskara, 1908), 2nd rev. ed., p. 29.

110. Modestin, *Zemljopis i statistika* (1905), p. 50; ibid. (1912), pp. 30, 53.

111. Vj. Klaić, *Zemljopis zemalja u kojih obitavaju Hrvati* (Zagreb: Dionička tiskara, 1880), I, p. 9.

112. Vjekoslav Klaić, *Bosna - Podatci o zemljopisu i poviesti Bosne i Hercegovine: Zemljopis* (Zagreb: Matica hrvatska, 1878), I, p. 71.

113. Klaić, *Zemljopis*, I, pp. 10–11.

114. Ibid., pp. 11–15.

115. Ibid., p. 13.

116. Klaić, *Bosna*, I, p. xii.

117. Klaić, *Zemljopis*, I, p. 30.

118. Matković, *Zemljopis za niže razrede* (1875), p. 189.

119. Mařik, *Kratak sveobći zemljopis* (1876), p. 13.

120. Hoić, *Zemljopis za gradjanske škole* (1880), p. 67; Hoić, *Zemljopis austro-ugarske* (1882), p. 70; Hoić, *Zemljopis za I licejski razred* (1908), p. 29.

121. Modestin, *Zemljopis i statistika* (1905), p. 66. "Dalmacija je naša," *Dragoljub kalendar za 1883* (Zagreb), pp. 46–48.

122. Modestin, *Zemljopis i statistika* (1905), p. 72; ibid. (1912), p. 86.

123. Lakatoš, *Statistika*, p. 23.

124. Matković, *Zemljopis za niže razrede* (1875), p. 189; Mařik, *Kratak sveobći zemljopis* (1878), p. 15; Hoić, *Zemljopis za više djevojačke škole* (1883), p. 32; Modestin, *Zemljopis i statistika* (1905), p. 77; ibid. (1912), p. 91.

125. Klaić, *Zemljopis*, II (1881), pp. 12–13.

126. Ibid., p. 237.

127. Mařik, *Kratak sveobći zemljopis* (1871), p. 35; Hoić, *Zemljopis austrijsko-ugarske* (1882), p. 65; Hoić, *Zemljopis za više pučke škole* (1891), p. 70; Modestin, *Zemljopis i statistika* (1905), p. 94; ibid. (1912), pp. 126–27.

128. Lakatoš, *Statistika*, p. 21. "Bosna-Vilajet," *Dragoljub kalendar za 1878* (Zagreb), pp. 32–37.

129. Hoić, *Zemljopis za gradjanske škole* (1880), pp. 77–78; Hoić, *Zemljopis za više djevojačke škole* (1883), p. 37.

130. Hoić, *Zemljopis austrijsko-ugarske* (1882), p. 120; Hoić, *Zemljopis za više pučke škole* (1891), p. 47; Hoić, *Zemljopis za I licejski razred* (1908), p. 52.

131. Josip Modestin, *Zemljopis za srednje škole* (Zagreb: Kraljevska zemaljska tiskara, 1905), p. 47; Modestin, *Zemljopis i statistika* (1912), p. 102.

132. Modestin, *Zemljopis i statistika* (1912), pp. 108–10. "Sarajevo," *Dragoljub kalendar za 1879* (Zagreb), pp. 47–52.

133. Klaić, *Zemljopis*, I, p. 5; Klaić, *Bosna*, I, pp. 71, 75.

134. Klaić, *Bosna*, I, p. 72.

135. Ibid., pp. 101–03.

136. Matković, *Zemljopis za niže razrede* (1875), p. 189; Mařik, *Kratak sveobći zemljopis* (1876), p. 13; Hoić, *Zemljopis za gradjanske škole* (1880), p. 67; Hoić, *Zemljopis za više djevojačke škole* (1883), p. 32; Hoić, *Zemljopis za I licejski razred* (1908), p. 29; Modestin, *Zemljopis i statistika* (1912), pp. 86–87; *Čitanka za treći razred pučkih škola* (1880), p. 81; ibid. (1907), pp. 101–06.

137. Modestin, *Zemljopis i statistika* (1912), pp. 93–110.

138. Matković, *Zemljopis za niže razrede* (1875), p. 94.

139. Mařik, *Kratak sveobći zemljopis* (1876), p. 54.

140. Hoić, *Zemljopis za gradjanske škole* (1880), p. 24; Hoić, *Zemljopis za više djevojačke škole* (1883), pp. 24–25; Hoić, *Zemljopis za više pučke škole* (1891), p. 82.

141. Hoić, *Zemljopis za gradjanske škole* (1880), p. 24.

142. Matković, *Zemljopis za niže razrede* (1875), p. 96; Mařik, *Kratak sveobći zemljopis* (1876), p. 55; Hoić, *Zemljopis za gradjanske škole* (1880), p. 25; Hoić, *Zemljopis za više djevojačke škole* (1883), p. 25; Ivan Hoić, *Zemljopis za II–VIII razred ženskoga liceja* (Zagreb: Kraljevska zemaljska tiskara, 1909), 2nd rev. ed., pp. 66–67.

143. Matković, *Zemljopis za niže razrede* (1875), pp. 91–93; Hoić, *Zemljopis za II–VIII ženskoga liceja,* (1909), p. 63.

144. Matković, *Zemljopis za niže razrede* (1875), pp. 181–83; Mařik, *Kratak sveobći zemljopis* (1876), pp. 28–31; Hoić, *Zemljopis za gradjanske škole* (1880), pp. 60–62; Hoić, *Zemljopis za više djevojačke škole* (1883), pp. 31–32; Hoić, *Zemljopis za I licejski razred* (1908), pp. 39–40; Modestin, *Zemljopis i statistika* (1905), pp. 89–92; ibid. (1912), pp. 122–25.

CHAPTER 5

1. Stanojević, *Narodna enciklopedija,* IV, supplement.

2. *Enciklopedija Jugoslavije,* III, p. 203.

3. Ibid., V, p. 355.

4. Ibid., IV, p. 541.

5. Ibid., VIII, p. 126.

6. Ibid., VIII, p. 553.

7. Jović, *Srpska istorija* (1882), pp. 7–8.

8. Milan S. Ubavkić, *Istorija Srba za osnovne škole u Kraljevini Srbiji* (Belgrade: Prosveta, 1891), p. 3.

9. Milenko Vukičević, *Istorija srpskoga naroda za srednje škole od dolaska Srba na Balkansko poluostrvo do polovine XV stoleća* (Belgrade: Dositej Obradović, 1904), I, p. 1.

10. Jovan Djordjević, *Istorija srpskoga naroda od najstarijega do najnovijega doba za srednje škole i za narod* (Vranje: Petar Jovanović, 1900), p. 4.

11. Ubavkić, *Istorija,* p. 5.

12. Jović, *Srpska istorija* (1896), p. 7; ibid. (1902), p. 7.

13. Mih. M. Stanojević, *Istorija srpskoga naroda za IV razred osnovne škole* (Belgrade: Velimir Valožić, 1908), p. 5.

14. Jović, *Srpska istorija* (1902), p. 15; M. Stanojević, *Istorija,* p. 15.

15. Djordjević, *Istorija,* pp. 7–8.

16. Vukičević, *Istorija,* I (1904), pp. 28, 30–31.

17. St. Stanojević and L. Zrnić, *Istorija srpskoga naroda za srednje i stručne škole* (Belgrade: Davidović, 1910), I, 2nd ed., pp. 21–22.

18. Vukičević, *Istorija,* I (1911), p. 3.

19. Djordjević, *Istorija,* p. 14. Mladen Karanović, "Istina i moć srpstva i pravoslavlja," *Sveti Sava Srpski narodni kalendar za 1910* (Novi Sad), pp. 18–26.

20. Djordjević, *Istorija,* pp. 9–11, 14; Svabić, *Istorija srpske crkve,* II,

pp. 4–17; Živković, *Istorija Hriščanske crkve*, (1897), 3rd enlarged and rev. ed., pp. 86–120, 144–46.

21. Djordjević, *Istorija*, pp. 163–64; Vukičević, *Istorija*, II (1906), pp. 1–7; 23–27; ibid., II (1912), pp. 23–29.

22. Djordjević, *Istorija*, p. 164.

23. Vukičević, *Istorija*, II (1906), p. 26.

24. Stanojević and Zrnić, *Istorija* (1908), II, p. 24.

25. Vukičević, *Istorija*, II (1902), pp. 80–84; ibid., II (1912), pp. 23–24; Djordjević, *Istorija*, pp. 166–68; Jović, *Srpska istorija* (1902), pp. 68–73.

26. Vukičević, *Istorija*, II (1912), pp. 28–29.

27. Ibid., II (1902), p. 1.

28. Stanojević and Zrnić, *Istorija*, II (1908), pp. 3–4.

29. Ubavkić, *Istorija*, p. 6; Vukičević, *Istorija*, I (1904), pp. 30–31; Stanojević and Zrnić, *Istorija*, I (1910), pp. 21–22.

30. Vukičević, *Istorija*, II (1906), p. 7.

31. Ibid., II (1906), pp. 7–8; 31; Jović, *Srpska istorija* (1902), p. 70; Stanojević and Zrnić, *Istorija*, II (1908), p. 7.

32. Jović, *Srpska istorija* (1882), p. 56.

33. Vukičević, *Istorija*, II (1902), pp. 72–74, 93–95; ibid., II (1906), pp. 23, 31; ibid., II (1912), p. 17.

34. Djordjević, *Istorija*, p. 18.

35. Jović, *Srpska istorija* (1882), p. 80.

36. Djordjević, *Istorija*, p. 18.

37. Stanojević and Zrnić, *Istorija*, I (1910), p. 121.

38. Vukičević, *Istorija*, II (1906), p. 8.

39. Ibid., II (1912), p. 17.

40. Ibid., II (1902), p. 74.

41. Ibid., II (1906), p. 9; Lj. Kovačević and Lj. Jovanović, *Istorija srpskoga naroda za srednje škole*, I (Belgrade: Državna štamparija, 1895–96), new rev. ed., pp. 67–69; Djordjević, *Istorija*, p. 18.

42. Vukičević, *Istorija*, II (1912), p. 17; Stanojević and Zrnić, *Istorija*, II (1908), pp. 34–35.

43. Vukičević, *Istorija*, II (1902), p. 47.

44. Ibid., pp. 47, 92–96; ibid., II (1906), p. 31.

45. Jović, *Srpska istorija* (1882), p. 92.

46. Ibid. (1896), p. 67.

47. Kovačević and Jovanović, *Istorija*, I (1895–96), p. 146.

48. Djordjević, *Istorija*, p. 90.

49. Kovačević and Jovanović, *Istorija*, I (1895–96), pp. 150–51; Djordjević, *Istorija*, p. 90.

50. Djordjević, *Istorija*, pp. 91, 123–24.

51. Ibid., pp. 160–61; Stanojević and Zrnić, *Istorija*, II (1908), pp. 10–11; Švabić, *Istorija srpske crkve*, II, pp. 34–37; Živković, *Istorija Hriščanske crkve* (1897), p. 100.

52. Stanojević and Zrnić, *Istorija*, II (1908), p. 11.

53. Vukičević, *Istorija*, II (1909), p. 11; ibid., II (1912), p. 8.

54. Djordjević, *Istorija*, p. 245.

55. Stanojević and Zrnić, *Istorija*, II (1908), p. 50.

56. *Enciklopedija Jugoslavije*, IV, p. 337.

57. Vukičević, *Istorija*, II (1906), p. 136.

58. Ubavkić, *Istorija*, p. 92.

59. Jović, *Srpska istorija* (1896), pp. 108–09; ibid. (1913), pp. 134–35; Djordjević, *Istorija*, pp. 236–37; Vukičević, *Istorija*, II (1902), pp. 367–71; ibid., II (1906), pp. 146–47; ibid., (1909), pp. 145–46; Stanojević and Zrnić, *Istorija*, II (1908), pp. 72–73; M. Stanojević, *Istorija*, pp. 131–32.

60. Djordjević, *Istorija*, pp. 250–51.

61. Vukičević, *Istorija*, II (1902), p. 368; ibid., II (1906), p. 146; ibid., II (1912), pp. 99, 115.

62. Stanojević and Zrnić, *Istorija*, II (1908), p. 72.

63. Vukičević, *Istorija*, II (1906), pp. 146, 166–67; ibid., II (1909), p. 146.

64. Ibid., II (1902), pp. 347–48.

65. Ibid., II (1909), pp. 132–34.

66. M. Stanojević, *Istorija*, p. 135.

67. Stanojević and Zrnić, *Istorija*, II (1908), pp. 76, 78.

68. Vukičević, *Istorija*, II (1909), p. 135.

69. Ibid. (1902), pp. 301–03; ibid., II (1906), p. 137; ibid., II (1909), p. 120; ibid., II (1912), pp. 93–95.

70. Stanojević and Zrnić, *Istorija*, II (1908), p. 70.

71. Jović, *Srpska istorija* (1913), p. 144.

72. Djordjević, *Istorija*, p. 254.

73. Vukičević, *Istorija*, II (1902), p. 367; ibid., II (1906), p. 165.

74. Stanojević and Zrnić, *Istorija*, II (1908), p. 91. "Bosna i Hercegovina moraju biti slobodne," *Kalendar narodnih novina za 1909* (Belgrade), pp. 62–70.

75. Jović, *Srpska istorija* (1896), p. 118.

76. Vukičević, *Istorija*, II (1909), pp. 139–40.

77. Ibid., I (1914), pp. 1–2.

78. Ibid., pp. 2, 6, 15; ibid., II (1914), pp. 2, 6, 23.

79. Ibid., II (1914), p. 17.

80. Ibid., I (1914), pp. iii–iv; ibid., II (1914), pp. iii–vi.

81. Ibid., I (1914), p. 7.

82. Jović, *Srpska istorija* (1913), pp. 17–19.

83. Vukičević, *Istorija*, I (1914), pp. 2–3.

84. Ibid., pp. 15, 23–24.

85. Ibid., p. 33.

86. Ibid., pp. 39–40.

87. Ibid., p. 40.

88. Ibid., p. 138.

89. Ibid., II (1914), p. 5.

90. Ibid., p. 28.

91. Ibid., p. 29.

92. Ibid., p. 17.

93. Ibid., p. 91.

94. Ibid., p. 92.

95. Ibid., pp. 92, 116.

96. Ibid., p. 115.

97. Ibid.

98. Ibid., pp. 115–16.

99. Ibid., pp. 116–17.

100. Ibid., p. 117.

101. Ibid.

102. Jović, *Srpska istorija* (1913), p. 18.

103. Ibid. (1902), p. 15; ibid. (1882), pp. 15–17, 104; ibid. (1896), pp. 43–44.

104. Vukičević, *Istorija* II (1914), p. 112.

105. Ibid., II (1912), p. 20.

106. Stanojević and Zrnić, *Istorija*, II (1908), p. 79.

107. Vukičević, *Istorija*, II (1912), p. 117.

108. Ibid., II (1912), pp. 117–18.

109. Djordjević, *Istorija*, p. 255.

110. Vukičević, *Istorija*, II (1912), p. 118.

111. Ibid., II (1909), p. 138.

112. Ibid., II (1912), p. 109.

113. Stanojević and Zrnić, *Istorija*, II (1908), pp. 80–81.

114. Vukičević, *Istorija*, II (1912), p. 118; ibid., II (1914), p. 114.

115. Jović, *Srpska istorija* (1913), pp. 154–55.

116. Vukičević, *Istorija*, II (1914), pp. 123–25.

117. *Enciklopedija Jugoslavije*, IV, p. 22.

118. Ibid., V, pp. 252–53.

119. Cuvaj, *Gradja* (1910), V, p. 293.

120. *Enciklopedija Jugoslavije*, VIII, pp. 111–12.

121. Cuvaj, *Gradja*, VI, pp. 37–38.

122. Ljudevit Tomšić, *Početnica hrvatske povjestnice za mladež pučkih škola* (Zagreb: Mučnjak & Senftleben, 1877), 3rd rev. and enlarged ed., p. 5; Vjekoslav Klaić, *Hrvatska povjesnica za više djevojačke škole i liceje* (Zagreb: Kraljevska zemaljska tiskara, 1894), p. 4. Hereafter cited as *HPVDS*. Stjepan Srkulj, *Povijest srednjega vijeka za više razrede srednjih učilišta* (Zagreb: Kraljevska zemaljska tiskara, 1912), pp. 49–53.

123. Ivan Hoić, *Povjesnica hrvatska za VIII gimnazijski razred* (Zagreb: Kraljevska zemaljska tiskara, p. 1897), 3rd ed., pp. 15–16. Hereafter cited as *Povjesnica VIII*.

124. Ibid., p. 16; Tomšić, *Početnica*, p. 5; Srkulj, *Povjest srednjega vijeka*, p. 58; Klaić, *HPVDS*, p. 6.

125. Tomšić, *Početnica*, p. 5.

126. Vjekoslav Klaić, *Povjest Austro-Ugarske monarkije za niže i više pučke škole* (Zagreb: L. Hartman, 1903), 3rd completely rev. and enlarged ed. by Milan Šenoa, p. 14. Hereafter cited as *Povjest A-U*. Ivan Hoić, *Opća povjesnica za niže razrede srednjih škola* (Zagreb: Kraljevska zemaljska tiskara, 1898), p. 123. Hereafter cited as *Opća povjesnica*.

127. Srkulj, *Povjest srednjega vijeka*, pp. 57–58.

128. Ibid., p. 58.

129. Hoić, *Povjesnica VIII* (1897), p. 4.

130. Ibid., pp. 4, 16.

131. Hoić, *Opća povjesnica* (1898), p. 124.

132. Srkulj, *Povjest srednjega vijeka*, p. 60.

133. Klaić, *HPVDS*, p. 7.

134. Tomšić, *Početnica*, pp. 6–7; Lasman, *Povijest crkve Hristove* (1917), 2nd rev. ed., pp. 62–65; Rubetić, *Kratka poviest crkve* (1896), 4th ed., pp. 28–29.

135. Hoić, *Povjesnica VIII* (1897), pp. 20–21; Rubetić, *Kratka poviest crkve* (1880), p. 27.

136. Hoić, *Povjesnica VIII* (1897), pp. 28–29; Srkulj, *Povjest srednjega vijeka*, p. 156; Tomšić, *Početnica*, p. 14; Ferdinando Belaj, *Povjest crkve*

Kristove za srednja učilista (Zagreb: Kraljevska zemaljska tiskara, 1892), 2nd rev. ed., pp. 95–97; Lasman, *Povijest crkve Hristove,* pp. 66–69; Rubetić, *Kratka poviest crkve* (1880), pp. 54–53; ibid. (1896), pp. 55–59.

137. Hoić, *Povjesnica VIII* (1897), p. 26.

138. Ibid., pp. 23–24; Tomšić, *Početnica,* p. 9; Srkulj, *Povjest srednjeg vijeka,* pp. 154–55.

139. Hoić, *Povjesnica VIII* (1897), p. 24.

140. Srkulj, *Povjest srednjega vijeka,* p. 155; Tomšić, *Početnica,* p. 11; Bogo Grafenauer et al., ed., *Historija naroda Jugoslavije* (Zagreb: Školska knjiga, 1953), I, pp. 192–93.

141. Klaić, *HPVDS,* pp. 17–18.

142. Hoić, *Povjesnica VIII* (1897), p. 32; Srkulj, *Povjest srednjega vijeka,* p. 156; Klaić, *HPVDS,* p. 18.

143. Klaić, *HPVDS,* p. 19.

144. Hoić, *Povjesnica VIII* (1897), pp. 31–33.

145. Ibid., p. 33.

146. Ibid., pp. 38–39; Tomšić, *Početnica,* pp. 18–19.

147. Hoić, *Povjesnica VIII* (1897), pp. 40–41; Srkulj, *Povjest srednjega vijeka,* p. 158.

148. Hoić, *Povjesnica VIII* (1885), pp. 32–33.

149. Ibid., pp. 41–42.

150. Ibid., pp. 42–43; Srkulj, *Povjest srednjega vijeka,* pp. 158–59.

151. Hoić, *Povjesnica VIII* (1897), p. 3.

152. Srkulj, *Povjest srednjega vijeka,* p. 257.

153. Ibid., pp. 163–64.

154. Hoić, *Povjesnica VIII* (1885), p. 15.

155. Ibid. (1897), p. 33; ibid. (1885), p. 33; Srkulj, *Povjest srednjega vijeka,* pp. 162–64; *Čitanka za treći razred općih pučkih škola* (1893), pp. 101–02; *Čitanka za četvrti razred* (1909), p. 123.

156. Srkulj, *Povjesnica srednjega vijeka,* p. 263; Hoić, *Opća povjesnica* (1879), p. 169.

157. Srkulj, *Povjesnica srednjega vijeka,* p. 263.

158. Hoić, *Povjesnica VIII* (1897), p. 54.

159. Srkulj, *Povjesnica srednjega vijeka,* p. 263.

160. Ibid., pp. 264–65; *Čitanka za treći razred* (1893), pp. 104–05; *Čitanka za četvrti razred* (1909), pp. 143–44.

161. Hoić, *Povjesnica VIII* (1897), pp. 66–67.

162. Srkulj, *Povjesnica srednjega vijeka,* pp. 337–38; Hoić, *Povjesnica VIII* (1897), p. 66; *Čitanka za treći razred* (1893), pp. 106–07.

163. Klaić, *HPVDS*, pp. 63–64; Tomšić, *Početnica*, p. 36; Hoić, *Povjesnica VIII* (1897), p. 70; Srkulj, *Povjesnica srednjega vijeka*, pp. 338–40.

164. Hoić, *Povjesnica VIII* (1885), p. 56; ibid. (1897), p. 70; Klaić, *HPVDS*, p. 64.

165. Srkulj, *Povjesnica srednjega vijeka*, pp. 339–40.

166. Hoić, *Povjesnica VIII* (1885), p. 56; ibid. (1897), p. 70; *Čitanka za drugi općih razred pučkih škola* (Zagreb: Kraljevska zemaljska tiskara, 1893), pp. 128–29.

167. Klaić, *Poviest A-U* (1875), p. 41; ibid. (1903), p. 33.

168. Hoić, *Opća povjesnica* (1898), p. 214.

169. Srkulj, *Povjesnica srednjega vijeka*, p. 260.

170. Ibid., p. 328; Klaić, *Povijest A-U* (1903), pp. 33–34; Hoić, *Povjesnica VIII* (1897), p. 66; Klaić, *HPVDS*, p. 60; Srkulj, *Povjesnica srednjega vijeka*, p. 326.

171. Hoić, *Povjesnica VIII* (1885), p. 54; ibid. (1893), p. 81.

172. Srkulj, *Povjesnica srednjega vijeka*, p. 328.

173. Hoić, *Povjesnica VIII* (1897), pp. 70–71.

174. Srkulj, *Povjesnica srednjega vijeka*, p. 328.

175. Hoić, *Povjesnica VIII* (1897), p. 70.

176. Klaić, *HPVDS*, p. 67; Hoić, *Povjesnica VIII* (1897), pp. 70–71; Srkulj, *Povjesnica srednjega vijeka*, pp. 326–29.

177. Srkulj, *Povjesnica srednjega vijeka*, pp. 328–29; Klaić, *Poviest A-U* (1903), p. 34; Hoić, *Povjesnica VIII* (1897), pp. 68–70.

178. Hoić, *Povjesnica VIII* (1897), p. 3.

179. Ibid., p. 74.

180. Ibid., pp. 87–91; Tomšić, *Početnica*, pp. 39–42.

181. Hoić, *Povjesnica VIII* (1897), p. 91.

182. Ibid., p. 90.

183. Klaić, *HPVDS*, p. 79.

184. Hoić, *Povjesnica VIII* (1897), p. 92.

185. Ibid.; Franjo B. Kořinek-Vjekoslav Klaić, *Povjesnica novoga vijeka za više razrede srednjih učilista* (Zagreb: Kraljevska zemaljska tiskara, 1907), 5th ed., p. 96.

186. Hoić, *Povjesnica VIII* (1897), p. 93.

187. Klaić, *HPVDS*, p. 89.

188. Hoić, *Povjesnica VIII* (1897), p. 3.

189. Ibid., pp. 96–97; Tomšić, *Početnica*, pp. 47–48; *Čitanka za četvrti razred* (1889), p. 104.

190. Tomšić, *Početnica*, p. 50; *Čitanka za drugi općih razred* (1889), pp. 130–33.

191. Klaić, *HPVDS*, p. 91.

192. Tomšić, *Početnica*, p. 50; Klaić, *HPVDS*, pp. 91–93.

193. Klaić, *HPVDS*, p. 91.

194. Tomšić, *Početnica*, pp. 50–51.

195. Hoić, *Povjesnica VIII* (1897), pp. 99–100.

196. Ibid., pp. 114–15.

197. Ibid., p. 116; *Čitanka za treći razred* (1880), pp. 103–04; *Čitanka za četvrti razred* (1889), pp. 104–05.

198. Hoić, *Povjesnica VIII* (1897), p. 98.

199. Ibid., pp. 118–19.

200. Ibid., p. 3.

201. Ibid., p. 119.

202. Ibid., p. 120.

203. Tomšić, *Početnica*, p. 51; Hoić, *Povjesnica VIII* (1897), p. 100.

204. Hoić, *Povjesnica VIII* (1897), p. 108.

205. Tomšić, *Početnica*, p. 54; Hoić, *Povjesnica VIII* (1897), pp. 109–10.

206. Hoić, *Povjesnica VIII* (1897), p. 110.

207. Srkulj, *Povjesnica srednjega vijeka*, p. 332.

208. Hoić, *Povjesnica VIII* (1885), p. 93; ibid. (1897), p. 112; *Čitanka za četvrti razred* (1889), pp. 110–11.

209. Klaić, *HPVDS*, p. 100; *Čitanka za četvrti razred* (1889), pp. 121–25.

210. Hoić, *Povjesnica VIII* (1897), p. 3.

211. Srkulj, *Povjesnica srednjega vijeka*, pp. 319, 324.

212. Kořinek-Klaić, *Povjesnica novoga vijeka* (1889), p. 293; Hoić, *Povjesnica VIII* (1897), p. 114.

213. Hoić, *Povjesnica VIII* (1897), p. 114.

214. Ibid., pp. 126–29; Tomšić, *Početnica*, p. 56.

215. Tomšić, *Početnica*, p. 56; Hoić, *Povjesnica VIII* (1897), p. 130.

216. Hoić, *Povjesnica VIII* (1897), p. 128–30.

217. Klaić, *Povijest A-U* (1875), p. 65; ibid. (1903), p. 58.

218. Hoić, *Povjesnica VIII* (1897), pp. 131–33; Klaić, *Povijest A-U* (1903), pp. 59–62.

219. Klaić, *HPVDS*, pp. 94–96.

220. Kořinek-Klaić, *Povjesnica novoga vijeka* (1907), p. 171; Hoić, *Povjesnica VIII* (1897), p. 128.

221. Kořinek-Klaić, *Povjesnica novoga vijeka* (1889), p. 94; Hoić, *Opća povjesnica* (1898), p. 237; Hoić, *Povjesnica VIII* (1885), p. 114.

222. Klaić, *HPVDS*, p. 114; Hoić, *Povjesnica VIII* (1897), p. 128.

223. Kořinek-Klaić, *Povjesnica novoga vijeka* (1889), p. 295.

224. Hoić, *Povjesnica VIII* (1897), p. 141.

225. Klaić, *Poviest A-U* (1875), p. 75.

226. Tomšić, *Početnica*, p. 59.

227. Hoić, *Povjesnica VIII* (1885), p. 121.

228. Kořinek-Klaić, *Povjesnica novoga vijeka* (1889), p. 295.

229. Ibid. (1907), p. 258.

230. Klaić, *Poviest A-U* (1903), p. 68; Hoić, *Opća povjesnica* (1898), p. 304.

231. Hoić, *Povjesnica VIII* (1885), p. 121.

232. Ibid.

233. Ibid. (1893), p. 146.

234. Kořinek-Klaić, *Povjesnica novoga vijeka* (1907), p. 260; Hoić, *Povjesnica VIII* (1893), p. 147.

235. Hoić, *Povjesnica VIII* (1893), p. 148.

236. Hoić, *Opća povjesnica* (1917), p. 356.

237. Ibid., pp. 356–58.

238. Ibid. (1879), p. 243.

239. Kořinek-Klaić, *Povjesnica novoga vijeka* (1907), p. 250; Hoić, *Opća povjesnica* (1879), p. 243.

240. Hoić, *Opća povjesnica* (1879), p. 243; Kořinek-Klaić, *Povjesnica novoga vijeka* (1889), p. 239.

241. Kořinek-Klaić, *Povjesnica novoga vijeka* (1889), p. 239.

242. Ibid. (1907), p. 251.

243. Hoić, *Opća povjesnica* (1879), p. 244.

244. Ibid.

245. Kořinek-Klaić, *Povjesnica novoga vijeka* (1907), p. 251; Hoić, *Opća povjesnica* (1879), p. 244.

246. Kořinek-Klaić, *Povjesnica novoga vijeka* (1907), pp. 251–52.

247. Ibid. (1889), p. 295.

248. Ibid. (1907), p. 275.

249. Kořinek-Klaić, *Povjesnica novoga vijeka* (1907), p. 276.

250. Ibid., p. 283.

251. Ibid., pp. 172–73.

252. Klaić, *Poviest A-U* (1875), p. 7.

253. Srkulj, *Povijest srednjega vijeka*, p. 57.

254. Ibid., pp. 152–54.

255. Hoić, *Povjesnica VIII* (1897), p. 100.

256. Ibid., p. 119–20.

CHAPTER 6

1. *Slovenski biografski leksikon* (Ljubljana: Jugoslavenska tiskarna, 1925–), II, pp. 140–42; 470–474; *Enciklopedija Jugoslavije*, VI, 581.

2. *Enciklopedija Jugoslavije*, III, p. 427; *Slovenski biografski leksikon*, I, p. 204.

3. *Slovenski biografski leksikon*, I, pp. 355–56; III, pp. 243–44.

4. Ibid., I, pp. 74, 78–79, 131–35; ibid., II, 193–96; *Enciklopedija Jugoslavije*, I, pp. 625–26; ibid., VI, pp. 104–05.

5. *Enciklopedija Jugoslavije*, IV, p. 457; *Slovenski biografski leksikon*, I, pp. 376–80.

6. *Enciklopedija Jugoslavije*, VII, p. 208; *Slovenski biografski leksikon*, III, pp. 330–32.

7. *Slovenski biografski leksikon*, I, pp. 493–94.

8. Ibid., I, p. 409; *Enciklopedija Jugoslavije*, IV, p. 488.

9. *Enciklopedija Jugoslavije*, VI, p. 390; *Slovenski biografski leksikon*, II, p. 231.

10. *Enciklopedija Jugoslavije*, VIII, p. 361; *Slovenski biografski leksikon*, IV, pp. 163–69.

11. *Slovenski biografski leksikon*, I, pp. 480–81; *Österreichisches Biographisches Lexikon* (Graz-Köln: Hermann Bohlaus, 1957–86). For Gindely, see ibid., I, pp. 441–42; for Hannak, II, p. 128; for Heiderich, p. 243; for Kozenn, IV, pp. 178–79; and for Mayer, V, pp. 423–24.

12. Jakob Sket, *Slovenska čitanka za tretji razred srednjih šol* (Klagenfurt: Družba sv. Mohorija, 1906), III, 2nd ed., pp. 34–37, 72–79.

13. Ivan Lapajne, *Koncenov zemljepis za ljudske šole* (Vienna: Edvard Hölzel, 1879), 2nd rev. ed., pp. 28–36; Fr. Orožen, *Zemljepis za meščanske šole: Tretja stopnja* (Ljubljana: Zadružna tiskarna, 1905), 2nd ed., pp. 37–61; M. Josin and E. Gangl, *Tretje berilo za štirirazredne in večrazredne občne ljudske šole* (Ljubljana: Ig. pl. Kleinmayr & Fed. Bamberg, 1902), pp. 133–35.

14. Orožen, *Zemljepis - tretja stopnja* (1905), pp. 56–61; Lapajne, *Koncenov*, pp. 34–36.

15. Orožen, *Zemljepis - tretja stopnja* (1905), pp. 37–61.

16. Jakob Sket, *Slovenska čitanka za četrti razred srednjih šol* (Klagenfurt: Družba sv. Mohorija, 1893), IV, pp. 120–21.

17. Henrik Schreiner and Fr. Hubad, *Čitanka za obče ljudske šole - za*

četrto in peto šolsko leto štiri - in večrazrednih ljudskih šol (Vienna: V cesarski kraljevi zalogi šolskih knig, 1904), part III, p. 250.

18. Henrik Schreiner, *Čitanka za obče ljudske šole - za šesto, sedmo in osmo šolsko leto štiri - in večrazrednih ljudskih šol* (Vienna: V cesarski kraljevi zalogi šolskih knjig, 1911), pp. 310; Josin and Gangl, *Tretje berilo* (1902), pp. 222–23.

19. Schreiner and Hubad, *Čitanka za četrto in peto* (1904), pp. 249–53; Josin and Gangl, *Tretje berilo* (1902), pp. 130–32.

20. Schreiner and Hubad, *Čitanka za četrto in peto* (1904), p. 246.

21. Ibid., pp. 247–248; Josin and Gangl, *Tretje berilo* (1902), pp. 226–29.

22. *Drugo berilo in slovnica za obče ljudske šole* (Vienna: V cesarski kraljevi zalogi šolskih knjig, 1895), pp. 126–27.

23. Ibid., pp. 127–28.

24. *Tretje berilo za občne ljudske šole* (Vienna: V cesarski kraljevski zalogi šolskih knjig, 1891), pp. 249–50; Josin and Gangl, *Tretje berilo* (1902), pp. 208–09.

25. *Tretje berilo* (1891), pp. 250–51.

26. Ibid., pp. 252–53; Josin and Gangl, *Tretje berilo* (1902), pp. 212–13.

27. *Tretje berilo* (1891), pp. 258–59.

28. Schreiner and Hubad, *Čitanka za četrto in peto* (1904), pp. 234–35.

29. Sket, *Slovenska čitanka za tretji razred* (1906), pp. 178–84.

30. Sket, *Slovenska čitanka za četrti razred* (1893), pp. 22–24.

31. Ibid., pp. 24–25; *Enciklopedija Jugoslavije*, V, p. 167.

32. Sket, *Slovenska čitanka za četrti razred* (1893), p. 28.

33. Schreiner, *Čitanka za obče ljudske šole - za šesto, sedmo* (1911), p. 122.

34. Peter Končnik, *Četrto berilo za ljudske in nadaljevalne šole* (Vienna: V c.k. zalogi šolskih knjig, 1883), p. 303; Josin and Gangl, *Tretje berilo* (1902), pp. 171–72.

35. Končnik, *Četrto berilo* (1883), pp. 304–306.

36. Schreiner, *Čitanka za obče ljudske šole - za šesto, sedmo* (1911), pp. 305–06.

37. Ibid., pp. 306–07.

38. Ibid., pp. 317–18.

39. Janez Jesenko, *Občni zemljepis* (Ljubljana: Narodna tiskarna, 1873), p. 201; Lapajne, *Koncenov*, p. 37; Janez Jesenko, *Avstrijsko-ogerska monarhija - Domovinoznanstvo za četrti razred srednjih šol* (Ljubljana: Narodna tiskarna, 1885), p. 82; Orožen, *Zemljepis - tretja stopnja* (1905), p. 62.

40. Jesenko, *Občni zemljepis*, p. 202.

41. Ibid., pp. 201–04; Orožen, *Zemljepis - tretja stopnja* (1905), pp. 61–62.

42. Franz Martin Mayer, *Lehrbuch der Allgemeinen Geschichte für die oberen Klassen der Realschulen* (Vienna: F. Tempsky, 1906), pp. 115–17; Andreas Zeehe and Wilh. Schmidt, *Österreichische Vaterlandskunde für die VIII Gymnasialclasse* (Laibach: Ig. v. Kleinmayr & Fed. Bamberg, 1901), p. 122.

43. Orožen, *Zemljepis - tretja stopnja* (1905), pp. 75–77.

44. Jesenko, *Občni zemljepis*, pp. 322–23; Sket, *Slovenska čitanka za tretji razred* (1906), pp. 138–43; V. Bežek, *Zemljepis za spodnje in srednje razrede srednjih šol - Opis dežel razen Avstro-Ogrske* (Ljubljana: Ig. pl. Kleinmayr & Fed. Bamberg, 1899), p. 63.

45. Sket, *Slovenska čitanka za tretji razred* (1906), pp. 138–39.

46. Ibid., pp. 139–42.

47. Ibid., p. 142.

48. Jesenko, *Občni zemljepis*, p. 323; Bežek, *Zemljepis*, p. 63.

Bibliography

PUBLISHED SOURCES

Saborski dnevnik kraljevinah Hrvatske, Slavonije i Dalmacije godina 1872–1875. Zagreb: Lav. Hartman, 1875.

Statistički atlas Kraljevine Hrvatske i Slavonije 1875–1915. Zagreb: Kraljevska zemaljska tiskara, 1915.

Statistički godišnjak Kraljevine Hrvatske i Slavonije 1906–1910. Zagreb: Kraljevskog zemaljskoga statističkoga ureda, 1917.

Statistički godišnjak Kraljevine Srbije. Belgrade: Državna štamparija, 1900–10.

Stenografski zapisnici sabora Kraljevine Hrvatske, Slavonije i Dalmacije, 1887–1918. Zagreb: Kraljevska zemaljska tiskara, 1902–21.

TEXTBOOKS
Serbian

Geography

Antonović, S., and I. Lazić. *Zemljopis za II razred srednjih škola.* Belgrade: Dositej Obradović, 1902.

———. *Zemljopis za II razred srednjih škola.* Belgrade: Geca Kon, 1912. 5th ed.

Antonović, S., and T. Radivojević. *Zemlja - Osnovna zemljopisna znanja za prvi razred.* Belgrade: Geca Kon, 1913. 9th ed.

Dragašević, Jovan. *Geografija za srednje škole.* Belgrade: Državna štamparija, 1881.

———. *Zemljopis Srbije i ostalog poluostrova balkanskog-za osnovne škole.* Belgrade: Državna štamparija, 1882. 5th rev. and enlarged ed.

[Dragašević, Jovan]. *Zemljopis Srbije i Turske za osnovne srpske škole.* Belgrade: Državna štamparija, 1871.

Gavrilović, Jovan. *Malii zemljopis knjažestva Srbie i Turskog carstva u Evropi za osnovne škole.* Belgrade: Knjigopečatni knjažestva srbskog, 1850.

Hrabrenović, Milan, and Vladimir T. Simić. *Atlas Kraljevine Srbije sa zemljopisom po rečnim slivovima za učenike -ce III razreda osnovne škole.* Belgrade: Dvorska knjižara, 1911. 3rd rev. ed.

Jović, Mihailo, and D. J. Putniković. *Zemljopis Srbije i srpskih zemalja za IV razred osnovne škole.* Belgrade: Savić, 1905. 3rd ed.

———. *Zemljopis Srbije po rečnim slivovima za III razred osnovne škole.* Belgrade: Dositej Obradović, 1902.

Karić, Vladimir. *Srbija-Opis zemlje, naroda i države.* Belgrade: Državna štamparija, 1887.

———. *Zemljopis kraljevine Srbije za III razred osnovnih škola.* Belgrade: Državna štamparija, 1889.

———. *Zemljopis za niže razrede srednjih škola po najnovijim izvorima - Politički zemljopis - Jevropa.* Belgrade: Štamparija srpske napredne stranke, 1883. Vol. 3.

Mali zemljopis za osnovne srpske škole. Belgrade: Državna štamparija, 1869. Also 1871.

Mali zemljopis za osnovne srpske škole. Belgrade: Državna štamparija, 1870.

Mali zemljopis Srbije i Turske. Belgrade: Pravitelstvena knjigopečatnica, 1863.

Miletić, Srećko A. *Zemljopis za srednje i stručne škole—Balkansko poluostrvo.* Belgrade: Dositej Obradović, 1908. Vol. 2.

Mitrović, Raša. *Zemljopis Kraljevine Srbije sa kratkim opisom sviju srpskih zemalja za učenike i učenice IV raz. osn. škole.* Belgrade: Velimir Valožić, 1900. 3rd ed.

Mitrović, Raša, and Mih. M. Stanojević. *Zemljopis Kraljevine Srbije sa kratkim opisom sviju srpskih zemalja za učenike i učenice IV razreda osnovne škole.* Belgrade: Velimir Valožić, 1902. Also 1906.

Niketić, Pet. M. *Zemljopis Kraljevine Srbije za III razred osnovnih škola.* Belgrade: Državna štamparija, 1894. 3rd rev. ed.

Nikolić, St. J. *Kraljevina Srbija i kratak pregled srpskih zemalja - za IV razred narodnih škola.* Belgrade: Sv. Nikolić, 1899. 2nd enlarged ed.

R. M. *Zemljopis Kraljevine Srbije za III r. osn. škole.* Niš: Z. Radovanović, 1895.

Radivojević, T. *Zemljopisna čitanka za srednje, gradjanske i djevojačke škole.* Belgrade: S. Stefanović, 1903.

Simić, Vladimir T., and Milan Hrabrenović. *Atlas Srbije i srpskih zemalja sa zemljopisom po rečnim slivovima za učenike -ce IV razreda osnovne škole.* Belgrade: Dvorska knjižara, 1909.

———. *Atlas Srbije i srpskih zemalja sa zemljopisom za učenike -ce IV razreda osnovne škole.* Belgrade: Mita Stajić, 1909. 2nd rev. ed.

Sokolović, Dim. J. *Zemljopis Kraljevine Srbije po rečnim slivovima sa životpisom i kartama rečnih slivova i lepim slikama za učenike -ce III raz. osn. nar. škole.* Belgrade: Dvorska knjižara, 1900.

———. *Zemljopis srpskih zemalja i balkanskog poluostrva za učenike IV razreda osnovnih škola.* Belgrade: Petar Čurić, 1890.

———. *Zemljopis srpskih zemalja i balkanskog poluostrva za učenike IV razreda osnovne škole.* Belgrade: Radikalna štamparija, 1894. 2nd rev. ed.

Sokolović, D., and I. J. Sokolović. *Zemljopis Kraljevine Srbije i srpskih zemalja sa slikama i kartama za učenike IV razreda osnovnih narodnih škola.* Belgrade: Velimir Valožić, 1900.

Spasić, Dr. M. *Zemljopisanie za predanie u III razredu osnovnih učilista kniažestva srbskog.* Belgrade: U knigopečatni kniažestva srbskog, 1848.

Šreplović, P. K. *Atlas Kraljevine Srbije sa zemljopisom i životopisma po novoj administrativnoj podeli za učenike -ce III razreda osnovne škole.* Belgrade: Prosveta, 1898.

———. *Atlas Kraljevine Srbije sa zemljopisom po rečnim slivovima; po programu; najkraći podsetnik za učenike III razreda osnovnih škola.* Belgrade: Velimir Valožić, 1914.

———. *Atlas Kraljevine Srbije sa zemljopisom po rečnim slivovima - za učenike III razreda osnovnih škola.* Belgrade: Prosveta, 1914.

———. *Atlas srpskih zemalja i balkanskog poluostrva sa zemljopisom za učenike -ce IV razreda osnovnih škola.* Belgrade: Prosveta, 1891.

———. *Novi atlas Kraljevine Srbije sa zemljopisom i životopisima po novoj administrativnoj podeli za učenike -ce III razreda osnovne škole.* Belgrade: Prosveta, 1892.

Stanojević, M. M. *Zemljopis Kraljevine Srbije i srpskih zemalja: Podsetnik na predavanja iz zemljopisa - za učenike i učenice IV razreda osnovne škole.* Belgrade: Velimir Valožić, 1912.

———. *Zemljopis Kraljevine Srbije i srpskih zemalja za učenike i učenice IV razreda osnovne škole.* Belgrade: Velimir Valožić, 1912.

———. *Zemljopis Kraljevine Srbije za III razred narodnih škola po rečnim slivovima.* Belgrade: Velimir Valožić, 1899.

Stanojević, Mih. M., and Raša Mitrović. *Atlas Kraljevine Srbije za III razred narodnih škola.* Belgrade: Velimir Valožić, 1902.

Stevanović, Mih. M. *Zemljopis za gradjanske i devojačke škole - za I, II i III razred.* Požarevac: Djordje Naumović, 1901.

Ubavkić, Milan S. *Zemljopis Kraljevine Srbije sa životopisma iz najnovije naše istorije - za učenike IIIeg razreda osnovne škole.* Belgrade: Napredna stranka, 1885.

Vasovic, Radovan. *Geografija za srednje škole.* Belgrade: Davidović, 1910.

History

Antonović, S., and Pet. M. Niketić. *Ilustrovana srspska istorija za osnovnu školu.* Belgrade: Pera Todorović, 1890.

Djordjević, Jovan. *Istorija srpskoga naroda od najstarijega do najnovijega doba za srednje škole i za narod.* Vranje: Petar Jovanović, 1900.

Ilovajski, D. *Opšta istorija za srednje škole: I. Stara istorija, II. Istorija srednjih vekova. III. Nova i najnovija istorija.* Kragujevac: Andrija Jovanović, 1894. 2nd rev. and enlarged ed. prepared by Dim. Dukić.

Jović, Mihailo. *Srpska istorija sa kratkom istorijom Hrvata i Slovenaca za IV razred osn. škole.* Belgrade, 1921. 39th ed.

———. *Srpska istorija sa slikama za IV razred osnovne škole.* Belgrade: Velimir Valožić, 1896. 14th ed.

———. *Srpska istorija sa slikama za IV razred osnovne škole.* Belgrade: Državna štamparija, 1902. 20th ed.

———. *Srpska istorija sa slikama za IV razred osnovne škole.* Belgrade: Velimir Valožić, 1913. 35th ed.

———. *Srpska istorija udesena za današnju osnovnu. školu.* Belgrade: Štamparija zadruge štamparskih radnika, 1882.

———. *Srpska istorija za IV raz. osn. škole.* Belgrade: Štamparija kraljevine Srbije, 1891.

———. *Srpska istorija za IV razred osnovne škole.* Belgrade: Geca Kon, 1919. 38th ed.

Kovačević, Lj., and Lj. Jovanović. *Istorija srpskoga naroda za srednje škole u Kraljevini Srbiji.* Belgrade: Državna štamparija, 1891. Vol. 1, part 2.

———. *Istorija srpskoga naroda za srednje škole u Kraljevini Srbiji za treći razred gimnazija i realka.* Belgrade: Državna štamparija, 1895–96. Vol. 1, new rev. ed.

Krstić, Nikola. *Istorija srbskog naroda.* Belgrade: Državna štamparija, 1862.

———. *Istorija srbskog naroda.* Belgrade: Državna knjigopečatnica, 1873.

———. *Istorija srbskog naroda za osnovne srbske škole.* Belgrade: Državna štamparija, 1867. Also 1869, 1870, 1872, 1880, 1882.

———. *Kratka istorija srpskoga naroda za osnovne srbske škole.* Belgrade: Državna štamparija, 1866.

Lazarević, L., and P. K. Šreplović. *Srpska istorija sa slikama za IV razred osnovne škole.* Belgrade: Velimir Valožić, 1903. 3rd ed.

Marković, Joksim St. *Srpska istorija za IV razred osnovne škole.* Belgrade: Državna štamparija, 1892. 8th ed.

———. *Srpska istorija za sadašnju potrebu niže osnovne škole.* Belgrade: Štamparija napredne stranke, 1885.

———. *Životopisi iz najnovije srpske istorije za omladinu niže osnovne škole.* Belgrade: Državna štamparija, 1889. 7th ed.

Milojković, A. *Istorija sveta za više osnovne škole u Kraljevini Srbiji*. Kragujevac: Andrija Jovanović, 1892.

Nenadović, Ljub. *Srbska istorija za osnovne srbske škole*. Belgrade: U knjigopečatni kniažestva srpskog, 1851.

Niketić, Pet. M. *Istorija sveta za osnovnu nastavu*. Belgrade: Štamparija zadruge štamparskih radnika, 1880.

Stanojević, Mih. M. *Istorija srpskoga naroda za IV razred osnovne škole*. Belgrade: Velimir Valožić, 1908. Vol. 2.

Stanojević, St., and L. Zrnić. *Istorija srpskoga naroda za srednje škole*. Belgrade: Davidović, 1908.

———. *Istorija srpskoga naroda za srednje i stručne škole*. Belgrade: Davidović, 1910. Vol. 1, 2nd ed.

Svabić, Pavle. *Istorija srpske crkve za učenike i učenice srednjih škola*. Belgrade: S. Horović, 1901. Vol. 2.

Ubavkić, Milan S. *Istorija Srba za osnovne škole u Kraljevini Srbiji*. Belgrade: Prosveta, 1891.

Vukičević, Milenko M. *Istorija Srba, Hrvata i Slovenaca*. Belgrade: Zdravko Spasojević, 1923. 2 vols. 10th ed.

———. *Istorija srpskoga naroda u slici i reci*. Belgrade, 1912.

———. *Istorija srpskoga naroda za srednje škole - od dolaska Srba na Balkansko poluostrovo do polovine XV stoleća*. Belgrade: Dositej Obradović, 1904. Vol. 1.

———. *Istorija srpskoga naroda za srednje škole: od polovine VII do kraja XV stoleća*. Belgrade: Sava Radenković, 1911. Vol. 1. 4th ed.

———. *Istorija srpskoga naroda za srednje škole: od polovine VII do kraja XV stoleća*. Belgrade: Davidović, 1914. 6th ill., rev., and enlarged ed.

———. *Istorija srpskoga naroda za srednje škole: od polovine XV stoleća do Berlinskog kongresa*. Belgrade: Petar Jovanović, 1902. Vol. 2.

———. *Istorija srpskoga naroda za srednje škole: od polovine XV stoleća do danas*. Belgrade: Aca M. Stanojević, 1909. Vol. 2. 3rd rev. ed.

———. *Istorija srpskoga naroda za srednje škole: od polovine XV stoleća do danas*. Belgrade: Davidović, 1906. Vol. 2. 2nd rev. ed.

———. *Istorija srpskoga naroda za srednje škole: od polovine XV stoleća do danas*. Belgrade: Sv. Sava, 1911. Vol. 2. 3rd rev. ed.

———. *Istorija srpskoga naroda za srednje škole: od polovine XV stoleća do danas*. Belgrade: Davidović, 1912. 5th rev. and enlarged ed.

———. *Istorija srpskoga naroda za srednje škole: od polovine XV stoleća do danas*. Belgrade: Davidović, 1914. Vol. 2. 6th rev. and enlarged ed.

Zrnić, L. *Istorija srpskoga naroda*. Belgrade: Državna štamparija, 1912.

———. *Opšta istorija za više razrede srednjih škola*. Belgrade: Državna štamparija, 1914. 3rd ed.

Readers (Čitanke) and Grammars

Čitanka za četvrti razred srpskih osnovnih škola. Constantinople: A. Želić, 1892.

Čitanka za drugi razred osnovnih škola knježevine Srbije. Belgrade: Državna štamparija, 1877.

Čitanka za treći razred osnovne škole u Otomanskoj Carevini. Constantinople: A. Selić, 1891.

Čuturilo, Stevo. *Bukvar za osnovne škole u kraljevini Srbiji*. Belgrade, 1892. Also 1910, 1920.

———. *Prva čitanka za osnovne škole u kraljevini Srbiji*. Belgrade: Državna štamparija, 1904.

Djordjević, P. P., and U. Blagojević. *Srpska čitanka za IV razred osnovnih škola u Kraljevini Srbiji*. Belgrade: Državna štamparija, 1906. 8th ed.

———. *Srpska čitanka za IV razred osnovnih škola Kraljevine Srbije*. Belgrade: Štamparija kraljevine Srbije, 1891. 2nd ed.

Druga čitanka za osnovne srpske škole. Belgrade: Državna štamparija, 1872.

[Hristić, Filip]. *Četvrta čitanka za osnovne srpske škole*. Belgrade: Državna štamparija, 1885.

———. *Čitanka za III razred osnovne škole*. Belgrade: Državna štamparija, 1883. New, especially rev. edition.

———. *Druga čitanka za osnovne škole*. Belgrade: Državna štamparija, 1872.

———. *Druga čitanka za osnovne srpske škole*. Belgrade: Pri knjigopečatni knjiažestva srpskog, 1850.

———. *Prva čitanka za osnovne srpske škole*. Belgrade: Pri knjigopečatni knjiažestva srpskog, 1859.

———. *Treća čitanka za četvrti razred osnovni srpski škola*. Belgrade: U knjigopečatni kniažestva Srbie, 1855.

———. *Treća čitanka za osnovne srpske škole*. Belgrade: Državna štamparija, 1867. Also 1872 and 1883, new completely rev. ed.

Ivković, Miloš. *Srpska čitanka za prvi razred srednjih škola*. Belgrade: Geca Kon, 1911.

Jovanović, Vojislav M., and Miloš Ivković. *Srpska čitanka za četvrti razred srednjih škola*. Belgrade: Geca Kon, 1913.

———. *Srpska čitanka za treći razred srednjih škola*. Belgrade: Geca Kon, 1913.

Marković, Mil., and Dj. J. Nedić. *Srpska čitanka za III razred osnovnih škola kraljevine Srbije*. Belgrade: Državna štamparija, 1894. 2nd ed.

[Natošević, Dj.]. *Čitanka za drugi razred osnovnih škola knjaževine Srbije*. Belgrade: Državna štamparija, 1873.

————. *Čitanka za drugi razred osnovnih škola knjaževine Srbije*. Belgrade: Državna štamparija, 1882.

————. *Čitanka za I razred osnovnih škola kraljevine Srbije*. Belgrade: Državna štamparija, 1893. 7th rev. ed.

————. *Čitanka za I razred srpske osnovne škole*. Belgrade: Državna štamparija, 1886. 5th rev. ed.

Novaković, Stojan. *Istorija srpske književnosti: Pregled ugadjan za školsku potrebu*. Belgrade: Državna štamparija, 1867.

————. *Istorija srpske književnosti: Pregled ugadjan za školsku potrebu*. Belgrade: Državna štamparija, 1871. 2nd completely rev. ed.

————. *Srpska čitanka za niže gimnazije i realke*. Belgrade: Državna štamparija, 1870. Vol. 1.

————. *Srpska čitanka za niže gimnazije i realke Kraljevine Srbije*. Belgrade-Kragujevac: Državna štamparija, 1893. Vol. 1. 6th ed.

————. *Srpska gramatika*. Belgrade: Državna štamparija, 1894. 1st complete ed.

Pašić, Sreten, and Milan Šević. *Srpska čitanka za srednje škole za I razred*. Belgrade: Državna štamparija, 1902. Vol. 1. 3rd rev. ed.

Pašić, Sreten, and Milan Šević. *Srpska čitanka za srednje škole za I razred*. Belgrade: Državna štamparija, 1902. Vol. 1. 3rd rev. ed.

————. *Srpska čitanka za srednje škole za I i II razred*. Belgrade: Državna štamparija, 1894. Vol. 1.

Protić, Ljub. M., and Vlad. D. Stojanović. *Srpska čitanka za II razred osnovnih škola u kraljevini Srbiji*. Belgrade: Državna štamparija, 1904. 1st ed. Also 1910, 7th ed.

————. *Srpska čitanka za III razred osnovnih škola u Kraljevini Srbiji*. Belgrade: Državna štamparija, 1910. Vol. 2. 8th ed. Also 1912, 9th ed.

————. *Srpska čitanka za IV razred osnovnih škola u Kraljevini Srbiji*. Belgrade: Državna štamparija, 1907. Vol. 3. 7th rev. ed.

Šević, Milan. *Srpska čitanka za srednje škole za II razred*. Belgrade: Državna štamparija, 1911. Vol. 2. 5th rev. ed.

————. *Srpska čitanka za srednje škole za III razred*. Belgrade: Državna štamparija, 1902. Vol. 3. Also 1909, 1911.

————. *Srpska čitanka za srednje škole za IV razred*. Belgrade: Državna štamparija, 1903. Vol. 4. Also 1911.

Vulović, Svetislav. *Srpska čitanka za više raz. gimnazija i realka srpskih uz predavanja srpskog jezika i novije istorije književnosti*. Belgrade: Državna štamparija, 1876. Vol. 3. And 1895.

————. *Srpska čitanka za niže gimnazije i realke*. Belgrade: Državna štamparija, 1874. Vol. 2.

Croatian

Geography

Bordjoski, Lazar. *Zemljopis za učenike III razreda srpskih vjeroispovjednih osnovnih škola u Kr. Hrvatskoj i Slavoniji.* Karlovac: Drag. Hautfeld, 1903.

Hoić, Ivan. *Zemljopis austrijsko-ugarske monarkije za gradjanske škole.* Zagreb: Kr. hrv. slav. dalm. zemaljska vlada, 1882.

———. *Zemljopis za I licejski razred.* Zagreb: Kr. hrv. slav. dalm. zemaljska vlada, 1908. 2nd rev. ed.

———. *Zemljopis za II–VIII razred ženskoga liceja.* Zagreb: Kr. hrv. slav. dalm. zemaljska vlada, 1909. 2nd rev. ed.

———. *Zemljopis za gradjanske škole.* Zagreb: Kr. hrv. slav. dalm. zemaljska vlada, 1880.

———. *Zemljopis za niže razrede srednjih škola.* Zagreb: Kr. hrv. slav. dalm. zemaljska vlada. 1916, 2nd ed.

———. *Zemljopis za VII razred viših djevojačkih škola.* Zagreb: Kr. hrv. slav. dalm. zemaljska vlada, 1894. 2nd rev. ed.

———. *Zemljopis za više djevojačke škole prvi stupanj.* Zagreb: Kr. hrv. slav. dalm. zemaljska vlada, 1883.

———. *Zemljopis za više djevojačke škole - prvi i drugi stupanj.* Zagreb: Kr. hrv. slav. dalm. zemaljska vlada, 1889. 2nd ed.

———. *Zemljopis za više djevojačke škole - prvi i drugi stupanj.* Zagreb: Kr. hrv. slav. dalm. zemaljska vlada, 1897. 3rd rev. ed.

———. *Zemljopis za više pučke škole.* Zagreb: Kr. hrv. slav. dalm. zemaljska vlada, 1891.

Klaić, Vjekoslav. *Bosna - Zemljopis.* Zagreb: K. Albrecht, 1878.

———. *Zemljopis zemalja u kojih obitavaju hrvati.* Zagreb: Dioniska tiskara - Društvo sv. Jeronima, 1880–83. 3 vols.

Mařik, Vjenceslav Zaboj. *Kratak sveobći zemljopis za mladež narodnih učionah.* Zagreb: Troškom spisateljevim, 1871. 4th rev. ed.

———. *Kratak sveobći zemljopis za mladež narodnih učiona.* Zagreb: L. Hartman, 1876. 7th ed.

———. *Kratak sveobći zemljopis za mladež narodnih učiona.* Zagreb: Mučnjak & Senftleben, 1878. 8th ed.

———. *Zemljopis trojedne kraljevine.* Zagreb: L. Hartman, 1873. 3rd rev. and enlarged ed.

Matković, Petar. *Hrvatska i Slavonija u svojih fizičnih i duševnih odnosajih.* Zagreb: Dragutin Albrecht, 1873.

———. *Zemljopis Austrijsko-Ugarske monarhije za niže razrede srednjih učilišta.* Zagreb: Kr. hrv. slav. dalm. zemaljska vlada, 1882.

———. *Zemljopis za niže razrede srednjih učilišta.* Zagreb: Kr. hrv. slav. dalm. zemaljska vlada, 1883. 3rd rev. ed.

———. *Zemljopis za niže razrede srednjih učilištah.* Zagreb: Lj. Gaja, 1878. 2nd ed.

Modestin, Josip. *Zemljopis i statistika Austro-Ugarske monarhije za srednja učilišta.* Zagreb: Kr. hrv. slav. dalm. zemaljska vlada, 1905. 2nd ed.

———. *Zemljopis i statistika Austro-Ugarske monarhije za srednja učilišta.* Zagreb: Kr. hrv. slav. dalm. zemaljska vlada, 1912. 3rd rev. and enlarged ed.

———. *Zemljopis za srednje škole po knjiži Dra. Eduarda Richtera.* Zagreb: Kr. hr. slav. dalm. zemaljska vlada, 1908. 2nd rev. and enlarged ed.

Streer, E. *Zemljopisna početnica za prvi razred srednjih učilišta.* Zagreb, 1879.

Tomić, Janko. *Hrvatska-to jest crtice iz zemljepisa Hrvatske, Slavonije, Dalmacije, Istre, Bosne, Hercegovine, itd.* Karlovac: I. N. Prettner, 1869.

History

Belaj, Ferdinando. *Povjest crkve Kristove za srednja učilišta.* Zagreb: Kr. hrv. slav. dalm. zemaljska vlada, 1892. 2nd rev. ed.

———. *Povjest crkve Kristove za srednje škole.* Zagreb: Kr. hrv. slav. dalm. zemaljska vlada, 1901. 3rd ed.

Heffler, Ferdo. *Slike iz povijesti crkve Hristove za učiteljske i više pučke škole.* Zagreb: Kr. hrv. slav. dal. zemaljska vlada, 1915.

Hoić, Ivan. *Opća poviest za gradjanske škole.* Zagreb: Kr. hrv. slav. dalm. zemaljska vlada, 1879.

———. *Opća povjesnica za niže razred srednjih škola.* Zagreb: Kr. hrv. slav. dalm. zemaljska vlada, 1888. Also 1896, 1898, 1901, 1907, 1912.

———. *Opća povjesnica za niže razrede srednjih škola.* Zagreb: Kr. hrv. slav. dalm. zemaljska vlada, 1917. 8th rev. ed.

———. *Povjesnica hrvatska za VIII gimnazijski razred.* Zagreb: Kr. hrv. slav. dalm. zemaljska vlada, 1885. Also 1893, 1897.

———. *Povjestnica novoga vijeka za niže razrede srednjih učilista.* Zagreb: Kr. hrv. slav. dalm. zemaljska vlada, 1889. 2nd rev. ed.

Klaić, Vjekoslav. *Atlas za Hrvatsku povijestnicu.* Zagreb: C. Albrecht, 1888.

———. *Hrvatska povjesnica za više djevojačke škole i liceje.* Zagreb: Kr. hrv. slav. dalm. zemaljska vlada, 1894.

———. *Poviest austro-ugarska monarkije za pučke, gradjanske i višje djevojačke učione.* Zagreb: L. Hartman, 1875.

————. *Povjest austro-ugarske monarkije za niže i više pučke škole.* Zagreb: L. Hartman, 1903.

Kořinek, Fr. B. *Povjestnica novoga vijeka za više razrede srednjih učilišta.* Zagreb: Kr. hrv. slav. dalm. zemaljska vlada, 1889. Also 1897. Rev. by Vjekoslav Klaić.

————. *Povjesnica novoga vijeka za više razrede srednjih učilišta.* Zagreb: Kr. hrv. slav. dalm. zemaljska vlada, 1907. 5th ed. rev. by Vjekoslav Klaić.

Lasman, Franjo. *Povijest crkve Hristove za više razrede srednjih škola.* Zagreb: Kr. hrv. slav. dalm. zemaljska vlada, 1917. 2nd rev. ed.

Ljubić, Sime. *Pregled hrvatske poviesti.* Rijeka: Emidija Mohović, 1864.

Rubetić, Cvetko. *Kratka poviest crkve Kristove za preparandije i gradjanske škole.* Zagreb: Kr. hrv. slav. dalm. zemaljska vlada, 1880. 2nd rev. ed.

————. *Kratka povjest crkve Kristove za realne gimnazije, učiteljske i gradjanske škole.* Zagreb: Kr. hrv. slav. dalm. zemaljska vlada, 1896. 4th ed.

Srkulj, Stjepan. *Povijest srednjega vijeka za više razrede srednjih učilišta.* Zagreb: Kr. hrv. slav. dalm. zemaljska vlada, 1912.

————. *Pregled opće i hrvatske povijesti.* Zagreb: Kr. hrv. slav. dalm. zemaljska vlada, 1905. Also 1909, 1912, 1920.

Tomšić, Ljudevit. *Početnica hrvatske povjestnice za mladež pučkih škola.* Zagreb: Mučnjak & Senftleben, 1877. 3rd rev. and enlarged ed.

Živković, Nikola Gr. *Istorija Hriščanske crkve za školsku mladež.* Zagreb: Dragutin Albrecht, 1880.

————. *Istorija Hriščanke crkve za školsku mladež.* Zagreb: Dragutin Albrecht, 1886. 2nd enlarged ed.

Readers (Čitanke) and Grammars

Basariček, Stjepan. *Čitanka za više pučke škole.* Zagreb: L. Hartman, 1890. Vol. 2.

Bukvar za niže pučke škole u Hrvatskoj i Slavoniji. Zagreb: Kr. hrv. slav. dalm. zemaljska vlada, 1910.

Čitanka za četvrti razred nižih pučkih škola u Hrvatskoj i Slavoniji. Zagreb: Kr. hrv. slav. dalm. zemaljska vlada, 1909.

Čitanka za četvrti razred nižih pučkih škola u Hrvatskoj i Slavoniji. Zagreb: Kr. hrv. slav. dalm. zemaljska vlada, 1910. Also 1912.

Čitanka za četvrti razred nižih pučkih škola u kraljevinama hrvatskoj i slavoniji. Zagreb: Kr. hrv. slav. dalm. zemaljska vlada, 1915

Čitanka za četvrti razred obćih pučkih škola. Vienna: U carskoj kraljevskoj nakladi školskih knjiga, 1889.

Čitanka za četvrti razred općih pučkih škola u Hrvatskoj i Slavoniji.

Zagreb: Kr. hrv. slav. dalm. zemaljska vlada, 1901. Also 1904, 1905, 1908.

Čitanka za četvrti razred nižih pučkih škola u Hrvatskoj i Slavoniji. Zagreb: Kr. hrv. slav. dalm. zemaljska vlada, 1915.

Čitanka za drugi razred nižih pučkih škola. Zagreb: Kr. hrv. slav. dalm. zemaljska vlada, 1894.

Čitanka za drugi razred nižih pučkih škola u Hrvatskoj i Slavoniji. Zagreb: Kr. hrv. slav. dalm. zemaljska vlada, 1914. Ed. B.

Čitanka za drugi razred općih pučkih škola. Zagreb: Kr. hrv. slav. dalm. zemaljska vlada, 1893.

Čitanka za II razred nižih pučkih škola. Zagreb: Kr. hrv. slav. dalm. zemaljska vlada, 1894. Also 1895, 1899, 1908, 1909.

Čitanka za drugi razred nižih pučkih škola u Hrvatskoj i Slavoniji. Zagreb: Kr. hrv. slav. dalm. zemaljska vlada, 1901. Also 1909.

Čitanka za II razred nižih pučkih škola u Hrvatskoj i Slavoniji. Zagreb: Kr. hrv. slav. dalm. zemaljska vlada, 1910. Also 1911, 1912, 1914.

Čitanka za drugi općih razred pučkih škola. Zagreb: Kr. hrv. slav. dalm. zemaljska vlada, 1886. Also 1887, 1888, 1889, 1890, 1892, 1893, 1897, 1898, 1900.

Čitanka za prvi razred općih pučkih škola. Zagreb: Kr. hrv. slav. dalm. zcmaljska vlada, 1894. Also 1895, 1897, 1899, 1900, 1901, 1905.

Čitanka za prvi razred općih pučkih škola u Hrvatskoj i Slavoniji. Zagreb: Kr. hrv. slav. dalm. zemaljska vlada, 1899.

Čitanka za treći razred nižih pučkih škola. Zagreb: Kr. hrv. slav. dalm. zemaljska vlada, 1892. Also 1894.

Čitanka za treći razred nižih pučkih škola u Hrvatskoj i Slavoniji. Zagreb: Kr. hrv. slav. dalm. zemaljska vlada, 1907. Also 1909, 1910, 1911, 1915.

Čitanka za treći razred nižih pučkih škola u kraljevinama hrvatskoj i slavoniji. Zagreb: Kr. hrv. slav. dalm. zemaljska vlada, 1915.

Čitanka za treći razred obćih pučkih škola. Zagreb: Kr. hrv. slav. dalm. zemaljska vlada, 1891. Also 1893, 1896, 1897, 1898.

Čitanka za treći razred općih pučkih škola u Hrvatskoj i Slavoniji. Zagreb: Kr. hrv. slav. dalm. zemaljska vlada, 1903. Also 1904, 1905, 1908.

Čitanka za treći razred pučkih škola. Zagreb: Kr. hrv. slav. dalm. zemaljska vlada, 1880.

Čitanka za treći razred pučkih škola i dodatak iz gramatike. Zagreb: Kr. hrv. slav. dalm. zemaljska vlada, 1880. Also 1883, 1888, 1889.

Divković, Mirko. *Hrvatska čitanka za I razred gimnazijski.* Zagreb: Kr. hrv. slav. dalm. zemaljska vlada, 1894. Also 1896, 1902, 1908, 1913, 1918.

————. *Hrvatska čitanka za III razred gimnazijski.* Zagreb: Kr. hrv. slav. dalm. zemaljska vlada, 1889. Also 1896, 1900, 1905, 1909, 1916, 1918.

———. *Hrvatska čitanka za IV razred gimnazijski*. Zagreb: Kr. hrv. slav. dalm. zemaljska vlada, 1897. Also 1901, 1911, 1918.

Druga slovnička čitanka za katoličke pučke učione u austriskoj carevini. Vienna: Kraljevska naklada školskih knjigah, 1879.

Filipović, Ivan. *Kratka poviest književnosti hrvatske i srbske za gradjanske i višje djevojačke škole*. Zagreb: Lav. Hartman, 1875.

Maretić, Tomislav. *Čitanka za drugi razred srednjih škola*. Zagreb: Kr. hrv. slav. dalm. zemaljska vlada, 1884. Also 1890, 1896, 1899.

———. *Hrvatska ili Srpska gramatika za srednje škole*. Zagreb: L. Hartman, 1899.

———. *Hrvatska ili Srpska gramatika za srednje škole*. Zagreb: Kr. hrv. slav. dalm. zemaljska vlada, 1906. 3rd ed. Also 1913.

Maretić, Tomislav, and Ivan Šarić. *Hrvatska čitanka za II razred gimnazijski*. Zagreb: Kraljevska zemaljska tiskara, 1906. Also 1910.

Marković, Franjo. *Hrvatska čitanka za IV razred gimnazije*. Zagreb: Kr. hrv. slav. dalm. zemaljska vlada, 1874. Also 1880.

Marković, Franjo, and Mirko Divković. *Dr. Franje Markovića Hrvatska čitanka za IV razred gimnazije*. Zagreb: Kr. hrv. slav. dalm. zemaljska vlada, 1891. Also 1897, 1901, 1911.

Mažuranić, Antun, Matija Mesić, and Adolfo Veber-Tkalčević. *Čitanka za I i II razred*. Vienna, 1869.

———. *Čitanka za III i IV razred*. Vienna, 1857.

———. *Ilirska čitanka*. Zagreb: Tiskarnica Ljudevita Gaja, 1856.

Pechan, Antun. *Povjest hrvatske književnosti za učiteljske pripravnike*. Zagreb: L. Hartman, 1910. 5th ed.

Petračić, Franjo. *Hrvatska čitanka za više gimnazije i nalike jim škole: Historija literature u primjerah*. Zagreb: Kr. hrv. slav. dalm. zemaljska vlada, 1880. Vol. 2.

———. *Hrvatska čitanka za više gimnazije i nalike jim škole: Uputa u poetiku i stilistiku*. Zagreb: Kr. hrv. slav. dalm. zemaljska vlada, 1877. Vol. 1.

Petračić, Franjo, and Hugo Badalić. *Fr. Petračića Hrvatska čitanka za više razrede srednjih učilista - poetika i stilistika*. Zagreb: Kr. hrv. slav. dalm. zemaljska vlada, 1888. Vol. 1. Also 1895, 1899.

Petračić, Franjo, and Ferdo Miler. *Hrvatska čitanka za više razrede srednjih učilista - povijest književnosti u premjerama*. Zagreb: Kr. hrv. slav. dalm. zemaljska vlada, 1895. Vol. 2. Also 1898, 1908.

Petračić, Franjo, and Djuro Zagoda. *Fr. Petračića čitanka za više razrede srednjih učilišta - poetika i stilistika*. Zagreb: Kr. hrv. slav. dalm. zemaljska vlada, 1904. Vol. 1. Also 1914.

Početnica za obće pučke škole. Zagreb: Kr. hrv. slav. dalm. zemaljska vlada, 1874. Also 1881, 1882, 1885, 1889, 1892, 1893, 1894, 1899, 1900, 1901, 1903, 1905, 1906, 1909, 1911, 1914, 1916, 1917.

Početnica za pučke škole u Hrvatskoj i Slavoniji. Zagreb: Kr. hrv. slav. dalm. zemaljska vlada, 1892. Also 1893, 1894, 1899, 1900, 1901, 1903, 1905, 1906, 1909, 1911, 1914.

Prva slovnička čitanka za pučke učione. Vienna: Kraljevska naklada školskih knjigah, 1875.

Šarić, Ivan. *Hrvatska čitanka za drugi razred srednjih škola.* Zagreb: Kr. hrv. slav. dalm. zemaljska vlada, 1906. Also 1910, 1916.

Slovnica i pismovnik za obćenite pučke učionice. Vienna: Kraljevska naklad učioničkih knjiga, 1891.

Smičiklas, Tade. *Čitanka za I razred gimnazije.* Zagreb: Kr. hrv. slav. dalm. zemaljska vlada, 1875. Also 1887.

———. *Hrvatska čitanka za III razred gimnazije.* Zagreb: Kr. hrv. slav. dalm. zemaljska vlada, 1880.

Šurmin, Djuro, and Stjepan Bosanac. *Čitanka iz književnih starina staroslovenskih hrvatskih i srpskih za VII i VIII razred srednjih škola.* Zagreb: Kr. hrv. slav. dalm. zemaljska vlada, 1896. Also 1901, 1905, 1908.

Zoričić, Petar. *Čitanka za pučke učionice u Hervatskoj i Slavoniji.* Zagreb: Franjo Suppan, 1850.

Slovenian

Berilo za tretji razred. Vienna: V. c. kr. zalogi šolskih knjig, 1879.

Bežek, V. *Zemljepis za spodnje in srednje razrede srednjih šol. Opis dežel razen Avstro-Ogrske.* Ljubljana: Ig. pl. Kleinmayr & Fed. Bamberg, 1899, pt. 2, 2nd ed.

Drugo berilo in slovnica za občne ljudske šole. Vienna: V cesarski kraljevski zalogi školskih knjig, 1895.

Drugo berilo in slovnica za obče ljudske šole. Vienna: V cesarski kraljevi zalogi šolskih knjig, 1911.

Janežič, Anton. *Cvetnik slovenske slovesnosti - Berilo za više gimnazije in realke.* Celovec: J. Blažnik, 1868. 2nd completely rev. ed.

Jesenko, Janez. *Občni zemljepis.* Ljubljana: Narodna tiskarna, 1873.

———. *Avstrijsko-ogerska monarhija - Domovinoznanstvo za četrti razred srednjih šol.* Ljubljana: Narodna tiskarna, 1885.

Josin, M., and E. Gangl. *Tretje berilo za štirirazredne in večrazredne občne ljudske šole.* Ljubljana: Ig. pl. Kleinmayr & Fed. Bamberg, 1902.

Končnik, Peter. *Četrto berilo za ljudske in nadaljevalne šole.* Vienna: V. c. k. zalogi šolskih knjig, 1883.

Lapajne, Ivan. *Koncenov zemljepis za ljudske šole.* Vienna: Edvard Hölzel, 1879. 2nd rev. ed.

Mayer, Franz Martin. *Lehrbuch der Allgemeinen Geschichte für die oberen Klassen der Realschulen: Die Neuzeit seit dem Ende des Dreizigjährigen Krieges.* Vienna: F. Tempsky, 1906. 3rd ed. Part 3.

Miklošič, Franc. *Slovensko berilo za osmi gimnazijalni razred.* Vienna: V zalogi C. K. bukev za šole, 1865.

———. *Slovensko berilo za 8 gimnazijski razred.*Vienna: V zalogi C. K. bukev za šole, 1881. 2nd rev. ed. by I. Navratil.

———. *Slovensko berilo za peti gimnazijalni razred.* Vienna: V zalogi C. K. bukev za šole, 1853.

Orožen, Fr. *Zemljepis za meščanske šole.* Prva stopnja. Ljubljana: Zadružna tiskarna, 1904.

———. *Zemljepis za meščanske šole.* Druga stopnja. Ljubljana: Zadružna tiskarna, 1903. 2nd ed.

———. *Zemljepis za meščanske šole.* Tretja stopnja. Ljubljana: Zadružna tiskarna, 1905. 2nd ed.

Schreiner, Henrik. *Čitanka za obče ljudske šole - Za šesto, sedmo in osmo šolsko leto štiri - in večrazrednih ljudskih šol.* Vienna: V cesarski kraljevi zalogi šolskih knjig, 1911. Vol. 4.

Schreiner, Henrik, and Fr. Hubad. *Čitanka za obče ljudske šole - za četrto in peto šolsko leto štiri - in večrazrednih ljudskih šol.* Vienna: V cesarski kraljevi zalogi šolskih knjig, 1904. Vol. 3.

———. *Čitanka za obče ljudske šole - za drugo in tretje šolsko leto štiri in večrazrednih ljudskih šol.* Vienna: V cesarski kraljevi zalogi šolskih knjig, 1902. Vol. 2.

Sket, Jakob. *Slovenska čitanka za tretji razred srednjih šol.* Celovec: Družba sv. Mohorija, 1906. Vol. 3. 2nd ed.

———. *Slovenska slovstvena čitanka za sedmi in osmi razred srednjih šol.* Vienna: V zalogi šolskih knjig, 1914. 3rd ed.

Sket, Jakob, and Josip Wester. *Slovenska čitanka za četrti razred srednjih šol.* Celovec: Družba sv. Mohorija, 1893. Vol. 4. 2nd revised ed.

———. *Slovenska čitanka za četrti razred srednjih šol.* Celovec: Družba sv. Mohorija, 1912. Vol. 4. 2nd revised ed.

———. *Slovenska čitanka za prvi razred dekliskega liceja.* Celovec: Družba sv. Mohorija, 1910. Vol. 1.

Tretje berilo za občne ljudske šole. Vienna: V. cesarski kraljevi zalogi šolskih knjig, 1891. Also 1892, 1896, 1902, 1907, 1914.

Zeehe, Andreas, and Wilh. Schmidt. *Österreichische Vaterlandskunde für die VIII Gymnasialclasse.* Laibach: Ig. v. Kleinmayr & Fed. Bamberg, 1901.

Montenegrin

Kovačević, Milo, and Lazar Perović. *Istorija srpskog naroda za treći i četvrti razred osnovnijeh škola.* Cetinje: Državna štamparija, 1898.

Popović, Djuro. *Čitanka za četvrti razred osnovnijeh škola.* Cetinje: Državna štamparija, 1904. 2nd ed.

———. *Čitanka za drugi razred osnovnijeh škola.* Cetinje: Državna štamparija, 1907. 4th ed.

———. *Čitanka za prvi razred osnovnijeh škola.* Cetinje: Državna štamparija, 1907. 6th ed.

———. *Čitanka za treći razred osnovnijeh škola.* Cetinje: Državna štamparija, 1907.

———. *Čitanka za III razred osnovnijeh škola.* Cetinje: Državna štamparija, 1912. 5th ed.

———. *Srpski bukvar.* Cetinje: Državna štamparija, 1907. 6th ed.

———. *Srpski bukvar.* Cetinje: Državna štamparija, 1913. 10th ed.

Popović, Djuro, and Jovan Roganović. *Zemljopis Knjaževine Crne Gore za učenike III razreda osnovne škole.* Cetinje: Državna štamparija, 1896. 2nd rev. ed. Also 1899.

Austrian, Hungarian, and Bosnian-Hercegovinian

Atanacković, Platon. *Druga knjiga o ezikosloviu i čitaniu za srpska narodna učilista u Austrijskom carstvu.* Vienna: C. kr. direkcie učilištnih knjiga, 1856.

Bač-Bodroška županija. *Zemljopis za bunjevsku i šokačku mladež.* Subotica: Dušan Petrović, 1894.

———. *Zemljopis za III razred srp. nar. škola u Bačbodroškoj županiji kao i za domaću potrebu.* Sombor: F. Biterman, 1883. Also 1900, 6th rev. ed.

Blagojević, Jov. *Opšti zemljopis za najstarije razrede osnovnih i niže razrede viših djevojačkih škola - po najnovijim izvorima.* Sombor: Milivoj Karakašević, 1878.

———. *Opšti zemljopis za najstarije razrede osnovnih škola kao i za opetovne i više djevojačke škole sa osobitim obzirom na Austro-Ugarsku monarhiju - po najnovijim izborima.* Sombor: Milivoj Karakašević, 1885. 2nd rev. and enlarged ed. And 1889, 3rd rev. ed.

Četvrta čitanka za osnovne škole u Bosni i Hercegovini s gramatičkim dodatkom. Sarajevo: Zemaljska vlada za Bosnu i Hercegovinu, 1887.

Četvrta čitanka za osnovne škole u Bosni i Hercegovini s gramatičkim dodatkom. Sarajevo: Izd. zemaljske vlade za Bosnu i Hercegovinu, 1912. 10th ed.

Čitanka za četvrti razred katoličkih glavnih i varoških učionah u Austrijskoj carevini. Vienna: Kraljevska prodavaonica školskih knjiga, 1861. Also 1867.

Čitanka za četvrti razred pučkih škola. Vienna, 1880. Also 1891, 1893, 1894.

Čitanka za četvrti razred srpske osnovne škole. Novi Sad: Milan Ivković, 1909.

Čitanka za četvrti razred srspke osnovne škole. Novi Sad: A. Pajević, 1892. Also 1909.

Čitanka za četvrti razred srpskih glavnih učilišta u Austrijskom carstvu.
Vienna: C. kr. direckie učilistnih knjiga, 1861.

Čitanka za II razred srpske osnovne škole. Novi Sad: A. Pajević, 1887. Also
1893, 1900.

Čitanka za drugi razred srpskih narodnih učilišta u Austrijskom carstvu.
Vienna: C. k. administracie učilistnih knjiga, 1855.

Čitanka za treći razred srpske narodne škole. Novi Sad: A. Pajević, 1882.
Also 1889, 1893, 1909.

Čitanka za treći razred srpske osnovne škole. Novi Sad: Milan Ivković,
1909.

Ćonić, Pavle, and Slavko M. Kosić. *Mala srpska čitanka (latinicom) za III
razred srpskih osnovnih škola.* Mostar: Paher & Kisić, 1908. Also 1910.

———. *Mala srpska čitanka (latinicom) za IV razred srpskih osnovnih
škola.* Mostar: Paher & Kisić, 1908. Also 1911.

———. *Srpska čitanka za I razred srpskih osnovnih škola.* Mostar: Paher &
Kisić, 1911. 2nd ed.

Čuturilo, Stevo. *Bukvar za crnogorske škole.* Pančevo: Braće Jovanovića,
1879.

———. *Druga čitanka za II razred osnovnijeh škola.* Pančevo: Braće Jovanovića, 1887.

———. *Prva bukvarska čitanka: Mješovita gradja za vježbanje u očigled-
noj nastavi, u govorenju, čitanju i pisanju - za drugo polugodište I
razreda.* Pančevo: Braće Jovanovića, 1880. Also 1887, 1923.

Djisanović, Veselin. *Srpska čitanka za V i VI razred osnovnih škola i za I i
II razred više djevojačke škole.* Sremski Karlovci: Srpska monastirska
štamparija, 1917.

*Druga čitanka za osnovne škole u Bosni i Hercegovini s gramatičkim
dodatkom.* Sarajevo: Nakladom zemaljske vlade za Bosnu i Hercegovinu, 1887. Also 1888, 1897, 1898, 1908, 1909.

*Druga čitanka za pučke škole u Bosni i Hercegovini sa slovnikim dodat-
kom.* Sarajevo: Zemaljska štamparija, 1884.

Druga slovnička čitanka sa zemljovidom Austro-Ugarske države. Vienna:
U c. k. nakladi školskih knjigah, 1879.

Druga slovnička čitanka za katoličke pučke učione u Austrijskoj carevini.
Vienna, 1863. Also 1868, 1869, 1873, 1874.

*Druga slovnika čitanke za katoličke pučke učione u Austrijskoj carevini sa
zemljovidom Austro-Ugarske države.* Vienna, 1875. Also 1877, 1879,
1887.

Druga stanka za katoličanske hrvatske škole ugarskoga kraljevstva. Gyur:
Andor Zechmeister, 1902. 5th rev. ed. Also 1905.

Franković, Franjo. *Hrvatska početnica za opće pučke škole.* Vienna: U carskoj kraljevskoj nakladi školskih knjiga, 1911.

Franković, Franjo Z. *Kratka zemljopisna početnica s dodatkom o Bosni za nižje učione.* Sarajevo: Vilajetska štamparija, 1869.

Gramatika bosanskoga jezika za srednje škole. Sarajevo: Zemljska vlada za Bosnu i Hercegovinu, 1903. 3rd ed.

Grčić, Jovan. *Istorija srpske književnosti - Prema nastavnom planu za srednje škole.* Novi Sad: Braća M. Popovića, 1903. And 1908.

Hadrović, Stjepan. *Zemljopis Bosne i Hercegovine.* Sarajevo: Bosanska pošta, 1902.

Hrvatska početnica za pučke učione. Vienna: U ces. kralj. nakladi školskih knjigah, 1884.

Ilirska čitanka za gornije gimnazije - sadržajuća izgled iz novije literature. Vienna: U. c. k. nakladi školskih knjigah, 1860. Vol. 2.

Kaludjerčić, Stevo. *Istorija srpskog naroda za III i IV razred srpskih osnovnih škola u Bosni i Hercegovini.* Mostar: Paher & Kisić, 1909. 2nd ed.

Kašiković, Nikola T., and Vojislav Borić. *Bukvar i prva čitanka za srpske osnovne škole u Bosni i Hercegovini.* Mostar: Paher & Kisić, 1908.

———. *Bukvar i prva čitanka za srpske osnovne škole u Bosni i Hercegovini.* Mostar: Trifko Dudić, 1913. 4th ed.

Kličin, Mita St. *Čitanka za II razred srpskih osnovnih škola u Bosni i Hercegovini.* Sarajevo: 1903. 2nd ed.

———. *Čitanka za drugi razred srpskih osnovnih škola u Bosni i Hercegovini.* Zombor: Milivoj Karakašević, 1911. 5th ed.

———. *Latinica za srpske narodne osnovne škole.* Sombor: Ferdinand Biterman, 1905. Also 1913.

———. *Latinica za treći razred srpskih narodnih škola u Bosni, Hercegovini i Crnoj Gori.* Sombor: Mil. Karakašević, 1907.

———. *Srpska čitanka za drugi razred srpskih pravoslavnih veroispovednih osnovnih narodnih škola.* Sremski Karlovci: Srpska manastirska štamparija, 1916.

Kušar, Marcel. *Čitanka za I razred srednjih škola.* Vienna: U carskoj kraljevskoj nakladi školskih knjiga, 1900.

———. *Čitanka za III razred srednjih škola.* Vienna: U carskoj kraljevskoj nakladi školskih knjiga, 1897.

———. *Čitanka za IV razred srednjih škola.* Vienna: U carskoj kraljevskoj nakladi školskih knjiga, 1895.

Miletić, Svetozar. *Nastava u zemljopisu za III i IV razred osnovnih škola.* Pančevo, 1881.

———. *Zemljopis za četvrti razred narodne škole.* Novi Sad: Luka Jočić, 1883, 2nd rev. ed.; 1890, 4th ed.; and 1894, 6th rev. ed.

———. *Zemljopis za četvrti razred narodne škole.* Sombor: Milivoj Karakašević, 1894. 6th reviewed and rev. ed.

Naković, M. *Zemljopis za hervatske narodne škole.* Budapest, 1873. 1st ed.

———. *Zemljopis za narodne škole s osobitim obzirom za zemlje Ugarske krune.* Gyur, 1880.

Nazor, Vladimir, Fr. Baf, J. Jakac, K. Pribil, R. Šarson, Dr. M. Tentor, and N. Žić. *Treća čitanka za hrvatske opće pučke škole.* Vienna: Kraljevska naklada školskih knjiga, 1913.

Nedeljković, Milan. *Opća geografija za srednja učilista.* Novi Sad: Braće M. Popovića, 1905. Also 1911, 3rd enlarged and rev. ed.

Peričić, J., V. Danilo, J. Dević, M. Zglav, and A. Kriletić. *Druga čitanka za opće pučke škole.* Vienna: U carskoj kraljevskoj nakladi školskih knjiga, 1900. Also 1908, 1917.

Peričić, J., V. Danilo, J. Dević, A. Kriletić, and M. Zglav. *Treća čitanka za občenite pučke učionice.* Vienna: Kr. naklada školskih knjiga, 1890. Also 1892, 1910, 1911.

Početnica za katoličke učionice u austrianskoj carevini. Vienna: C. k. prodaonice školskih knjigah, 1854. Also 1862.

Popović, Jov. *Zemljopis za srpske narodne škole u ugarskoj.* Pančevo: Braće Jovanovića, 1877. Also 1893, 6th rev. ed.

Popović, Stevan V. *Opšti zemljopis za srpske narodne škole u Ugarskoj.* Novi Sad: Braće M. Popovića, 1880.

Povijest Bosne i Hercegovine za osnovne škole. Sarajevo: Nakladom zemaljske vlade za Bosnu i Hercegovinu, 1893. Also 1898.

Povijest srednjega vijeka za više razrede srednjih škola u Bosni i Hercegovini. Sarajevo: Zemaljska štamparija, 1902.

Prosvjetni bukvar. Sarajevo: Srpska dioničarska štamparija, 1910.

Prva čitanka za osnovne škole u Bosni i Hercegovini. Sarajevo: Nakladom zemaljske vlade za Bosnu i Hercegovinu, 1886. Vol. 1. Also 1896, 1903, 1906.

Prva čitanka za osnovne škole u Bosni i Hercegovini. Sarajevo: Nakladom zemaljske vlade za Bosnu i Hercegovinu, 1888. Vol. 2. Also 1892, 1896, 1903, 1906, 1911, 1912, 1914.

Prva čitanka za osnovne škole u Bosni i Hercegovini. Sarajevo: Nakladom zemaljske vlade za Bosnu i Hercegovinu, 1913.

Prva čitanka za pučke škole u Bosni i Hercegovini. Sarajevo: Nakladom zemaljske vlade Bosne i Hercegovine, 1883. 2 parts.

Raca, Djordje M., and Miloš Popar. *Čitanka- latinica i pouke iz srpskog jezika za II razred srpskih osnovnih škola u Bosni i Hercegovini.* Sarajevo: Trifković, 1911.

Slike iz istorije srpske za učenike osnovnih škola u kratko izvedene. Pančevo: Braće Jovanovića, 1891.

Slovnica Hrvatska i pismovnik za pučke učione. Vienna: Kr. naklada učioničkih knjigah, 1877. Also 1879, 1883.

Slovnica Hrvatska i pismovnik za pučke učione. Vienna: Kr. naklada učioničkih knjiga, 1891.

*Slovnica za četvrti razred katoličkih glavnih učionah u carevini Austri-
janskoj.* Vienna: Kr. naklada učioničkih knjigah, 1862. Also 1867, 1868.

*Slovnička čitanka za pervi razred katoličkih učionah u carevini Austri-
janskoj.* Vienna: U. c. r. kr. nakladi školskih knjigah, 1853. Also 1855.

Srpska čitanka za četvrti razred narodne škole. Budapest: Svojina ugarske
kraljevine, 1871. Also 1908.

Srpska čitanka za drugi razred narodne škole. Budapest: Svojina ugarske
kraljevine, 1879. Also 1900.

Srpska čitanka za treći razred narodne škole. Budapest: Svojina ugarske
kraljevine, 1871. Also 1873, 1877, 1881, 1908.

Šušljić, Milan P. *Zemljopis za IV razred srpskih osnovnih škola u Bosni i
Hercegovini.* Sarajevo: Trifković, 1912.

Šušljić, Milan, and Risto Šušljić. *Zemljopis za III razred srpskih osnovnih
škola - Bosna i Hercegovina po riječnim slivovima.* Sarajevo: Trifković,
1911.

Terzin, Djura. *Zemljopis pretpojmovi i opis torontalske županije za III raz.
srp. nar. škola.* Novi Sad: Djordje Ivković, 1903. Also 1905, 3rd rev. ed.

———. *Zemljopis za srpske pravoslavne veroispovedeine osnovne škole.*
Nadjkikinda: Jovan Radak, 1913. 4th rev. ed.

Torontolska županja. *Zemljopis za III razred srpskih nar. škola.* Sombor:
Ferdinand Biterman, 1889. 3rd ed. And 1894, 5th rev. ed.

*Treća čitanka za osnovne škole u Bosni i Hercegovini s gramatičkim do-
datkom.* Sarajevo: Nakladom zemaljske vlade za Bosnu i Hercegovinu -
zemaljska štamparija, 1886. Also 1896, 1898, 1912, and 1914.

Vukičević, Nikola Dj. *Ogledalo hristianske dobrodietel'i - Žitiia svetih'.*
Vienna: Kr. direkcie učitelistnih knjiga, 1863.

———. *Otačastbenica i opšti zemljopis za srpsku decu sa osobitom obzirom na zemlje u kojima naš narod živi - po najnovijim i najboljim
izvorima.* Pančevo: Braće Jovanovića, 1873. Also 1874, 2nd ed.

Zemljopis za Bunjevačku i Šokačku mladež. Subotica, 1894.

Zemljopis za IV razred osnovnih škola u Bosni i Hercegovini. Sarajevo:
Nakladom zemaljske vlade za Bosnu i Hercegovinu, 1885. Also 1886
and 1905.

*Zemljopis za srpske narodne škole u Ugarskoj sa obzirom na najnovije
zaokruženje županija u Ugarskoj - po najnovijm Madjarskim izborima
izradjen.* Pančevo: Braće Jovanovića, 1878. Also 1881, 2nd rev. ed.; 1892,
4th rev. and enlarged ed.

Zemljopis za srpske narodne škole u ugarskoj. Pančevo: Braće Jovanovića,
1892. 4th rev. and enlarged ed.

Zemljopis za III razred osnovnih škola u Bosni i Hercegovini. Sarajevo: Nak. zemaljske vlade za Bosnu i Hercegovinu, 1885.

Zemljopis za III i IV razred srpskih narodnih škola po najnovijim i najbojim izvorima u kratko izveden. Pančevo: Braće Jovanovića, 1875.

Zemljopis za III razred osnovnih škola u Bosni i Hercegovini. Sarajevo: 1893. 2nd rev. ed. Also 1898 and 1901.

Zemljopis za III i IV razred srpskih narodnih škola - po najnovijim i najboljim izvorima. Pančevo: Braće Jovanovića, 1875.

Zglav, Miho. *Slovnica i pismovnik hrvatskog ili srpskog jezika za opće pučke škole.* Vienna: U carskoj kraljevskoj nakladi školskih knjiga, 1916.

Živanović, Jovan. *Srpska čitanka za niže gimnazije.* Pančevo: Braće Jovanovića, 1884.

———. *Srpska čitanka za donje gimnazije.* Pančevo: Braće Jovanovića, 1892. Vol. 1, 2nd rev. ed.

Živković, Grigorije (Nikola). *Istorija hriščanske crkve za školsku mladež.* Tuzla: Nikola Pisenberger, 1897. 3rd enlarged and rev. ed.

BOOKS

Aleksić, Ljiljana, Danica Milić, and Vladimir Stojančević, eds. *Srbija u završnoj fazi velike istočne krize (1877–1878).* Belgrade: Prosveta, 1980.

Bakotić, Lujo. *Srbi u Dalmaciji od pada mletačke republike do ujedinjenja.* Belgrade: Geca Kon, 1939.

Banac, Ivo. *The National Question in Yugoslavia: Origins, History, Politics.* Ithaca, N.Y.: Cornell University Press, 1984.

Barac, Antun. *A History of Yugoslav Literature.* Ann Arbor: University of Michigan Publications, 1973.

———. *Hrvatska književnost od preporoda do stvaranja Jugoslavije.* Zagreb: Jugoslavenska akademija znanosti i umjetnosti, 1954. 2 vols.

Behschnitt, Wolf Dietrich. *Nationalismus bei Serben und Kroaten 1830–1914. Analyse und Typologie der nationalen Ideologie.* Munich: R. Oldenbourg, 1980.

Belić, A. *Vukova borba za narodni i književni jezik - rasprave i predavanja.* Belgrade: Prosveta, 1948.

Besarović, Risto. *Iz kulturne i političke istorije Bosne i Hercegovine.* Sarajevo: Svjetlost, 1966.

Bičanić, Rudolf. *Doba manufakture i Hrvatskoj i Slavoniji 1750–1860.* Zagreb: Jugoslavenska akademija znanosti i umjetnosti, 1951.

Bogdanov, Vaso. *Društvene i političke borbe u Hrvatskoj 1848/49.* Zagreb: Jugoslavenska akademija znanosti i umjetnosti, 1949.

———. *Historija političkih stranaka u hrvatskoj*. Zagreb: Novinarsko izdavačko poduzeće, 1958.

———. *Starčević i stranka prava prema Srbima i prema jedinstvu južnoslavenskih naroda*. Zagreb: Školska knjiga, 1951.

Bošković-Stulli, Maja. *Usmena književnost kao umjetnost riječi*. Zagreb: Mladost, 1975.

Budisavljević, Srdjan. *Stvaranje države Srba, Hrvata i Slovenaca*. Zagreb: Jugoslavenska akademija znanosti u umjetnosti, 1958.

Buturac, Josip. *100 godina hrvatskog književnog društva 1868–1968*. Zagreb: Hrvatsko književno društvo Sv. Ćirila i Metoda, 1969.

Ćerić, Salim. *Muslimani srpskohrvatskog jezika*. Sarajevo: Svjetlost, 1968.

Čingrija, Melko. *Dubrovnik i hrvatsko pitanje*. Dubrovnik: Jugoslaveni Dubrovnika, 1939.

Ćorovic, Vladimir. *Bosna i Hercegovina*. Belgrade: Srpska književna zadruga, 1925.

Čubrilović, Vaso. *Istorija političke misli u Srbiji XIX veka*. Belgrade: Prosveta, 1958.

———. *Odabrani istorijski radovi*. Belgrade: Narodna knjiga, 1983.

Čubrilović, Vaso, ed. *Velike sile i Srbija pred prvi svetski rat*. Belgrade: Srpska akademija nauka i umetnosti, 1976. Naučni skupovi, IV. Odeljenjc istorijskih nauka, I.

Čulinović, Ferdo. *Državnopravna historija Jugoslavenskih zemalja XIX i XX vijeka*. Zagreb: Školska knjiga, 1959. 2 vols.

———. *Nacionalno pitanje u jugoslavenskim zemljama*. Zagreb: Institut za historiju države i prava, 1955.

Ćunković, Srećko. *Školstvo i prosveta u Srbiji u XIX veku*. Belgrade: Pedagoški muzej, 1971.

Cuvaj, Antun. *Gradja za povijest školstva Kraljevina Hrvatske i Slavonije od najstarijih vremena do danas*. Zagreb: Kr. hrv. slav. dalm. zemaljska vlada, 1910–11. 11 vols. 2nd rev. enlarged ed.

Cvijićeva knjiga. Belgrade: Srpska književna zadruga, 1927. Series 30, no. 201.

Dedijer, Vladimir. *The Road to Sarajevo*. New York: Simon & Schuster, 1966.

Dedijer, Vladimir, Ivan Božić, Sima Ćirković, and Milorad Ekmečić. *History of Yugoslavia*. New York: McGraw-Hill, 1974.

Despalatović, Elinor Murray. *Ljudevit Gaj and the Illyrian Movement*. Boulder, Colo.: East European Quarterly, 1975.

Deželić, Gj. *Hrvatska narodnosti ili duša hrvatskoga naroda*. Zagreb: Lav Hartman, 1879.

Djordjević, Dimitrije. *Carinski rat Austro-Ugarske i Srbije 1906–1911*. Belgrade: Istorijski institut, 1962.

————. *Revolutions nationales des peuples balkanique 1804–1914.* Belgrade: Istorijski institut, 1965.

Djordjević, Dimitrije, ed. *The Creation of Yugoslavia 1914–1918.* Santa Barbara, Calif.: Clio Books, 1980.

Djordjević, Milan P. *Srbija i Jugoslaveni za vreme rata 1914–1918.* Belgrade: Sveslovenska knjižara, 1922.

Djordjević, Živojin. *Istorija vaspitanja u Srba - Udžbenik nacionalne istorije pedagogike.* Belgrade, 1958.

Djurić, Vojislav, ed. *Knjiga Djure Daničića.* Belgrade: Srpska književna zadruga, 1976. Series 64, vol. 460.

Doklestić, Ljubiša. *Makedonite vo Srbija i nivoto učestvo vo nejziniot stopanski i opštestven život vo XIX vek.* Skopje: Nova Makedonija, 1969.

————. *Srpsko-makedonskite odnosi vo XIX-ot vek do 1897 godina.* Skopje: Nova Makedonija, 1973.

Draganović, K., and J. Buturac. *Poviest crkve u Hrvatskoj. Pregled od najstarijih vremena do danas.* Zagreb: Hrvatsko književno društvo sv. Jeronima, 1944.

Dragnich, Alex N. *The First Yugoslavia—Search for a Viable Political System.* Stanford, Calif.: Hoover Institution Press, 1983.

————. *Serbia, Nikola Pašić, and Yugoslavia.* New Brunswick, N.J.: Rutgers University Press, 1974.

Dubrovčani su Srbi. Dubrovnik: Srpska Dubrovačka štamparija A. Pasarića, 1903.

Ekmečić, Milorad. *Ratni ciljevi Srbije 1914.* Belgrade: Srpska književna zadruga, 1973.

Enciklopedija Jugoslavije. Zagreb: Jugoslavenski leksikografski zavod, 1955–71, 8 vols.

Erjavec, Fran. *Slovenci i Srbi - Kulturno i političko istorijska studija.* Windsor, Canada: Glas kanadskih Srba, 1953. Vol. 1.

Filipović, Mil. S. *Sabrana dela Vuka Karadžića - Ethnografski spici.* Belgrade: Prosveta, 1965. Vol. 17.

Foretić, Dinko, ed. *Dalmacija 1870.* Zadar: Matica hrvatska, 1972.

Franković, Dragutin, ed. *Povijest školstva i pedagogije u Hrvatskoj.* Zagreb: Pedagoško-književni zbor, 1958.

Franković, Dragutin, Mihajlo Ogrizović, and Dragutin Pazman. *Sto godina rada hrvatskoga pedagoško-književnog zbora i učiteljstva u Hrvatskoj 1871–1971.* Zagreb: Pedagoško-književni zbor, 1971.

Gaj, Ljudevit. *Kratka osnova horvatsko-slavenskoga pravopisana, poleg mudrolubneh, narodneh i prigospodarneh temelov i zrokov.* Budapest: Iz tiskarnice kralevskoga vseučilisca, 1830. Reprinted by Liber, 1983.

Gestrin, Ferdo, and Vasilij Melik. *Slovenska zgodovina od konca osemnaj-stega stoletja do 1918.* Ljubljana: Državna založba Slovenije, 1966.

Grafenauer, Bogo, Dušan Perović, and Jaroslav Šidak, eds. *Historija naroda Jugoslavije.* Zagreb: Školska knjiga, 1953–54. Vols. 1–2.

Gravier, Gaston. *Les frontières historiques de la serbie.* Paris: Armand Colin, 1919.

Gross, Mirjana. *Počeci moderne hrvatske. Neoapsolutizam u civilnoj hrvatskoj i slavoniji 1850–1860.* Zagreb: Globus, 1985.

————. *Povijest pravaške ideologije.* Zagreb: Institut za hrvatsku povijest, 1973.

————. *Vladavina hrvatsko-srpske koalicije 1906–1907.* Belgrade: Institut društvenih nauka, 1960.

Gross, Mirjana, ed. *Društveni razvoj u Hrvatskoj.* Zagreb: Liber, 1981.

Horvat, Josip. *Ante Starčević. Kulturno-povjesna slika.* Zagreb: Tipografija, 1940.

————. *Frano Supilo.* Belgrade: Nolit, 1961.

————. *Ljudevit Gaj.* Belgrade: Nolit, 1960.

————. *Povijest novinstva hrvatske 1771–1939.* Zagreb: Stvarnost, 1962.

————. *Supilo - Život jednoga hrvatskoga političara.* Zagreb: Tipografija, 1938.

Hrvatska seljačka sloga. Stranka prava i njezini protivnici. Zagreb: Prava hrvatska radnička tiskara, 1910.

Ibler, Janko. *Hrvatska politika 1903–1906.* Zagreb: Kraljevska zemaljska tiskara, 1914 and 1917. 2 vols.

Ivić, Aleksa. *O srpskom i hrvatskom imenu.* Belgrade: S. B. Cvijanović, 1922.

————. *Seoba Srba u Hrvatsku i Slavoniju - Prilog ispitivanju srpske proš-losti tokom 16 i 17 veka.* Sremski Karlovci: Srpska manastirska štampa-rija, 1909.

Ivić, Pavle. *Srpski narod i njegov jezik.* Belgrade: Srpska književna zadruga, 1986. 2nd ed.

Jakšić, Grgur, and Vojislav J. Vučković. *Spoljna politika Srbije za vlade Kneza Mihaila. Prvi Balkanski zavez.* Belgrade: Istorijski institut, 1963.

Janković, Dragoslav. *Istorija države i prava Srbije XIX veka.* Belgrade: Na-učna knjiga, 1958. 3rd rev. ed.

————. *O političkim strankama u Srbiji XIX veka.* Belgrade: Prosveta, 1951.

————. *Srbija i Jugoslovensko pitanje 1914–1915 godine.* Belgrade: Institut za savremenu istoriju, 1973.

Jelavich, Barbara. *History of the Balkans.* Cambridge: Cambridge Univer-sity Press, 1983. 2 vols.

Jelavich, Charles. *Tsarist Russia and Balkan Nationalism: Russian Influ-*

ence in the Internal Affairs of Bulgaria and Serbia, 1879–1886. Berkeley: University of California Press, 1958.

Jelavich, Charles, and Barbara Jelavich. The Establishment of the Balkan National States, 1804–1920. Seattle: University of Washington Press, 1977.

Jonke, Ljudevit. Hrvatski književni jezik danas. Zagreb: Školska knjiga, 1971.

———. Hrvatski književni jezik 19 i 20 stoljeća. Zagreb: Matica Hrvatska, 1971.

Jovanović, Jovan M. Južna Srbija od kraja XVIII veka do oslobodjenja. Belgrade: Geca Kon, 1941.

Jovanović, Slobodan. Druga vlada Miloša i Mihaila. Belgrade: Geca Kon, 1933.

———. Jedan prilog za proučavanje srpskog nacionalnog karaktera. Windsor, Canada: Avala, 1964.

———. Moji savremenici. Windsor, Canada: Avala, 1961–62. 6 booklets.

———. Političke i pravne rasprave. Belgrade: Geca Kon, 1932.

———. Vlada Aleksandra Obrenovića. Belgrade: Geca Kon, 1934. 3 vols.

———. Vlada Milan Obrenovića. Belgrade: Geca Kon, 1934. 3 vols.

Jugoslavenki odbor u Londonu. Zagreb: Jugoslavenska akademija znanosti i umjetnosti, 1966.

Južbasić, Dževad. Jezičko pitanje u austro-ugarskoj politici u Bosni i Hercegovini pred prvi svjetski rat. Sarajevo: Svjetlost, 1973.

Kapidžić, Hamdija. Naučne ustanove u Bosni i Hercegovini za vrijeme austrougarske uprave. Sarajevo: Arhiv Bosne i Hercegovine, 1973.

Karadžić, Vuk Stefanović [V. S. K.]. Kovčežić za istoriju, jezik i običaje - Srba sva tri zakona. Vienna: U štamparija jeremenskog manastira, 1849.

———. Sabrana dela. Belgrade: Beografski grafički zavod, 1965–1974. 36 vols.

Karaman, Igor. Privreda i društvo hrvatske u 19 stoljeću. Zagreb: Školska knjiga, 1972.

Kardelj, Edvard (Sperans). Razvoj slovenačkog nacionalnog pitanja. Belgrade: Kultura, 1958.

Kessler, Wolfgang. Politik, Kultur und Gesellschaft in Kroatien und Slawonien in der ersten Hälfte des 19 Jahrhunderts. Historiographie und Grundlagen. Munich: R. Oldenbourg, 1981.

Klaić, Vjekoslav. Hrvati i Hrvatska - Ime Hrvat u historiji slavenskih naroda. Mainz: Liber, 1978.

Koneski, Blaže. Kon makedonskata prerodba - Makedonskite učebnici od 19 vek. Skopje: Institut za nacionalna istorija, 1959. 2nd ed.

Kos, Milko. *Istorija slovenaca od doseljenja do petnaestog veka*. Belgrade: Prosveta, 1960.

Kostić, Lazo M. *Istina o hrvatskoj tisućletnoj državnosti - istorijsko-politička studija*. Chicago: American Institute for Balkan Affairs, 1967.

―――. *Katolički Srbi - političko-istoriska rasprava*. Toronto: Sveti Sava, 1963.

―――. *Šta su Srbi mislili o Bosni. Političko-istorijska studija*. Toronto: Pisčevo, 1965.

―――. *Verski odnosi Bosne i Hercegovine - Demografska-istorijska studija*. Munich: Pisčevo, 1965.

Kovačević, Ljub. *Srbi u Hrvatskoj i veleizdajnička parnica 1909*. Belgrade: Davidović, 1909.

Krestić, Vasilije Dj. *Srpsko-hrvatski odnosi i jugoslovenska ideja*. Belgrade: Narodna knjiga, 1983.

Krizman, Bogdan, and Bogumil Hrabak, eds. *Zapisnici sa sednica delegacije kraljevine SHS na mirovnoj konferenciji u Parizu 1919–1920*. Belgrade: Institut društveni nauka, 1960.

Krneta, Ljubomir et al., eds. *Istorija škola i obrazovanja kod Srba*. Belgrade: Istorijski muzej Srbije, 1974.

Krokar, James P. "Liberal Reform in Croatia, 1872–1875: The Beginnings of Modern Croatia under Ban Ivan Mažuranić." Ph.D. diss., Indiana University, 1980.

Kuntic, Ljerka. *Kvaternik i njegovo doba (1825–1871)*. Zagreb: Znanje, 1971.

Kuster, Franja. *Glavni demografski podatci o Kraljevini Srbiji*. Belgrade: Državna štamparija, 1928.

Kvaternik, Eugen. *Politički spisi rasprave, govori, clanci, memorandumi, pisma*. Zagreb: Znanje, 1971. Ed. by Ljerka Kuntić.

Lakatoš, Josip. *Narodna statistika*. Osijek: Radoslav Bačić, 1914. 2nd ed.

Lederer, Ivo J. *Yugoslavia at the Paris Peace Conference—A Study in Frontiermaking*. New Haven: Yale University Press, 1963.

Leshchilovskaia, I. I. *Illirizm - k istorii horvatskogo natsional'nogo vozrozhdeniia*. Moscow: Nauka, 1968.

Macartney, C. A. *Hungary and Her Successors: The Treaty of Trianon and Its Consequences, 1919–1937*. London: Oxford University Press, 1937.

McClellan, Woodford D. *Svetozar Marković and the Origins of Balkan Socialism*. Princeton: Princeton University Press, 1964.

MacKenzie, David. *Ilija Garašanin: Balkan Bismarck*. Boulder, Colo.: East European Monographs, 1985.

Marjanović, Milan. *Londonski ugovor iz godine 1915*. Zagreb: Jugoslavenska akademija znanosti i umjetnosti, 1960.

―――. *Savremena Hrvatska*. Belgrade: Davidović, 1913.

Marković, Svetozar. *Sabrani spisi.* Belgrade: Kultura, 1960–65.

Milutinović, Kosta. *Štrosmajer i jugoslovensko pitanje.* Novi Sad: Institut za izučavanje istorije Vojvodine, 1976.

Mužić, Ivan. *Hrvatska politika i jugoslavenska ideja.* Split: Ivan Mužić, 1969.

Myl'nikov, A. S. *U istokov formirovaniia natsii v tsentral'noi i iugo-vostochnoi evrope.* Moscow: Nauka, 1984.

Nešković, Borivoje. *Istina o Solunskom procesu.* Belgrade, 1953.

Niković, Radislav. *Prosveta obrazovanje i vaspitanje u Srbiji.* Belgrade: Zavod za izdavanje udžbenika socialističke republike Srbije, 1971.

Novak, Viktor. *Antologija jugoslovenske misli i narodnog jedinstva (1390–1930).* Belgrade: Državna štamparija, 1930.

———. *Franjo Rački u govorima i raspravama.* Zagreb: Hrvatski štamparski zavod, 1925.

———. *Vuk i Hrvati.* Belgrade: Naučno Delo, 1967.

Noyes, George Rapall, trans. *The Life and Adventures of Dimitrije Obradović.* Berkeley: University of California Press, 1953.

Osterreichisches Biographisches Lexikon. Graz-Köln: Hermann Bohlaus, 1957–1986.

Palavestra, Predrag. *Književnost mlade bosne.* Sarajevo: Svjetlost, 1965. 2 vols.

Papić, Mitar. *Školstvo u Bosni i Hercegovini za vrijeme Austrougarske okupacije (1878–1918).* Sarajevo: Veselin Masleša, 1972.

———. *Stazama prosvjete i kulture.* Sarajevo: Zavod za izdavanje udžbenika, 1966.

Pavelić, Ante Smith. *Dr. Ante Trumbić - Problemi hrvatsko-srpskih odnosa.* Munich: Knjižica hrvatske revije, 1959.

Pavličević, Dragutin. *Narodni pokret 1883 u Hrvatskoj.* Zagreb: Liber, 1980.

Peco, Esad. *Osnovno školstvo u Hercegovini za vrijeme austrougarske vlasti, 1878–1918.* Sarajevo: Zavod za izdavanje udžbenika, 1971.

Pejović, Dj. D. *Razvitak prosvjete i kulture u Crnojgori 1852–1916.* Cetinje: Istorijski institut u Titogradu, 1971.

Perić, Ivan. *Suvremeni hrvatski nacionalizam - izvori i izrazi.* Zagreb: "August Cesarec," 1976.

Perić, Ivo. *Dalmatinski Sabor 1861–1912 (1918) god.* Zadar: Centar Jugoslavenske akademije znanosti i umjetnosti u Zadru, 1978.

Petković-Popović, Radmila, and Vukoman Salipurović. *Srpske škole i prosveta u zapadnim krajevima Stare Srbije i XIX veku.* Belgrade: Opštinska zajednica obrazovanje priboj, 1970.

Petrović, Rade. *Nacionalno pitanje u Dalmaciji u XIX stoljeću (Narodna stranka i nacionalno pitanje 1860–1880).* Sarajevo: Svjetlost, 1968.

Petrovich, Michael Boro. *A History of Modern Serbia, 1804–1918*. New York: Harcourt Brace Jovanovich, 1976. 2 vols.

Picchio, Ricardo, and Harvey Goldblatt, eds. *Aspects of the Slavic Language Question: Church Slavonic, South Slavic, West Slavic*. New Haven: Yale Concilium on International and Area Studies, 1984. Vol. 1.

Pleterski, Janko. *Nacije Jugoslavija Revolucija*. Belgrade: Izdavački centar Komunist, 1985.

Polić, Martin. *Parlementarna povijest Kraljevine Hrvatske, Slavonije i Dalmacije: Sa bilježkama iz političkoga, kulturnoga i društvenoga života 1860–1880*. Zagreb: Franjo Suppan, 1900. 2 vols.

Popović, Daka. *Vuk i njegovo doba. Prilog kulturnog-političkoj istoriji*. Novi Sad: Ljubomir Bogdanov, 1940.

Popović, Dimitrije. *Borba za narodno ujedinjenje 1908–1914*. Belgrade: Geca Kon, 1936.

Popović, Dušan J. *Srbi u Vojvodini*. Novi Sad: Matica Srpska, 1963. 3 vols.

Popović, Miodrag. *Vidovdan i častni krst. Ogled iz književne arheologije*. Belgrade: Slovoljubve, 1976.

Prelog, Milan. *Slavenska renesansa 1780–1848*. Zagreb: Naklada jugoslovenske štampe, 1924.

Prodanović, Jaša M. *Istorija političkih stranaka i struja u Srbiji*. Belgrade: Prosveta, 1947. Vol. 1.

Purivatra, Atif. *Nacionalni i politički razvitak muslimana*. Sarajevo: Svjetlost, 1969.

Redžić, Enver. *Prilozi o nacionalnom pitanju*. Sarajevo: Svjetlost, 1963.

Rogel, Carole. *The Slovenes and Yugoslavism, 1890–1914*. Boulder, Colo.: East European Quarterly, 1977.

Schmidt, Vlado, et al. *Osnovna šola na Slovenskem 1869–1969*. Ljubljana: Slovenski šolski muzej, 1970.

Šepić, Dragovan. *Italija, saveznici i jugoslavensko pitanje 1914–1918*. Zagreb: Školska knjiga, 1970.

———. *Supilo diplomat*. Zagreb: Naprijed, 1961.

Seton-Watson, Hugh, et al., eds. *R. W. Seton-Watson and the Yugoslavs: Correspondence, 1906–1941*. London and Zagreb: British Academy and Institute of Croatian History, 1976. 2 vols.

Seton-Watson, R. W. *The Southern Slav Question and the Habsburg Monarchy*. London: Constable, 1911.

Šidak, Jaroslav. *Kroz pet stoljeća hrvatske povijesti*. Zagreb: Školska knjiga, 1981.

———. *Studije iz hrvatske povijesti XIX stoljeća*. Zagreb: Institut za hrvatsku povijest, 1973.

———. *Studije iz hrvatske povijesti za revolucije 1848–49*. Zagreb: Institut za hrvatsku povijest, 1979.

Šidak, Jaroslav, Mirjana Gross, Igor Karaman, and Dragovan Šepić. *Povijest hrvatskog naroda g. 1860–1914*. Zagreb: Školska knjiga, 1968.

Šišić, Ferdo. *Jugoslovenska misao. Istorija ideje jugoslovenskog narodnog ujedinjenja i oslobodjenja od 1790–1918*. Belgrade: Balkanski institut, 1937.

———. *Pregled povijesti hrvatskoga naroda*. Zagreb: Matica hrvatska, 1962. Rev. by Jaroslav Šidak.

Šišić, Ferdo, ed. *Korespondencija Rački-Strossmayer*. Zagreb: Jugoslavenska akademija znanosti i umjetnosti, 1928–31. 4 vols.

Skarić, Vladislav, Osman Nuri-Hadžić, and Nikola Stojanović. *Bosna i Hercegovina pod austro-ugarskom upravom*. Belgrade: Geca Kon, 1938.

Skerlić, J. *Eseji o srpsko-hrvatskom pitanju*. Zagreb: Jugoslavensko nakladno dioničarsko društvo, 1918.

———. *Omladina i njena književnost (1848–1871) - Izučavanja o nacionalnom i književnom romantizmu kod Srba*. Belgrade: Napredak, 1925. New rev. ed. by Vladimir Ćorović.

Slijepčević, Djoko. *Srpska oslobodilačka ideja*. Munich: Iskra, 1983.

Slovenačka. Belgrade: Srpska književna zadruga, 1927. Series 30, no. 202.

Slovenski biografski leksikon. Ljubljana: Jugoslavenska tiskarna, 1925–.

Stančić, Nikša *Hrvatska nacionalna ideologija preporodnong pokreta u Dalmaciji: (Mihovil Pavlinović i njegov krug do 1869)*. Zagreb: Centar za povjestne znanosti, 1980.

Stanković, Djordje Dj. *Nikola Pašić i Jugoslavensko pitanje*. Belgrade: Beogradski izdavačko-grafički zavod, 1985. 2 vols.

———. *Nikola Pašić: Saveznici i stvaranje Jugoslavije*. Belgrade: Nolit, 1984.

Stanojević, Stanoje. *Narodna enciklopedija srpsko-hrvatsko-slovenacka*. Zagreb: Bibliografski zavod, 1925–1929. 4 vols.

Starčević, Ante. *Izabrani spisi*. Zagreb: Hrvatski izdavalički bibliografski zavod, 1943. Ed. by Blaž Jurišić.

———. *Misli i pogledi: Pojedinac-Hrvatska-Svijet*. Zagreb: Matica hrvatska, 1971. Ed. by Blaž Jurišić.

———. *Pasmina slavoserbska po Hervatskoj*. Zagreb: L. Hartman, 1876.

———. *Politički spisi*. Zagreb: Znanje, 1971. Ed. by Tomislav Ladan.

———. *Program i pravilnik Hrvatske stranke prava prihvaćen na glavnoj skupstini 22 kolovoza 1907*. Zagreb: Klub hrvatske stranke prava, 1907.

Starčevića hrvatska stranka prava. Zagreb: Hrvatska radnička tiskara, 1907.

Stojančević, Vladimir. *Miloš Obrenović i njegovo doba*. Belgrade: Prosveta, 1966.

Stokes, Gale. *Legitimacy through Liberalism: Vladimir Jovanović and the*

Transformation of Serbian Politics. Seattle: University of Washington Press, 1975.

Südland, L. V. [Ivo Pilar]. *Južnoslavensko pitanje - Prikaz cjelokupnog pitanja*. Zagreb: Matica hrvatska, 1943.

Sugar, Peter F., and Ivo J. Lederer, eds. *Nationalism in Eastern Europe*. Seattle: University of Washington Press, 1969.

Tešić, Vladeta, et al. *Sto godina prosvetnog saveta Srbije, 1880–1980*. Belgrade: Zavod za udžbenike i nastavna sredstva, 1980.

Tošić, Desimir. *Srpski nacionalni problemi - Ethnografska karta Jugoslavije*. Paris: Oslobodjenje, 1952.

Vosnjak, Bogumil. *A Bulwark against Germany*. London: George Allen & Unwin, 1917.

Vučković, Vojislav J. *Politička akcija Srbije u južnoslovenskim pokrajinama habsburške monarhije 1859–1874*. Belgrade: Naučno delo, 1965.

———. *Srpska kriza u istočnom pitanju (1842–1843)*. Belgrade: Srpska akademija nauka, 1957.

Wandruszka, Adam and Peter Urbanitsch. *Die Habsburgermonarchie 1848–1918: Die Völker des Reiches*. Vienna: Verlag der Österreichischen Akademie der Wissenschaft, 1980. Vol. 3, 2 pts.

Wilson, Duncan. *The Life and Times of Vuk Stefanović Karadžić, 1787–1864: Literacy, Literature, and National Independence in Serbia*. Oxford: Clarendon Press, 1970.

Winters, Stanley B., and Joseph Held, eds. *Intellectual and Social Developments in the Habsburg Empire from Maria Theresa to World War I*. Boulder, Colo.: East European Quarterly, 1975.

Žaček, Vaclav. *Bosna u tajnim političkim izvjestajima Františeka Zacha iz Beograda (1843–1848)*. Sarajevo: Akademjia nauka i umjetnosti Bosne i Hercegovine, 1976.

———. *František A. Zach*. Prague: Melantrich, 1977.

Živanović, Milan Ž. *Solunski proces hiljadu devetsto sedamnaeste - Prilog za proučavanje političke istorije Srbije od 1903–1918 god*. Belgrade: Srpska akademija nauka, 1955. Posebna izdanja, vol. 243.

———. *Dubrovnik u borbi za ujedinjenje 1908–1918*. Belgrade: Istoriski institut, 1962.

Živojinović, Dragan R. *America, Italy and the Birth of Yugoslavia (1917–1919)*. Boulder, Colo.: East European Quarterly, 1972.

Zwitter, Fran, Jaroslav Šidak, and Vaso Bogdanov. *Les problèmes nationaux dans la monarchie des habsbourg*. Belgrade: Comité national yougoslave des sciences historiques, 1960.

ARTICLES

Banac, Ivo. "Main Trends in the Croatian Language Question." In *Aspects of the Slavic Language Question*, ed. Riccardo Picchio and Harvey Goldblatt, pp. 189–259. New Haven: Yale Concilium on International and Area Studies, 1984.

Biber, Dušan. "Jugoslavenska ideja in slovensko narodno vprašanje v slovenski publicistiki med balkanskimi vojnami v letih 1912–1913." *Istorja XX Veka - Zbornik Radova* (Belgrade) 1 (1959): 285–326.

Bogdanov, Vaso. "Historijska uloga društvenih klasa u rješavanju južnoslovenskog nacionalnog pitanja." *Rad* (Jugoslavenska akademija znanosti i umjetnosti-JAZU) 300 (1954): 5–154.

———. "Historijski uzroci sukoba izmedju Hrvata i Srba." *Rad* 311 (1957): 353–477.

———. "Hrvatski narodni pokret 1903/4." *Rad* 321: 225–478.

"Bosna i Hercegovina u Hrvatskoj pripovjeci." *Ljetopis matice srpske* 208 (1901): 110–20.

"Ćirilica u našoj pučkoj školi." *Hrvatski učitelj* 3 (1879): 145–47.

D. J. "Pobornici i protivnici ćirilice." *Hrvatski učitelj* 3 (1879): 177–81.

Djakić, Vojislav. "Nacionalno vaspitanje." *Nastavnik* 1 (1890): 117–29.

E-nne. "Nekoliko reči o nastavi iz srpske istorije u osnovnoj školi." *Učitelj* 22 (1902–03): 782–88.

F. R. "Ćirilica u hrvatskoj pučkoj školi." *Hrvatski učitelj* 3 (1879): 81–85.

Fleišer, Vjekoslav. "Dr. Ante Starčević. *Bog i Hrvati* (1897): 65–72.

Goldinger, Walter. "The Nationality Question in Austrian Education." *Austrian History Yearbook* 3, no. 2 (1967): 136–56.

Gostiša, I. "Hrvatska literarna historija u srednjim učilistima." *Nastavni vjesnik* 1 (1893): 197–207.

Gross, Mirjana. "Croatian National-Integrational Ideologies from the End of Illyrism to the Creation of Yugoslavia." *Austrian History Yearbook* 15–16 (1979–80): 3–33.

———. "Hrvatska politika u Bosni i Hercegovini od 1878 do 1914." *Historijski zbornik* 19–20 (1966–67): 9–68.

———. "Nacionalne ideje studentske omladine u Hrvatskoj uoči svjetskog rata." *Historijski zbornik* 21–22 (1968–69): 75–143.

———. "O ideološkom sustavu Franje Račkoga." *Zbornik zavoda za povijesne znanosti JAZU* 9 (1979): 5–33.

———. "Social Structure and National Movements among the Yugoslav Peoples on the Eve of the First World War." *Slavic Review* 36, no. 4 (1977): 628–43.

———. "Zur Frage der jugoslawischen Ideologie bei den Kroaten." In *Die Donaumonarchie und die südslawische Frage von 1848 bis 1918*, ed. by

Adam Wandruszka, Richard G. Plaschka, and Anna M. Drabek, pp. 19–45. Vienna: Österreichischen Akademie der Wissenschaften, 1978.

Hranilović, H. pl. "Šta nam treba u zemljopisu." *Nastavni vjesnik* 10 (1902): 465–483, 588–613.

"Hrvatski učitelj." *Hrvatski učitelj* 1 (1877): 49–52.

Jelavich, Charles. "The Croatian Problem in the Habsburg Monarchy in the Nineteenth Century." *Austrian History Yearbook* 3, no. 2 (1967): 83–115.

———. "Garašanin's Načertanije und das großserbische Programm." *Südost-Forschungen* 27 (1968): 131–47.

———. "Serbian Textbooks: Toward Greater Serbia or Yugoslavia?" *Slavic Review* 42, no. 4 (1983): 601–19.

———. "Serbian Nationalism and the Question of Union with Croatia in the Nineteenth Century." *Balkan Studies* 3 (1962): 29–42.

"Jugoslavenstvo i učiteljstvo." *Hrvatski učiteljski dom* 6 (1913): 121–23.

Korunić, Petar. "Jugoslavenska ideja u hrvatskoj politici, 1866–1868." *Zbornik zavoda za povijesne znanosti JAZU* 11 (1982): 1–107.

———. "Jugoslavenska ideja u hrvatsko i slovenskoj politici za revolucije 1848–1849 g." *Radovi JAZU* 14, no. 1 (1981): 91–228.

MacKenzie, David. "Ljuba Jovanović-Čupa and the Search for Yugoslav Unity." *International History Review* 1 (1979): 36–54.

———. "Serbian Nationalist and Military Organizations and the Piedmont Idea, 1844–1914." *East European Quarterly* 16, no. 3 (1982): 323–44.

Marjanović, Čed. "Obrazovanje ženskinja i naše srednje škole." *Učitelj* 26 (1906–07): 358–62, 425–32.

"Naša inteligencija i prosvjeta." *Hrvatski učiteljski dom* 7 (1914): 61–62.

Obradović, Laza J. "Nastava u istoriji i negovanje patriotizma." *Učitelj* 13 (1893): 799–812.

Okanović, Stev. M. "Narodna istorija u vaspitnoj školi." *Učitelj* 30 (1910): 1–10.

P. "Hrvatski jezik u srednjim učilistima." *Hrvatski učitelj* 13 (1889): 1–3.

Pasarić, J. "Ivan Franjin Gundulić." *Hrvatski učitelj* 12 (1888): 17–21.

Petković, Drag. "Kakve su i kakve treba da su čitanke u našoj narodnoj školi." *Učitelj* 25 (1905–06): 95–102.

Petrović, K. "O nacionalnom vaspitanju u nas." *Učitelj* 10 (1891): 292–314.

Petrovich, Michael B. "The Croatian Humanists: Cosmopolites or Patriots?" *Journal of Croatian Studies* 20 (1979): 17–36.

Prodanović, J. M. "Milan Šević: Pitanje o srpskim čitankama." *Nastavnik* 24 (1913): 53–59.

"Prosveta u Srpstvu." *Učitelj* 27 (1908): 600–616.

R. St. "Istorija u osnovnoj školi." *Učitelj* 19 (1899–1900): 363–67, 447–51.

Rožić, V. "Gramatička obuka hrvatskoga jezika u srednjim školama." *Nastavni vjesnik* 10 (1902): 354–65.

S. K. "Odziv na članak: 'Ćirilica u hrvatskoj pučkoj školi.'" *Hrvatski učitelj* 3 (1879): 97–99.

Šević, Milan. "Pitanje o srpskim čitankama." *Nastavnik* 23 (1912): 193–209.

Šepić, Dragovan. "Jugoslavenski pokret i Milan Marjanović 1901–1919. (In memoriam Milanu Marjanoviću)." *Zbornik historijskog instituta JAZU* 3 (1961): 531–62.

————. "O misiji Lj. Stojanovića i A. Belića u Petrogradu 1915 godine." *Zbornik historijskog instituta JAZU* 3 (1961): 449–98.

————. "Srpska vlada i počeci Jugoslavenskog Odbora." *Historijski Zbornik* 13, nos. 1–4 (1960): 1–45.

Šidak, Jaroslav. "Hrvatsko pitanje u Habsburskoj monarhiji." *Historijski pregled*, nos. 2–3 (1963): 101–22, 175–94.

————. "Južnoslovenska ideja u ilirskom pokretu." *Jugoslovenski istorijski časopis*, no. 3 (1963): 31–42.

————. "Prilog razvoju jugoslavenske ideje do g. 1914." *Naše Teme*, nos. 8–9 (1965): 1290–1317.

"Šidakov Zbornik." *Historijski Zbornik*, nos. 29–30, (1976–77).

"Školske knjige." *Školski prijatelj* 6 (1873): 286–87, 294–95.

"Sloboda udžbenika." *Učitelj* 26 (1906–07): 531–35.

"Srpske škole u Austro-ugarskoj." *Učitelj* 22 (1902–03): 256–62, 298–304.

Stančić, Nikša. "Hrvatstvo, srpstvo i jugoslavenstvo u Dalmaciji u vrijeme narodnog preporoda." *Časopis za suvremenu povijest* 2 (1970): 229–38.

————. "Problem Načertanije Ilije Garašanina." *Historijski Zbornik* 21–22 (1968–69), 179–96.

S[tojanović], N[ikola]. "Srbi i Hrvati." *Srpski književni glasnik* 6–7 (1902): 1149–59.

Šumkarac, Voj. Stev. "Nas patrijarhalni i moderni patriotizam." *Učitelj* 22 (1902–03): 746–51.

Trstenjak, Davorin. "Prije svega i nada sve: dužnost!" *Napredak* 40 (1899): 257–60, 273–75, 369–71, 385–89.

"Udžbenici, njihov značaj i upotreba," *Učitelj* 23 (1903–04): 172–76, 266–69.

V.K. "Slava Ljudevitu Gaju!" *Svačić - kalendar za 1910* (Zadar), pp. 119–22.

Valentić, Mirko. "Koncepcija Garašaninova 'Načertanije' (1844)." *Historijski pregled* 7 (1961): 128–37.

Zrnić, L. "Narodnost." *Nastavnik* 19 (1908): 1–9.

Zwitter, Fran. "The Slovenes and the Habsburg Monarchy." *Austrian History Yearbook* 3, no. 2 (1967): 157–88.

JOURNALS

Danica Ilirska. Zagreb: Franjo Suppan, 1835–43.

Hrvatski učitelj - Časopis za školu i dom (Zagreb: Dionička tiskara, 1879–1914).

Hrvatski učiteljski dom - Glasilo hrvatskoga pedagoško-književnog zbora, saveza hrv. učiteljskih društava i hrvatske steno-predujamne zadruge (Zagreb: Hrvatski pedagoško-književni zbor, 1908–1918).

Kršćanska škola (Zagreb, 1897–1914).

Napredak: Časopis za učitelje, uzgajatelje i sve prijatelje mladeži (Zagreb: Hrvatski pedagoško-knjižcvni zbor, 1898–1914).

Nastavni vjesnik - Časopis za srednje škole (Zagreb: Narodnih novina, 1893–1918).

Nastavnik - List profesorskoga društva (Belgrade: Državna štamparija, 1890–1913).

Prosvctni Glasnik - Službeni list ministarstva prosvete i crkveni poslova (Belgrade: Državna štamparija, 1881–1914).

Školski prijatelj - Časopis za promicanje pučkoga školstva (Zagreb: Ljudevit Gaj, 1868–76).

Slovenski Jug. Belgrade: 1903–12.

Učitelj - Pedagoško-književni list: organ učiteljskog udruženja (Belgrade: Radikalna štamparija, 1883–1914).

ALMANACS (KALENDARI)

Bog i Hrvati - Ilustrovani hrvatski narodni kalendar sa poslovnim zabavnim prilogom te šematizom, sajmovnikom i adresarom (Zagreb: Antun Scholz, 1894–1912).

Danica (Zagreb: Društvo svetojeromina, 1878–1914).

Dragoljub ili upisnik kalendar za javne urede, odvjetnike, kr. javne i obćinske bilježnike, agente, private pisarne, trgovce, obrtnike te ine poslovodje itd. (Zagreb: L. Hartman, 1862–1907).

Hrvatski ilustrovani pučki koledar za rimo-katolike grčko-istočne i izraeličane (Bjelovar: Lavoslav Weis, 1910–15).

Kalendar - Školski za profesore i učitelje srednjih zavoda i viših i nižih škola (Zagreb, 1897–1901).

Kalendar matice srpske (Novi Sad: Matica Srpska, 1902–05.).

Kalendar narodnih novina (Belgrade: Davidović, 1908–12).

Kalendar - Mali Srbobran. Narodni srpski kalendar (Zagreb, 1905–13).

Maerif - Muhamedanski kalendar (Zagreb, 1894–99).

Marija-Bistrički katolički koledar (Zagreb: Lav Hartman, 1891–1906).

Napredak - Hrvatski narodni kalendar (Sarajevo, 1907–14).

Narodni koledar (Zadar: Matica Dalmatinska, 1878–98).

Orao - Veliki ilustrovani kalendar (Novi Sad: Srpska narodna zadružna štamparija 1876–1900).

Prosvjeta (Sarajevo: Srpska dioničarska štamparija, 1910–14).

Prosvjeta - Srpski narodni kalendar (Sremski Karlovci: Srpska manastirska štamparija, 1905).

Srbobran - Narodni srpski kalendar (Zagreb: Srpska štamparija, 1893–1914).

Srpska crkva (Belgrade: Ljub. J. Bojović, 1912–14). Izdanje odbora gospodje "Knjaginje Ljubice."

Srpski omladinski kalendar (Novi Sad: Platonova štamparija, 1869, 1870).

Strossmayer (Zagreb: Dionička tiskara, 1907–12).

Svačić - Hrvatski ilustrovani koledar (Zadar: Hrvatska knjižarnica, 1904–10).

Sveti Sava (Novi Sad: Štamparija učiteljskog dioničarskog društva "Natošević," 1910–14).

Vardar (Belgrade: Izdanje društva "Kola srpskih sestara," 1906–14).

COURSE CATALOGUES (IZVEŠTAJI)

Gimnazija Kralja Milana I (Belgrade: Državna štamparija). 1900–1901; 1901–02.

Gimnazija Kralja Milana I u Nišu (Belgrade: Državna štamparija). 1898–99; 1899–1900; 1903–04; 1911–12.

Gimnazija u Leskovcu Izvestaj (Belgrade: Merkur Milorada Stefanovića). 1908/1909, 1910–11.

Godišnje izveješće gradske više, obće pučke djevojačke i obćih pučkih dječačkih učiona Zagreba (Zagreb: C. Albrecht). 1879/80; 1885/86; 1890/91.

Godišnji izveštaj o I beogradskoj gimnaziji (Belgrade: Državna štamparija). 1896/97; 1902–03; 1903–04; 1904–05; 1906–07; 1909–10; 1910–11; 1913–14.

Godišnji izveštaj o srpsko-narodnoj osn. školi u Zagrebu (Zagreb: Srpska štamparija). 1895–96; 1912–13.

Godišnji izveštaj o stanju bogoslovije beogradske (Belgrade: Državna štamparija). 1885.

Godišnji izveštaj pučkih i šegrtskih škola slobodnoga i kralj. glavnoga grada Zagreba (Zagreb: Dionička tiskara). 1912–13.

Izveštaj Bogosloviji Svetoga Save (Belgrade: Državna štamparija). 1900–1901; 1901–02; 1902–03; 1903–04; 1908–09; 1909–10; 1910–11; 1911–12.

Izveštaj - gimnazija u Leskovcu (Belgrade: Milorad Stefanović). 1908–09; 1910–11.

Izveštaj kralj. mužke učiteljske škole i vježbaonice u Zagrebu (Zagreb: Kr. zemaljska tiskara). 1890/91; 1899/1900; 1905–06; 1909–10; 1910–11.

Izveštaj o gimnaziji Kralja Aleksandra I (Belgrade: Državna štamparija). 1898–99; 1899–1900; 1900–1901; 1901–02.

Izveštaj o srpskim učitelskim školama u Somboru (Sombor: F. Biterman). 1899/1900; 1912/13.

Izveštaj o srpskoj pravoslavnoj učiteljskoj školi u Somboru (Sombor: Vl. Bajić). 1899/1900; 1912/13.

Izveštaj o srpskom pravosl. bogoslovskom učilištu u Sremskim Kralovcima (Novi Sad: Pavlović and Jočić). 1891–92; 1894–95; 1899–1900; 1904/05; 1905/06; 1909/10.

Izveštaj o stanju srpske pravoslavne Bogoslovsko-učiteljske škole u Prizrenu (Kruševac: Djordje Budimović). 1894/5; 1904–05.

Izveštaj o višoj i nižoj pučkoj djevojačkoj školi ursulinskoga samostana u Varaždinu (Zagreb: Mirko Kos). 1907–08.

Izveštaj - Srpska kraljevska Negotinska gimnazija (Negotin: Miloš Marković). 1908–09; 1911–12.

Izveštaj srpske vel. gimnazije Kralovačke (Sremski Karlovci: Srpska manastirska štamparija). 1899–1900; 1904/05; 1909/10.

Izveštaj velike gimnazije u Mostaru (Mostar: V. M. Radović). 1894/95; 1901/02; 1910/11.

Izvješće gradske niže i više pučke djevojačke škole, ženske stručne škole i zabavišta za malu djecu u Varaždinu (Varaždin: J. B. Stifler). 1901–02; 1904–05.

Jahresbericht des k.k. Obergymnasiums zu Laibach (Laibach: Ig. v. Kleinmayr & Fed. Bamberg). 1880; 1885; 1899/1900; 1901/02; 1905/06.

Jahresbericht des k.k. Staatsgymnasiums in Krainburg (Krainburg: Ig. v. Kleinmayr & Fed. Bamberg). 1895/96; 1900/1901; 1905/06; 1910/11.

Jahres-Bericht des k.k. Staats-Gymnasiums in Marburg (Vienna: Im Verlage des k.k. Staats-Gymnasiums). 1900; 1910; 1911–12.

Program C.K. velike državne gimnazije u Zadru (Zadar: C. K. Gimnazija). 1901–02; 1905–06; 1910–11.

Programm des k.k. Staats-Gymnasiums in Cilli (Cilli: Johann Rakusch). 1893/94; 1897/98; 1904/05; 1909/10; 1914/15.

Programma dell'i r. Ginnasio Superiore di Capodistria (Capodistria: Cobol & Priora). 1894.

Srpska kraljevska muška učiteljska škola u Jagodini prvi godišnji izveštaj (Belgrade: Prosveta). 1898–99; 1901–02; 1902–03; 1903–04; 1904–05; 1908–09; 1909–10.

Srpska Kralj. Negotinska gimnazija: Izveštaj (Negotin: Miloš Marković). 1908–09; 1911–12.

Index